Las Madres

Las Madres

Latinas in the Heartland Who
Led Their Family
to Success

Dennis Raphael Garcia

University Press of Kansas

© 2024 by the University Press of Kansas
All rights reserved

Published by the University Press of Kansas (Lawrence, Kansas 66045), which was organized by the Kansas Board of Regents and is operated and funded by Emporia State University, Fort Hays State University, Kansas State University, Pittsburg State University, the University of Kansas, and Wichita State University.

Library of Congress Cataloging-in-Publication Data

Names: Garcia, Dennis Raphael, author.
Title: Las madres : Latinas in the heartland who led their family to success / Dennis Garcia.
Other titles: Latinas in the heartland who led their family to success
Description: [Lawrence] : [University Press of Kansas], [2024] | Includes index.
Identifiers: LCCN 2024011392 (print) | LCCN 2024011393 (ebook) | ISBN 9780700637973 (cloth) | ISBN 9780700637980 (paperback) | ISBN 9780700637997 (ebook)
Subjects: LCSH: Padilla, Candelaria Garcia, 1865-1927—Family. | Mexican American women—Biography. | Mexican American women—Social conditions—20th century. | Rodriguez family. | Padilla family. | Garcia family. | Garcia, Irene, 1920-2001—Family. | Rodriguez, Rafaela, 1906-1990—Family. | Mexican Americans—Genealogy. | Aguascalientes (Mexico)—Genealogy. | BISAC: SOCIAL SCIENCE / Ethnic Studies / American / Hispanic American Studies
Classification: LCC E184.M5 G347 2024 (print) | LCC E184.M5 (ebook) | DDC 929.20973—dc23/eng/20240907
LC record available at https://lccn.loc.gov/2024011392.
LC ebook record available at https://lccn.loc.gov/2024011393.

British Library Cataloguing-in-Publication Data is available.

FOR CANDELARIA, RAFAELA, and IRENE,
For all the love you gave and sacrifices you made

Contents

Candelaria Garcia Padilla Family Tree ix
List of Illustrations xi
Preface xiii
Prologue: Dodge City, Kansas, 1920 xv

Part I: Candelaria
1. The Challenges of Hacienda Life 3
2. Candelaria's Children, Courtship, the Military Threat 18
3. The Flight to El Paso, Fernando's Arrival 34
4. Life and Death in El Paso, the Santa Fe in Kansas 48
5. The "Village" Labor Camp, the Teen Bride 66
6. The Barest Segregated School and Church, the Great War 84
7. Surviving the 1918 Pandemic, the Taking of Rafaela 101
8. Candelaria's Grandchildren, the Cold of November 1927 121

Part II: Rafaela
9. Steadfast Through the Dust Bowl and Depression, Irene's Diploma 161
10. Leaving the Village, World War II Begins, Irene's Marriage 180

Part III: Irene
11. Victory, the Baby Boom Arrives, Death by TB 203
12. Enedina's Ordeal, Arrivals and Passings, Higher Education 223
13. Work and Stress, Radio DJs, Floodwaters 243
14. Election Campaign, Miracle Birth, Cayetano's Fall 258

15. The Disclosure, the Board of Education, the Last Relief 281
16. The Rivalry Ends, Life Is for the Living 299
Epilogue 313

Postscript: Las Madres Legacy *319*
References *321*
Index *323*

Family Tree

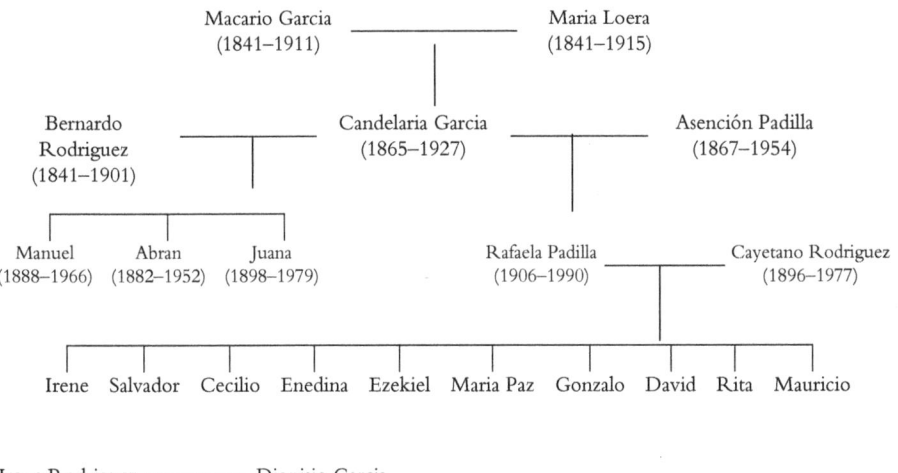

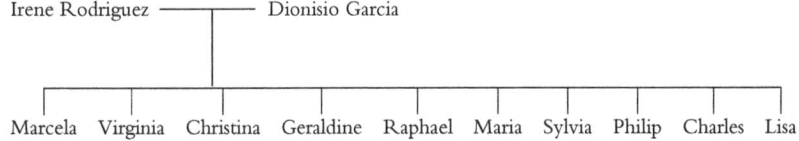

Marcela	Virginia	Christina	Geraldine	Raphael	Maria	Sylvia	Philip	Charles	Lisa

List of Illustrations

Photo gallery follows page 132.

Candelaria and Asención Padilla with grandchildren
Girls from the Mexican Village riding a tricycle
Members of the Santa Fe Mexican Band
Interior of Sacred Heart Catholic Church
Rafaela Padilla with friends
Rafaela Padilla with friends
Wedding photo of Rafaela Padilla and Cayetano Rodriguez
Rafaela Rodriguez with sons
Rafaela Rodriguez family celebrates a birthday
Family portrait of the children of Rafaela Rodriguez
Rafaela Rodriguez
Irene Rodriguez
Hipolita ("Pola") Rodriguez, Antonio Rodriguez, and Irene Rodriguez
Irene Rodriguez and Dionisio Garcia wedding portrait
Irene Garcia and Dionisio Garcia at wedding dance
Irene Rodriguez Garcia and Micaela Rodriguez
Garcia Family Seasons Greetings Portrait
Irene and Dionisio Garcia dancing
Irene Garcia in her kitchen
Enedina Rodriguez and friends
Gonzalo Rodriguez high school graduation
Dionisio Garcia in US postal uniform
Ladislao Rodriguez

Rosella Rodriguez and Salvador Rodriguez, with godson
Asención Padilla
Mexican Village children and Francisca Rodriguez
Wedding Ceremony in Our Lady of Guadalupe Church
Our Lady of Guadalupe congregation
Rhythm Aces Band
American G.I. Forum Independence Day parade float
Garden City, Kansas, Mexican Fiesta
Candelaria and Asención Padilla headstone
Candelaria Padilla
Sanborn Insurance map, Dodge City, Kansas
Rafaela Rodriguez and Irene Garcia with the Munoz family
Antonio "Tony Montana" Rodriguez
Irene Rodriguez, First Holy Communion

Preface

Las Madres is the story of three generations of women in my mother's family. It recounts the difficult challenges each of them faced in their lifetimes in pursuit of the same goal: the advancement of the well-being of their families from poverty to success and security. The main characters are Candelaria (1865–1927), who was born in Mexico; her daughter Rafaela (1906–1990), who was born in El Paso, Texas; and Rafaela's daughter Irene (1920–2001), who was born in Dodge City, Kansas. Irene was my mother, and I am the Raphael referred to in the text.

Each of these Latina women followed a separate path on their journey to the same individual and joint objective, security, and freedom from want. Though they traveled with apprehension and uncertainty into unknown places and arenas, they were courageous, patient, and steadfast in their pursuit.

Las Madres dispels any notion that immigrants and their families who come to the United States are given a life of ease. Very few people living on the high plains of Kansas in 1900 "had it easy," especially Mexican railroad workers and their families. Their story reminds readers that there is no one true path toward achieving an end. The ability to adjust, anticipate, and persevere are the gateways to achieve the dreams one holds tightly.

I suggest to the reader to keep close at hand a marker for quick access and reference to the Candelaria Garcia Padilla family tree. Initially, the family tree will help maintain clarity until the reader becomes familiar with the relationships of the characters.

Las Madres is based on a true story. I have added a handful of characters that might or might not have existed and have given them a name. For example, I know my great-grandparents were married before a priest, but the records do not clearly state the priest's name.

This book relies on the oral histories and experiences told by family members and friends and those who generously provided documents, records, and photos. My thanks to them for sharing their stories. Information was also gleaned from official documents and records from the military, census, immigration, property, and certificates of birth, death, marriage, and divorce.

Virtually all of the dialogue before 1917 reasonably reflects conversations the characters might have had, given what is known of their personalities and circumstances.

After 1917, actual dialogue, as recalled by those who heard, or were told, the story begins to seep in. By 1960, virtually all the dialogue was actually spoken, heard, or recalled and passed on.

I have changed the names of a few characters to avoid harm to relationships with my family that might exist today.

Thank you to my wife, Celeste, for her invaluable research and support for this project. And I am greatly appreciative of the editing and development of the manuscript provided by Amy Sherman. Thanks are also due to the University Press of Kansas and their staff who supported the publication of this book.

A note on the use of the term "Mexican." I use the term to refer to members of the following groups of people: (1) A person born in Mexico and living in Mexico; (2) a person born in Mexico but living in the United States; (3) a person of Mexican ancestry born in Mexico or in the United States. The meaning will depend on context.

Prologue
Dodge City, Kansas, 1920

In 1920, in the Mexican Village in Dodge City, Kansas, the birth of a child brought joy and hope, essentials for living in the Village. But in the first hours of October 19, the dark scraggly Shadow of Death slipped into the Village shanty. It hung in the lantern-lit home like the dangling tip of a tornado slowly twirling, waiting for the right moment to descend and steal the lives of fourteen-year-old Rafaela Rodriguez and the child in her womb. On blankets covering the dirt floor of her home, Rafaela lay suffering the throes of hard labor. Just hours earlier, her water had broken, signaling the start of the delivery.

When nature's design worked in sequence, birth was truly a wonder. But with disorder or a failure of an organ, the pathway to life outside the womb became a gauntlet of hidden and unknown dangers within the mother, putting her and the child at greater risk. Two of those dangers, infection and internal bleeding, could be catastrophic. The risks only escalated without a physician. In the days before the delivery, Rafaela's mother, Candelaria Garcia Padilla, described to her the pain she should expect in giving birth. But at her age, Rafaela could not comprehend the nature and depth of her mother's words. Candelaria did not explain to Rafaela the danger and the possibility of death, in order to tamp down Rafaela's fears and anxieties—those emotions might further complicate the delivery. Candelaria feared that Rafaela's body had not produced all that was necessary to withstand the gauntlet.

Marcela Gutierrez, Rafaela's mother-in-law, and Francisca Rodriguez, her sister-in-law, attended Rafaela in her home when she began labor. Both women had attended other births in Mexico. Professional medical care was rarely available in the Village, and like many Village residents, Rafaela's family did not have the money to pay for such care.

To lessen Rafaela's pain, the women encouraged her to walk for as long as possible. They gave her water, wiped her sweat, applied heat compresses to relax her muscles, and lit a votive candle seeking the protection of Our Lady of Guadalupe. When she could no longer walk, they lay her on the blankets on the floor.

Shortly after midnight, as Rafaela's uterus contracted with increasing strength, duration, and frequency, she began pushing the baby out of her womb. The birthing process had reached the critical stage. At this point, any failures in the process or functions of the tissues and organs become apparent and must be resolved for a safe and successful birth. With the increasingly painful contractions, Rafaela thought that only the baby's head could cause such pain. Her attendees encouraged her to keep pushing, but progress was slow. It was not uncommon for first-time deliveries to require a longer time in labor, and more so for Rafaela, who was only a child herself. Her labor pains were excruciating. She believed them to be unending and futile. Finally, the baby's head was visible, indicating that two potential major risks had been avoided: a breech delivery and a closed womb. Rafaela responded to Marcela's call for more pushing, but the unbearable pain, anxiety, and exhaustion eventually overwhelmed her. She fainted.

When Rafaela regained consciousness, she was alone on the floor, and in pain, but not in labor. She had no baby or attendees, and she didn't know why they were not at her side helping her. Fear began to overtake her. She thought that her baby had died and that they had taken it so that she would not see it lifeless. Feeling hurt, she began to cry. She sat up and wanted to call out, but she was exhausted and had little strength. Then she realized she was sitting in the fluids and tissue of the afterbirth, the placenta. There was no flow of bright red blood indicating internal bleeding of the womb. Alone in the house, Rafaela tearfully lifted the *olla*—a clay pot of hot water—from the coal-burning potbellied stove, washed herself, and gathered the blankets and towels from the floor.

A short time after Rafaela had gathered herself, Francisca returned and told her that she had delivered a healthy girl. Francisca also told her that she was allowed to see her daughter but that the baby would stay with her and Marcela in their Village home next door. They had denied Rafaela that most tender of moments, the initial bonding of a newborn on the mother's chest. Candelaria knew well that death might take the life of her daughter or grandchild, but it remains unclear whether she knew of Marcela and Francisca's plans for the baby. Marcela and Francisca had conspired—apparently without any objection from Cayetano Rodriguez, Rafaela's twenty-four-year-old husband and Marcela's son and Francisca's brother—that if the baby survived, they would take the child from Rafaela and assert that she was too young to care for the child and that it would be better for the child to be raised in their household.

The degree to which Candelaria protested the actions of the Rodriguez women also remains unknown. What is known is that Candelaria and her husband, Asención Padilla, had vehemently opposed the marriage of their daughter to Cayetano, a man ten years her senior. There is no information suggesting that Candelaria was present during the delivery. Perhaps she did not attend in order to register her continuing rejection of the marriage, or maybe the Rodriguez women, or Rafaela herself, did not want Candelaria present. Possibly, Candelaria and Asención objected fiercely but relented due to some cultural norm whereby the father's family had the final say in matters of custody and child-rearing.

Regardless, the painful and tragic outcome was that Rafaela and her daughter survived the ordeal of birth, only to be separated by the interests and beliefs of her husband's family. Perhaps as a concession to Rafaela and the Padilla family, Rafaela was allowed to name her daughter. She chose the name Irene, after Saint Irene of Tomar, Portugal, whose feast was celebrated by the Roman Catholic Church on October 20.

The events surrounding Irene's birth in the early morning hours of October 19 set in place an interlaced web of loving affection and resentment among Rafaela, Irene, and Francisca. That resentment held fast for decades to come. Rafaela and Irene, with an age difference of some siblings, were just beginning the journeys of their lives. Candelaria, who was at that time fifty-five, knew their futures would include happiness and hardships, some expected and some not. But on this morning, on the cool, breezy, treeless, open plains of southwestern Kansas, three generations of Padilla-Rodriguez women walked through the proverbial valley of the shadow of death, and survived.

Part I
Candelaria

1

The Challenges of Hacienda Life

Candelaria Garcia entered the world in 1865, in the middle of a century of great turmoil, as countries and governments in Europe and the Americas rose and fell. She was born when the three-centuries-old order of European nations and their New World empires began to crumble. Mexico rebelled against Spain and won its independence in 1821. By 1826, virtually all of Spain's colonies in Mesoamerica had rebelled as well and ended Spanish rule. Nine years later, Texas revolted against Mexico and established its own independence and ultimately joined the United States in 1845. The following year, the United States and Mexico fought a war that settled the boundaries between the two. In 1857, Mexico endured a civil war between the liberals and the conservatives. The liberals—mostly the poor and people of "mixed" blood—demanded land, economic, and social reforms, while the conservatives—the wealthy Mexico-born Spanish, the Catholic Church, and the military—wanted Mexico's wealth and political power to remain in the hands of those of Spanish blood.

In Mexico, the availability of many rights and privileges of individuals, especially those who had been taken into slavery, were tied to their bloodlines. Since the seventeenth century, Spain and the Church had been constructing and tracking classifications of race in support of their efforts to control and manage both slave labor and the conversion of Indigenous peoples. From the beginning, the Spanish Crown left the recording of births, marriages, and deaths to the Church. Church baptismal records were one of the primary tools for gathering information to support their efforts. Many Church records in the early 1800s indicated the bloodline of a person: "Indio" for Indigenous, "Negro" for African, "Mulato" for a mix of European and African, "Mestizo" for a mix of European and Indigenous, and "Español" for Spanish. The Church's control of the birth and death registry created great leverage over the poor and the campesinos, as it possessed the strongest proof of lineage, legitimacy, and ownership.

Candelaria's ancestors emerged out of those centuries of European dominance, and she began her life at the precarious bottom of the order. Her parents, Maria and Macario Garcia, were born in 1841 in a region of Mexico's Central Plateau within the state of Aguascalientes. The region was known as El Saucillo and encompassed a group of haciendas, ranchos, towns, and villages. At one time, El Saucillo exceeded eighty-thousand acres, with its border touching the small town of Rincón de Romos. Rincón de Romos was a reference point for El Saucillo inhabitants and for travel into northern Mexico. The Church in Rincón de Romos registered the births, marriages, and deaths occurring on the nearby ranchos. Maria's place of birth was the rancho at San Jose de Gracia, and Macario's the rancho at San Jacinto. Both were fifteen miles from Rincón de Romos—San Jose to the south and west, San Jacinto to the north and east. Macario's and Maria's records bear no indication, but given Candelaria's fair skin and reddish hair, it's likely that they were mestizo, with Spanish blood.

Maria and Macario Garcia were among the campesinos—the rural poor, who had little say in the decisions of the wealthy and the powerful. An alliance of two European powers, the Spanish monarchy and the Catholic Church, dominated and shaped the lives of the ranch and farm laborers, who were mostly Indigenous and people of mixed blood. The impact of the alliance was profound—lives were drained and shortened in servitude to the Crown, the wealthy, and the Church. For the generations of families trapped in this serfdom, the constant concerns were daily bread and survival of the many hardships they encountered: infant death, disease, dangerous and exhausting labor, and war.

During the 1600s and 1700s, the Crown and wealthy landowners built many haciendas on acreage that varied in size and operation. The meaning and use of the term "hacienda" can be imprecise and confusing. Often it is used to refer to the land estates in general, including the smaller estates called "ranchos." But usually, it refers to the walled villages on the land estates that were the heart or command center of the ranching operation. Hacendados (landowners) allocated space within the walls to themselves for their personal comfort and command of hacienda operations. The comfort area was palatial and included a large main residence filled with elegant furniture and drapes available only to the social elite. Many living and dining room floors were made of marble. Kitchens were well-equipped and stocked with fresh water, meat, and food supplies. A team of household servants kept the residences in good order and tended to trees and fountains that greeted palace entrants. The grandeur of the residence also served as a reminder to those living within the hacienda walls of where power and authority lay. The business area often included an office from where the hacendados, or their administrator, the mayordomo, directed the operations of the hacienda and met with the campesinos and Church officials.

The hacendados used the remaining space within the walls to construct, in essence, a village to serve the needs of their particular hacienda and to a lesser degree the needs of the campesinos. Some of the more common structurers in the village included a small chapel, horse stables, corrals for cattle, sheep, and other livestock, water troughs, water tanks, a cookhouse, bakery, kiln, and cobbler, a dry-goods store, and granaries. The village also maintained spaces for supplies, materials, and milling and a pit for waste. Spaces just outside the ten-to-fifteen-foot-high walls included gardens, orchards, and fields of maize, wheat, and beans and a threshing floor. On some haciendas, campesinos used a small area just outside the hacienda entrance for communal activities such as cooking, children's play, and end-of-workday gatherings.

In these times, Indigenous and enslaved people, mestizos, and mulattos often outnumbered the European fortune seekers within the ranchos and haciendas. The hacienda housed most of the laborers, mostly Mestizos and Indigenous people, in ten-by-ten rooms made of adobe and stone. The walls were attached to the fortress wall, which also served as the back wall for the rooms. A number of these windowless rooms, each with its own door, stood side by side sharing common walls. Dirt floors were the rule, with the occasional exception of stone or tile. Residents preferred clay pantiles for roofing but used dried cornstalks if needed. Some hacendados attached the rooms to the inside of the fortress wall, while others chose the outside. The campesinos left on the outside were vulnerable to attack from roving bandits and rebelling Indigenous warriors. When tower sentries sounded alarms that hacienda intruders were imminent, the campesinos were charged with rushing livestock and equipment into the safety of the walls before retreating into their rooms. Favored campesinos who had been rewarded with rooms within the walls also find safety. Nonetheless, it can be said without jest that the care for the animals and equipment often exceeded the care for the campesinos.

With so little space in the rooms, families kept only essential household items. Tables, chairs, and benches were very few and small. Most rooms contained a shallow pit that allowed for a meager amount of heating and very light cooking. A minimum number of utensils, clay plates, pots, mugs, and cookware were kept within, ready for use as needed. Large clay jugs held a supply of drinking water for a family that might include as many as two adults and six or seven children. Bedding and blankets cushioned the dirt floors on which the families slept. Many families also set aside a small space for an altar for prayer. The altars often included an image of a holy saint or a crucifix draped with a rosary, with small lighted candles on either side. From these meager rooms the men, women, and children on El Saucillo began the workday in support of the cattle ranchos or mines.

By the time Maria and Macario considered marriage, they were already part of the hacienda system. From birth, the expectation on the hacienda was that Maria would do as the prior generations of women in her family had done—marry and raise children. By age six, she had begun to learn the skills for the traditional and never-ending tasks of women and children on the hacienda. She helped prepare meals for family and hacienda workers. She observed and helped older and stronger women exerting great amounts of energy grinding corn for tortillas. They used a *metate*, a rectangular grinding stone with a depression, and a *mano*, a stone similar in shape and size to a rolling pin. Maria learned to sew, mend, and launder clothing. Alongside her mother, she gathered fruits and vegetables out of the hacienda gardens and orchards and labored in the fields during harvest. She learned to care for and nurture children of the hacienda. And she accepted the teachings of the Church and participated in prayer and religious rites.

Macario learned his father's trade and became a blacksmith, a vital resource for ranching and mining. Horses, mules, and other beasts of burden moved heavy loads of ore from the mines, plowed the fields, and transported people and goods within the hacienda. Blacksmiths shod the hooves of the animals and fashioned metal hardware, tools, wagon wheels, gates, and latches for barns, corrals, and other structures. Macario's tools were heavy and difficult to wield in the heat of the forge, but despite the tiring and heavy lifting, the life of a blacksmith was better than the life of a miner.

This hacienda way of life—some might argue the way of death—kept a harsh grip on the life of the campesinos. For those living in Mexico in the 1800s, with at best an average lifespan of thirty years, death always lingered close by. Prior to Macario's birth, his sister died at age six. He was five years old when his mother died. Just nine months later, his new twenty-one-year-old stepmother and the child she was carrying also died. Maria's father and a brother died of fever on the same day, when she was eleven years old.

In the face of this history and hardship, and armed only with determination and a prayer for God's protection, Maria and Macario promised each other their lives and to work and sacrifice for one another. They shared the universal hope: that they and their children might live in peace and without hunger. They married on December 17, 1859. Maria was nineteen and Macario eighteen. They paid the mandatory fee to the Church to record the marriage in its registry at Rincón de Romos. They began their married lives at Macario's rancho at San Jacinto, following the path of generations before them on El Saucillo.

At the time, Mexico's relatively new, but troubled, government had obtained loans to operate from French, British, and Spanish creditors. The debt to Britain was approximately seventy million pesos, to Spain ten million pesos, and to France three million pesos. When Mexico announced in 1861 that it would suspend loan payments for two years, military forces from the three European countries sailed to Mexico to collect the debt. Though France described its venture as a matter of trade, its true objective was to send a force to take control of Mexico. The ships landed on the Mexican Gulf Coast at Veracruz in December 1861. After three months, the British and Spanish realized that France's ambition was to occupy Mexico and withdrew their forces. The French Imperial Army alone made its way to Mexico City, the nation's capital, and encountered heavy resistance from the Mexican Republic's forces.

All of Mexico understood that the fall of Mexico City was critical for French occupation. From the capital city, France could send its armies to the resource-rich areas of the country, including the silver mines and haciendas of Zacatecas and Aguascalientes. To reach the silver mines, the French army had to march through Rincón de Romos. San Jacinto was off the main route between Rincón de Romos and the city of Zacatecas. There was no military reason for the French imperial troops to stray from the direct line other than to steal the food stocks and supplies of San Jacinto. Nevertheless, warning had spread to towns and villages that women and children were not always spared the bloodletting of war and the Imperial Army. Maria and Macario knew that if they stayed in San Jacinto, the marching soldiers could easily come for them.

Maria gave birth to their first child, Catarina, in San Jacinto on May 1, 1863. A month later, on June 7, 1863, the Imperial Army marched into Mexico City. They installed Maximilian von Habsburg from Austria as emperor and proclaimed Mexico a Catholic empire. Mexican Republic resistance to the French invasion was not universal. Many criollos (Mexican-born wealthy Spaniards), the Church, and wealthy Mexicans opposed Mexico's new land reform and liberal racial policies. They welcomed and supported the Imperial Army and a return to a conservative monarchy government. The Imperial Army, supported by conservatives opposing the Mexican Republic's liberal government, was now in position to send troops into the Mexican countryside to tame and control any resistance.

Days after the capital's fall, Macario, Maria, and baby Catarina left San Jacinto for the town of Ojocaliente, Zacatecas, on Mexico's Central Plateau, near the present-day state border with Aguascalientes. The move to Ojocaliente, another sixteen miles farther away, made an encounter with the French even less likely.

On February 2, 1865, still in Ojocaliente, Maria gave birth to her second daughter. Macario left the naming of the baby to Maria. The Church maintained a yearly calendar, with each day celebrating and honoring a different saint, holy event, or member of the Holy Family. Since the fourth century, the Church had celebrated the feast day of Candlemas on February 2, the fortieth day after Christmas, marking the end of the Epiphany season—the time of recognition of Christ's presence on earth. It was a common practice in Mexico and other countries for Catholic parents to name their children after the patron saint celebrated on the day of their birth. Maria chose a name to honor the Holy Mother and named her Candelaria. Macario agreed with her choice. By naming her Candelaria, Maria believed that Our Lady of Guadalupe would watch over her and protect her from harm. Countries across the globe celebrated Candlemas Day in various ways, but the common thread was lighting every candle in the home. Maria and Macario did so in their humble room on that day.

Just two months after Candelaria's birth, the US Civil War ended when General Robert E. Lee surrendered to General Ulysses S. Grant. The Civil War's end began a series of events that reached Candelaria and her parents. With the defeat of the Confederacy and the Union intact, the United States turned its attention to Mexico and the French violation of the Monroe Doctrine. The United States began providing war materials in support of Mexico's Republican Army. Napoleon III's hope that the Confederacy would block the United States from direct access to Mexico ended. Facing additional pressures in Europe, he reconsidered his position and thought it better to have diplomatic rather than hostile relations with the United States. To the surprise of many, Napoleon III announced in March 1866 that the Imperial Army would withdraw and return to France by the end of May.

The French departure dramatically improved Mexico's Republican Army's advantage over the remaining Imperial Army forces that chose to stay and fight with Mexican conservatives seeking a monarchy. With a weakened adversary, the Republican Army began steadily recapturing capital cities and towns under Imperial Army and conservative control. Some Imperial troops abandoned their posts to consolidate their forces in stronger defensive positions. On January 31, 1867, the Imperial Army briefly held the capital city of Zacatecas but quickly retreated when they learned the Republican Army was advancing on the city.

The Imperial Army and conservatives began their escape heading south and cutting across the San Jacinto rancho. The following day, the Imperial Army stopped its retreat, turned, and stood its ground at San Jacinto. Four years earlier, Maria and Macario had fled San Jacinto for safety from the same Imperial Army. The Battle of San Jacinto ended in a matter of hours when the outnumbered and poorly positioned Imperial Army was unwilling to sacrifice itself for the sake of empire. The French forces quickly resumed their retreat. The Imperial Army that remained in Mexico and conservative forces regrouped at Querétaro, approximately two hundred miles southeast of San Jacinto. By mid-May they were encircled there and in Mexico City. French Emperor Maximillian saw that defeat was inevitable and tried to escape through Republican lines. He was captured, court-martialed, and executed by firing squad on June 19, 1867. The brutal and bloody French Intervention finally came to an end.

For a short while, Macario and Maria remained in Ojocaliente with Candelaria before returning to San Jose de Gracia in 1868. No records of Candelaria's older sister, Catarina, beyond her birth, are known. She might have died as an infant or in her first years of life. Maria and Macario were likely unable to pay the Church fees required to record her passing and burial on ground blessed by the Church. For the many deeply religious campesinos, the inability to pay for registry and holy burial added to the pain and heartache of the loss of a loved one. In one respect, Maria and Macario were fortunate—history knows Catarina lived, but for many other campesinos across the haciendas, their existence remains unknown.

In the decade that followed, Maria gave birth to eight more children. Two of the eight died when Candelaria was a toddler, and three others passed away between 1873 and 1876, each child under the age of three. Only Candelaria and the three remaining children—Visente, Maria Pascula, and Delfina—lived to adulthood. By the time Candelaria was eleven years old, she knew the heartache and sadness of death. She saw her mother and father in great sorrow with the loss of each of their children.

The hacienda did not provide schooling for Candelaria. Formal instruction for campesino children was extremely rare and did not extend far beyond the ability to write their names. The elites of government and the wealthy regarded education for children on the hacienda as too expensive and a threat to its dominance. The formal education of wealthy children was left to the Church, which provided instruction with large doses of Catholic teachings. On the hacienda, Candelaria learned from her mother. And just as Maria's mother had taught her the work of women and children on the hacienda, so did she instruct Candelaria. By the time Candelaria had reached her teens, she was preparing meals, grinding corn for tortillas, gathering fruits and vegetables from the orchards and gardens, and caring for children. And like her mother, she had faith in prayer.

In his work as a blacksmith, Macario met a carpenter named Bernardo Rodriguez. From time-to-time Bernardo took equipment and wooden pieces to Macario for metal work. Their specialized skills earned them slightly higher pay relative to the day laborers within the hacienda, more home space inside the wall, and greater access to supplies and materials. This shared status led to a friendship between the two.

Bernardo was born in 1841—the same year that Maria and Macario were born—near Asientos, Aguascalientes, eighteen miles east of Rincón de Romos. He was living in San Jose de Gracia in 1866, when he married Patricia Ybarra. Bernardo introduced Patricia to Macario and Maria after Sunday Mass, and the two couples enjoyed conversation when they met at weddings, baptisms, and Church holidays. Patricia gave birth to five children but suffered the heartache of losing two, an infant son to dysentery in 1875 and a five-year-old daughter to smallpox in 1879. A few months later, in February 1880, the family suffered yet another devastating heartache—Patricia died as well. She suffered from a type of heart disease, *hidropesía*. She was thirty-seven when she died and left behind three daughters, ages thirteen, nine, and seven.

After Patricia's funeral mass, Maria made a considerate offer to Bernardo. "Bernardo, I know the pain that is in your heart today. And I know the days ahead will be difficult. If you are in agreement, I am willing to care for the girls while you work." She reassured him, "I will not be overburdened, and besides, Candelaria can help me until you are able to make other arrangements."

Surprised, Bernardo answered, "Gracias, Señora. Gracias. Thank you for your kind offer, but that is too much to ask of you and your family."

"Don't worry, Bernardo. It is not a problem. We are friends, and that is the least I can do for Patricia."

"Please allow me some time to consider your offer. I will send word soon." Bernardo knew he needed immediate care for his daughters, and Maria's offer was certainly the most helpful and convenient resolution. After waiting for a few days, Bernardo sent word to Maria that he accepted her offer and would bring the girls to her for care.

A month later, Bernardo approached Maria and Macario with a new proposal. They met in the Church courtyard in Rincón de Romos. In a tone of optimism and with a touch of apprehension, Bernardo said, "I am grateful for all you have done for me and my daughters. I thank you. And

I have been trying to find a way to resolve this situation because I know it can't continue. With all due respect, I am asking you for Candelaria's hand in marriage."

Maria and Macario sat in stunned silence. Neither had anticipated this. Maria turned to Macario, who was looking straight at Bernardo. Bernardo, seeing no response, tried to salvage his request using what he believed was the strength of his proposal. "I know my request is surprising, but I'm able to provide for her. She will be safe and have the things that she needs."

Macario gathered his thoughts and led with the obvious. "Bernardo, my friend, you are so much older than she is. Your daughter and Candelaria are nearly the same age."

Maria asked, "How can there be the love of a husband and wife? You don't know what kind of woman she will be, all you know of her is what you see when she is with your children. She doesn't know what kind of man you are."

"You are right to have concerns," Bernardo said to them. "I assure you that I will accept my responsibility to care for her. I know that life is hard on El Saucillo, but I can make it easier for Candelaria. And we will learn to love one another, as our parents, grandparents, and ancestors did when they married. She will always be close to you here in San Jose."

Neither Maria nor Macario rejected his proposal directly, so Bernardo thought it better to end the discussion before they did. "You need not decide at this moment. Respectfully, I ask you to discuss the matter between yourselves, and with Candelaria."

Macario agreed, "Yes, Bernardo, that is the best thing to do. Maria and I will talk about your request. Gracias. We will talk again soon."

Candelaria had turned fifteen just a month prior to Bernardo's proposal. She was attractive and petite, at five feet two inches tall, and had European features and thick, long, braided, auburn hair. She was an obedient child and mindful of her parents' wishes. When called upon, she worked alongside Maria in the fields and orchards with little complaint. Neither Maria nor Candelaria received any pay for their work. The hacienda system did not compensate women and children for their labor.

In 1880, a fifteen-year-old bride was not unheard of on El Saucillo. From the beginning, the Crown did not concern itself with matters of marriage, leaving that arena to the Church as well. The Church's rules for marriage often protected the interests of parental consent and property rather than the bride and groom's mental and physical fitness for marriage. Church authorities set the minimum age for marriage for girls at eleven and for boys at thirteen. The age for girls was set so low in the belief that they were merely going from one dependent home to another, but with the additional duties of a spouse. Priests also had the power to consider the circumstances surrounding a proposed marriage and grant waivers or set conditions for an otherwise disallowed marriage. For example, an exception might be made where men outnumbered women in a particular location or where blood relatives lived in a remote area with sparse population.

As Maria and Macario walked to their room after meeting with Bernardo, Maria said, "This cannot be. She is too young!"

Macario was calm. "Yes, I know."

"Mija thinks he's an old man," Maria said, thrusting out her hand in disbelief. "She is not ready for this."

"I know," Macario said again.

"And what does she know about being a wife?"

"She knows nothing," Macario said, finally offering an answer. He then surprised Maria with his view of the proposal. "Maria, Bernardo speaks an important truth we must consider. He can provide for her. He holds an important position here, and the mayordomo likes his work and will protect him."

"Have you gone mad, Macario? Her life will be difficult; she will suffer, married to that man!"

"Everyone suffers on the hacienda, but she might suffer less than most. I agree that in the beginning her life will be difficult, but you will be there to help if she has any problems. As time passes, she will adjust so that life will be better for her and any children God might grant her."

"Don't even say that! God forbid. I want Candelaria's children to have a father, not a grandfather," Maria retorted sharply.

Macario moved the discussion forward. "I think we should talk to Candelaria and tell her about the proposal and tell her what we are thinking."

Maria, in frustration, exclaimed, "Macario, I am thinking no! I am against this marriage. You can tell her what you are thinking. If she asks me what I think, I will tell her what I am telling you. No!"

As in most countries in Europe, Mexican society expected women to defer to the judgment of men. Maria expressed her judgment as forcefully as she dared, but she knew that in the end, Macario's decision would rule the day. She could only pray that Macario would see the harm that Candelaria might suffer at her age in a marriage to Bernardo.

Days later, Maria and Macario sat with Candelaria at a table on the patio outside their room. Macario had told her that they wanted to discuss a serious matter. Candelaria was puzzled and could not imagine what matter that might be.

Macario began, "Mija, I have something very important to discuss with you." Candelaria nodded. "I knew since you were little that someday we would talk about these things, but I did not know that the day would arrive so soon."

Candelaria was still puzzled. "What do we need to talk about, Papá?"

"Bernardo Rodriguez has asked your mother and me about you."

"About me?" Candelaria could not think of any reason why he would do so. She wondered if there were a problem with how she helped care for his children. "Did I do something wrong with his daughters?"

"No, mija, you and your mother have cared for the children properly. Bernardo has asked us for your hand in marriage."

Candelaria, not comprehending, was more unsure than startled. "What did he ask you?"

"He wants to marry you. He has asked us for your hand in marriage."

This time, Candelaria understood. She could not think beyond the word "marriage." She looked at Macario, then at Maria, and without emotion uttered the word, "Marriage." She repeated the word but this time questioning the very idea. "Marriage?" Then again, in disbelief, "Marriage to me?"

"Yes. Mija, your mother and I are thinking about your future and the life you will live." Maria nodded in agreement even though her beliefs differed entirely from her husband's. Macario continued, "Bernardo can provide for you and that is what is most important."

Candelaria ignored her father's reasoning. "He is too old. I want to be married someday, but not to an old man. I want someone who is my age. Don't you want me to marry someone my age?" Bernardo, in addition to being her parents' age, was not a particularly handsome man. He was five foot five inches tall—an average height at the time—thick in build, and tanned, with large, thick hands that served him well as a carpenter.

"If there is a younger man in San Jose today who can provide for you, then yes, you should marry him. But there is no one like that here.

Bernardo needs a wife who can support him and help him with his children. And you need a man who can support you today and in the future. If you don't marry him now, you may lose the chance to live a better life."

Maria added without showing her opposition to the marriage, "I will be here when you need help with anything."

At this point the discussion overwhelmed Candelaria. She put her hands over her eyes as the tears began to roll down her cheeks. Her crying ended Macario's desire to continue making his case. He relented and taking the tack Bernardo had used, said to Candelaria, "We don't have to decide anything today. Let's think about this and we can make a decision later."

Candelaria left the table and stepped out of the room. Maria stood and thrust her hand out at Macario and said, "I told you so." She followed Candelaria to console her.

In the days that followed, Candelaria asked Maria, "Do you agree with Papá?"

"Mija, I, too, want you to marry a man who is responsible and able to provide for you. But I don't agree that Bernardo is that man. He is old and experienced in the world, and you are not. If you marry him, he will always be stronger than you in many ways. And you will have to do as he says and not anger him."

"You must explain this to Papá."

"I did. But your father won't listen."

"What's wrong with him?"

"Mija, he loves you. He believes this marriage is best for you, especially as you grow older."

Candelaria offered a way out. "Maybe we can ask the priest to speak with Papá."

"I already have," Maria confessed. "He agrees with your father and Bernardo."

Candelaria did not speak for a few seconds. Maria could see that she was gathering her thoughts. Finally, she asked, "If I have to marry him, will I have to sleep next to him too?"

Maria could not answer in a way that calmed Candelaria's apprehension. She said, "That is a decision to be made by a wife and husband."

Again, the tears flowed down Candelaria's cheeks. She was trapped—short of entering a convent, there was no alternative life on El Saucillo but that of a spouse and mother. For weeks she resisted and told her parents that she did not want to marry Bernardo, but they disregarded her opposition. She hoped that if she delayed, they might tire and end any further attempts to persuade her. Bernardo regularly asked Macario if there was progress with Candelaria, and each time Macario deflected his inquiry, telling him that she needed more time to decide. Macario began to feel the weight of the delay and began to pressure Candelaria for her cooperation. In mid-April, after many tears, it was Candelaria who tired and ended her resistance. She told her parents, "If you still think that it is best that I marry Señor Rodriguez, I will." Maria held her in her arms, saying, "All will be well, and you will know in time that you have done the right thing." Macario also embraced his teary-eyed daughter and tried to comfort her. "Remember that your mother and I will help and support you."

Candelaria's character was one of obedience rather than rebellion, and at fifteen she lacked the emotional and mental maturity to defy her father's wishes. Her parents did not see that placing her in the hands of this older man, in effect, enslaved her into a life of subservience.

On learning that Candelaria had relented and agreed to his proposal, Bernardo moved quickly. He told the priest, who made no attempt to impose the traditional year of mourning before marrying a second time. Instead, the priest suggested a thirty-day waiting period and set the date for May 16. Bernardo also borrowed a small amount of money from the hacendado to cover the costs of a small wedding celebration and the Church's recording fee. The loan was not unusual; hacendados regularly lent small amounts of money to favored campesinos. These loans were also in the interests of the hacendados, as the debt served to further tie the campesinos to the hacienda.

As the wedding date approached, Candelaria became more and more anxious. By the wedding's eve, she was terrified. Given the Church's stance on modesty and chastity, Maria had not explained to her the matters of intimacy as a wife or conception. Maria's one counsel was that she pray for strength. Maria also suggested a prayer commonly recited by wives before marital relations in those times. The words were, in essence: "I do this, Lord, not out of lust but in service of my duty to produce children." Candelaria was left with no real expectations or understandings of the emotional strain and physical pain of sexual relations, especially with a man twenty-four years her senior. She thought she might suffer harm and that pregnancy would be the immediate result. Her wedding night would not be one of romantic affection for her new husband. It would instead be a matter of enduring and surviving the advances of an inconsiderate and impatient man.

With the blessing of the Church and the consent of Maria and Macario, Candelaria married Bernardo in San Jose de Gracia on May 16, 1880, just three months after his first wife passed away.

2

Candelaria's Children, Courtship, the Military Threat

Within the first few months of her marriage, Candelaria became pregnant. She gave birth on April 27, 1881, but her child did not survive. Candelaria named the baby girl Maria Anastasia, Anastasia meaning "she who will rise again." Candelaria turned to her mother for consolation and support, and Maria recounted her own experiences. She encouraged her daughter to have faith that God would bless her and Bernardo with another child. Eleven months later, Candelaria gave birth to a son, Abraham, who was later called Abran. He survived not only his birth but his childhood as well—a remarkable feat under the circumstances. Infant mortality was high on the haciendas. The poverty and harshness of life on El Saucillo had their impacts, and good nutrition and medical care remained out of reach for the campesinos. Abran's survival was not repeated when Candelaria, at age twenty in June 1885, gave birth to her third child, Modesto. He, too, did not survive. Despite Maria and Macario's assurances of a better life in a marriage to Bernardo, life for Candelaria on the rancho at San Jose remained very harsh. In the years 1885 through 1901, Candelaria gave birth to seven children who did not reach adulthood. Most died within a year of being born—only Abran, Manuel, born in 1888, and Juana, born in 1898, would survive into adulthood.

After the war with France, Mexico's president, Porfirio Diaz, began a thirty-year reign in 1876 and successfully attracted investors from the United States and Great Britain, among others. Regrettably, Diaz ensured that the foreign investors and Mexico's wealthy received the larger share of the benefits of industrialization. Little of the wealth generated reached the pockets of the campesinos, and the difference between the rich and the poor increased. As the political and social unrest rose in rural areas, a number of roving raiders and militias, who once fought against the French, began to plunder the ranchos and rural towns. Diaz responded with a mounted armed police force under his direct command and out of the Republican Army's control. But his force, known as the Rurales, was, at best, ineffective in eliminating the banditry and, at worst, brutally oppressive toward opponents of Diaz. The countryside, including Aguascalientes and Zacatecas, lacked stability and security and left the campesinos to arm themselves in fear of both the militias and the Rurales.

Amid this poverty, war, and exhausting labor and the sorrow of losing a child, one might wonder how Candelaria, or anyone, could find even a few moments of joy during the day. But the people of El Saucillo did. They enjoyed each other's company and were passionate in their music and dance. Men and women greeted each other with a hearty embrace that conveyed the sentiments *I'm happy to see you* and *I'm happy to see that you're still alive and well*. For Candelaria, with her mother in close vicinity, her faith, and a continuing hope for a better life, she found the physical and emotional strength to survive and take the next step forward.

Incredibly, fate called on her to take that next step just one month after she lost her seventh son in July 1901. Bernardo became ill and died of pneumonia on August 15, at age sixty. He lived his life—birth, marriage, children, death, and burial—on the ranchos within twenty miles of Rincón de Romos. With Bernardo's passing, Candelaria was a thirty-six-year-old widow with three children: nineteen-year-old Abran, thirteen-year-old Manuel, and two-year-old Juana. The loss of their breadwinner forced the family to adapt to avoid falling into deeper poverty. They moved to a smaller room on the rancho in San Jose but still within the hacienda walls and safe from the brewing rebellion, militias, and roving bandits. Determined, Candelaria and Abran combined their earnings, Abran from the carpentry skills he had learned from Bernardo, and Candelaria from any paying domestic or housekeeping work she might find. Their earnings were unstable and uneven, but the family was determined, and they survived.

With their focus on day-to-day living, the family did not anticipate a man of stern character becoming a part of the family and profoundly altering its course.

❦

The Church's records for the Padilla family reach back to the mid-1700s and show that the family lived on El Saucillo for at least one hundred and fifty years. Asención ("Chon") Padilla was born on December 8, 1867, on the rancho at San Jose De Gracia. He was the only child of Rafael Padilla and his second wife, Matilde Rodriguez Padilla. Chon was named after the Ascension feast day, the Catholic holy day celebrated on the fortieth day after Easter honoring the ascent of Jesus Christ into heaven. Rafael and Matilde married in Rincón de Romos on January 14, 1866; he was thirty-seven and she was twenty. They remained on the rancho and stayed clear of the French Intervention, which ended a few months before Chon's birth. The family survived the harsh conditions on the rancho for the next two decades and made a home in the small room assigned to them.

Death was always busy on the haciendas, and it came to San Jose in November 1890, when Rafael broke his leg out on the rancho. One of the men tried to stabilize his leg with a makeshift splint in preparation for the return to the hacienda. Medical treatment, beyond bandaging and a supply of oils and bottled tonics, was not readily available. Most haciendas did not have a resident doctor to attend to the medical needs of the hacendados or campesinos. There was no remedy other than to ask the hacendado to summon the nearest doctor and wait. The doctor for Rafael was delayed, and by the time he reached the hacienda the gangrene had begun its lethal march. It was apparent to Rafael and Matilde that death was inevitable.

On his deathbed, Rafael spoke to his twenty-two-year-old son. "Mijo, I have only one request of you," he whispered slowly.

"Si, Papá, whatever you ask," said Chon.

"Take care of your mother. No matter what happens, take care of your mother. If someday you should marry, it doesn't matter. Take care of your mother."

"Of course, Papá. I promise you."

"Bueno. Bueno."

Chon and Matilde sat at his side until Rafael's life came to its end. He was sixty-two years old.

As Chon had promised, he took care of his mother and worked as a day laborer on the rancho at San Jose. He had a reputation as a stern, quick-tempered man with a macho demeanor—a tough guy. He was a *pistolero*, a man comfortable with a pistol. Given the brigands and increasing political tensions on the haciendas and rural countryside, his familiarity with firearms is understandable. With thick black hair and lean at a height of nearly six feet, taller than most men of his time, it is fair to describe him as tall, dark, and handsome. His physical presence created a sense of confidence and security. He also had the ability to grow and harvest gardens that yielded a bounty of corn, tomatoes, squash, chilies, cilantro, mint, and other vegetables and herbs. He lowered his guard and was a man at peace only in the garden with his hands in the soil nurturing sustenance for the body and soul.

From time-to-time, Candelaria had observed Chon tending his garden in the area within the hacienda set aside for the families who labored on the rancho. Their paths crossed when Chon accompanied Matilde to the rancho-owned dry goods store and other village shops. They also had met on occasion through the years at baptisms, weddings, funerals, and other hacienda events, but they did not speak to one another beyond a polite greeting. During the middle of Candelaria's observance of the Catholic tradition of a widow's year of mourning, she and Chon encountered each other at the rancho lumber stall. She was sitting on the buckboard of a horse-drawn wagon with three-year-old Juana in her lap as she waited for Abran to fill the wagon bed. Chon was there to gather material for a corral. When he saw Candelaria, he removed his hat and approached. "Buenos días, Señora."

She properly returned the greeting. "Buenos días."

Chon continued respectfully, "I did not have the opportunity before today to tell you that I am sorry for the loss of Don Bernardo, may he rest in peace."

Candelaria thanked him, "Gracias for your kindness, Asención."

"If you need help at any time, I am at your service. Just send for me."

"Gracias," she responded.

After a brief moment of expectation, he was unable to raise any other topic of conversation, so he brought it to an end. "Please excuse me, but I must join the other men."

"Of course."

He put on his hat and returned to the small group of workers.

Candelaria was surprised by his approach and expression of condolence. Chon's gesture was thoughtful and kind and a little unusual given his reputation. Nonetheless, he had made a favorable impression. When Abran climbed aboard the wagon, he asked, "Was that Señor Padilla talking with you?"

"Yes."

"What did he want?" he asked.

Candelaria reassured her son that nothing was amiss and explained, "He wanted to offer his condolences for your father's passing." She softly gave Juana a little hug and kissed her on the head. Her response put Abran at ease, and he did not ask any more about Chon. But he did have another subject he wanted to discuss. As he drove the wagon, he said to Candelaria nervously, "I want to tell you about my plans."

"What plans, mijo?"

Without looking at her and keeping his attention on driving the wagon, Abran said, "I'm going to get married."

Candelaria was surprised. She thought for a second, then squinted her eyes at him as though trying to see through a fog. With some disbelief, she asked, "Who are you going to marry?" But before he could respond she answered her own question. "Alvina?"

"Yes. I'm going to marry Alvina."

Alvina was born in the same year as Abran and, like him, raised in San Jose. Candelaria had noticed in past celebrations that Abran spent much of his time in conversation with the very petite, black-haired, brown-eyed young woman. They were frequent dancing partners, but she never thought they were considering marriage. "Stop. Stop the wagon," she ordered.

Abran slowed the wagon to a stop and turned to face his mother. When he saw Candelaria's expression, he knew it was time for the conversation he had mentally practiced for several weeks. "Abran, are you serious about this? Does she know what you are thinking?"

"Yes, I'm serious. Of course she knows. She wants to get married as well."

Candelaria was trying to piece together the events that had led Abran to a proposal of marriage. "Whose idea was it to get married?"

"Mamá, both of us had the same idea. When I asked her to marry me, she said she was thinking about marriage as well." Abran paused, then said, "We're in love."

Candelaria felt some relief that Alvina was a consenting bride with affection for her husband-to-be. She asked, "Abran, have you asked her parents for her hand?"

"No, Mamá, I have not asked them. I wanted you to come with me when I ask for her hand and their blessing."

"Of course, mijo," she said quickly. "Have you chosen a wedding date?"

"Sometime in the spring, I will ask the padre for a dispensation since the year of mourning for Papá will not end until August. There is another favor I want to ask of you." Candelaria looked at him, waiting for his request.

"Can we live with you until we can get our own space?"

"Of course. Is Alvina willing to do that?"

"She is."

Candelaria wanted to assure Abran that she supported the marriage. "I'm happy for you, and I wish both of you many years of happiness in your marriage."

"Thank you, Mamá. Shall we go?" Candelaria, with Juana still in her lap, nodded in agreement. With his mother's blessing in hand, Abran clicked his tongue and the horse started the wagon on its way.

Abran and Alvina married in May 1902. The young couple believed they would spend their lives on the hacienda as their parents and grandparents had. Candelaria and Chon sat together during the humble wedding celebration in the chapel yard. They chatted about the hopes and dreams of the newlyweds. "I pray that Abran and his bride have long lives filled with happiness," Candelaria proudly said to Chon. "This is the beginning of a new life for Abran."

"Much of life is very difficult," Chon reminded her.

"Yes, Chon, you're right, it is. But with God, all is possible. I will pray that they have children, and that their family overcomes the hardships of life, and that they know many blessings."

Chon could only yield to her faith in the future. "Of course, let's hope so."

In the weeks that followed, Chon kept Candelaria in his thoughts.

He found her attractive and felt comfortable in her presence. Chon had reached the age of thirty-four and remained unmarried. After their encounter at Abran's wedding, he began to consider marriage and becoming a husband and father all at once. He had no experience in either role, but with untested confidence he believed he was capable. He decided to pursue marriage in earnest.

Chon had little faith in Catholicism and believed the Church did not act to serve the needs of the campesinos. But he knew that Candelaria was a devout woman and followed the teachings of the Church. He asked the local priest, Francisco Sanchez, to facilitate the courtship. Chon believed that Candelaria might have more confidence in his proposal with the presence and approval of the padre.

After hearing Chon's request, Padre Sanchez responded, "Asención, I am pleased that you came to the chapel seeking the Church's assistance. Candelaria is a good woman, a holy woman, and deserves a good life in holy matrimony."

Chon quickly agreed. "Yes, padre."

"But I see obstacles, Asención. In the first place, Candelaria is still in her time of mourning for the loss of her husband. It will be three or four months before her year ends."

Reluctantly, Chon replied, "I understand. Is there anything else?" He was already feeling the onset of frustration with the priest.

Padre Sanchez responded with certainty, "I need to see you at Sunday Mass. I can't recall the last time I saw you with your mother in the pews. A holy marriage requires the presence of God through the Church. And speaking of your mother, what will happen to her? Are you leaving her to live alone?"

Chon had anticipated that question. "Of course not, padre. I will continue to support her as I always have." He then offered a defense of his absence from Mass. "Padre, I want to attend Mass with my mother every Sunday. But you know I work out on the rancho, and many times I am miles away and cannot return."

The priest relented. "Well, Asención, let's see how you do in the time she finishes her mourning period. And I am happy to see you are not forgetting your mother."

Hiding his frustration, Chon said, "Certainly, padre. I will do my best."

As one might expect, Chon made few appearances at Sunday Mass in the months that followed. But he was in attendance on a Sunday in September. After celebration of the Mass, Padre Sanchez approached Chon and said, "Asención, I am pleased to see you."

"I am happy to be here, padre," he said, unconvincingly.

The good padre continued, "I assume the reason you are here is to again ask for my assistance with the widow Candelaria."

"Yes. That is still my hope."

"Very well, her year of mourning has ended, and I will speak to her during the week. I can share her response with you after Mass next Sunday. Of course," he added with a touch of skepticism, "that is, if you are not working out on the rancho."

Chon ignored the padre's jab, relieved that the courtship was finally underway. "Thank you, padre. Thank you, I will be here on Sunday."

Days later, Padre Sanchez told Candelaria of Chon's request. The words were so unexpected, she replied, "Please repeat what you said."

"Asención Padilla has asked if you would consent to a courtship—in my presence, of course."

Candelaria looked at him to see if there was any jest in his expression. "Courtship and marriage? Asención Padilla?" she asked in a tone laced with doubt.

Padre Sanchez tried to assure her. "I'm aware that Señor Padilla can be a difficult man at times, but I believe his request is sincere and genuine. He is a responsible man who takes care of his widowed mother. Now, if you have an interest, I will convey your answer to him. And remember, I am willing to accompany the two of you as you become more acquainted." The good padre apparently never considered that his presence might impede the acquainting.

Candelaria responded, "Padre Sanchez, in truth I thought that perhaps someday I might remarry, but not this soon after my husband's passing. And I hardly know Señor Padilla. I was married for twenty-one years. Most of my life has been spent in marriage, and half the time I was carrying a child. I'm not sure I want more marriage."

The padre countered, "Keep in mind, Candelaria, that a woman in a holy marriage is a blessing from Dios." He paused to allow her to consider his counsel, and then pressed her, "Do you have an answer?"

She ended his near-sermon by replying in a manner that was curious but not revealing. "Tell him that I consent to the courtship in your presence, but agreeing to courtship does not mean yes to marriage. If Señor Padilla is willing to agree to those conditions, then you can arrange a time for us to meet."

"Candelaria, I think that is a wise decision. I will tell him as you have answered," the priest replied.

She left her thought unsaid: *Yes. A holy marriage would be a blessing indeed.*

Padre Sanchez arranged for the three of them to meet on the following Sunday in the chapel courtyard. Sitting at the modest wooden benches and tables, they talked for a short while over coffee, chocolate, and pan dulce that Candelaria provided. The good padre discreetly allowed Candelaria and Chon private conversation by stepping away and turning his attention to conversation with Abran and Alvina. Candelaria and Chon's second meeting consumed an entire afternoon and included a full meal of chicken, beans, corn tortillas, and a sweet bread dessert—again, made by Candelaria. The highlight of the meal for Chon was the extra portion of meat. They capped their meeting with a stroll around the small tree-lined plaza and fountain. They walked side by side, with Chon towering over Candelaria and the good padre trailing at a reasonable distance.

Initially their conversation was easy and lighthearted, but then Candelaria turned to matters of the heart. "Asención, before you ask for my hand in marriage, I want you to understand what you are asking. I am a widow with two grown children and a three-year-old daughter. I will not leave them with anyone. They will stay with me for as long as they choose. If you want me as your wife, you must want them as your children and support all of us. And you must protect us from harm, especially Abran and Manuel. I do not want them shot or dragged away by some gang or army. I do not wish to bury any more children."

Chon was taken aback by her conditions and the intensity with which she made them known.

He tried to answer, "Candelaria, I will—"

But before he could say more, she continued. "My husband must be a man of faith and not addicted to drink or chasing women." Her words were as formidable as his physical presence.

Chon tried to answer with conviction, "Candelaria, I will do my best to do the things that you ask. And you know that I can provide. I have supported my mother since my father died years ago."

She acknowledged his efforts. "Yes, I know you have taken care of your mother, and that is a sign you are a responsible man. But still, please take the time to think about what I have asked of you." Looking up at him, she asked him directly, "Will you do that, please?"

He nodded, and said, "Yes, I will."

"Good. After you have considered these things, and if you still wish to propose marriage, I will consider it and give you an answer."

Candelaria's firm demands left Chon momentarily unsure about the road he had chosen to travel. She was forceful in her position, and he was not accustomed to taking orders from anyone other than the mayordomo. In the days after their Sunday afternoon visit, he did reconsider the wisdom of a marriage under her conditions. In the end, he wanted to be married to Candelaria and believed they would resolve the challenges before them. Days later, Chon told Padre Sanchez that he was ready to ask for her hand.

When the priest told Candelaria that Chon wished to speak to her soon, she agreed to meet with the two of them at her small adobe and stone candlelit room. When the two men reached Candelaria's door, the good padre said to Chon, "Remember, I will remain silent and not intervene unless someone has a question or some problem arises."

As he knocked on the door, Chon affirmed, "Entiendo."

Candelaria welcomed them in, with Chon following the priest, who wore a brown cassock. Her adobe home was typically small, with a curtain dividing the room into a living area and a smaller space for cooking. She led them to a small table where the question would be posed. She offered them coffee, but both men politely declined. Sitting across from her, Chon was unusually mild in demeanor. He spoke without hesitation and, looking directly at her, said, "Candelaria, I am here to ask for your hand in marriage, and I propose that we marry in the Church."

Candelaria's first concern was always the well-being of her children. She had concluded that with no readily available secure alternatives, and the immediate uncertainties of life on El Saucillo, her family's security was better served by marriage. Chon had some harsh tendencies, but he had his better traits, too. He was committed to caring for his mother, he did not avoid work, and he performed any labor the mayordomo asked of him. Most importantly, she believed he accepted that her children would be coming with her, and she in turn accepted that his fifty-six-year-old mother, Matilde, would accompany Chon.

She placed her hand in his and answered, "Yes, Asención. I will be your wife."

The padre gently dropped his fist on the table in approval. "Good, very good. May the Lord bless you and your families." He then said, "Candelaria, if you are still offering, I will take that cup of coffee now."

"Certainly." She stood and looked at Chon, who was smiling. "And you, Señor Padilla?"

"Yes, please. And thank you, Candelaria."

With the stress of the decision now behind her and hope in her heart, she lifted the pot from the *comal* covering the shallow fire pit and poured coffee into mugs. She set one before Chon and the other before the priest.

Chon was thirty-five years old when they married, and Candelaria was just shy of her thirty-eighth birthday. They married in the rancho chapel and duly registered their marriage in the municipal records of Rincón de Romos on January 4, 1903.

Six months after her marriage, as Candelaria filled a large *jarra* with water, she saw four men on horseback enter the hacienda gate riding two by two. One of the lead riders appeared to be a soldier of some rank, as he wore a peaked cap with a visor, an olive-colored coat with insignia on the shoulders, and a medal on his chest. He wore a belt around his waist and a side arm holster supported by straps across his chest. His black leather riding boots completed his military ensemble. The other men wore short tan-colored jackets, and pants over their boots. They wore sombreros and bandolero belts and holstered their rifles in leather saddle scabbards. Their presence and manner were menacing as they rode in the direction of the stables.

An hour later, a woman from the main residence found Candelaria, with Juana at her side, working with other women in the activity area of the hacienda. The woman said to her, "Candelaria, the mayordomo has summoned you to his residence." Candelaria was startled—in all the years she had lived on the hacienda, she had entered the residence on only a handful of occasions.

She asked the woman, "Do you know for what reason?"

"No, Señora. All I know is that he wants to speak with you."

Candelaria took Juana by the hand and followed the woman to the residence. As she waited in the foyer, she surveyed the rich furnishings and decor without jealousy or bitterness. Soon a male servant approached and said, "Señora, please follow me."

Candelaria held Juana's hand as they entered the mayordomo's office. He and another man at his side stood behind a large wooden desk. The mayordomo greeted her, "Buenos días, Señora."

"Buenos días, Señor."

"Thank you for coming, Señora. Please allow me to introduce my guest. May I present Capitán Andres Valencia?"

Candelaria, in a show of deference, said in a low tone, "At your command, capitán."

The mayordomo continued, "Capitán, may I present Señora Padilla." With a slight nod of the head, the capitán replied, "Encantado, Señora." The mayordomo motioned with his hand and asked her to be seated. "Gracias," Candelaria replied as she sat down in a very comfortable chair with armrests. She lifted Juana onto her lap while both men took their seats. She then recognized the man next to the mayordomo. It was the military officer she had seen earlier, but without his cap.

The mayordomo began, "Señora, I am asking you to speak with Capitán Valencia because I am unable to locate your husband. I thought you might answer the capitán's questions for Asención."

She could not imagine what information the capitán needed from Chon. "Certainly, capitán, if I am able to do so."

Capitán Valencia stated his purpose. "Señora, I have been ordered by President Diaz to ensure the safety of the people in Aguascalientes and Zacatecas. The people in these states require protection from bandits and rebels. In order to carry out my orders, the men of Mexico must step forward and serve their country in the Republic's army."

Candelaria realized then that the capitán was in San Jose to recruit soldiers for the *federales*, Mexico's Republican Army. At the start of the twentieth century, the tension of an oncoming revolution in Mexico was increasing year by year. Teenage boys and men were conscripted or recruited by competing militias, rebels, and the Mexican Republic forces. Men like Chon were also in high demand: mature, healthy, strong, defiant, and comfortable with firearms.

"The mayordomo tells me that you have two sons who are of age to serve as soldiers. I would like to speak with them today."

The day Candelaria feared had come to pass. The capitán was pursuing Abran and Manuel. She did not offer him the whereabouts of Chon and Abran. "I cannot say where they are. My husband and son left the hacienda early this morning to work out on the rancho. And, my youngest son is only twelve," she said, understating Manuel's age by two years.

"What time will they return?" Capitán Valencia pressed her.

"They will not return today. They are out on the rancho for three days moving cattle and building a corral."

Many haciendas on El Saucillo had an uneasy arrangement with Mexican officials regarding the taking of campesinos for military service. The hacendados argued that their experienced workers were more valuable to Mexico producing food than as soldiers fighting an occasional battle. Often the hacendados were not highly responsive to the military's requests for recruits and delayed or completely avoided sending men.

Capitán Valencia sensed Candelaria's resistance, and that of the mayordomo as well. After a slight pause he continued, "I must make my way to the other ranchos in El Saucillo, but I will return in fifteen days." He looked at Candelaria and said, "I expect to see your husband and sons here at that time."

"Certainly," she assented.

The mayordomo concluded the meeting, saying pleasantly, "Thank you again, Señora."

Candelaria stood and began to walk toward the door with Juana at her side. Before she reached the door, Capitán Valencia said to her, "Señora, forgive me, but I have just one more question."

"Yes, capitán?"

"How old is your husband?"

Candelaria immediately understood the unspoken threat. *If the boys don't report to me, I will go after your husband.* "My husband is thirty-five years old," she said lightly.

"Ah, then he is still a young man. Gracias, Señora," replied the capitán.

Candelaria did not linger. The pain of the children she lost had never left her, and the ever-present fear of losing yet another raced to the forefront of her mind. The capitán was threatening her sons and husband, and she was determined to defy him.

On Chon's return, Candelaria waited to speak with him about her meeting with the capitán until they were alone. Later, in the activities area and away from Abran and Manuel, she recounted her conversation. "The mayordomo called me to his residence the day you left."

Unconcerned, Chon looked at her for a second, "And why was that?"

"An army capitán wanted to speak with you. His name was Valencia."

"I don't know anyone by that name. Why didn't he wait for me to return? He should talk with me."

"The capitán was here only for the day. He said he was going to other ranchos."

"What business does that bastard have with me?"

"The business was not with you; he asked about the boys. He wanted to speak with them."

Chon began to anger as he realized the captain's purpose: he was looking for soldiers. His mind filled with many thoughts all at once. He weighed the consequences of the federales taking the boys and any possible responses to avoid their conscription. Candelaria saw his frustration but allowed him a few moments of thought before breaking her silence. She reminded him, "We talked about this before we were married."

"Yes, I haven't forgotten." Once he considered the lay of the land, he quickly made his decision. "We will never convince the federales that the country is better served with the boys working on the hacienda. We must go to a safer place," Chon declared. His rush to make decisions often led to poor results, but on this occasion his call hit the mark.

"How are we going to do that, Chon? He is looking for soldiers all over El Saucillo. Valencia will eventually find us, and he'll be back here in twelve days."

"We must get out of his reach. If the boys refuse to join the federales, they will be imprisoned or shot to keep the rebels from taking them," Chon said, not answering her question.

She tried again. "Where is out of reach?"

Chon realized that to keep his promise to Candelaria to ensure her safety and that of the children, he must act quickly. He looked at Candelaria and said with certainty, "We need to go as far north as we can. Chihuahua, possibly all the way to Juarez on the border, perhaps even to the United States."

Candelaria was taken aback. She had lived most of her life on the rancho at San Jose and never far from her parents. She knew little about city life, and even less about a city on the border. Thinking that his plan might be an overreaction, she asked, "Must we move so far away?"

"Yes. We'll ride the train to Juarez," Chon said. "If El Capitán is returning, as you say, then we must tell the boys and my mother right away that we are leaving. We don't have many things, so we'll take only the important items we can carry. Besides, if the neighbors see us packing the blankets and what little we have, we will reveal our intention to leave."

Chon and the campesinos on El Saucillo had learned from the men who built Mexico's Central Railway, and from those assigned to the station at Rincón de Romos, that laborers were needed in the United States via Juarez, Chihuahua. Among the investments to modernize Mexico's factories, agriculture, transportation, and other industries, the railroads were perhaps the industry with the greatest unforeseen impact on central and northern Mexico. They were built in the early 1880s for the movement of commerce, but like other modern industries, they took laborers from the haciendas. The exodus of the campesinos over decades altered and diminished the importance of the hacienda system. The railroad companies needed laborers to protect their investments in Mexico's Central Railway, and the Santa Fe was one of the railways in the United States that offered higher wages to lure campesinos from the haciendas and ranchos. The Santa Fe's and Chon's aims were straightforward and nearly identical: Chon wanted to go to the United States to work for the Santa Fe, and that was precisely what the Santa Fe wanted.

In seeking refuge in the North, Chon blindly put his faith in the tales of the rail workers who had returned from the United States. He had no certain knowledge about the railway work in the United States, but he saw no other immediate alternative. A step toward the United States and away from the haciendas was something neither his nor Candelaria's family had taken in more than two centuries. They did not know the language, the landscape, or the customs of the United States. But with a sense of survival, and drawing on their courage and prayers, they overcame the fear of leaving El Saucillo.

The hacienda paid the campesinos on Saturday evenings at the end of the workday. Sundays were the only days of rest unless the mayordomo agreed to additional time. Chon devised a plan whereby he and Abran would save most of their final two weeks of pay before Valencia's return. When Candelaria explained the plan to Abran, his response surprised her. He wanted to stay on the hacienda so that Alvina would remain close to her family. Candelaria tried to convince him to leave with her and Chon. "Abran, I understand how Alvina feels, but you are not safe here! That capitán is looking for you, or if some militia takes you, you might die in battle."

"Mamá, no army is going to take me," he assured her.

"You can't stay here; the capitán knows you are here."

With the certainty of immortality that one has at his age, Abran said, "I will stay with Alvina's family. I'll be safe with them. The capitán will not look for me there."

Candelaria began to realize that Abran had reached the age when he could make decisions for himself and his family. She reluctantly conceded to his wishes, though his assurances did not lessen her fear for him. "Mijo, if this is what you have decided, then I accept your wishes. I will pray for you. But if at any time you and Alvina want to join us, you are always welcome."

"Thank you, Mamá. I will give you and Chon part of my next pay and will help you in any way I can." He embraced her and said, "I love you, Mamá."

"And I love you, mijo, y que Dios les bendiga," she whispered.

3

The Flight to El Paso, Fernando's Arrival

Matilde gave Chon a small leather pouch of coins to help pay for the journey. She had saved the coins for his inheritance after she passed. Combining the coins with the money Abran gave him, Chon had sufficient funds to buy passage for the five of them: Chon, Matilde, Candelaria, Juana, and Manuel.

On the first Sunday after Candelaria's meeting with the capitán, she and Chon told her parents of their decision to leave. Chon knew that Macario, as a blacksmith, had access to a hacienda wagon that might be used to transport them to the train depot in Rincón de Romos. Chon asked Macario, "Would you be willing to help us?"

"Of course, Chon. What can I do?"

"We want to leave next Sunday on the afternoon train to Juarez. We need transport to the depot. Are you able to take us early next Sunday morning?"

Macario usually asked for prior approval from the mayordomo for personal use of hacienda equipment. But more troubling was approval for leaving the hacienda. Hacendados and mayordomos informally cooperated to keep campesinos from moving between haciendas and thereby controlled the workforce. Additionally, they would not permit campesinos to leave if they were in debt for loans or purchases at the hacienda dry goods store. Requesting approval to use the wagon would likely lead to the discovery of Candelaria's and Chon's intention to leave, but Macario decided that given his long standing and position at the rancho, the guards at the entrance would allow him to leave and return without any challenges. Keeping his concerns to himself, he said, "Yes, I can do that for you. Of course."

"Thank you, Macario. Thank you. We will always be grateful for all you are doing for us," Chon said.

During the week, Candelaria and Matilde stuffed bags with three days of clothing for everyone. They filled a smaller bag with heirlooms, photos, mementos, and religious items. Chon hid in his clothing a small bag containing a loaded handgun. They left all their other possessions in their place. On the eve of their departure, Chon and Abran picked up their pay as usual while the women prepared a basket of tortillas, meat, and beans for the first day's travel. That night no one slept well except Juana. The tension of the impending trip was too great to allow for sleep.

The families awoke just before daylight and met Maria and Macario at the stables. Before boarding the two-horse-drawn wagon, Candelaria asked for their blessing. Maria and Macario suppressed any fears about their daughter's departure and granted her request. Candelaria knelt before her parents as they each extended a hand above her head. They recited a short prayer asking for God's protection and mercy and that He grant them peace and prosperity.

Chon and Macario then helped the women and Juana into the wagon. They positioned themselves as close to the buckboard seat as possible. Macario gave them all blankets for warmth or seating comfort. Chon climbed aboard and took his place next to Macario, who held the reins. He clicked his tongue and the horses began to pull. When they reached the hacienda entrance, the sentry waved him through without question, just as Macario had predicted. The journey was underway.

A short distance from the rancho, Macario stopped the wagon to allow Chon to pull out his revolver in the event they encountered highwaymen or other hostiles. The ride to Rincón de Romos was long, bumpy, and uncomfortable, but they arrived at the depot in the early afternoon without incident. Macario embraced everyone and said goodbye. He left immediately so that he might return to the hacienda before nightfall. Candelaria and her family waited three hours in the summer heat before the train's noisy arrival. They boarded and took seats on the wooden benches with metal frames that seated two on both sides of a center aisle. With a loud blast of the steam whistle and the slow roll of its large wheels, the black locomotive slowly began pulling a line of wooden passenger cars. As the train moved through town, Candelaria saw from her window seat the graveyard where her children were buried: Anastasia, Modesto, Cesario, Maria Isaac, Ventura, Jose, and Vicente. Moving her fingers from bead to bead after each Hail Mary, she prayed the rosary for their souls and for the safety of their journey.

Three days later at the hacienda, the mayordomo told Capitán Valencia that Asención Padilla and his family had not been seen for some time and their whereabouts were unknown.

❋

Steam locomotives in 1900 reached speeds of forty miles per hour or more, but when carrying passengers, they traveled at safer speeds of twenty to thirty miles an hour. The speed of the train depended on the quality of the tracks, the terrain, and the condition of the locomotive itself. Tracks were often laid imprecisely, with inconsistent space between the rails or with weak and uneven bedrock supporting the rail ties. As a result, the cars rocked, screeched, and bounced as they traversed the rails. The ride was often a noisy affair.

Candelaria's nearly eight-hundred-mile journey to Juarez required eight days. The trip included thirty or more stops in towns and cities for passengers, water, coal, and overnight stops. Candelaria and Chon decided to stay in hotels only in the bigger cities where the accommodations were more reliable. They slept in the passenger car when the security of the smaller trackside inns appeared less certain. On the first afternoon, the train began its northward progress to Zacatecas, the capital city. At the Zacatecas overnight stop, the family rented one room at the trackside inn. The accommodations were meager but sufficient for the family of five. They ate the food they had brought with them for their evening meal.

On leaving Zacatecas the next morning, the train headed for the city of Torreón in the state of Coahuila. Torreón is located on the south end of the Chihuahuan Desert, which extends in a northwesterly direction into Arizona and as far north as Albuquerque, New Mexico. The climb from Zacatecas to Torreón, from approximately 2,000 feet to 3,700 feet in elevation, required three days. On the second night, the family remained aboard the train and bought their meals from the local vendors who set up trackside booths and tables. They slept in unoccupied seats. They kept their windows open, and with the small windows set in the raised roof of the car, there was enough airflow for comfort. At either end of the aisle, candles supplied enough light for them to see the way to the small lavatory with a toilet and wash bowl. Each car had a small water barrel and cup near the car entrance, but Candelaria was cautious about family members drinking from the barrel. She tried to keep a small canteen filled with water from trackside cafes and restaurants for family use, especially for Juana.

Much of the time, Candelaria spent chatting with Matilde, playing with Juana, and talking with other female passengers. Chon and Manuel were less sociable and kept to themselves, with Chon sternly telling Manuel that upon arrival he was expected to find a job and work. During the day, Juana often napped in Candelaria's lap, giving her mother the chance to look out her window at the countryside. She saw fewer and fewer farms, ranchos, and livestock. The grass and bushes of Aguascalientes gave way to the drier landscape of Zacatecas. Candelaria had never traveled so far from San Jose.

Though Torreón has a high elevation, summers were hot, and as they continued northward the heat became more uncomfortable. The family cooled themselves with wet towels and drank water throughout the day. The only relief at that altitude was the cooler mornings and evenings.

The family took full advantage of the overnight stop in Torreón. They rented a room, ate at the restaurant, and laundered their clothes. They remained hopeful and in good spirits. But they were about to be tested. They faced a slow climb to the capital city of Chihuahua over three days in the middle of the Chihuahuan Desert.

By the time the train approached the city of Chihuahua, the family was suffering different levels of fatigue. Candelaria's struggle to keep Juana occupied became more challenging. The few initial distractions no longer held Juana's attention; the walks up and down the aisle did little to lessen her energy level. The view outside the window was an unchanging landscape of rocky hills with few shrubs or plants of any kind. The afternoon heat remained stifling. Only when the train stopped for the night did the family's hopes begin to rise. One more day of travel remained. They rented a room and readied themselves for the final part of the journey to Juarez.

The next morning, the family felt excitement and anticipation. Juarez was a half-day ahead. As the train began to move, Candelaria continued her practice of starting each day of travel praying a rosary for safety. Shortly after midday, the train reached the Juarez depot and slowly rolled to a stop. They had reached the northernmost point of Mexico at last. Everyone disembarked, with Chon in the lead. He and Manuel helped Matilde and Candelaria, with Candelaria holding Juana's hand. They rented a hotel room to gather themselves in preparation for crossing into the United States the following day.

The next morning, they spoke to a priest and asked for help in crossing. The priest suggested that they enter with as few material items as possible. If they were asked, they should say that they were going to El Paso for three days to visit Matilde's ill sister. The priest also provided the street name and number in the barrio tenements for their stay. This information would be also helpful in the event US border inspectors asked about their stay. The priest then escorted them to the trolley stop for the newly installed El Paso Electric Railway that would take them across the Rio Bravo. The priest's assistance ended with a blessing, for which Chon thanked him. He also offered a small contribution in gratitude, which the priest accepted.

When the trolley reached the bridge, a Mexican official stepped aboard. Two armed federales stood a few feet from the trolley steps. The official stopped at each seat and asked the riders if they were Mexican citizens. When he reached Chon, he asked, "How many, and when do you expect to return?"

Chon was calm. "There are five of us. Three days."

The official looked at everyone and then asked Manuel, "How old are you?"

"Twelve," Manuel answered.

The official immediately wrote on a notepad, tore off the page, and gave it to Chon, saying, "Bring this paper with you when you return."

"Si, Señor. Gracias," Chon said, as he took the paper and put it into his shirt pocket.

The official continued down the aisle and soon stepped off the trolley. He signaled to the operator and the trolley began its slow roll across the Rio Bravo. When the trolley finished crossing, everyone was directed to disembark for inspection. Candelaria followed the command and, in so doing, stepped into the twentieth century.

The US inspector, like his Mexican counterpart, asked the family in Spanish to declare their citizenship, to which the group answered, "Mexicano." He asked Chon, "What is the nature of your business in the United States?"

"We have come to visit my mother's sister, who is gravely ill."

The inspector looked at Matilde and asked, "Your sister lives in El Paso?" Matilde felt apprehension but managed a convincing nod. The inspector then asked, "What street does she live on?" The priest had prepared Matilde for this question, and she answered with an accent, "Kansas Street." The inspector did not react. Instead, he began filling in a form and handed it to Chon. "You and your family have a three-day pass to enter the United States. But you must leave by the end of the third day. Do you understand?"

"Si, señor. Gracias," Chon said again.

At that time, there were few inspectors, and the US port of entry at El Paso kept sketchy records of daily or short-term Mexican crossers into the United States. Mexicans crossing alone and couples were often waved through without any questions. As a result, entrants who overstayed were difficult to pursue. The immigration inspectors kept better records of crossers from other countries—individuals from across the globe, including Germans, Greeks, Italians, Turks, Japanese, and Chinese, entered the United States through the El Paso Port of Entry.

Candelaria and the rest of the family climbed back onto the trolley with their bags. It took them to the stop across from the Kansas Street address given to them by the priest.

The family began their lives in the United States in one of the few wood-framed houses on Kansas Street. It was a boardinghouse with a long hallway that led to four windowless rooms with tile floors. The house had a small reception area and a space that served as a common living, dining, and kitchen area for the residents. The boardinghouse space was slightly larger than the hacienda rooms, but the wood frame and tile floors created a sense of far more comfort. Candelaria rented two rooms, one for her, Chon, and Juana; the other for Matilde and Manuel. Tired but relieved, they spent their first day in the United States. That night, after Candelaria put Juana to sleep, she lay next to a sleeping Chon, took out her rosary, and silently prayed in thanks for God's protection during their journey.

Candelaria's foremost motivation for fleeing Mexico was the safety of her family. But another motivation was to escape the sense of unworthiness that mixed-blood campesinos were made to feel at the hands of the Spanish-blood-only elites. Regrettably, she quickly learned that racial prejudice was also a significant part of the United States.

As the Rio Grande, as it is called north of the border, approaches El Paso from the west, its course dips southward and flows around the city, then resumes an easterly course on its way to the Gulf of Mexico. The U-shaped dip around the city resulted in a bulge on the border with Mexico. The bottom of the dip was approximately three-fourths of a mile long and created a pocket thirteen city blocks deep and sixteen blocks across. Within the pocket, two barrios emerged: Chihuahuita on the western side, and El Segundo on the eastern side. Virtually all the people in the de facto segregated barrios were of Mexican descent. The boardinghouse at the Kansas Street address where Candelaria and Chon rented their rooms was near the center line between the two barrios and less than five hundred feet from the banks of the Rio Grande.

In the decade prior to Candelaria's arrival, El Paso's population surged with Mexican nationals and non-Mexican immigrants from central and eastern Texas. This influx was separate and apart from the usual of flow of Mexicans passing through El Paso to find work in the interior of the United States. Many from central Texas were citizens of the United States, and regardless of their nationality, they intended to live and work in El Paso permanently. The city did not have the housing capacity for their increasing numbers, particularly for the Mexicans who crowded into the barrio tenements and shanties.

In the late 1800s and early 1900s, the El Paso barrios were the first stop for thousands of Mexicans on their way to the interior of the United States. For the incoming Mexicans, barrio housing was inexpensive, and the furnishings, as might be expected, were very, very meager. Neither the landlords nor the tenants made material improvements to the units, as everyone hoped and understood that with few exceptions, their stays in the adobe dwellings, tenements, and shanties were temporary. Families vacated the dwellings as soon as better housing became available or when families moved north into the interior of the country for better work.

Candelaria's determination to reach El Paso kept her sons out of the grasp of Mexico's armies and militias. She was relieved and pleased with her effort. But any impression that more comforts were readily available in the new city was swept away in the days that followed. When she stepped out of the boardinghouse, she saw and heard dozens and dozens of people moving about on foot, in wagons, and on horseback. Small shops and businesses were sprinkled in among the dwellings on either side of the unmarked dirt streets. The shops included grocers, bakeries, butchers, restaurants, laundry and cleaning services, sewing, and dry goods stores. Many of the structures were two stories with living quarters on the top floor and the business on the ground floor. Most of the shops were made of wood or brick. Candelaria had seen similar types of services on the hacienda, but she never expected to see so many and varied shops with a constant flow of clientele entering and leaving. Scattered throughout the two barrios were many small one- or two-story brick buildings that housed manufacturing plants, metal works, and machine shops. Many of these were on the north edge of the barrios, farther away from the Rio Grande and the barrio dwellings.

There were essentially three types of housing in the barrios: adobe houses that accommodated a single family; tenement housing consisting of a long, narrow, two-story brick building that accommodated multiple families; and the shanties, which were essentially boxes constructed from throwaway materials and mud. The more common dwellings were the adobe houses—one-room structures built with sun-dried adobe bricks made of clay and straw. Most had dirt floors, and their roofs were made of dirt and straw if no other materials were available. Very few had windows, and none had running water. They were irregular in size and shape, with the smaller ten-by-ten units usually occupied by workers or small families, and the larger units of twenty-by-fifteen, give or take three feet, occupied by larger families or a small family business. The families in the dwellings used curtains or blankets to divide the space into rooms. Families shared an outside privy. The primary difference between the barrio dwellings and the rooms on the haciendas was the potbellied stoves and stove pipes in each barrio dwelling for cooking and heating.

Candelaria was surprised by the dilapidated dwellings and the poverty in the barrio—she had expected El Paso residents to have better housing. When she ventured out of the barrio toward downtown El Paso, she began to see the quality of homes and buildings that she expected of a big city. There were newly built hotels, government buildings, banks, and other structures rising five or more floors. Most were built of brick or stone and a new material, concrete. On rare occasion, she strolled into the new buildings just to get a sense of their interior, the beauty of the displayed art, the furnishings and feel of the furniture, the smell of fresh paint and materials, and the echo of her footsteps on wood or marble floors.

Candelaria knew that many people lived in El Paso, but she had vastly underestimated the city's population of forty thousand. So many people in one place was a new experience for her. She began to recognize the Franklin Mountains and the mountain peak later named Mount Cristo Rey, located north and west of the city, and she used the landmarks to mark her bearings in relation to the barrios and the Rio Grande.

Despite the poverty and hardship Candelaria saw in the barrios with each passing day, she also saw and felt a growing sense of security that allowed her to begin to hope for a better life in her family's future. She saw people of Mexican descent running their own businesses and working in the hotels, banks, and government buildings. She knew that type of work might be difficult for her children to obtain, but those positions were within their reach. *Con Dios, todo es posible.*

Candelaria immediately set out to establish a reliable routine for the family. The boardinghouse did not have an icebox, but it was within walking distance from the barrio shops. Most of Candelaria's days began with a walk to the shops with Juana in hand and Manuel along to carry the provisions. After buying the groceries for the day's meals, the trio returned to the boardinghouse, where Candelaria made breakfast for all and lunch for Chon to take with him as he searched for work. El Paso businesses and local families did not hesitate to hire the Texas and Mexican immigrants in the city, paying low wages for their work as day laborers for railroads, lumber mills, slaughterhouses, and smelters. Many women worked as household servants, washerwomen, seamstresses, and other domestic laborers.

Each morning, Chon began his search by walking the three-fourths of a mile from the boardinghouse to the Santa Fe Railway roundhouse, located on the west edge of the Chihuahuita barrio near the border. Within a few days of his first attempt, the Santa Fe began to select him regularly for daily labor, and within weeks, because of his good work and steady attendance, they hired him. The Santa Fe wanted him for any task that required hard labor or heavy lifting. During his initial search for work, Chon carried his concealed revolver, as he was wary of his new surroundings in the barrio.

In the initial days, he walked alone along the railroad tracks to reach the roundhouse and was prepared for any attempted robbery or assault. With time, he began to feel more secure and comfortable with the other men working alongside him and competing with him for work. At Candelaria's constant urging, he left the pistol at the boardinghouse, hidden in his belongings.

As the heat of summer subsided and cool mornings began to appear with the arrival of fall, Candelaria and her family reached a level of stability. She grew accustomed to the rhythms of living in the barrio and the big city. Chon's work was reliable and he had regular pay. Candelaria was seldom at odds with Matilde, who was sympathetic to Candelaria's struggles to temper Chon's harsh manner.

But Chon's persistent complaint that Manuel did not work became a concern. Chon believed that Manuel was old enough to work and contribute to the family. His comments to Manuel were hardly supportive or encouraging. Instead, they were critical and suggested that Manuel's failure was for lack of effort.

Candelaria saw that Chon was asking too much of Manuel for his age and that he was making the matter more troublesome for the family with his manner and tone. Initially, she did not try to intervene, in the hope that a respectful father-son relationship might develop, but Chon's methods remained mean-spirited and unproductive. Candelaria knew that it was unlikely Chon would change his approach with Manuel, so she decided to speak to him and explain that he must temper his conduct.

She waited for a moment when Chon's mood might improve the chance that he would accept her effort to stop him from pushing Manuel so harshly. On a cool October night, she waited for Chon to ready himself for a good night's sleep. When he sat next to her, she said, "Chon, I want to talk with you about important things." Chon looked at her but could not see any expression that might help him determine what she might want to discuss.

"That's fine," he said. "What do you want to talk about?"

"We have to talk about you and Manuel," she said, hoping that he would not erupt with frustration.

"Manuel? And why is that?"

"Because, Chon, you are too hard with him when you talk about work."

Chon immediately became defensive. "You know what? I talk to him like that because he needs to know that life is hard and work is hard. He better get accustomed to it."

"I understand what you are saying, Chon. But he is only fifteen. He's a boy, he is still growing, he is short and thin. You can't expect him to do the heavy work of a grown man."

Chon retorted, "He doesn't have to do the work of a grown man, he just needs to find work of some kind so that he can help pay for rent and food."

"Chon, it is not just about finding work, it's the way you talk to him. You raise your voice and say things that are mean and hurtful. You make him feel ashamed."

"Candelaria, do you think his bosses are going to speak to him in a nice soft voice? They are going to cuss at him and order him around."

"If you keep talking to him like that he is going to rebel. He won't do anything you say, and he will leave this house as soon as he can."

Chon continued to defend his view. "He can work. I was out on the hacienda when I was his age. I don't want to hear excuses."

Candelaria's dread that Chon would be unyielding was realized. She then tried an approach from an angle she had been considering during the previous days. She paused for a few seconds before she began her second attempt. "Chon, is this the way you are going to treat your own children?"

"Yes. But I don't have to worry about that because I don't have any children."

To which Candelaria quietly responded, "Are you sure?"

"Of course."

"I'm not so sure," she said, looking at him. They were silent for a few moments before Chon looked back at her. She raised her eyebrows to signal what she was telling him. He finally asked, in a much gentler tone, "What do you mean, Candelaria?"

"I mean, Chon, you're going to be a father."

Chon sat still in quiet disbelief. He straightened up a little and asked, "Are you sure?"

"Chon, I have been pregnant for half of my adult life. I know when I'm carrying a child." There was another moment of silence. Then Chon asked, "When is the baby coming?"

"In the spring, May or June. Aren't you happy?"

"Yes, of course. But it's such a surprise. I had no idea."

"It's all right, Chon, men never do." She leaned slightly toward him to kiss him. He leaned toward her to receive it and shared the moment of affection.

Chon got in bed and reached out to turn down the light of the kerosene lamp. When he laid his head on the pillow, he said, "I can't believe it." She reached over and gently rubbed his shoulder. He said, "I'll try to be better with Manuel."

"Good. I know you can," said Candelaria. With that, she began silently praying the rosary but fell asleep before she finished.

❦

In the fall and winter months that followed, the family's focus turned to the arrival of the baby. Chon did try to be more patient with Manuel and to control his temper. His efforts produced positive results. He was more attentive to Candelaria and her needs and sometimes expressed his hope for a son. She responded without critique that he should hope and pray for a healthy baby. She also asked if the family could leave the boardinghouse and move to an adobe tenement where they might enjoy more space and privacy. Matilde would have a curtain-made space for herself, while Juana and Manuel would share sleeping space in the living room–kitchen area, and the baby would sleep with her and Chon in a separate space. Chon was not enthusiastic about the idea. The move would mean sacrificing the few comforts of the boardinghouse, including water collected from city faucets north of the barrios. But he agreed that the family needed more space. Besides, tenement rental rates were lower than those of the boardinghouse, and the small savings covered the added expenses of a newborn.

Candelaria's fall and winter pregnancy passed without issue. She was relatively comfortable, and she was grateful she had avoided a pregnancy during the unbearable ninety-degree heat of July and August. In May, the heat began its return along with frequent dusty, blustery spring winds. During this time, Candelaria and Juana often walked the dirt street of the barrio to the nearby bank of the Rio Grande, where they strolled barefoot along the water's edge. For Juana, splashing in the water was a fun playtime; for Candelaria, the cool water on her feet was a respite from the heat and dust. They sat together on a blanket in the shade of a tree near the riverbank. There, Juana played while Candelaria tried to explain that soon she would have a new brother or sister. On occasion, Manuel, still without work, joined them.

On the morning of May 30, Candelaria felt strong cramps with increasing frequency along with backaches, unmistakable signals of active labor. She knew the day of delivery had finally arrived. In between the intervals of cramps, she made a breakfast and lunch for Chon and told him that she was in labor. "I'm feeling many pains; the baby will come today, si Dios nos da licencia." *God willing.*

Chon was positive but almost impatient. "I hope so. We have been waiting for this baby a long time. Will you be okay?"

"Yes, of course. Your mother and the midwife will be with me. You will be a father by the time you return home from work." There was never a thought that Chon would miss a day of work. The Santa Fe did not take kindly to unexpected absences. The railway valued reliable, hardworking men, and when layoffs occurred, those with a record of missing work were the first to be discharged. At the doorway, as he was about to leave for the roundhouse, Chon stopped, bent down, and embraced and kissed Candelaria, saying, "I hope all goes well today."

"All will be well," she told him.

"Make sure Manuel is around to help you. He can take care of Juana."

"Chon, you worry about the wrong things. I am sure Manuel will help if he is needed." She grabbed him by the arm, turned him around slowly, and gently pushed him out the doorway, saying, "Be careful at work today."

Candelaria waited until Matilde sat down for breakfast before announcing that she was in labor. She also woke up Manuel and told him to go and bring the midwife. By noon, the midwife, her helper, and Matilde were moving about the house heating water for a compress to ease the pain of the contractions, gathering towels and large bowls, and preparing the bed for birth with blankets and sheets.

In the midafternoon, Candelaria, suffering great pain, strained mightily at the urging of her attendees. Breathless and exhausted, she delivered the baby into the hands of the midwife, who wiped the mucus and blood from the baby, cut the umbilical cord, and happily announced, "It's a boy!" Candelaria felt relief upon hearing the cries of the infant and pleased that Chon's hope for a son had been answered. The midwife swaddled the baby in blankets and placed him on Candelaria's chest. After a few minutes, she moved him to her side and encouraged him to begin nursing.

Late in the afternoon, Matilde told Manuel to wait outside the house and tell her when Chon was approaching. When Manuel announced Chon's arrival, Matilde moved to the doorway to greet him. When he stepped inside, she announced, "Chon, you are a father! God has blessed you with a son, and I have a grandson!"

Chon stood in quiet disbelief for a moment and then said, "De veras?"

"Si, mijo. Felicidades. He is beautiful, you will be so proud."

"Candelaria?"

"She is tired, but mother and baby are well. I will see if she is awake so you can talk to her. Asención, you must first be kind to her, then ask to see your son."

"As you say," Chon replied. After a minute with Candelaria, Matilde opened the door and signaled to Chon that he should enter. With a gentle smile, Candelaria reached for his hand as he approached. "How are you feeling?" he asked her.

"Bien. Bien, Chon. You have a son." He nodded. "Do you want to hold him?"

"Yes," he said tentatively.

Matilde took the baby and held him in one arm while with the other she moved Chon's arm into position to properly hold the baby. Matilde placed the tiny bundle in Chon's arm and large hands and commanded, "Make sure you hold up his head."

Candelaria said to Chon, "I want you to see him, he is so cute." Chon lifted the blanket to peek at his son. The sight of his child tapped the store of his emotions that he kept tightly sealed. His eyes watered as he gazed at the life in his hands. After a minute, he returned the baby to Candelaria's side and asked, "Did you decide on a name?"

"Yes, I told you the name I like, Fernando. And besides, today is the feast day of San Fernando."

Without the slightest resistance, Chon said, "If that is what you want, then Fernando it shall be."

"Good," said Candelaria. Exhausted but with great contentment, and knowing that Fernando would soon wake to nurse, she slipped into well-deserved sleep.

4

Life and Death in El Paso, the Santa Fe in Kansas

In 1905, Candelaria and Chon decided to leave the boardinghouse for a less expensive adobe unit. By the time they began their search, the population in El Paso's barrios had risen to fifteen thousand people. Chon found an adobe unit a block farther south and west of the boardinghouse, on the corner of Ocampo Alley and East Tenth Street. The unit had one door, one window, no running water, and a dirt floor. Like most units, it consisted of one room divided with blankets or curtains into spaces for living and sleeping and a space for a small square iron stove or a potbellied stove with a stovepipe.

With the exception of the slightly larger living space and iron stoves, there was essentially no difference in comfort from the hacienda spaces on El Saucillo. Rent for the adobe units in the area ranged from one to four dollars per month. Rent for the unit that Chon selected was two dollars a month, resulting in a savings of three dollars per month. At the time, Chon earned one dollar for a full day's work. Candelaria and Chon were willing to sacrifice the minor comforts of the boardinghouse and save for a better unit in the future. But they did not understand the hidden risk of moving into the adobe units and tenements—the barrio's water supply was poisoned with pollutants.

Since the city did not provide water in the southern part of El Paso, drinking water for the barrios was drawn from shallow wells. With the rising number of arrivals to the barrio, the quality of the well water steadily declined. The wells were contaminated by the lack of sewer lines, garbage collection, and the runoff from infrequent rains on the unpaved streets. The inevitable result was a community vulnerable to fevers, diarrhea, vomiting, stomach pains—even death, from bacterial diseases such as typhus, cholera, dysentery, and hepatitis. Cases of tuberculosis also appeared in the barrios from time to time.

El Paso was divided on the future of the barrios. Some in the public and city government believed the structures should be demolished and replaced with new homes. Others argued that the city was avoiding its obligations to supply clean water, garbage collection, and other services and improvements. Additionally, demolition would leave the residents homeless and create greater challenges for the city. The city and landowners were not willing to pay for improvements, and the residents did not have the means to pay. So, the dispute remained unresolved when Candelaria and family moved into their new home on Ocampo Alley.

Despite their living conditions, Candelaria and her family lived in a period of stability and calm through the first half of the year. Their focus was on the care of baby Fernando. Juana, newly enrolled in school, was always at her mother's and Matilde's side, intently watching as they tended to him. Fernando lightened their efforts with an occasional smile and cooing at their touch and affections. Chon was not a doting father—he did not change diapers, and he offered little help with Fernando's care. He regarded such chores as women's work and left them to his wife and mother. But if Candelaria asked Chon to hold Fernando and rock him, he did so.

The disruption of the family's brief stability began in late May, when Matilde suddenly became ill. Until the onset of her illness, she was in good health at age fifty-nine. At first, she felt fatigued, and by the end of the day she complained of muscle aches. She sat on a bed of blankets while Candelaria and Chon offered home remedies of warm broth and herbal teas. The soup and tea eased her discomforts, but the relief was short-lived, as her symptoms worsened during the night. She became feverish and suffered bouts of heavy sweating. The following morning, Candelaria sent Manuel to bring the midwife to examine Matilde and possibly identify the illness.

After Candelaria explained Matilde's symptoms over the previous day, the midwife told her, "Señora, you need to break the fever. Keep applying wet towels to her forehead to bring the fever down. Make her drink as much tea or water as possible, but use boiled water. She should eat some soup if she can."

"Of course," Candelaria responded.

The midwife warned, "If the fever does not break by this afternoon, you must have a doctor or nurse examine her. Fevers are a dangerous sign."

Candelaria nodded and said, "Gracias; thank you for all your help."

"De nada, Señora."

Candelaria relayed the midwife's recommendations to Chon and assured him that she would be at Matilde's side while he was working.

When Chon returned at the end of the workday, Candelaria reported that Matilde showed no improvement. "Her fever did not break. She drank very little water and could not eat. I tried to talk to her, but she did not respond." Chon went to his mother's side, placed his hand on her forehead, and touched her cheek with the back of his hand. He felt the fever's heat.

Candelaria became fearful, thinking Matilde might be dying. "Chon, she does not look well. She needs a doctor." Barrio residents who did not have sufficient funds to pay for a doctor often asked the priests to use their influence to convince doctors and nurses to provide medical care at little or no cost. If they were able, some parishioners paid the Church for its help in small amounts through Sunday tithing.

Candelaria sent Chon to ask the Sacred Heart parish priest if he could send a doctor to see his mother. Chon hurriedly walked the six blocks to the Church rectory, where he spoke to the priest. In a very concerned tone, he said, "Padre, I apologize for interrupting your evening. My name is Asención Padilla."

"Do not worry, Señor Padilla. How can I be of service?"

"My mother is very sick and she needs a doctor. I don't have the money for a doctor to come see her. Do you know a doctor who can help us without payment?"

"Is your mother on her deathbed? Do I need to administer the last rites?"

"Padre, I don't believe she is near death, but she is very ill and needs a doctor."

"Very well, Señor Padilla. I don't know if I can find a doctor or nurse for you this evening. You may have to wait until tomorrow. I will do what I can."

"Gracias, padre, I appreciate anything you can do."

On his return, Chon told Candelaria that a doctor was unlikely to come until the morning at the earliest. Matilde's condition had not improved. They braced themselves for another difficult night.

Candelaria put cool towels on Matilde's forehead through the night, but the fever remained unbroken. In mid-morning, a nurse arrived to examine Matilde. She asked Candelaria about Matilde's condition over the last two days. The nurse felt Matilde's forehead and back, felt her pulse, and spoke to her, hoping for any response. She told Candelaria, "Her fever is very high. She might have an infection caused by some bacteria, perhaps typhus." Explaining further, the nurse said, "The bacteria attack some part of the body, and then spread to the rest of the body. I think the bacteria are spreading; that is why the fever won't break. I will confer with the doctor. She is in danger."

Just the day before, Candelaria had thought Matilde might be dying. Still, hearing the nurse's warning stunned her. For a moment, she couldn't believe it. She began to feel the weight of telling Chon the severity of his mother's illness.

As the nurse prepared to leave, she said to Candelaria, "Keep applying the cool towels and try to get her to drink some water. Hopefully, the fever will break. I will return if the doctor has a tonic or medicine to give her. Señora, it's time to pray."

When Chon came home from work, he knew upon entering the tenement that Matilde's condition was grave. Many candles were lit around the image of Our Lady of Guadalupe. Candelaria, with a rosary in hand, sat next to a silent Matilde. She said to Chon, "She is not doing well. A nurse saw her this morning and said that her fever might be typhus or some other infection. She drank very little water today and could not speak."

Chon sat next to his mother and touched her face.

Candelaria told him, "You should talk to her. She will hear you. Tell her you love her, and make your peace with her. I'm going to ask the priest to come and give her the last rites. Do you agree?" Chon only nodded. She left him alone with Matilde.

Candelaria directed Manuel to go to the Church and ask the priest to come and administer the last rites. The priest responded within an hour and administered the holy oils and recited the prayers for those near death. When he left, Candelaria and Chon sat with Matilde. In a low soft voice, Candelaria repeated over and over the Hail Marys of the rosary: "Ave Maria, llena de gracia, the Lord is with thee . . . Santa Maria, Madre de Dios, pray for us sinners, now and at the hour of our death." Chon recited the prayer a few times but mostly sat in silence.

The next morning, Saturday, May 20, Matilde took her last breath.

Concordia Cemetery is in the rocky desert on El Paso's east side. Sections of the cemetery were purchased or set aside by the city and county of El Paso for different religious and racial groups, such as Catholics, Mormons, Jesuit priests, the Chinese community, and Black soldiers. Chon arranged for the county to take Matilde's body and prepare it for burial the next day in the Catholic section.

Just eleven days into Candelaria's and Chon's grief over Matilde's passing, Death was again at their door. A spike of typhoid, cholera, or some other bacteria was raging in the barrios. The immune systems of the elderly and children were often unable to fend off the infections. At the first sign of Fernando having a fever, Candelaria became terrified. She and Chon had both seen epidemics on El Saucillo. They knew few medicines were available to stop the fevers. Survival was determined by the individual's ability to fight off the infection.

After the first day, Fernando began to show no interest in nursing. As he slept, Candelaria applied wet cloths to cool his forehead. She held him as much as possible to comfort him. She dabbed his thin hair, wet with sweat. He was not doing well. He took water but nothing else. Recognizing Fernando's condition, Chon asked for and, surprisingly, received time off from work.

Through the second day the fever continued, Fernando stopped nursing, and he cried less and less. With each passing hour, Candelaria knew Fernando was unlikely to survive. As the third day wore on, the impending tragedy became more apparent. Candelaria began to cry and prayed to God, "Why Lord, why do you let this happen to me? How can you place this cross upon me? Why must you test my faith?" When the tears slowed, she silently prayed, *If this is Fernando's fate, then Thy will be done. Our Lady of Guadalupe, intercede for me, pray to God that He gives me the strength to carry whatever burden I must bear.*

In the afternoon on the third day, Tuesday, June 13, Fernando lay still in Candelaria's arms. The pain and heartache Candelaria had dreaded once again entered her soul. She held Fernando as long as possible, knowing she would not comfort him again. Chon lifted the blanket and kissed Fernando on the forehead. Candelaria knew Chon was brokenhearted. The pain of the loss of his son, and his mother fifteen days earlier, was more than he could hold within. He held a handkerchief in his hand to wipe away any tear that might escape his eyes, lest he be seen as a weakened man. He suffered moments of anger and helplessness, as well as guilt because he had not been able to protect their son from the illness that took his life.

Candelaria, holding Fernando in a blanket, walked with Chon to Sacred Heart Church. Manuel and Juana stayed behind in the adobe house. When the priest saw them at the door, he immediately recognized them. He saw the tears and sadness in their eyes and knew their suffering. He said without any forethought, "May God have mercy on you."

Candelaria, in deep sorrow, said, "Padre, we have lost our son. Can you please give him the last rites?"

"Of course, Señora. Of course."

After the priest administered the holy oils and blessings, Chon and the priest arranged for the burial. Chon explained that with payments for the cost of Matilde's burial, he did not have the money for another burial in the Catholic section at Concordia. The priest suggested that Fernando could be buried in the pauper's section of the El Paso County cemetery. Infant mortality was high in El Paso—in a three-month period a few years earlier, infants died at the rate of one a day—and the cemetery had an area called the "infant nursery" where they could be buried. The priest arranged the burial with the county.

The next morning, the family, including Manuel and Juana, met the priest at the Church. They rode in a horse-drawn wagon to Concordia, where the priest briefly recited prayers and sprinkled holy water on the small wooden box holding Fernando. Candelaria, wearing a somber black lace mantilla veil and drawing strength from her faith, held Juana's hand and a rosary and quietly wept as Fernando was laid to rest in an unmarked grave.

Candelaria knew from experience that the pain subsides over time, but it never leaves. Fernando was the eighth child she laid to rest. Each death left a lasting emptiness in her soul, but despite the accumulation of heartache and sorrow, she did not become immobile with grief. She always carried the burden of Fernando's loss, each day putting one foot in front of the other and minding her responsibilities as a wife and mother. Her heartache for Fernando was foremost in her mind, of course, but at the same time she worried about Chon and the pain he suffered. She hoped for moments of lightheartedness in each day and that Chon would see and follow her example, rather than become angry or bitter.

Candelaria seldom had the chance to control the events that overwhelmed her or the ability to alter them. She responded with prayer and hoped that she might survive. She believed that faith brought the strength to survive and overcome. She held on to her belief that children were blessings from God who bring joy to life and provide security to parents in their old age. She accepted the heartbreaking cold reality that infants and mothers very often die during or shortly after birth.

El Paso County took some steps to reduce the number of infant deaths. The county dispensary provided limited support for expectant mothers and small children with medicines and medical supplies. Charitable groups collected cans of condensed milk and household goods for distribution in the barrios. They also encouraged residents to boil their water, open their doors for better ventilation, use dirt closet toilets, and limit their use of open toilets. Many of the volunteers acted out of generosity, while a few acted out of fear that the "servant class" of barrio residents might spread disease to other parts of the city. Despite the combined efforts of the county and charities, the number of infant deaths remained significant.

Four months after Fernando's death, Candelaria found that she was again expecting a child. She focused on the blessings, rather than the gauntlet lying in wait. When she was certain of her pregnancy, she told Chon. Outwardly, he displayed a cautious contentment in support of his wife. But hidden within was an uneasiness and apprehension that the infant and Candelaria were again at risk of death.

After the passing of Matilde and Fernando, and hearing the comments of midwives and women about the number of infants and children dying, Candelaria began taking extra precautions with their drinking water. She boiled any barrio water to be used for drinking and cooking. She directed Chon to bring city water home anytime he was in the northern part of the city. Chon was skeptical that the water caused the illness that had taken his mother and son. But after Candelaria's announcement that she was carrying a child, he accepted that the water precautions were well-taken and followed her orders.

In 1906, Manuel was seventeen years old and finally working as a laborer at the electric plant. Chon's work at the Santa Fe continued without interruption. Juana was seven and remained a constant at her mother's side. To get relief from the early summer heat, Candelaria and Juana walked along the banks and shade trees of the Rio Grande. Candelaria's pregnancy was without incident as when she carried Fernando. During the later months, the baby's movements and kicks were not as frequent as Fernando's movements. But they continued, and that gave Candelaria confidence for the delivery. Chon remained quietly cautious about the baby's development. He did suggest that if the baby were a boy, he should be named after Chon's father, Rafael. Candelaria agreed without question.

In the first week of June, Candelaria sent word to the midwife that delivery was a matter of days away. Late in the evening on Tuesday, June 5, Candelaria's water broke. Chon asked, "How soon before the baby arrives?"

"I cannot say with certainty, but I hope by tomorrow morning."

Chon surprised Candelaria by saying, "If I ask *el jefe*, he might give me permission to miss work. But I will have to report in the morning to get an answer."

"Of course, I want you here, if there are no problems at work."

"Muy bien, I will go in early and return as soon as I can."

Candelaria began to feel hard labor pains at 3:00 in the morning. She sent Chon to tell the midwife. When the midwife and her assistant arrived, he left to ask the Santa Fe for the day off. The boss granted his request, and by the time he returned, about 9:00 a.m., Candelaria was in active labor. The midwife told Chon that he could stay at her side for the moment, but when Candelaria began delivering the child, he should wait on the other side of the curtain or outside of the house. Within the hour, the midwife told Chon it was time for him to leave the room. Chon stepped outside, but he could still hear Candelaria groaning in pain.

Finally, the sounds of Candelaria's effort ended. Chon peered behind the curtain and saw the midwife and aide moving about. When he heard the cries of a baby, his apprehension of death and tragedy began to subside. After a few minutes, the midwife invited Chon into the room. He could see the quiet bundle of life next to Candelaria. Before he could speak,

Candelaria said, "Chon, you have a beautiful daughter. I know you wanted a boy, but she is beautiful!" Chon did feel minor disappointment, but uncharacteristically for him, he understood that this was a time to support Candelaria. "Don't worry, I just want the two of you to be healthy. Can I hold her?"

Candelaria transferred the baby to his arms. He looked under the blanket. For the moment, she was calm and quiet. Chon said to Candelaria, "She has so much hair!"

"Just like her father," she said. She then suggested, "Chon, let's name her after your father. Rafaela is a pretty name."

"That's a good idea. Let's do that."

Rafaela's birth was without any incident, and mother and baby were in good health. As Rafaela began to nurse, Candelaria softly said, "Gracias a Dios."

Over the next two years, Rafaela remained healthy. With each passing month, she became the blessing that was promised. The household remained stable during this time. Chon's work remained steady, as did Manuel's at the electric plant. Juana was nearly ten and in grade school. Rafaela was a calm and playful child and always happy to be in the company of her big sister. Chon was patient with Rafaela, but he began to recede into harsh impatience toward Manuel.

❦

Two years after Rafaela's birth, Candelaria became a grandmother in June 1908. Abran cabled from Rincón de Romos that Alvina had given birth to a son, Antonio.

A year later, Candelaria and Chon became acquainted with Florencio Loera and his family. Florencio had recently bought two attached large adobe tenements on the corner of Kansas Street and Tenth Street. He and his family operated a small bakery and grocery store in one unit and used the other as the residence. The tenements, facing Kansas Street, were on the south end of the same block as the boardinghouse where Candelaria and her family had lived when they first arrived in El Paso. Florencio and his son, Francisco, worked for a railway and helped in the store in the evenings. Another son, Homobono, was a baker and managed the store.

Florencio encouraged Chon to buy an adobe house facing Tenth Street behind the store. According to Florencio, the residence had more space than the Ocampo Alley house they currently lived in, and it was available for a good price. Chon described the adobe house to Candelaria and argued that owning the tenement would benefit the family. The monthly payment was slightly more than their current rent and provided more space for everyone. Chon suggested that when the family eventually moved, the new sale price might exceed their purchase price. But Chon did not realize that the price was so low because of the health conditions in the barrios and the threat of demolition of the tenements and shanties. Candelaria was not entirely convinced that the resale of the tenement would result in any gains, but she did like the convenience of the grocery next door. She left the decision to Chon.

Chon's purchase was limited to the house, not the land. The lack of land sales was common in the barrios and kept the real property in the hands of the owners. Chon and Candelaria moved into the house on Tenth Street, and it did not take long for Manuel and the seventeen-year-old Loera daughter, Felipa, to lay eyes on one another. By early 1910, their acquaintance had developed into a romance. It was the first in a series of life-changing events over a tumultuous decade in the life and history of not only Candelaria but Mexico and the United States as well.

In February 1910, Chon responded to a foreman's summons to the Santa Fe offices. As he made his way, he wondered why el jefe had called for him. On his arrival at the small windowless office, the door was open and the foreman waved him in. "Come in, come in, Chon. Please sit down." After Chon seated himself as directed, the foreman said, "I do not have much time, so I am going to speak directly."

"Of course," said Chon respectfully.

"I am going to give you a chance to make more money. I believe you are interested in making more money, is that right?"

"Yes, sir," Chon answered with confidence, despite having a little skepticism.

"The Santa Fe needs labor to construct some passenger stations, freight buildings, and lay new track. We're looking for hard workers—men who know what they're doing. It will not be easy. You'll work hard, but we will increase your pay. How much do you make now, Chon?"

"One dollar per day."

"You'll get paid $1.25 per day. Does that sound good to you?"

"Yes, of course," Chon said, still hiding his doubt. The Santa Fe had never increased his pay.

Chon's feelings of gratitude and good fortune subsided quickly as the foreman continued. "There's one other thing, Chon. The work is outside of El Paso. The crew will have to travel to Kansas. That's where the work is."

Foregoing his usual practice of quick decisions without regard to long-term consequences, Chon paused before responding.

El jefe then asked him, "Chon, do you know where Kansas is?"

Chon recognized the Kansas street name and recalled hearing the name in conversation with Santa Fe laborers returning from laying track in El Norte. They described their time in Kansas as hard work in bad weather, a thousand miles away.

The foreman said as he got out of his chair, "See this map behind me? It shows the Santa Fe's railway lines in the country." He grabbed a tack from the top of his desk and jabbed it into the center of the United States. "That's it, right in the middle of the damn country."

Chon stood and leaned forward to better see and understand where he might work.

"What's the matter? Don't you want to make some extra money? The Santa Fe will provide meals and a place for you to sleep. You'll save money and can send it home to your wife."

Chon straightened up and replied, "That is all fine, jefe. But I will be so far from my family. How long will I work there? Will I be able to return and visit my family?"

"Sure. Sure. If you have an extra-long stay there, you'll get time to come and see your wife and kids. Your crew will leave in the middle of March and stay until the work is done, probably May or June. Understand, Chon, you are a good worker, and I want you on that crew, but you need to tell me tomorrow, because when I have a full crew signed up, no one else will be added to the list."

"Bueno, jefe, I'll tell you tomorrow."

"All right, Chon, but don't wait too long—you'll lose your chance."

When Chon explained the foreman's offer to Candelaria, she was more surprised than he had been. She, too, knew that the railways in El Paso sent Mexican laborers to many parts of the United States, but she never thought the Santa Fe might choose Chon. She asked him, "Do you want to leave for so long?"

"No. But I do want the extra money to buy the things we need and someday move out of this barrio. If I decide to go, Manuel can help you with the girls."

"Why does el jefe need an answer so soon? You are not leaving right away."

"The Santa Fe likes to have crews ready for the spring and its long days with sunlight. If el jefe doesn't have crews ready to leave, they might get rid of him."

Candelaria was not concerned about being left with the children. A decade prior she had raised the children without a husband. But in El Paso, she seldom dealt in matters that required English or interaction with government officials—she left those tasks to Chon. In his absence, and if Manuel were unavailable, she would have to manage with the little English she spoke. Ultimately, she reasoned that if the work in Kansas resulted in an actual increase in pay, as Chon described, his time away would justify his absence. And she admitted to herself that she would not miss the tension that Chon's rough edges brought to the household. She told her husband, "If you are certain about the money, then you should go. But please, don't get hurt. Manuel will help me if I need it. If they don't pay the extra money, you get back here right away."

"Muy bien, that's what I will do. I'll go to Kansas."

In late March, Chon's foreman announced that the trip to Kansas required three days, including stops at major stations along the way. At dawn on departure day, Chon and the other crew members tossed their gear into a boxcar and climbed aboard for the long ride. He packed his revolver, keeping it out of sight in his bag. He was aware that tempers on the railway, fueled by alcohol, gambling, and close quarters, sometimes flared to the point of assault and an exchange of gunfire. Traveling with his pistol gave him a sense of safety and confidence that he could defend himself should he encounter any such conflicts.

Chon's steam locomotive left El Paso heading due north with an overnight stop at Albuquerque, at the northern tip of the Chihuahuan Desert near the center of the New Mexico Territory. The Santa Fe did not consider for a moment lodging the crew at its largest, newly built Harvey

House. Instead, the crew spent the night on a thin bed of straw fighting the crisp air of the high desert.

The next morning, the train began its climb to the Rocky Mountains. Much of the day was a long, slow, winding climb into Colorado via the Raton Pass tunnel at the border town of Raton, New Mexico. The sharp turns at the pass, and the two-year-old tunnel, were so narrow that the rock walls seemed within an arm's reach. On clearing the tunnel at its highest elevation, the train rumbled down and around the east side of the Sangre de Cristo and Spanish Peaks Mountains toward Pueblo, Colorado. Pueblo sat one hundred miles to the north at the base of the eastern side of the Rocky Mountains. After the overnight stop there, and taking on additional Santa Fe crews, the locomotive made a sharp right turn, headed east, and began its daylong run to Dodge City, Kansas. From Pueblo to Central Kansas, the Santa Fe's main line generally ran parallel to the Arkansas River, whose source lies in western Colorado. From Central Kansas, the main line veered northeast to Kansas City and Chicago, while the Arkansas River veered southeast into the Mississippi River. Ironically, Chon's journey to Kansas took him to the place explored by men from Mexico more than 350 years prior: in 1541, Francisco Vazquez de Coronado and his expedition reached the Arkansas River near Dodge City.

During the train ride, Chon heard other crews talking about the work ahead of them. He became confused, as he believed the work was in Topeka. But other crewmen explained that their destination was Dodge City. The Santa Fe station in Dodge was the area headquarters, and from there, crews were assigned projects along the main line. On arrival, he and the other men again slept in boxcars, bunk cars, and tents, rather than in the fancy, red-brick, two-story Fred Harvey Hotel. Two days later, Chon and his crew were sent eighty miles east of Dodge on the main line to Stafford, Kansas, a small town with a population of slightly more than six hundred. With the arrival of the new crews, the number of Santa Fe employees at the Stafford site reached nearly ninety single Mexican men and six men with families.

Chon's crew maintained a length of track approximately ten miles long, referred to as a "section." Their primary task was to build track ballast for the main line and its spurs. With pick and shovel, they built a track bed of gravel or crushed stone to support the wooden rail ties and steel rails. The rail ties were ten feet long and weighed two hundred pounds, while the steel rails were ten yards long and weighed one thousand pounds. Two men with tongs laid the wood ties in place across the track bed, followed by a number of men with heavy tongs who laid the steel rails onto the ties. The crew then used sledge hammers to drive iron spikes into the wood ties to secure the steel rails. The work was not for weak men. It was dangerous, sometimes deadly, and required strength of body, mind, and spirit. Limbs and bones broke under the weight of falling pieces of heavy metal or the crush of moving pieces of machinery. Moving trains mauled men who fell underneath their wheels, and smashed the life out of the ones who could not make the leap to safety.

The hardships suffered by Chon in Kansas were not solely the result of industrial machinery but also the harsh weather on the southern plains. Temperatures in early spring remained very cool through the tornado season of May and June. Section crews were often unprotected from tornados, thunderstorms, hail, and strong winds. Summers were hot, with temperatures reaching the 90s. Winters included snowfall and, occasionally, brutal blizzards. Winter temperatures in the mid-teens were not uncommon. And nearly always, the wind blew, particularly October through May.

Chon received his first pay on a Saturday after two weeks in Stafford. He followed the other men to the local post office, stood in line at the money order window, and sent money to Candelaria in El Paso. He followed this ritual every Saturday for the next three months.

After Chon's crew finished their work in Stafford, the Santa Fe sent them back to Dodge City to await assignment to their next project. Along with the regular money order, Chon sent a telegram to Candelaria telling her that he wanted her and the children to leave El Paso for Dodge City. He emphasized the abundant work and better pay in Kansas and less sickness than in El Paso.

Chon's suggestion took Candelaria by surprise. A move would disrupt the family's stability—Juana was still in school and Manuel was still working at the electric plant. She had also been harboring hopes that she and the family might visit her aging parents in San Jose de Gracia. Seven years had passed since she had seen them or Abran, and she was yet to hold her two-year-old grandson.

Candelaria told Manuel about the possible move to Kansas as they sat at their small kitchen table. Manuel promptly said, "I do not want to leave El Paso." Candelaria had not expected such a quick and certain reply from her son. "And why is that?" she asked in the most matter-of-fact tone she could muster.

"Because . . . I don't want to. Mamá, why should I to go to a place where I have never been? So Chon can watch and criticize everything I do? And I have a job here." After a slight hesitation, he said firmly, "I don't want to be apart from Felipa." With that, Manuel revealed the real reason he wanted to stay in El Paso.

Candelaria did not respond right away. She stood up and poured a mug of coffee for each of them. As she set a mug in front of Manuel, she thought that perhaps he had arrived at his moment of independence. She sat down and asked, "Does Felipa know you feel this way about her?"

"Yes."

"Does she feel the same way about you?"

"Yes, I am sure she does."

Candelaria knew that Manuel and Felipa were comfortable in each other's company, but she had not considered that marriage might be a possibility. She asked Manuel, "What are your intentions with this girl?"

"My intention is to marry her."

"Have you asked her to marry you?"

"No, not yet, but I will."

Candelaria took a sip of coffee and then offered a suggestion. "Mijo, if that is your intention, then you must begin thinking about how you will ask her parents for her hand."

Manuel's desire to stay in El Paso added to Candelaria's misgivings about a move to a distant and unknown town. She added the possibility of Manuel's marriage to the list of concerns she sent to Chon. But Chon was insistent, countering that Manuel should get married and bring his wife with him. He knew the Santa Fe preferred to hire married men with families to reduce the loss of single men and the cost of training their replacements. Single men were not tied to their jobs to support a family. They easily relocated for better pay And were quick to return home for family or a bride. Chon reminded her that the Santa Fe paid a higher wage than the electric plant. He also told Candelaria that trains were military targets, and a trip to Rincón de Romos to see her parents would be dangerous. There were continuing reports of skirmishes between Mexican rebels, bandits, and wealthy hacendados.

Candelaria responded without agreeing. Instead, she continued to press him for more information. She cabled and asked when they might move and what his plans were for the adobe house. Asking Chon these questions gave Candelaria more time to contemplate her deepest concerns: keeping the family together and keeping the children safe and healthy. In the end, she believed her destiny, even if in faraway Kansas, would be under God's protection. Chon wrote to say that he would return to El Paso in late August and accompany the family back to Kansas. He planned to sell or leave the tenement to Francisco Loera to keep or sell as he wished.

Candelaria relayed Chon's suggestion to Manuel that he marry Felipa and bring her to Kansas with the family. Manuel, who had never considered taking Felipa so far from her family, was taken aback by the proposal. But if Felipa was willing to leave her parents in favor of Manuel, then Candelaria's reluctance to accept Chon's plans would be resolved. She set the resolution of the dilemma in motion by telling Manuel of the possible August move and asking, "Manuel, have you already asked Felipa for her hand?"

"Yes. But not formally."

"What do you mean, 'formally'?"

"Not with a ring and setting a date."

"Mijo, you need to ask formally and get a formal yes very soon. You must meet with her parents as well and ask for her hand. I will go with you and you need to talk with the priest to set a date for the wedding." When he did not answer, she pressed him, "Do you understand what I'm telling you?"

With slight irritation, he finally said, "Si, Mamá. Entiendo."

"Bueno, I want to be sure you do."

Soon afterward, Manuel announced that Felipa had accepted not only his marriage proposal but also his proposal to leave El Paso for Kansas. Candelaria and Manuel met with his fiancé's parents, Florencio and Concepción, who gave their blessing to the match. The Church priest was not so quick. He insisted that the couple complete the customary three weeks' banns of marriage. The custom, in which the Church publicly announced impending marriages during the Mass for three consecutive Sundays prior to the wedding, was devised to allow anyone who might know or have a religious or civil objection to state their case.

Candelaria sent a telegram to Chon to say that she would join him in Kansas and that Manuel and his bride would come as well.

The Santa Fe allowed Chon to return to El Paso in the last week of August to move the family. The date did not allow for the Church's banns of marriage to run its course, so Manuel devised an alternative solution to marry Felipa in a county court in El Paso and remarry in the Church at a later date. Candelaria was troubled by this because she believed that the state of marriage was sacred and that a marriage without God's blessing would suffer. But she saw no other path for Manuel and Felipa to have a proper ceremony in some form. She considered their marriage lacking until blessed by the Church, but under the circumstances, a civil marriage was necessary.

The events of August passed quickly, not only for Candelaria but also for Felipa's parents. Soon after giving their blessing to Felipa and Manuel, their youngest daughter, Virginia, and her beau, Anacleto, also approached them for their blessing in marriage. Virginia, at sixteen—two years younger than Felipa—was about to lose the company of her only sister and confidant. Perhaps fearing the loneliness, Virginia felt compelled to follow in her sister's footsteps to the county court, quite literally. Virginia and Anacleto Valenzuela married on August 17, as did Manuel and Felipa.

Chon returned the following week and packed the family for the three-day, bumpy ride to Kansas. As always, he packed his revolver, while Candelaria carried her rosary. On this trip northward, the family rode in passenger cars. Chon, making his third trip between Dodge City and El Paso, previewed and highlighted the sights and beauty of the high desert and Rocky Mountains of New Mexico and Colorado. After the overnight stop in Pueblo, the locomotive made its hard right turn and steamed down the eastern front of the Rockies and on to the southern plains of western Kansas.

❧

Dodge City's emergence from open prairie to a small farming and ranching town began with two pivotal events in 1872: the arrival of the railroad, and the land survey to set boundary points for housing and commercial construction. Three years later, cattle herds from Texas began arriving in Dodge after Kansas restricted Texas cattle from the eastern part of the state. Kansas imposed the quarantine to prevent the spread of cattle diseases to the local herds. The Texas cattle ranchers turned to Dodge for railway access, and it soon became a busy cow town of a thousand residents that included gamblers, saloons, brothels, and shootings.

The Santa Fe Railroad crossed the Colorado line and reached Pueblo in 1876 before arriving in Santa Fe in 1880. With the advance of the railway, the trading parties and wagons that had once passed through Dodge on the Santa Fe Trail came to a stop. In Dodge, the Santa Fe Railroad's peak years of cattle shipments were in 1883–1884, but the shipments essentially ended when the state set its quarantine further west. Despite the loss of the cattle business, the Santa Fe and Dodge continued to prosper with passenger traffic, shipments of wheat, and coal from Colorado.

Dodge City began to emerge as an important stop on the Santa Fe's sparsely populated route between Topeka and Pueblo. The Santa Fe built a new red brick station in 1896. It added a Harvey House hotel and restaurant in 1901. In the ensuing decade, the Santa Fe continued to improve and add on to its facilities with freight houses, coal houses, lumber yards, shops, a powerhouse, and a roundhouse.

During this time, the Santa Fe brought Mexican nationals and their families to Dodge to build and maintain the essential engine of American economic progress, the railroads. The initial workforces were single men temporarily assigned to Dodge. The Santa Fe placed them in a camp on the south side of the tracks, across from the passenger depot, platform, and the new Harvey House. Near or just outside of Dodge, other camps contained as many as one hundred men. They slept in tents, in working and abandoned boxcars, and in bunk cars. With the Santa Fe's continuing success, Dodge was selected as the site for their Western Division offices. The expansion required more building construction, new track, and more labor. Soon the Mexican workforces became permanent. Not only did the Santa Fe allow those men to bring their families to Dodge, but it began to specifically recruit men with families to help stabilize the workforce and avoid abandonment by the single men. Estimates are that by 1930, the Santa Fe had brought more than six thousand Mexican laborers to Kansas.

5

The "Village" Labor Camp, the Teen Bride

Dodge City's population of nearly 3,500 supported a city hall, a park, a library, waterworks, elementary schools, and a high school. Local businesses included grocery, hardware, and drugstores. Commercial enterprises included the Santa Fe, and the Chicago, Rock Island & Pacific Railways, an oil station, hotels, banks, churches, saloons, a daily newspaper, an ice plant, and a movie theater. But outside of the development limelight, a growing assembly of tents, used boxcars, and shanties made of throwaway lumber and material began to emerge on the south side of the Santa Fe tracks and railyards on Dodge's southeast side. The Santa Fe's Mexican workforce and their families lived there on Santa Fe property alongside the southernmost set of tracks. This setting awaited forty-five-year-old Candelaria and her family in the fall of 1910.

At 10:30 p.m., on the 568 train from Pueblo to Dodge City, the night conductor walked through each passenger car announcing, "Next stop, Dodge City, Kansas—thirty minutes!" Candelaria, attempting to measure in her mind the challenges before her, said to Chon, "Tell me again about this place where we are going to live."

Chon was direct in his descriptions and spoke with little concern for any disappointment that she might feel. "It's made of wood, not adobe.

The roof is wood and metal sheets covered with tar paper. It sits next to the tracks with a few Santa Fe houses in a field owned by the Santa Fe. Some families with children live in old boxcars. Every place has its own outside privy. Our place has a yard big enough for a garden, and the rent is only fifty cents a month."

"Chon, I'm not that interested in the outside. Tell me about the inside."

"It is like the house in El Paso, only with more space. It has a dirt floor and a stove toward the middle of the room. It has two small windows on each side but no electricity."

"Where do you get water, and wood for the stove?"

"The Santa Fe put in a spigot where people pump water out of a well. We'll use coal for fuel. I store it in a wooden box behind the house. The only wood we'll use is the lumber the Santa Fe throws away."

"Did you get a *comal*?"

"No, not yet. We can buy one tomorrow and get whatever provisions we need. There is a woman a couple of houses away. She makes money making breakfast for the men going to work. We can buy breakfast from her." Candelaria concluded from Chon's descriptions that she needed to rearrange the family home anew to accommodate the two families.

On their arrival in Dodge City, Candelaria, Rafaela, Juana, and Felipa waited in the passenger room of the two-story, red brick depot while Chon and Manuel collected their baggage. Once inside the depot, Candelaria realized she was in deeply unfamiliar and alien surroundings. All the signs and office doors were in English. Most of the passengers in the room were light-skinned and spoke English. A few others spoke a language that she didn't recognize. The only Spanish she heard came from a few Santa Fe workers engaged in conversation.

Chon convinced one of the Mexican baggage handlers to lend him a small wooden cart and a lantern. The handler agreed on the promise that Chon return both items in the early morning. Chon then led the families to Central Avenue, where they crossed over six sets of tracks. Then they walked on a dirt lane parallel to the tracks in an easterly direction. As they did so, Candelaria realized they were alongside a train yard with men busy with noisy locomotives and train cars. After a short walk, Chon led them to an area where Candelaria saw dim lighting in the darkness a few yards away in the distance. As they approached, she saw that the lights came from lanterns illuminating what appeared to be tents and small shanties.

Chon opened the door to one of the shanties, but all Candelaria could see were shadows on a wall. She hoped there would be more space than in the adobe units in El Paso. When Chon lit the lanterns in the shanty, she was finally able to gauge the space and decided that there was, indeed, more space for privacy. Candelaria put aside any disappointment she might have felt and began to plan for the best use of the larger space, including a small altar for Our Lady of Guadalupe.

The family readied themselves for much-needed sleep, laying out blankets on the dirt floor and dimming their lanterns. Candelaria kept Juana and Rafaela close to keep them at ease and comfortable. When all were drifting into sleep, she began to silently pray a rosary of thanks for their safe journey. But the sharp whistle of a freight train interrupted her prayers, and she felt the vibrations of the heavy train cars on the rails as they rumbled past, just a few yards from their shanty. She wondered if the noise was a constant fixture of each day. When the rhythmic *clank-clank, clank-clank* sounds of the wheels passing over the rail joints slowly subsided, she completed the rosary and slipped into sleep, ending one journey in her life and beginning the next.

The next morning, Candelaria opened her eyes to the sound of loud train whistles and the crash of railcars coupling as they maneuvered around the rail yard for service. She stepped outside of the shanty and saw groups of men walking toward the railyard with lunch buckets in hand. They looked like the workers starting the workday in El Paso, though not in the same numbers. An even smaller number of workers had ended their work night and walked toward the shanties. She realized for the first time that Chon's description was accurate—some families were living in abandoned boxcars. She saw that the lanes and paths of the encampment were unpaved and dusty. Women with toddlers moved through the shanties and tents. The older children were already outside, shouting and at play.

From her door, Candelaria surveyed the horizons to see what landmarks she might use to get her bearings. To the north, a small hill, dotted with buildings and houses, rose behind the train depot. Immediately to the east were railway tracks that disappeared into the distance, and in the forefront, just beyond a row of shanties and tents, lay a flat pasture with a few cattle and horses. Farther east in the background was a group of treeless short hills. Approximately a half-mile to the south stood a tree line that meandered east and west. Apart from the tree line, the landscapes to the south and west were flat and treeless. Only a few businesses and industrial buildings interrupted the westerly view. Unlike El Paso with the Franklin Mountains rising on its west side, Dodge City had few distinguishing landmarks.

Later that morning, as the family walked to see the breakfast woman, Candelaria saw that the better part of her new home was the size of the yard. Chon had correctly assessed that there was sufficient space for a garden and small animal pens. He introduced Candelaria to the breakfast woman and bought breakfast for the family. They ate corn tortillas filled with eggs and fried potatoes. The breakfast woman welcomed Candelaria and told her she was happy to be serving tortillas de maiz that morning. When corn masa was unavailable, she used flour instead. Candelaria thanked her and complimented her on the delicious breakfast.

After their meal, the family set off to the shops on the other side of the tracks to buy goods and provisions. Candelaria felt a surprising awkwardness when she first entered the grocery shop—she was unfamiliar with many of the goods on display. All the signage was in English. Manuel and Felipa spoke enough English to ask for some items, but there was no friendly banter between the shopkeeper and his customers. They translated Candelaria's requests for specific items she regularly bought in El Paso. But the grocer did not stock cilantro, chilies, masa for tortillas de maíz, prickly pear, squash, or chocolate. Families in the encampment relied on individuals returning from El Paso to bring with them a cache of the favored spices, herbs, and other food items. Candelaria eventually left with the staples: flour, coffee, milk, eggs, beans, rice, bacon, and small cuts of beef and poultry. Because their new home had no refrigeration of any kind, her trips to the grocer would be frequent.

When the family returned to their shanty, Candelaria arranged, then rearranged, the items in their home. Sturdy cardboard boxes or small wooden crates served as a table and chairs and shelving for cans and dry goods stacked one atop the other. Cooking utensils, baskets, and washtubs hung on nails on the walls. Some items of clothing also hung on nails as well.

They enjoyed a warm September and mild fall, but when winter came, Candelaria and the family were dismayed by the harsh cold, the snow, and the ferocity of the winds that whistled through their shanty. Chon nailed discarded pieces of wood and cardboard to the walls for insulation. But he avoided using discarded railroad ties for heat. They were treated with chemicals, and when burning they produced a foul odor, made breathing difficult, and caused skin blisters on contact. Out of necessity, the family bought coats, hats, gloves, scarves, and heavy clothing to endure their first Kansas winter. Chon and Manuel, who was hired as a laborer soon after his arrival, suffered the brunt of the season while working out in the elements. Regardless of cold or snow, as many as twenty trains a day, with their loud whistles, continued to rumble through Dodge.

On the worst of the winter days, Candelaria sometimes asked herself if suffering all the cold and other discomforts of the encampment justified leaving Mexico and El Paso. She always came to the same conclusion: yes. All the hardships might shorten her life, but she believed that in Dodge her children and grandchildren would live beyond their infancy and childhood. No army or revolutionaries were going to steal her sons for warfare or kill them outright. She did not want to lose them to the disease and poisoned water in El Paso. She wanted all her children and grandchildren to have secure lives without want.

The following year, the number of shanties and tents continued to increase. The Santa Fe's property did not lie within the city limits of Dodge and was not part of an incorporated town. It had no official name, nor town officials. Spanish speakers referred to the Santa Fe property as *la yarda*, or *colonia*. English speakers and newspapers used the terms "Little Mexico," "settlement," "Spanish Mission," or "Mexican Village." Over time, the English speakers settled on the term "Mexican Village." At that time, neither Dodge City nor Ford County provided a public school for the Village children. Nor was Dodge City's Sacred Heart Catholic Church readily accessible to the Mexican families. To attend Mass, Village families and residents walked on dirt lanes to the track crossing, dodged passing trains to cross over to Central Avenue, and then climbed Central's steep hill to reach the church. The trek from the Village to the church covered a mile and a half. In times of biting cold and strong winds, the Village families sheltered in their homes, abandoned Sunday services, and yielded to the elements rather than risk harm and illness.

In the spring of 1911, the Santa Fe office sent word to Chon that a telegram had come for him. When the envelope was handed to him, he saw that the message was for Candelaria. It was from Abran, who was by this time twenty-eight years old. The message read: "Mamá, I now live and work in Coalinga, California. I send money to Alvina, who is in Mexico with her mother. I am well and will visit you as soon as I am able. May God bless you. Abran." Candelaria was overjoyed by Abran's message. She was pleased that he was supporting his family and removed from Mexico's growing revolution. The possibility that she might see him soon and that her children might gather under one roof raised in her a joyful hope. But she also missed her parents, and she longed especially for the company of her mother, Maria, whom she had not seen for eight years.

By the time she received Abran's telegram, Candelaria had settled into a daily routine. Candelaria and Felipa prepared a breakfast to send Chon and Manuel off to work. The two women filled their husbands' lunch buckets with the staples: corn tortillas, shredded meat if available, beans, potatoes, scrambled eggs, a chili pepper, and a jar of coffee. Corn tortillas were preferred in the Village, but with the scarcity of the maíz, the popularity of flour tortillas rose over time. Chon, the gardener, planted corn, squash, peppers, cilantro, and other herbs in the yard behind their home.

Candelaria and Felipa did the house chores and took care of Rafaela and Juana. The dirt floors were swept daily to remove any loose soil and leave a hardened surface. The table, chairs, and makeshift shelves were frequently dusted as well. The laundry was done with a washboard and tin tub. Clothes were dried on a clothesline outside the shanty, weather permitting. In the freezing winter, they hung the laundry to dry inside the house. After a day of play on the dirt grounds of the Village, the children bathed by standing in a tin tub while the women poured stove-warmed water over them. To Candelaria's dismay, Juana did not attend school, so Candelaria insisted that Juana help with the chores.

During the warm days of late spring, Candelaria and the girls walked to the nearby Arkansas River for a picnic on its riverbank. The tree line that Candelaria saw on her arrival grew along the north bank of the river. Candelaria laid out a blanket in the shade where she and the girls escaped the noisy Village. She had traveled nearly a thousand miles from El Paso, and yet she found herself in a similar place—sitting on the bank of a river that separated Mexico and the United States. Spain and the United States in 1819 signed a treaty setting the border lines at the Arkansas River and present-day Dodge City.

In late November, the Santa Fe office again summoned Chon for a telegram. He later gave the unopened envelope to Candelaria, who hoped it was from Abran, and included the dates of an upcoming visit. She opened the envelope with great anticipation. The telegram read: "Dearest Mother, Alvina advised me that grandfather Macario died from edema on November 19, 1911, in Rincón de Romos. May he rest in peace. Abran." Candelaria put her hand to her mouth at the shocking news. In disbelief, she asked Felipa to reread the message in the hope that she had misread it. Candelaria sat at the table as tears welled in her eyes.

Chon saw the emotion in her face and wondered what possible news could have brought her to tears. "What's the matter? What is it?"

Candelaria looked up at him and said, with tears slipping from her eyes, "Mi papá, se murió."

Shocked, Chon said, "No, Candelaria, no es posible." She nodded at him. "How could that be?"

Candelaria said in a near whisper, "He had some kind of illness, something called 'edema.' But I don't know what that means." She quickly wiped away the tears and said to Chon, "I don't want the girls to see me crying."

Setting aside his usual harshness, Chon tried to console her, saying, "Lo siento. I am so sorry. When did this happen?"

"The telegram says on the nineteenth."

"Dios mío. How old was he?"

"Seventy."

"He lived a long life. May God bless his soul."

By this time, Juana was anxious to know if her big brother was coming to visit. She refused to stay in the other side of the room and insisted that she be included in the adults' conversation. She went to Candelaria and asked, "Was that telegram from Abran? Is he coming soon?"

Candelaria, in a tone of disappointment but not sorrow, said to Juana, "Yes, it's from Abran, but he can't come to visit us right now. He doesn't know when, but he will come."

Juana pressed, "Why not?"

"Because right now he has to stay in California and work."

"Well, I hope he comes soon," Juana complained.

"Me too. You should go play with your sister." Juana did, which gave Candelaria the time to gather her thoughts and emotions. She lit a small votive candle for the soul of her father and said a prayer. She decided she did not want to further crush Juana's expectations for Abran's visit by revealing Macario's death. Instead, she would wait for a time when Juana was free from other disappointment or sadness.

The next afternoon, Candelaria asked Felipa to take care of the girls while she went to the church. She put on a coat and black shawl, made her way across the many sets of tracks, and walked up the hill through the cold and wind to Sacred Heart. There was no image of Our Lady of Guadalupe, so she lit a candle at the side altar and knelt on the padded rail in front of the image of the Blessed Virgin Mary. She prayed a rosary that Macario rest in peace and that Visente, her younger brother by four years, might have the strength to care for their mother.

❖

The Santa Fe continued to recruit and bring Mexican labor to Dodge to meet the needs of its growing operations. As many as 100 to 150 section crewmen worked the main line at any one time. Some followed the work and moved on to the next project, but others stayed with the intent to settle in Dodge. There was no housing for these men and their families, nor did many of Dodge's residents choose to sell or rent homes to Mexicans. Additionally, the Santa Fe wanted the men close and ready to work at a moment's notice. The resolution of these interests was to keep the residents in the Village with low rent at fifty cents a month. Many workers accepted the poorest of housing to avoid the Mexican Revolution and send more of their pay to their families in Mexico. Those who intended to stay in Dodge permanently used the small savings from low rents to add minor comforts to their shanties in the Village.

The increase in the number of Mexicans in the Village and surrounding areas of southwest Kansas irritated many white immigrants and first-generation Kansans. The words and actions of public officials reported in newspapers often reflected the intolerance toward Village residents and Mexicans generally. The comments and actions stripped away the humanity of the Mexicans and enabled those in the white public without a moral conscience to treat them as lesser beings and undeserving of common decency.

In March 1912 in Stafford, Kansas—eighty miles east of Dodge and the site of Chon's first work assignment—the local newspaper, the *Stafford Courier*, reprinted an article from the Syracuse, Kansas, *Journal*. The article supported a bill introduced by US congressman George A. Neeley to stop Mexican employment by western railways. The newspaper supported passage of the bill, arguing that Mexicans displaced American workers, paid no taxes, cost the American taxpayers, sent money to Mexico, and had a large criminal element among them. Unscrupulous politicians and individuals repeated the *Courier*'s lament over Mexican immigrants during the course of the twentieth century. The same lament, often in the same words, has continued into the twenty-first.

In August 1913, the *Dodge City Daily Globe* reported on the Santa Fe's response to a petition submitted by the inhabitants of Kinsley, Kansas, thirty-seven miles east of Dodge. The petitioners wanted the Mexican workers fired and replaced with white men, but C. W. Kouns, general manager of the Santa Fe, countered that "white men as a rule will not work on the section any more, and the talk of trying to force the Santa Fe to discharge its Mexican laborers is nonsense." Kouns explained that the Santa Fe struggled to maintain the track for a lack of workers and that the Mexican laborers relieved the stress and performed the work in a satisfactory manner.

In another article published in July 1912, the *Courier* wrote that regarding the "so-called Aztec civilization . . . it can be authoritatively asserted that it was simply the 'higher type of barbarism' and in no sense civilization as we understand the term at the present." The paper left unsaid its assertion that a civilized society may disregard the humanity of descendants of a barbarous people. The *Courier* also failed to apply the same standards to disqualify Europeans from the benefits of a just society. After a millennium of warfare on the European continent and barbaric atrocities like the Spanish Inquisition, the descendants of Europeans nonetheless did not suffer the same loss of the unalienable rights, life, liberty, and the pursuit of happiness. Tragically, one of the worst acts of barbarianism was at Europe's doorstep when the *Courier* published its article. Eleven months later, the Great War began the furious slaughter of approximately twenty million people.

When publishing stories about the Village and Mexicans, area newspapers often used terms such as "invasion," "greasers," "hombre," and "gang," instead of "crew" or "team." One paper described a windstorm that blew the roof off a bunk car and exposed the Mexicans inside to the heavy rains. The paper continued with a contemptuous comment that the rain saved them the trouble of washing the next day. In May 1914, the *Globe* reported that members of the Pretty Prairie Commercial Club entertained ten towns in central Kansas with a fourteen-car parade. The parade route included Hutchinson, which is on the Santa Fe's main line. Part of the entertainment included a skit in which the men of Pretty Prairie adorned themselves with brownface and Mexican attire, marched up to a US flag, and saluted on command.

Candelaria and Village residents felt the sting of the attitude and the restrictions that were imposed on them because of race. Many Dodge businesses barred Mexicans from their shops, stores, and restaurants. They were discouraged from sending their children to public schools, barred from the public swimming pool, and limited to balcony seating in the movie theater. Many Village residents did not cross the tracks into Dodge without good reason and were careful to patronize only those businesses that accepted them

Candelaria and her family did not find easy comforts living on the south side of the tracks. Her focus remained on her daily purpose: to keep her family safe, healthy, and together. Any dreams of comforts beyond those life essentials would have to be saved for the future.

Despite the barriers, in the fall of 1912, Candelaria made the effort to have six-year-old Rafaela attend the public school. She walked Rafaela to the school in Dodge's East Side District north of the tracks. The classroom was a difficult and challenging experience for the Spanish-speaking Rafaela. Not only was her learning compromised by the language barrier, but the teasing by some classmates also drained her enthusiasm. It is noteworthy that at that time, Dodge City High School taught German but not Spanish.

Out of the growing pool of Villagers, several musicians joined together to form the Santa Fe Mexican Band. A stringed trio, two guitarists, a fiddler, and other individual performers emerged as well. During spring and summer evenings, the trio and vocalists performed in the yards of homes or other gathering places. Adults and children alike were drawn to the performers and listened to the traditional songs and music of Mexico. For most of the small adult audience, the music distracted them from the fatigue of their labors and was a comforting reminder of their families and homeland. On occasion, listeners seized by passion and emotion impulsively joined the musicians in harmony.

It was during one of these performances that Geronimo Gomez first saw Juana. Geronimo was born in Mexico in 1890 and was a very light-skinned, blue-eyed Spaniard with a strong Catholic faith. In 1912, he was twenty-two years old, single, and, of course, worked for the Santa Fe. He entered the United States in 1907 after his parents passed away and lived alone in Dodge. When Geronimo spied her, Juana was standing with Candelaria, Felipa, Manuel, and Rafaela, enjoying the Village serenade. She was thirteen, just a few months from her fourteenth birthday in November.

With the steady stream of laborers, the Village population approached one hundred residents who were mostly young single men. But there was no corresponding group of single women, and the possibility of marriage with the white women of Dodge was exceedingly unlikely. Some of the Village men returned to their homes in Mexico or moved to other towns in search of spouses, while others looked closer to home for brides in their early teens—as young as twelve and thirteen. Parents in the Village kept vigilant and warned their daughters to avoid the men.

The way the girls were lost to the men can be described in different terms depending on the circumstances: stolen, kidnapped, abducted, seduced, snatched, runaway, and carried away. Most of these takings in the Village did not involve physical violence. Instead, the men swayed the girls and young women with promises of love and unending happiness. If a young man seduced a girl with a promise of marriage and then retreated from that promise, he faced the threat of violence. The girl's family might demand that unless he restored the family's honor with marriage, he would suffer consequences.

Not every girl was taken. Many were given away in marriage with the acquiescence of her parents and a priest. Some parents gave consent and blessings to their daughter's choice after a formal request for her hand in marriage. Regardless of the circumstances, hardships awaited these teenage brides, as Candelaria could ably attest. Candelaria was aware from talking with other mothers in the Village that men were on the prowl for brides. She was adamant that she would not be a party to any arranged marriage. She wanted her daughters to marry in the Church and to wed men of their choice who were able to provide security and affection.

Like her mother, Juana was petite, at five feet tall. She was fair-skinned and had dark curly hair that revealed shades of auburn in the sunlight. Geronimo moved closer toward the group, hoping to catch her eye. She made eye contact, but it was a quick passing glance, more out of curiosity than attraction.

Candelaria and the girls left for home without another glance. As they did so, Geronimo asked Marco, a member of his section crew, "Do you know who that beauty was, the short one, standing with the older woman and her daughter?" His friend paused and looked at Geronimo with a grin, "Why? Are you interested?"

"Yes. She is so pretty."

"I know which girl you're talking about. I think that's the Padilla family. You better be careful with the old man; he's not very friendly. If you really want her to notice you, go to ten o'clock Mass on Sunday. I have seen her there with her family. You will get a good look if you sit in a nearby pew."

"I've gone to Mass but never noticed her," Geronimo said.

"You were probably too busy praying," Marco teased with a chuckle. "I'll ask around for you and see if anybody knows her. Until then, if she is that important to you, Mass is your best chance."

A week after Marco's promise to learn about the beauty Geronimo had spotted, he reported, "That beauty you asked about? I have some information for you. Her name is Juana Rodriguez. She and my neighbor's daughter, Maria, are friends. The old man is her stepfather. Padilla is his last name."

Geronimo said cheerfully, "Bien hecho, Marco, well done."

"De nada," Marco told him, and issued a warning. "Geronimo, you better be careful. The gossip is that the old man always talks about his '*pistola*.'"

"I'll be all right, Marco. It's just talk."

"Well, if anyone ever asks about you, I don't know anything."

Geronimo began to place himself in locations where he might encounter Juana, seemingly by chance. He stood close when the musicians performed and knelt close at Mass. Juana did notice his frequent appearances and they exchanged glances and friendly smiles. By this time, she found him very attractive, especially his blue eyes. Geronimo's biggest advance in his pursuit occurred on an early summer evening, when he had gone to Marco's to talk about their work in Kinsley the following week. As they stood in front of Marco's home, Juana and Maria passed. Geronimo called out to them, "Pardon me, pardon me." As he began walking toward them, he asked, "Can you ladies stop for a minute?"

Maria said, "Sure, may I help you?"

Geronimo, with Marco at his side, said, "Buenas tardes. I just want to say hello and introduce myself."

The girls both replied with the traditional greeting. "Buenas tardes."

He went on, "My name is Geronimo Gomez, and may I present Marco Sanchez?"

Maria said, "I know who he is." She looked at Geronimo and said, "Mucho gusto. This is my friend, Juana." Juana nodded at Geronimo and greeted him similarly.

Geronimo turned to Juana. "I have seen you at Church and wanted to meet you." He did not waste any time. "I want to tell you that I think you are beautiful."

Juana and Maria looked at each other and giggled.

"I'm serious."

Juana thanked him for the compliment.

While Marco remained silent, Geronimo pushed on, "I would be pleased to know more about you, Juana. Do you think that is possible?"

She stood still for a second, then after a small twist side to side, answered with a smile, "Yes. I would like that. But we can't talk right now, I have to go home. We can talk later."

"Muy bien, until later, then," said a pleased and smiling Geronimo. He kept his gaze on Juana as she and Maria walked away. After a few steps, Juana turned slightly and looked back at Geronimo and, seeing him, smiled as well. Each of them soon began to imagine themselves as sweethearts, but their imaginations differed significantly.

Over the next two months, they met at every available opportunity, visiting at Marco's home, standing next to each other at the evening serenades, or chatting after Mass out of Candelaria's view. Almost always Maria accompanied Juana, acting essentially as a chaperone. They were careful to avoid any public display of affection. When they found themselves alone, they held each other and shared long passionate kisses. Juana's emotional and physical responses were new, and she felt an intoxicating excitement. She believed she was experiencing the kind of romance that women and men talk and sing about.

Word soon reached Candelaria about Juana and Geronimo. Candelaria had taken notice of Juana's response in Geronimo's presence and thought perhaps a romance was brewing. But when Village talk confirmed her concern, she reluctantly concluded that the time to warn Juana had arrived. On a late September morning, after Chon had left for work, Candelaria asked Juana for help making flour tortillas. Candelaria used a rolling pin to flatten the *testales*—balls of tortilla dough—and placed one on the griddle. Juana teased the testal and flipped it after it bubbled. She kept it on the griddle until it browned slightly. This process was repeated until all the dough was used. During this ritual, Candelaria said to Juana, "Mija, do you want to tell me about this young man, Geronimo?"

Juana had not been expecting this question, and the bigger shock was that Candelaria knew his name. She delayed answering, trying to think of a proper answer. "What did you say?"

"Geronimo. What should I know about him?" Candelaria's tone was serious but not one of anger. Juana still could not respond. She avoided eye contact and flipped a tortilla.

"Did you think that I did not know about him?"

Finally, Juana said, "We're friends. How did you know his name?"

Candelaria put down her rolling pin, looked at Juana, and said, "You need to understand that in a place like this, there are no secrets. Everyone knows everybody's business, and everybody tells everyone else." Candelaria resumed rolling out a testal with a *klak, klak-klak*. "His last name is Gomez, is it not?"

"Sí, Mamá."

"I have seen the two of you look at each other. Is he your boyfriend?"

Juana's answer was a little bolder. "Yes, and I'm his girlfriend." At this point, Felipa, who knew the rumors, took Rafaela outside for a walk to allow for their privacy and to avoid taking a side in the matter.

Juana's answer was what Candelaria had dreaded. "Mija, I hope you are not getting serious about this man. You are too young to think about marriage."

"Mamá, I am not thinking about marriage, and neither is he."

"I know he is a handsome boy, but good looks and working for the Santa Fe does not mean a happy marriage. I married your father when I was fifteen—that was too young, and I have lived a hard life."

Juana interrupted her. "Mamá, you were not too young, Papá was too old for you, and he had children."

Candelaria ignored her comment and continued, "Mija, I don't want you to suffer a life of hardship. You need to wait until you are older and can marry in the Church. A marriage outside the Church will suffer." She made one last plea. "Please wait to marry, whether it's Señor Gomez or someone else. I want you and your children to be happy."

As Juana wrapped the tortillas in a kitchen towel to keep them from hardening, she tried to assure her mother. "We will wait, and we'll get married in the Church, if ever that day comes."

Candelaria hugged Juana, knowing that someday soon Juana would marry someone and leave her. Candelaria's only hope of keeping Juana close in her life was that she might live nearby.

One of the hazards of working for railways was the moving workplace. The work took laborers from their homes, sometimes for days, weeks, or months, even permanently. The Santa Fe had moved Chon from El Paso to Kansas, and now it wanted Geronimo to move to Hutchinson, Kansas, 120 miles east of Dodge. He had no choice; he had to move to Hutchinson or lose his job. He did not want to lose his ability to provide for himself and a family, nor did he want to stop his pursuit of Juana. For Geronimo, the resolution was straightforward: marry Juana and move her to Hutchinson.

At midweek, Geronimo met with Juana at Marco's home. He told her, "Mi amor, I've been assigned to work in Hutchinson. And I will be there all next week."

Juana did not realize the impact of his words right away. "What are you saying, Geronimo?"

"The Santa Fe is sending me to Hutchinson, permanently."

"Do you mean you're moving away?"

Geronimo nodded.

"Why?"

"Juana, I did not ask for this. The Santa Fe is moving me because they need me there and because they can move anybody, anytime. If I don't go, I won't have a job."

Filled with doubt, Juana asked, "Will I see you anymore?"

"Yes, of course. Juana, I'm not going to stop. Te adoro." He also believed, without saying so, that Juana might be swept off her feet by some other man in his absence. He paused for a second and decided that it was time to propose. "Will you marry me? We can see each other every day if we get married right now. And I will have a job to support you."

Juana had expected that Geronimo might propose marriage someday, but she was more troubled by her promises to Candelaria just days before.

She explained to him that she had assured her mother that she would wait to marry and would marry in the Church.

Geronimo said, "We can marry in the Church, as soon as possible. And we can come back to Dodge to see your mother. The ride to Hutchinson is only four hours."

Finally, Juana said, "Yes. I will marry you." They kissed and embraced each other but Juana's thoughts quickly returned to Candelaria. "Let me tell my mother and ask if she wants you to come to the house and ask for my hand. I don't even know if she and Chon will speak with you."

"If they don't speak with me or give us their blessing, we can still get married in the court," Geronimo said.

Juana asked him, "What day are we getting married?"

"It depends on what your parents say. But either way, I will be back next Sunday. We can get married in Hutchinson if we must." They parted with a short goodbye kiss, each full of excitement and apprehension about the week ahead of them.

To delay a possible emotionally charged outburst with Chon and Candelaria, Juana waited until the following Thursday to reveal her intentions. This time Felipa stayed in the room and listened. "Mamá," Juana said, "I have something to tell you that will not make you happy." Candelaria's first thoughts were that Juana was about to announce a wedding date or, worse yet, that she was carrying a child. She poured herself a mug of coffee and asked as she sat at the table, "What is it you want to tell me?"

"Geronimo and I are getting married right away."

Candelaria looked at Juana and saw determination in her young daughter's eyes and expression. The rush suggested to Candelaria that Juana was indeed expecting a baby.

Juana went on, "I know that I told you a few days ago that we would wait, but something new has changed everything." Candelaria waited for Juana to continue. "The Santa Fe is sending Geronimo to work in Hutchinson, permanently."

"Why can't you wait? What is the rush? You have time to set a date in the Church."

"Mamá, we love each other and do not want to be apart. We want to be together. Mamá, why should I stay here? He is a good man, he has a good job with the Santa Fe, and he can provide for us. Do you think there is a better man in this Village who will love and care for me? It is difficult living here in this space, and you know Chon does not make it easy to live here." Juana's plea found sympathy with Felipa. She ended emphatically, "I know it might be better to wait, but this is my chance to live a different life, and I don't want to lose it."

After allowing Juana to give her explanation, Candelaria asked, "How old is he?"

"Twenty-two."

"What day are you planning to get married?"

"As soon as possible. He will be here Sunday."

"You know you won't be able to marry in the Church on Sunday," Candelaria said with disappointment.

"Yes, I know. Will you give us your blessing?"

Candelaria looked directly at Juana and said firmly, "I cannot, until you marry in the Church."

Juana thought for a few seconds and then asked, "Do you want Geronimo to come and ask for my hand?"

"That is not a good idea, especially with Chon. Geronimo had better stay away from this house."

"Mamá, if we do not get married here Sunday, then we'll go to Hutchinson together on Sunday evening."

Candelaria responded with uncertainty and resignation. "If this is your destiny, then I will pray that you will be safe, and I will leave it in God's hands. I will tell Chon tomorrow so he will have a few days to calm down. Maybe that will keep him from yelling at you, and me." Candelaria reached for Juana and gave her a hug and a kiss on the forehead, then kissed Rafaela in the same way. Candelaria could not have anticipated that her daughter's departure was just days away and that there would be some distance between them. Her last words to Juana on the matter were a firm instruction. "Respect your husband, but never let him strike you—for any reason. Never."

Candelaria began to prepare the evening meal though she was deep in thought and memory about the events in her own life. That night, when everyone else had fallen asleep, Candelaria fought her way through her anger, frustration, and sadness. She prayed a silent rosary asking that Juana find the strength to keep the faith for the journey on which she was about to embark.

The next day, Candelaria told Chon of Juana's plans. Knowing his likely response, she tempered his anger by saying that Geronimo was going to have the care of Juana and that her absence would lessen their own burdens. Candelaria managed to convince Chon that the real offense was not Juana's leaving but the way Juana and Geronimo chose to leave.

The following Sunday afternoon, Felipa and Manuel walked with Juana to the train depot where Geronimo waited. Manuel and Felipa embraced Juana and shook hands with Geronimo. They waited together for the train to arrive. Back at the house, Candelaria explained to Rafaela that her big sister had gone to live in another town with her new husband. Rafaela asked, "She has a husband now?"

"Yes, mija, she does. But she will come and visit us when she can," Candelaria reassured her. But six-year-old Rafaela only understood that Juana was not coming home that night.

Once Juana and Geronimo boarded the train and the wheels began to turn, they waved goodbye to Felipa and Manuel from their window. They married two days later, on Tuesday, October 15, 1912. Juana was a month from her fourteenth birthday.

6

The Barest Segregated School and Church, the Great War

The Santa Fe Railway and Dodge City continued to expand in commerce and population, and the railway and the city built more facilities to accommodate the growth. The number of shanties in the Village grew as well, with the population approaching 150 residents. In 1913, the Santa Fe constructed a bigger, larger roundhouse to service the increasing number of locomotives and freight cars. The site selected for the new roundhouse was just east of its original location and was currently occupied by the Village. The residents of the Village were forced to literally pull up stakes and move farther east to accommodate the construction. The new Village was nearly square, with the east-west boundary 160 yards long and the north-south boundary 150 yards long.

Chon and Manuel salvaged the wood and materials of their shanty and built another in the northeast corner of the Santa Fe property. Chon collected extra materials and increased the size of their new shanty, although the dirt floors remained. Their shanty stood in a group that faced southward, with a set of tracks running east and west a few yards to the rear. A track spur on the east boundary of the Santa Fe property ran north and south. A farmer grazed a few head of cattle in the field on the other side of the spur. While the added space was an improvement for the Padilla family, the noise of the railyard continued, and the odor of the grazing cattle fouled the air at times.

Shortly after the Village relocated, Juana sent word from Hutchinson that Geronimo had left the Santa Fe and taken a job for better pay with the Rock Island railway. She reported that the Rock Island was moving them to Iowa. Candelaria was saddened when Manuel explained Iowa's general location. Juana had not yet returned to visit her—instead, she was moving even farther away. Over time, Rafaela asked less often about her big sister's return.

❦

In February 1913, the Mexican government was suffering murderous chaos. Victoriano Huerta, a conservative military officer under Porfirio Díaz, led the overthrow of the democratic government of President Francisco Madero. Huerta declared himself president and had Madero and his vice president, José Pino Suarez, jailed and shot on February 22. Acting in part to protect American business interests, US Ambassador Henry Lane Wilson supported Huerta and assisted in planning the coup d'état. Huerta believed that President William Howard Taft would recognize his government; however, in March, the new president, Woodrow Wilson, refused to do so. In April, President Wilson sent ships to the port of Veracruz to intercept arms and munitions sold to Huerta. Although the arms were transported on a German ship, some of the weaponry was manufactured by an American arms company. United States naval forces remained in Veracruz for seven months.

In central Mexico, rebel forces continued to seize control of cities and states. Pancho Villa captured the city and state of Zacatecas on June 23, 1914. Villa sought to weaken the alliance between the federal conservatives and the high-ranking officials of the Catholic Church. One of Villa's earliest decrees required all Catholic priests to immediately leave Mexico at the nearest port of entry. At the time of Villa's victory in Zacatecas, one of the priests forced to leave the country was Padre Hilario Hernandez. He was born in Spain and was serving in Monterrey, Mexico, at the time of Villa's decree. He crossed into the United States at the Texas border and was assigned to serve the Mexican community in Dodge City.

When Padre Hernandez began serving the Village, Sacred Heart Parish was part of the Diocese of Wichita. At that time, the diocese planned to expand and construct new facilities in Dodge, including a convent for girls and young women. The bishop of the diocese, John J. Hennessy, an Irish-born immigrant, led the project. In September 1912, Bishop Hennessy paid $8,000 to the Methodist Church for the land under Soule College, located on Dodge's far north side. The college consisted of an administration building and a dormitory/classroom building, both four-level structures. The diocese's newsletter, the *Catholic Advance*, reported in April 1914 that building improvements for the two structures were underway. The *Advance* also reported the cost of one of the buildings at $100,000 and the other at $68,000. Costs for improvements were listed at $32,000. The diocese changed the name from Soule College to Saint Mary of the Plains Academy, for the high school, and Saint Mary of the Plains College. With improvements, Saint Mary of the Plains Academy's boarding capacity reached two hundred students. The diocese set the reopening for September 1914, and in the interim Saint Mary of the Plains Academy operated the coed day school it established in 1913. The diocese facilitated attendance for thirty day-school students by providing a horse and wagon service between Dodge City proper and the campus.

After his arrival, Padre Hernandez held weekday services in Spanish at 7:00 a.m. and Sunday services at 8:00 a.m. for any Villagers willing and able to cross the tracks to Sacred Heart Church. For Candelaria and other devout Catholics, Padre Hernandez's presence enabled them to practice the rituals of the Catholic faith. He led Villagers in prayer and counseled them in their language. He also administered the Holy Sacraments: baptism, confession, Holy Communion, matrimony, and the last rites. The sacraments of Holy Orders—the ordination of priests and Confirmation—were usually performed by a bishop.

Soon after Padre Hernandez arrived in Dodge, Manuel announced to Candelaria that he, too, was taking a job with the Rock Island in Iowa. Manuel's announcement was yet another hurt to Candelaria's heart. She had lost children at birth or soon thereafter, and their deaths often dimmed the spirit of her soul. Her greatest hope after her first husband died was to keep Abran, Manuel, Juana, and Rafaela together in one household or at least nearby if they married. With Abran in Mexico and Juana and now Manuel in faraway Iowa, she felt she had failed in her efforts. But she could not argue with Manuel and Felipa's decision. Manuel was twenty-five years of age, Felipa twenty-two, and they lived in a small crowded shanty. Juana and Geronimo had told Felipa and Manuel about the better pay and living conditions in Iowa, and Manuel had long awaited the opportunity to be out from under Chon's harshness. Juana, especially, welcomed the prospect of having family nearby. Candelaria understood her children's hope to live better lives. She had the same hope when she left Mexico and followed Chon to Kansas.

When Manuel and Felipa were about to leave, they asked Candelaria and Chon for their blessing. Manuel and Felipa knelt before them as Candelaria held her hand over their heads and recited a prayer for their health and safety. Chon held out his hand, but only said, "May God bless you." The young couple rode the Rock Island from Dodge to Des Moines, Iowa, where they met with Juana and Geronimo.

❧

Just as Saint Mary of the Plains Academy was about to open its doors for the fall semester, events across the Atlantic began Europe's descent into death and destruction. On June 28, 1914, Archduke Franz Ferdinand, heir to the Austro-Hungarian throne, and his wife, Sophie, visited Sarajevo, Bosnia. An assassin threw a hand grenade at their passing motorcade. The couple escaped injury, but an hour later their driver turned onto the wrong street. When the driver tried to reverse the motorcar, the gears locked and became immobile. A Bosnian Serb then approached the motorcar and shot and killed the archduke and his wife. Enraged, the government of Austria-Hungary demanded that it be allowed to investigate the murders to establish that Serbian elements were responsible. Serbia refused these demands, and a month later, on July 28, Austria-Hungary declared war on Serbia. Russia sided with Serbia, Germany sided with Austria-Hungary, and within days the Great War was underway.

Two months after the start of the Great War, Juana sent word from Iowa that she and Geronimo were expecting a child. Juana's announcement brought happiness and a light heart to Candelaria, but, as always, her joy was tempered by the dark knowledge of the risks of childbirth and the possibility of death. In mid-December, Candelaria received a message from Waterloo, Iowa, that Juana had given birth on December 4. Both Juana and her son, Nicolas, survived the ordeal and were doing well.

Abran, Candelaria's oldest son from her first marriage, did not follow Candelaria to El Paso in 1903. He and his wife, Alvina, stayed behind with her family. In 1911, just three months after Mexico's revolution began, Abran traveled to California to find work and avoid conscription by rebel and government forces. He worked as a farm laborer in the San Joaquin Valley near Coalinga, Fresno County, California, and used his carpentry skills when possible. He sent most of his earnings to Alvina to support her and their son, Antonio. In January 1915, after four years away from his family, Abran returned to Rincón de Romos. But the joy of Abran's homecoming was dampened days later when on February 1, Maria, Candelaria's mother and Abran's grandmother, died of pneumonia at the age of seventy-three. Abran mourned his grandmother's passing, but he was more concerned with the impact it would have on Candelaria. Abran had not seen his mother in eleven years, and given the painful news he had to deliver, he decided to go to Dodge City to tell her in person and support her during her time of grieving.

In mid-February, Abran rode the train from Rincón de Romos to El Paso. He was cautious to avoid Villa's army, which controlled northern Mexico. On reaching El Paso, Abran telegraphed Candelaria to tell her that he would arrive within the next ten days. She was thrilled and prayed for his safety on the journey.

On a cold February night, Chon waited in the Santa Fe passenger depot for Abran's arrival on the 11:00 p.m. train from Pueblo. When Abran's locomotive rolled into Dodge, Chon stepped out of the depot and spotted Abran among the disembarking passengers. Even in the poor lighting, Chon saw him repeatedly turning and looking for who might be there to meet him. Chon walked toward him and was just about to reach him when Abran saw him. They greeted each other with a firm hug and pat on the back.

Chon stepped back and cheerfully said, "Welcome, Abran. Welcome. You look well."

"Thank you, Chon. Thanks for coming to meet me."

Chon politely asked about his wife and their son. "Alvina y Antonio, como están?"

"Están bien, gracias a Dios."

The two men gathered Abran's bags and crossed the tracks on foot. As they made their way to the shanty, Abran asked, "How is my mother?"

"Bien, muy bien."

"I understand that Juana and Geronimo moved out of Dodge."

"Yes, they live in a state north of here, Eowa, or something like that. Manuel and Felipa also went to Eowa. Just your mother and Rafaela and I live in our humble house." This news surprised Abran, who had not expected that Manuel and Felipa would leave Candelaria.

When Candelaria heard the men talking as they approached, she opened the door and then backed away to allow them space for them to step in. She looked at Abran as he set down his bags. With happiness, she reached for him, and they gave each other a full, long embrace. She kissed him on the cheek, stepped back, and said, "Let me see you, mijo!" She then held his cheeks in her hands as her eyes filled with tears, and said, "Your face is the same, but you are heavier, and thicker!" She squeezed his hands and said, "There is no doubt, you are a grown man!" She pulled him by the hand to a chair and sat him down at the table.

Candelaria asked, "How is Alvina and my grandson, Antonio?"

"He is a big boy now, seven years old, with a lot of energy," he said with pride.

"Y mi mamá, how is she?"

Abran knew the question was inevitable, and there was no way to avoid the answer. His face turned serious and somber as he answered, "Mamá, I have very sad news about Grandmother."

Candelaria knew from Abran's expression and words that Maria was not well. She asked in apprehension, "Mijo, what are you saying?"

"Mamá, Doña Maria has passed away."

"No, mijo!" Candelaria shook her head. "No es posible!" she murmured in disbelief. "When? How?"

"She died on the first day of February. She died of pneumonia. I had just returned from California. She became ill, and after three or four days, she passed away."

As Candelaria began to cry, Abran stood and embraced her and gave her comfort. She buried her head in her son's chest and wept. He gently rocked her and said, "I'm so sorry, Mamá. She was a strong woman. All we can do now is pray for her soul that she may rest in peace with God."

When Candelaria's tears subsided, she asked Abran, "Where is she buried?"

"On the Rancho de San Jose."

When Abran and his mother separated from their embrace, Chon hugged Candelaria as well. He said to her, "I'm sorry. May God bless her soul." She thanked him, appreciating his effort at kindness. As she wiped away tears with a handkerchief, she said to them, "I should have gone to visit her before she passed."

Abran defended her. "Mamá, how were you going to do that? They are fighting a war in Mexico; people are getting killed. I was very careful when I went to San Jose. It is very expensive to travel, and it's dangerous. And crossing into the United States is more difficult since the revolution began."

Candelaria conceded, "Perhaps you're right, mijo. I will have to wait until the war is over before I can go back to visit her grave. I can't believe I must wait." She asked Abran, "Mijo, will you walk with me to the church tomorrow morning so I can pray for her?"

"Of course, Mamá."

"We can take Rafaela with us."

"Of course. How old is she now?"

"Eight years old; she is like your Antonio, growing up very quickly."

That night, Candelaria slept very little. Chon placed his arm around her, trying to ease her sadness, but many emotions and thoughts about Maria kept her awake. She found it difficult to accept that she would never again hold her mother's hand, kiss her cheek, feel her warm embrace, or take comfort from her voice and counsel. She wished she had made a better effort to visit her in Mexico. Candelaria had wanted to tell Maria before she passed away that any resentment from her arranged marriage to her first husband, Bernardo, was set aside, if not forgotten. Her heart carried a heavy burden knowing the chances to fulfill these wishes were forever lost.

In the morning, in between quiet moments of tears, she made breakfast for everyone and a lunch for Chon to take to work. Later in the morning, she, Abran, and Rafaela walked the mile and a half to Sacred Heart Church. They lit a votive candle near the altar at the front of the church and returned to the pews at the rear of the church, where she prayed a rosary for her mother's soul.

Abran stayed with Candelaria for a few weeks before returning to Mexico. During his stay, he helped Chon prepare the ground for planting his garden and helped Candelaria with her housework. Abran was still living with Candelaria when Kansas conducted its March 1915 census, and each family member's name was duly recorded. Before he returned to Mexico, he told Candelaria that he hoped to bring Alvina and Antonio to Dodge within two years. He promised to care for her and Chon as they grew old. She took some comfort from his promise to be close to her. The other item that brightened her future was a telegram from Manuel, in Iowa, to say that Felipa was expecting a child in August.

❧

At the time of Abran's visit to Dodge, the Wichita Catholic Diocese continued with its expansion of its facilities. The *Globe* reported on March 3, 1915, that Father John Handly planned to construct a settlement house for the Village. Handly, who made a personal contribution, and friends outside of Ford County raised a "considerable amount of the money" for the project. The single structure would contain a day and night school, a church, and a community house for the Village. Grades 1–3 would use the day school, with classes for the older grades in the night school. Classes for the older girls would include "sewing, cooking and other domestic branches." Classes for the boys would include office skills, such as "telegraphy, typewriting, stenography, etc." On Sundays, the church would use the building to conduct services. The community house was designed to encourage the Villagers to "develop some community interest." Handly offered that the neglected Village "drifted into bad ways" and that these improvements would "keep them occupied at better things."

The next day, the *Dodge City Journal* carried a similar story, reporting that Bishop Hennessy wanted the Village school to be the first of a system for Mexican villages in the Wichita diocese. The *Journal* noted that the future school included "modern appliances" and "reading room facilities." The article also noted that the bishop had given his permission to begin the construction of the new Sacred Heart Church and to break ground for the Mexican school within "a few days."

Nearly two months later, on April 22, the *Globe* reported that the church had begun relocating the old wood-framed Sacred Heart Church. The move to the rear of the current lot was necessary to accommodate the new church building in its place. The diocese also repeated its assertion that the Mexican school would "be equipped with modern appliances" and a "reading room." The plans for the new Sacred Heart Church site included a "steam heating plant" that would also heat a future "parochial school" and a "priests' house." The *Globe* further reported on June 10,

"When the new Sacred Heart church building is completed in the fall the present building is to be moved to the east side for the Mexicans." Church officials added that moving the old church to the east side made it "convenient for the parishioners to reach." But the east side site was north of the tracks and farther east of the Village, which required Villagers to cross multiple sets of tracks, then to double back. Any convenience for the Villagers would be minor at best.

Also on June 10, the *Globe* reported a new development in the diocese's construction plans. Father Handly announced that the diocese intended to build an all-boys school near the site of the new Sacred Heart Church on Central Avenue. The new school was to accommodate parish boys who were "deprived of parochial school privileges," while the all-girls Saint Mary of the Plains Academy was up and running. With respect to the priests' house and Village school, the *Catholic Advance* reported on July 3, "The new home for the Mexican Fathers will be completed in a few weeks." The *Advance* also reported that "the Mexican . . . children will have a suitable school in the future."

Word of a new school being constructed nearby was welcome news for Candelaria and other parents in the Village. Whether on the ranches of Mexico or the high plains of Kansas, they wanted education for their children. Many of the adults in the Village had completed only two or three years of schooling, and many others had received no education at all. With the news in the *Advance*, they believed their children were on the threshold of better lives. Villagers, including Candelaria, also took some comfort in the planned relocation of the old church to the east side of Dodge. But a small number of Villagers were skeptical of the diocese's building plans—Chon among them. He gave little credence to the news of a new school and church. Like the biblical doubting Thomas, he would not believe until he could see and touch them.

By the summer of 1915, the building plans for the Village church and school, with all the "modern appliances" and "reading rooms," were in tatters. In the end, no settlement house or school with modern appliances and a reading room were built. Instead, the diocese, led by Father Handly, constructed in the Village a one-story, wood-frame building to serve as both a chapel and a school. The structure was approximately fifty feet long and half as wide. The diocese offered no explanation to the Village for the collapse of its plans. On September 16, the Dodge *Journal* quoted a statement from Father Handly that was somewhat defensive and disjointed, with overtones of racial intolerance:

> In my work for the Mexicans I have had ever in view the interests of the American Catholics of Dodge City. . . . The churches at Ingalls, Copeland, Elkhart and Wright, and the Catholics scattered in other towns, made it necessary for me to spend two or three days of work every week away from the Dodge City parish. I did not believe I could do the local parish justice under this handicap, and I began at once to tackle the problem thus presented.
>
> It was plain to me that the American and Mexication [sic] congregations should be separated. Best results always come from such separation of widely divergent nationalities. The difference in language alone is enough to make this imperative.

Father Handly then described his efforts to raise money for the Village church:

> I appealed to friends of the cause outside of Dodge City and have collected close on to $5,000 from them, by means of begging letters. With this money I built a school house in the Mexican Village which is now being used also as a church. A benefactor in New York City has given me money to move the old church to Chestnut Street for the use of the Mexicans, after the new church is finished on Central Avenue.

Handly did not disclose until two years later in a letter to the *Globe* that then governor Arthur Capper had helped him obtain permission to build the Village school on Santa Fe property. Later, as a US senator, Capper demonstrated his segregationist views when he introduced a proposed amendment to the Constitution to ban interracial marriages.

Though Father Handly's comments were confusing, the fact was that only one structure was built in the Village. Some members of the Catholic community described it as a chapel. Regardless of the description, the two-room school and chapel were under one roof. Neither the school nor the chapel had running water, indoor restrooms, or electricity.

Father Handly drew a distinction between the interests of "American" Catholics and Mexican Catholics. But the spiritual interests of Catholics living in the Village—including those who were US citizens by birth, like Rafaela—and of the non-citizen Germans and Europeans of Dodge and Ford County were not distinct. The interests of all were the same—eternal salvation through the teachings of Jesus Christ.

The difference in language did not divide the Catholic congregation. The Latin Mass at Sacred Heart, whether for the white congregation or the Mexican congregation, was used for nearly four hundred years to unify all Catholics. In any church they might enter across the planet, the Latin Mass was a comforting familiarity. Whether the German, Spanish, or English languages were spoken, the Sacred Heart congregation took spiritual comfort from the Mass, though the Gospel and liturgy were recited in Latin. The practice, if not the policy, at Sacred Heart already had Villagers sitting in the back pews for reasons unrelated to language.

The separation of the congregations by the diocese did not yield the "best results" for the Villagers of Mexican heritage. The expansion of the diocese facilities in 1915 did little to support their physical health and condition. Other interests were better served: the Santa Fe kept its workforce close at little or no expense, and the diocese avoided the expense of a new or used church and kept its congregations separated. The local public school district operated three elementary schools that rarely included non-white students. The new Village chapel/school saved the school district the expense of constructing and operating another school. Sacred Heart Parish, the diocese, and the school district acted in a manner consistent with civil governments' implementation of the separate-but-equal doctrine of *Plessy v. Ferguson*—long on separate, very short on equal.

In the mist of the confusion around the what and the why of the diocese construction, Candelaria accepted the minimal comforts of the Village chapel and school. She received the happiest news of the summer when a daughter was born to Manuel and Felipa on August 27, 1915, in Des Moines. Mother and daughter were healthy. They named the baby Rafaela, after Manuel's sister. Late in the year, there was more good news; Juana and Geronimo were expecting their second child the following summer. Three months after that announcement, Manuel and Felipa sent word that they were expecting another child, with a due date in October 1916.

The scope of the diocese's building construction remained a topic in the new year. The January 1, 1916, issue of the *Globe* noted that Father Handly had "built a $1,300 combination chapel and school in the Mexican Village, and a handsome, two-story, steamed heated residence for the Mexican priests" on Chestnut Street. The story indicated that the heated house "cost almost $4,000." The article also reported that fifty children were enrolled in the Village school, and church attendees numbered nearly two hundred.

While the diocese often used the term "church," which conjures an image of a large stone building with concrete steps at the entrance, a tall steeple, and a cross atop its roof, the Village structure was at best a wholly inadequate small chapel. One room served as a chapel with a vestibule and sacristy and the other as a school. The report did not mention that the structure had no water fountain or indoor plumbing and was heated by coal. Children drank water from the same water container and cup and thereby spread whatever sickness might lie within. The children also endured the winter cold on their walk to the outdoor privy. In a later edition, the Dodge *Journal* published an article on the church written by Father Handly. Among many descriptions of the Village, Handly wrote:

> Most of their homes are huts built of old crossties. But inside! How clean many of them are! How brave their array of pasteboard saints and blessed candles! It is most pathetic this desperate clinging to reminders of better days, in the midst of such dreary and universal degradation. These people are worth the best we can give them. We owe it to them because they are our brothers in Christianity, and because if we help them, they will become good Americans.

In his comments, Handly acknowledges that the diocese had a duty to provide more for Catholic Villagers, and he admitted that the Church's actions had yet to relieve their poverty.

The dedication of the newly constructed Sacred Heart Church was on August 2, 1916. The *Globe* reported that the new church cost $40,000 and described the exterior as attractive and the interior as magnificent. The interior was decorated with numerous images and paintings of the Catholic faith, including a $1,000 painting of the Crucifixion. That painting alone cost only $300 less than the construction of the entire Village chapel and school. The June 8 edition added that the "old church is to be used for a school for boys." There was no mention of moving the old church to the east side of Dodge, as originally announced. During this time, the diocese also made improvements to the academy, including the purchase of a ten-thousand-gallon water tank.

❧

On July 26, 1916, in Decorah, Iowa, Juana gave birth to a son and named him Jose Santana. Again, both mother and child survived the birth and were healthy. At the same time, Manuel and Felipa had tired of being separated from their families and of the Iowa winters. They decided to return to El Paso and Felipa's family. In the interim, they wanted their baby to be born in Dodge, where Candelaria could help care for the newborn and fourteen-month-old Rafaela.

When they moved to Dodge in September, Candelaria, for the first time, held one of her grandchildren. She held Rafaela close to her face and told her, with loving sweetness, "Que hermosa eres! You are so beautiful." She kissed her on the forehead and held her close on her shoulder. Candelaria continued to hold her granddaughter as much as her chores allowed, sometimes completing her work while carrying the baby in one arm. For a short time at least, Candelaria was able to put aside the daily hardships of her life and enjoy the sweet moments with baby Rafaela. On October 7, Felipa gave birth to her second child, Florencio, named after her father. He was born in a shanty attended by Village midwives, Candelaria, and the women who prayed the rosary with her. Felipa and Florencio, too, were healthy and eluded the dangers of childbirth.

❧

While these intimate, familial events ran their course in the Village, events unseen across the planet were running their course as well. To this point, the United States had avoided entering the Great War. Initially, President Wilson and the public were unwilling to suffer US casualties in a European fight. During the war, German submarines and naval forces constantly attacked commercial shipping of the Allied Powers, including France, the United Kingdom, and neutral countries like the United States. As the war dragged on, Germany attacked more and more passenger ships, resulting in an increasing number of deaths of US citizens. After nearly three years of losses on the high seas, Wilson and the public changed course and began to support entry into the war. Officials in the US government and private business began to prepare for a buildup of materials and men.

The likelihood that the United States would enter the Great War began to rise, as did the hysteria about spies and enemy saboteurs penetrating the U.S.-Mexican border and attacking the United States. Those who sought to discourage or eliminate Mexican immigration took advantage of this hysteria, along with claims of disease prevention, to advance their aims. In January 1917, customs officials at the US border in El Paso instituted an abusive practice against Mexico's poor that was meant to shame and dehumanize Mexicans and to deter them from entering the United States. Cruelty was the intent. As each person crossed the border, a customs official determined, by unspecified factors, whether the person seeking entry was "second-class." If so, the person was stripped of their clothing and left naked while their clothing was steam-sterilized and fumigated with a weak acid solution. A customs inspector then examined their bodies for lice; if present, the inspectors shaved the heads of the travelers and subjected them to treatments with harmful chemicals. Presumably, if a person was determined to be other than second-class, they avoided the humiliation of the fumigation and "bath."

The fumigation and chemical bath policy did little to improve the sanitation problems of El Paso, which were a consequence of the failure of the federal government and the city to provide adequate running water, indoor plumbing, paved streets, and trash collection for the residents of the barrios. Instead, the federal government's focus was on fumigating clothes administering delousing powder and chemical baths to sanitize Mexican visitors and residents. In late January, thousands of Juarez residents gathered at the border crossing to protest these practices. The local press labeled the protests "Bath Riots." Despite the cruelty and ineffectiveness of the policy, US Customs continued the fumigation and bath abuse of the Mexican border crossers for decades.

Unbelievably, the fumigation and chemical bath abuse reached the Village. On February 5, the *Globe* reported the abuse with an article titled "Mexicans Object to Winter Baths." The story described the arrival of the Santa Fe's "delousing train" on a Saturday night, with Santa Fe "sanitary experts" scheduled to cleanse the Village the following morning. The experts targeted Village dwellings as well as people. Over the objections of many residents, they sanitized the Village homes with chemicals and subjected some Villagers to chemical baths out in the February cold. The Villagers who refused were subjected to "strenuous methods." The process began with men, women, and children disrobing and leaving their clothing to be subjected to eighty pounds of steam pressure that reached 180 degrees. The naked people were then herded into separate railroad cars, one for men and one for women and children. Their bodies were then scoured with a mixture of half kerosene and half vinegar. Villagers were then directed to a third car, where they were given paper towels to remove the chemicals and dry themselves. At that point, their clothing was returned. During the inhumane process, these so-called experts completed the chemical "sanitizing" of the dwellings. From Dodge, the Santa Fe delousing train continued its tour of the Santa Fe system of Mexican labor camps.

❧

Germany understood that the continued sinking of US shipping vessels would likely lead to a declaration of war. Nonetheless, they gambled that they could defeat the Allied Powers before US military forces could respond. With public outrage against Germany at a fever pitch, the US Congress took the opportunity in February to pass the Immigration Act of 1917. The law expanded the list of prohibited "defective" immigrants to include those over the age of sixteen who were illiterate. Under the new law, Mexican immigrants were required for the first time to present passports and pay a tax for entry. In the Southwestern and Midwestern states, the law was particularly popular with those who believed Mexicans and the Spanish language were a threat to the white Anglo-Saxon social fabric. Other advocates of the law were simply consumed with hatred and contempt for anyone of a different race or color. The effective date for the Immigration Act was set for May 1. Railroads and other industries in the Southwest immediately rushed their paperwork to add Mexican laborers to their workforce in advance of the restrictions.

The United States' entry into the Great War became seemingly inevitable after the Zimmerman telegram episode. In January 1917, Germany's ambassador to Mexico sent a coded telegram to the Mexican government suggesting that when the United States declared war, Mexico should join Germany's fight against the United States. The telegram assured Mexico that Germany would support Mexico taking back Texas, New Mexico, Arizona, and parts of Colorado. British decipherers decoded the telegram and passed on the contents to the US government a month later. Though the Mexican government ignored the telegram, Wilson was outraged, as was the public when its contents were released in March 1917. The debate over whether the United States should enter the Great War withered and shifted instead to when.

Speculation grew in cities and towns across the country, including Dodge, that a military draft was inevitable. With all the talk about men called into service if the United States entered the war, Felipa worried about Manuel. She asked him in a serious tone, "Do you think that you will serve in the army?"

He said confidently, "Don't worry, mi amor. Los Estados Unidos might not even go to war. It's all rumor. People just like to talk."

"Well, then why all this talk about Mexico fighting with Germany? That does not appear to be good for Mexico or Los Estados Unidos."

"Understand, mi amor, even if the Estados Unidos goes to war, they will not want me to fight. I'm not a citizen, and I'm twenty-eight years old. They don't want old men, they want young, healthy men."

"Listen to me, Manuel. If you get sent to war, I am not going sit here in Dodge with the babies. I'm taking them to El Paso to live with my family. You know how hard it is to live here in the Village, and with Chon. I'm telling you, I will leave! Florencio is six months old now, and my family and I can take care of the children." Manuel had no basis to disagree with Felipa. He conceded to her, even though he had some lingering belief that the United States would not enter the war. "Está bien, está bien. If it appears that I must go into the army, we'll go to El Paso. I can work there with the Santa Fe until the army takes me."

"Good, do you promise me?"

"Yes, mi amor. I promise."

Candelaria was deeply troubled when she learned of Manuel and Felipa's plans. A move to El Paso was not her biggest concern—it was her fear that the army might call Manuel to war. She questioned why governments, be it Mexico or the United States, were so quick to take men and boys for their warfare. She had suffered many hardships and taken tremendous strides to get her children to safety in the United States and Dodge City. Her mother, Maria, had repeatedly, through word and act, taught her that as a mother, Candelaria's most important duty was to protect her children.

With Manuel's plans, she was frustrated that she had failed to protect him. She believed her family's history was repeating itself, and she felt she was in the same place as when she decided to leave Mexico—protecting her son from the army. *How did this happen?* she asked herself.

7

Surviving the 1918 Pandemic, the Taking of Rafaela

On April 2, 1917, President Woodrow Wilson asked the US Congress for a declaration of war against Germany. Congress approved his request, and on April 6, 1917, nearly three years after the savagery of the Great War began, the United States officially entered the war. Wilson named General John J. Pershing, who was the commander of Fort Bliss in El Paso, to command the US forces in Europe.

Two months after the US declaration of war, railroad, mining, and southwestern agricultural lobbyists convinced Congress to allow the Department of Labor to carve out exceptions to the new Immigration Act. The lobbyists emphasized the loss of US manpower marched off to war. The exceptions adopted by the department kept intact the source of cheap labor for US industries and permitted tens of thousands of Mexicans to enter and work in the United States. In effect, some in the United States worked to keep Mexicans out while others worked to keep them in.

The US government's declaration of war and the announcement of a military draft solidified Felipa's fears. True to his promise, Manuel arranged a transfer to El Paso. Candelaria helped Manuel and Felipa prepare for their move despite her sadness and disappointment. The eight months she had spent with her grandchildren had passed in an instant. On the day of their departure, she prayed a rosary for their safety and, for a time, for their quick return. Candelaria, Chon, and eleven-year-old Rafaela returned to the routines of a household of three, with the additional routine of Rafaela's attendance at the Village school. Rafaela had stopped attending the public school after her second year, but Candelaria insisted that she go back to school.

When Manuel and Felipa returned to her family home on Tenth Street in El Paso, the family welcomed them with a small celebration filled with joy and doting on the babies. They also warned Manuel and Felipa to avoid going into Juarez and thereby risk the fumigation and chemical baths they might suffer on reentry.

Later, on June 1, the El Paso *Herald* published a notice issued by the new commander at Fort Bliss, Brigadier General George Bell Jr. His notice required all Mexicans in El Paso to register for military service. The general's order also clarified that despite their registration, Mexican citizens would not be drafted into military service. The *Herald* also reported that General Bell ordered the notice to be distributed to Mexicans in El Paso. According to the *Herald*, his purpose was to halt the alarm among many Mexicans that led to their abandonment of the United States for Mexico. The scheduled date for registration was June 5. On that day, Manuel, Felipa's brother, and her sister's husband all dutifully registered for the US military. Manuel's registration, and that of the thousands of men of mestizo and Indigenous blood across the United States, amounted to an ironic reversal overlooked by history—mestizo men organizing to cross the Atlantic and wage war against European nations on European soil.

From the time of his registration, Manuel and Felipa began living steady and stable lives despite the health issues of El Paso. Manuel left the Santa Fe for work as a wiper with the El Paso Electric Railway. The work was difficult and dirty, but the job provided a modest life for the family. In early July, Manuel sent a telegram to Candelaria telling her that the family had arrived safely and that the children were well. He also shared some unexpected news: Abran and Alvina had a new baby boy, Ladislao, born in Rincón de Romos on June 27. Manuel sent a similar telegram to Juana in Iowa, adding that he and Felipa were happy to be back in El Paso.

Juana had been in a hurry to leave Dodge, but after two years in Iowa's cold social climate and weather, she was determined to return. Though she was just eighteen years old, she took charge and told her husband that they were leaving Iowa as soon as possible. By the end of the year, Juana, Geronimo, and the two boys, Nicolas and Jose Santana, were living in their own home across the lane from Candelaria in the Village. Candelaria was thrilled to see her grandsons. She had imagined them as small infants and was surprised to see that they were already toddlers. And another grandchild was on the way; Juana was pregnant with a third child, due in April the following year.

❧

Fifty miles west of Dodge is Haskell County, Kansas, with a population of approximately seventeen hundred. In late January and early February 1918, Dr. Loring Miner, a physician who practiced in Haskell County, noted a number of patients with unusually severe flu-like symptoms. This flu struck down the strongest and healthiest individuals in the community. Their sickness progressed to pneumonia in two or three days, some within hours. They suffered horrific pain, bloody coughing, and bleeding from the nose, ears, and eyes. Their bodies turned blue for lack of oxygen. Mercifully, they died within a few hours. Dr. Miner soon realized that this flu was unlike any he had seen—it was brutal and quick to kill. He alerted the US Public Health Service of his observations of the disease. Over the next six months, his report describing this illness was the first and only written report filed with the Health Service.

At the time of the outbreak, several men in Haskell County were in the army and stationed at Camp Funston, on Fort Riley, in northeast Kansas. The men who were exposed to the flu virus in Haskell County traveled back and forth to Fort Riley. The camp's average population numbered fifty thousand, most of whom were training to fight in the Great War. The first report of the flu at Fort Riley occurred in early March, and three weeks later more than a thousand soldiers were hospitalized; thousands more were infected and ill. The spread was rapid, as the incubation of the virus was estimated at two to three days. From Fort Riley, thousands of soldiers traveled to other camps within the United States, while still others traveled to Europe to fight the war. The global spread of the flu had begun.

Science and medical historians cannot identify with complete certainty the exact location in Haskell County of the source of the 1918 flu virus. But the vast majority agree that the evidence suggests strongly that the flu virus originated in Haskell County. At the time, many farmers in Haskell

County still lived in sod houses. A 2018 story in the *Wichita Eagle* described the living conditions on the Kansas prairies in 1918, reporting that it was "where dirt-poor farm families struggled to do daily chores—slopping pigs, feeding cattle, horses and chickens, living in primitive, cramped, uninsulated quarters." Haskell County was also in the pathway for more than a dozen migratory bird species. Late twentieth-century medicine and science discovered that when bird influenza viruses and human viruses infect the same pig cell, their genes can mix. In the exchange, the mix might create a new deadly virus and corresponding influenza crisis. All the necessary elements for the deadly mix of a new virus were present. Additionally, the absence of any other reports at the time of such severe and lethal influenza in the United States or on the planet further supports the conclusion that Haskell County was the origin.

Perhaps if governments and health officials had made the sanitary conditions for raising livestock a point of emphasis and supported poor farmers with materials and equipment, the risk of a new flu virus might have been minimized. Instead, their attentions were focused on the supposedly unsanitary conditions of poor Mexicans entering the United States and Mexicans living in the Village and other labor camps on the railways. In the end, after two years, the 1918 flu had completed its course across the planet. During that time, the virus killed fifty million to one hundred million people worldwide, including 670,000 in the United States, approximately twelve thousand in Kansas, and hundreds more in the Mexican barrios of south El Paso.

Just as the flu was spreading at Fort Riley, Juana gave birth to her third son, Prudencio, in the Village on April 28, 1918. With the newly constructed chapel just yards away, Candelaria and other women prayed the rosary during the delivery while the midwives of the Village tended to Juana. When it became clear that mother and child had survived, Candelaria returned to the chapel to say a prayer of thanks. At that time, she also looked back on her decision to come to the United States with her children. Abran, Manuel, and Juana had reached adulthood, and Rafaela was thriving. She had five grandchildren born in the United States, and all had survived their birth. One-year-old Fernando was the only infant who was lost. Manuel was registered with the US Army, but he had not been called to war. Though her children's lives were filled with hardships, she had accomplished most of what she set out to do.

With Prudencio and his siblings in the Village, Candelaria again spent her days helping with the care of her grandchildren. She especially enjoyed the two families gathering for a Sunday meal after Mass. The Sunday meal became a family tradition. Candelaria ensured that plenty of servings of meat, usually chicken, vegetables, beans, and tortillas were on the table. Some of the vegetables were grown in Chon's garden. Juana's boys were always comfortable in their play at abuela's house, with eleven-year-old Rafaela supervising. During the week, Rafaela often went to Juana's home to help with the washing, cleaning, and caring for the boys.

Rafaela again stopped attending school when Prudencio was born. She did not find the Village school, Coronado, named by the students, a welcoming place of excitement and inspiration. A classmate harassed her constantly and started fights with her. She struggled with the materials and the English instruction. Candelaria wanted Rafaela to continue, but Chon believed schooling, especially for girls, was of little value. He thought that helping Candelaria would be a better use of her time. So, with Chon's support, Rafaela convinced Candelaria to allow her to leave school.

The first wave of the 1918 flu pandemic began in March, with the virus killing hundreds of soldiers on military bases. As spring moved into summer, the virus spread into cities across the United States. It reached its peak in mid-July. Thousands of people, particularly in the eastern states, died horrific deaths. Though the Village and Dodge were only fifty miles from Haskell County, they escaped the wrath of the first wave. Rail passengers constituted most of the outside contacts with Dodge City and rural communities with small populations.

By July, Dodge residents knew the flu was menacing, but most believed the illness was confined to the East Coast. The *Globe* published articles about the impact of the virus in Germany, Spain, and the European battlefields of the Great War. At the end of August, Kansans and other rural areas of the country began to feel the deadly effects of the pandemic. Young men who had contracted the virus in the military camps were being sent home for burial.

The second wave erupted in September and it overwhelmed the country. In mid-September, the Great Lakes Naval Station near Chicago reported four thousand men ill and dying from the flu. Chicago quickly saw a surge in cases. In the third week of September, the National Health Service advised Kansas and other states to be on guard and to report any cases. At the same time, the Kansas Health Department asserted that the flu had not reached the state. In late September and early October, the *Globe* carried stories of flu cases and public restrictions in Saint Louis and Kansas City, Missouri. People in Kansas and other central states clearly saw that the deadly disease was quickly spreading westward.

On October 9, the governor of Kansas and the State Board of Health issued a ban on public meetings of fifteen or more, including churches, schools, and theatres. The Ford County Board of Health issued the same ban. But in Dodge, the ban was not uniformly enforced. Political meetings, fundraisers, and similar events continued. The next day, the *Globe* reported that Hollywood actor and director Douglas Fairbanks Jr. had given a speech to a crowd in Dodge from the back of a train in support of war bonds. In the days that followed, the *Globe* and the *Dodge City Journal* began to report on and name residents suffering from influenza. Individuals suffering in the Village were unnamed: "Several cases of the 'flu' were in Little Mexico," and "two residents of Little Mexico died Sunday . . . victims of the 'Flu.'"

In a small community like the Village, news of illness and death spread quickly. Neighbors comforted the grieving family with meals, prayers, and their company, knowingly or unknowingly risking infection. If the family of the deceased could not purchase a coffin, a Village resident with carpentry skills built a simple wooden casket. Many of the cemetery plots on Dodge's west side were owned by Dodge City and the churches. If a Catholic family could not purchase a lot, their deceased were laid to rest in an unmarked paupers' lot in the Catholic section.

In an effort to inform the public, the *Globe* reported on October 14 the US Public Health Service's conclusion that the flu epidemic was "probably not Spanish in origin." The Health Service added, "If the people of this country do not take care the epidemic will continue so widespread throughout the United States that soon we shall hear the disease called 'American' influenza." Three days later, with the headline NO QUARANTINE, the *Globe* reported that except for the state and county restrictions on large gatherings, "everybody is free to come and go and business of all kinds is being conducted as usual." For the Village, the same freedom was denied. The Dodge *Journal* reported, "It was necessary to patrol Little Mexico yesterday to keep the population inside the quarantine lines and the Hom [*sic*] Guards were called upon to do this service." The article, in one sentence, went on to demean and insult Village residents, stating that health officers had "difficulty in getting the Mexican population to understand the complicated workings of the quarantine order against Spanish influenza in this free country." The article concluded by referring to the Village as "Jose."

By October 20, everyone in Ford County knew the influenza was flourishing in the county. The county health officer reported an average of thirty new cases daily, and at least one daily death, including a Mexican boy. The county health officer also ordered that the quarantine of the Village should continue. In the first week of November, the average number of new county cases fell to fifteen cases a day, and the number of deaths per week was lower, at two, compared to twelve the week before. County health officials estimated the number of Village cases at fifteen. The county also estimated that overall, during the epidemic the Village had 150 cases. The quarantine of the Village continued despite the improvement.

The November 2 issue of the *Globe* cited a drop in flu cases in the county and proclaimed in a short front page story, FLU EPIDEMIC NEARS END! But the headline was a wish and a hope, as residents continued to become infected. At Saint Mary's Academy, classes ended and the school converted the space into an emergency hospital with the capacity for 175 patients. The only catastrophe that came to an end in 1918 was the Great War. Germany did not have the resources and materials to keep fighting the United States and the Allied Powers, and the flu was depleting the ranks of all the armies. The warring parties finally realized the futility of the war and declared an armistice. It went into effect on the eleventh day of the eleventh month, at the eleventh hour, and essentially ended the Great War. However, the return of the armies to their home countries continued the spread of the virus across the planet.

In December, Village and Ford County residents continued to battle the virus with the number of cases generally in decline. The strict quarantine of the Village had been suspended, but toward the end of the month, sixteen new cases were reported in the county, twelve of which were in the Village. The sick were immediately isolated from other residents, and health authorities delayed a decision on reinstating a strict quarantine. The Dodge *Journal* identified four non-Village residents who contracted the virus, but none of the Village cases were named. Instead, the *Journal* described the Villagers as "inmates."

Ironically, the segregation practices aligned with the public health recommendations for preventing the virus infection, and perhaps the segregation practices in Dodge reduced the chances of infection. Village residents, who numbered approximately 250, were even more isolated, as they were ostracized from the general public. The new chapel and school building kept them on their side of the tracks, literally. Their visits to shops and stores were kept to a minimum, with some establishments barring Villagers entirely. Nearly all Village men worked outdoors—even the roundhouse had large open entrances and a high roof. Few Villagers attended Sunday Mass at Sacred Heart, and they were cautious to shop only at stores that welcomed them. Their limited contacts and time in public enclosures minimized their exposure to the virus in the community. Candelaria, Chon, and Rafaela were not stricken with the virus. Unlike other flu viruses, the 1918 virus struck hard at young healthy adults, which meant that Juana and Geronimo were most at risk, but by a random stroke of biological luck, they escaped as well.

The third wave of the pandemic rose during the early months and spring of 1919 and finally subsided in the summer. In the middle of the spike, Candelaria received welcome news from Manuel: Abran and his family were in El Paso and on their way to Dodge. The battles of the Mexican Revolution had nearly ended, the flu was in decline, and Antonio, age ten, and Ladislao, twenty months old, were healthy. As he had promised years before, Abran was returning to be close to Candelaria and Chon. The time for him, Alvina, and the boys to move to Kansas had arrived.

Candelaria was able to see for the first time, and hold in her arms, two more grandsons. She had always hoped to hold each of her grandchildren at least once. Although she was able to realize her hope with Ladislao, Antonio was already too big to lift, so she gave him a long, rocking hug instead and told him how tall and handsome he was. She held back her tears so that he would not think that his presence saddened her. For Candelaria, it was a time of great happiness—although living in a crowded space was inconvenient at times, they had escaped the flu, the men were working, and the families helped each other. On Sundays, the families carried on the tradition of gathering for a meal after Mass.

Electricity had reached Dodge by 1890, and over the next two decades, health and sanitation utilities, waterworks, and sewers were available to Dodge residents. They enjoyed the conveniences of streetcars, automobiles, and telephones. But while Dodge was progressing into the twentieth century, Village residents struggled along in nineteenth-century living conditions. Nevertheless, the Village was changing from a temporary labor camp to a permanent settlement of families. Families in the Village began to add small items of comfort to their poor shanties. The men gathered scrap wood, purchased other pieces of lumber, and tapped into the Village's pool of skilled laborers, including Abran, who brought his carpentry skills to the Village. He and Chon built a small add-on space to Chon and Candelaria's shanty. Slowly but steadily, families added additional spaces onto their shanties, attached small porches, fenced their yards and gardens, and built chicken coops and small corrals for their animals. A few flower pots began to appear on the porches in front of the homes. But the Village remained without electricity, running water, plumbing, and paved lanes. Heavy rains and melting snows turned the lanes and dirt paths into a muddy mess. There were no shops in the Village, other than a recently opened small grocery store. It was not a city within a city, nor was it a company town.

The small grocery store in the Village had been opened in 1917 by Arturo Ceballos and his wife, Preciliana, and offered the popular staples of beans, rice, potatoes, flour, milk, eggs, meats, candies, and herbs and spices from Mexico when they were available. It was the only structure in the Village with electricity and, later, a telephone. The Ceballos family also operated a small dance hall alongside the store. Villagers still knew the venom of racism of many in Dodge City. Even Arturo Ceballos, perhaps the most prominent person in the Village, felt the sting. The Dodge City *Journal* reported that on May 23, 1918, local authorities arrested and jailed him on charges of failing to register for the military. Ceballos duly registered two days later. Apparently, local law enforcement had informed the U.S marshal in Wichita, who then re-arrested him on May 29, and took him into custody for the same charge and on suspicion of being a German spy. Ceballos's arrest for espionage prompts the question: Why would the German Kaiser use a Mexican for spying when there were thousands of German nationals and descendants in Kansas?

In 1919, the *Journal* also reported that a Mexican woman in the Village, the mother of six, had "a 'litter' of Mexicans." Another article reported that three Mexican men had been arrested and taken into custody in Dodge and held for a neighboring sheriff. He claimed that the men had unlawfully switched employment from the Rock Island to the Santa Fe. The sheriff falsely claimed that the men were required to work for a certain length of time for one employer only and took custody of the men solely to deport them.

A third article in the *Journal* appeared in April and left no doubt that many in Dodge wanted segregated housing. The article was titled "Citizens of East Side Protest Against Mexicans Acquiring Homes There." The article reported that citizens were "up in arms" over the "invasion" of Mexicans seeking housing on the East Side. According to the article, the Phoenix Industrial Club sought "to devise a means of segregating the Latins in a community of their own." The article pointed out that railroad companies who employ Mexicans "furnish a site for a colony of laborers." The supporters of segregation argued that the "residents of the various 'Little Mexicos' are usually housed in box cars usually furnished by the railroads or in rudely constructed shacks built with railroad ties and the holes chucked with mud." The officers of the Phoenix Club wanted the "Mexicans to live in a colony outside the city limits." It was undeniable that segregation was the goal.

❧

The exact date that thirteen-year-old Rafaela met twenty-three-year-old Cayetano Rodriguez is unknown, but it was likely in early June 1919. Cayetano had been working for the Santa Fe for three years. They might have been neighbors or met at the Village chapel after Mass. Perhaps they were introduced to one another during a wedding or baptism celebration where he and other musicians performed. Cayetano was a self-taught fiddler and performed with other Village musicians. Perhaps the beautiful music of love ballads and the notes from his fiddle made him more attractive in Rafaela's eyes than boys her own age.

Cayetano was born in 1896 to Arcadio Rodriguez and Marcela Gutierrez on a small ranching town in Mexico named Calera de Victor Rosales. The town, commonly referred to as "Calera," was eighteen miles north of Zacatecas. Cayetano was fourteen when the Mexican Revolution began in 1910. Four years later, in June, Villa and his División del Norte were in Calera preparing to attack the city of Zacatecas. After taking the city, his forces searched nearby towns and villages to collect food supplies and livestock to feed the División. To prevent the theft, Arcadio and his sons, Leon, age twenty-one, Cayetano, age nineteen, and Felipe, age fifteen, dug a trench to hide their pigs and goats a short distance away from their adobe house. The boys corralled the animals into the trench and cleaned out the animal pens to remove any trace of recent use.

A short time later, a Villista rode his horse up to the doorway of the house. He was rugged, brown-skinned, unshaven, and had a black mustache. He wore his pants over his boots, a dusty jacket over a plain shirt. The bandoleros across his chest and waist were filled with cartridges. His sombrero had a wide brim with an upturned edge, a short conical crown, and a leather chinstrap.

"Everyone out of the house!" he yelled. One by one, the family filed out with just enough space to walk past the horseman into the yard. When all were out, the horseman nudged his horse forward to the doorway so that the horse stuck its head and neck into the doorway. The rider then backed the horse out and turned to face the family: Arcadio, Marcela, their sons, and their daughter, Francisca.

From his saddle, the Villista sternly announced, "The General Francisco Villa, Commander of the División del Norte, has declared that all families in the State of Zacatecas have a duty to support the Constitutionalist forces. All residents of Calera are commanded to contribute a fair amount of their grains, provisions, and livestock to the División del Norte."

Arcadio said cautiously, "Mi Capitán, with all respect, we are campesinos. We have very little food and no animals. Please spare us from this order."

The Villista unholstered his revolver and waved it at the two women who accompanied him. They were soldaderas—female soldiers who fought and died on the battlefield alongside Villa's troops. The two brown-skinned women wore plain, long-sleeved blouses, and dark, long, straight skirts. They carried long guns and wore bandoleros across their chests and brimmed sombreros with rounded crowns and chin straps. On the Villista's command, they slung their rifles over their backs and entered Arcadio's home. The family could not risk suffering harm, so they stood in silence and hoped the soldaderas would not discover the animals.

The soldaderas gathered cornmeal, flour, salted pork, beans, rice, and coffee beans and piled them into a cart filled with other captured supplies. One of the soldaderas searched the back of the house for livestock, but seeing only a few chickens, she reported that there were none. The horseman holstered his firearm and said to the family, "General Villa thanks you for your generous contribution." He turned and left, with the soldaderas pulling the cart close behind.

Arcadio and Marcela considered the Villistas thieves, not patriotic champions of liberty and freedom for the campesinos. He also recognized his family had little safety and were vulnerable to the armies and that the Revolution would not end soon. He said to Marcela, "I can only protect this family if we go north, and maybe to the United States, like everyone else. Those thieves will be back, and next time they'll rob us of our sons. The federales are killing Villa's soldiers, and he needs to replace them."

Without hesitation, Marcela volunteered, "My brother in Juarez, Refugio, he will help us."

"Yes, that's a possibility."

Marcela said to her husband with calm certainty, "And we are taking our parents and my sisters."

"Of course. Of course, no one will be left behind."

Marcela, at age fifty-two, was the oldest of three sisters. The middle sister, Maria, at age forty-four, was the single mother of Micaela Sanchez. Micaela was married to Pedro Rodriguez, also from Calera but not related to Arcadio's Rodriguez family. In early 1915, twelve members of the Gutierrez and Rodriguez families began their move northward to the United States. The family reached Juarez over a period of months with intermittent stops to allow the men to find work and pay for their train fares to Juarez. Along the way in mid-July, Micaela gave birth to a daughter. With her birth, Pedro felt the pressure to get to Juarez as soon as possible, not only for his family's safety but also for better wages. He soon made his way to Juarez, and with the help of Maria's brother, Refugio, became a "day crosser." He worked as a laborer in both cities.

During a visit to see Micaela and his daughter, Pedro suggested that Cayetano and Leon return with him to Juarez. They agreed and planned for the rest of the family to follow later. In mid-May 1916, Pedro and the brothers rode the train to Juarez. The men constantly feared capture by the rebels for the battlefield. As they approached Juarez, the brothers dressed in women's clothing and shawls to cover their faces to avoid detection. The ruse was successful and they crossed the Rio Bravo into El Paso. Within days the trio were working as day laborers for the Santa Fe and saving money to bring the rest of the family over.

Arcadio and Marcela were relieved that their sons had safely crossed the border. But in August, Marcela's father, Francisco, died of dementia at the age of eighty-nine. His widow, Catarina, and the remaining family gathered itself, reset its bearings, and pressed on to the border. With the help of Refugio, the families were in Juarez by the end of 1916. By that time, Cayetano and Leon were already working for the Santa Fe in Dodge City.

At the beginning of 1917, Arcadio, Marcela, and her sisters waited in Juarez for travel money from the men. Micaela was also anxious to tell Pedro that they were expecting another child in June. As they waited, entry into the United States had become more difficult with the passage of the new Immigration Act and the chemical bath policy. The families intended to avoid the policy by presenting themselves at the border in their finer clothing and showing sufficient cash to avoid being labeled by US border inspection officers as second-class citizens.

But during the family's wait for entry, Arcadio tragically succumbed to his liver disease on March 23, at age fifty-seven. Marcela buried her husband in Juarez days later.

Shortly after Arcadio's death, Pedro returned to Juarez from Dodge City and was present in mid-June when Micaela delivered her second child, Antonio. Within weeks, Pedro gathered Micaela, her mother, and the children and crossed the border at El Paso on their way to the Village in Dodge. Three months later, Cayetano and Leon finally had saved enough pay to send for Marcela, Francisca, and Felipe. They were lawfully admitted at El Paso on October 1, 1917, without submission to the chemical baths. They, too, rode the Santa Fe directly to the Village in Dodge. The Rodriguez and Gutierrez families were fortunate that their flight from the Revolution occurred at a time of high demand for labor in the United States. The families arrived in Dodge City just months before the outbreak of the 1918 flu in nearby Haskell County.

❦

In 1919, Cayetano was a handsome young man. At five feet four inches tall, he was of average height and build compared to most Mexican men. His features had little European influence and his skin color had a golden cinnamon tone. He had very black, thick hair with a low hair line, and he wore a thin mustache. He and his family noted with pride that their indigenous blood was from the Huichol people from the Occidental Mountain Range of the Sierra Madre in central Mexico. Their homeland was largely in the bordering states of southwestern Zacatecas and northeastern Nayarit.

With his handsome face and the shine of a polished musician, Cayetano began his pursuit and conquest of Rafaela. Rafaela was lightly tanned, thin, and stood five-foot one. She had auburn hair and features that were more European than Cayetano's. She knew how to write, despite her limited education, and they communicated with each other by exchanging notes through friends. At thirteen, Rafaela was quite vulnerable to compliments. Cayetano assured her that he was in love with her and that their lives would be filled with wedded bliss. Rafaela believed his words, as any young teen might—especially a girl whose life was limited to dirt floors, one-room homes, and treatment as a diseased undesirable in her new city. She welcomed any hope for a better life.

Their romance by courier continued during the fall and became an item of Village gossip. When Juana learned of the talk, she was immediately concerned. She did not want her little sister to go through the same hardships she had suffered as a teenage spouse and mother. Juana relayed the unsettling news to Candelaria, who became upset and fearful for Rafaela. Candelaria carried the wound she suffered from having been a teenage girl forced to marry a much older man. She blamed herself when she failed to keep thirteen-year-old Juana from becoming a child bride. In late 1919, there were still far more young men than women in the Village, and it was not a rare occurrence that a teenage girl was seduced and eloped with—or, as some might argue, was taken by—a young adult man.

Before talking with Rafaela, Candelaria told Chon the news in a way that she hoped might not evoke an overreaction. She waited until after he ate a full meal and was calm. "Chon, I have something to tell you about Rafaela," she said quietly.

"De que?"

"I've heard gossip that a young man is after her. I have asked women in the Village about him. People say he is handsome and popular with the ladies."

"She is too young for boyfriends," Chon said dismissively.

"Asención. You are not listening to me. She is a child, and he is not a boy, he is a grown man."

Instantly, Chon's calmness changed to hostility. "Any *cabrón* that comes around here will learn to stay away. I'll shoot him if necessary."

"Ay, Chon! Don't say those things," Candelaria pleaded. "I don't know if she is interested in this man. If she is, we will have to convince her that she is too young to marry and that life is very difficult when you are a teenage wife and mother. If we argue with her, she will defend him. And if you threaten him, we'll push her to him."

Chon countered, "She is my only child. And I am in the right to protect her. Didn't you ask me to protect the children when we got married?"

"Yes, Chon, that is what I asked of you. But we must take care to protect her in a way so she doesn't go to him."

Chon backed down from his *shoot first, ask questions later* approach. But, he warned, "if talking doesn't work, we'll do things my way."

Candelaria hoped that Chon's threats were only words of macho bravado. He had made similar statements through the years but never acted on them.

Candelaria waited until Chon was out of the house and only Juana was present in support when she confronted Rafaela. Juana was less concerned that Rafaela had a boyfriend at her age and far more worried about the man and his reputation. When they were finally together, Candelaria asked, "Mija, I understand there is talk in the Village, that you have a boyfriend, and that his name is Cayetano Rodriguez. Is that true?"

Rafaela was quiet for a few moments, not knowing how to respond. She looked at Juana, who gave her only a short nod. She reluctantly said, "Yes, I do."

Candelaria continued, "Am I correct that his name is Cayetano Rodriguez?"

Rafaela was quiet in nature. She rarely became emotional or spoke loudly and with animated gestures. She answered her mother's questioning in a manner consistent with her usual demeanor. "Yes."

"Rafaela, you are too young to have a boyfriend. He is a man, not a teenage boy. What do you know about him?"

"I know that he loves me and cares for me very much."

Candelaria challenged her, "What else do you know about him?"

"I know he works for the Santa Fe, and he plays the violin in a band."

"And do you like him?"

"Yes, he's very nice and a gentleman."

"Gentleman? I hear he has girlfriends and that he is popular with the ladies in the Village. Did you know that?"

Rafaela defended Cayetano. "I don't think that is true. You just don't want me to have a boyfriend."

"Mija, you're too young to have a boyfriend who is so much older than you. Does he tell you he wants to marry you?"

"No."

"Rafaela, do not think about marrying any man, especially this one. You are not ready to deal with this type of person for a husband. He lives at home with his mother and aunt. He is not a responsible man for marriage. And your father agrees with me."

"I'm not thinking about marriage. He likes me, and I like him, that's all."

"Please, mija, I married too young, your sister did too. Look at the difficult lives we lead. If you marry so young, you will suffer as we do."

"Mamá, he is my boyfriend and we're not getting married."

Candelaria stopped the discussion. She had said all she could and didn't want to risk pushing Rafaela to Cayetano by saying more.

In the weeks before Christmas, Cayetano continued to pursue Rafaela with small gifts and promises of a happy life. At the same time, Cayetano learned that Chon was angry at his continued pursuit and was openly making threats against him. He decided that the window of opportunity to complete his conquest might be closing. Despite all of Candelaria's pleading in opposition and patience, just days before Christmas, Cayetano persuaded Rafaela to join him with the promise that they would marry. They planned to meet at the Village school and stay at a house of one of his friends. Days after Christmas, Rafaela walked out of her mother's home to meet him. She left without any idea of what might happen when she joined him. She thought they would have the chance to be together out of her family's view, when they could kiss and hold hands. She did not realize that Cayetano might have different ideas of a romantic time alone with a girl.

When Rafaela did not return home that night, Candelaria realized that her worst fear had come to pass. Rafaela was with Cayetano. She turned to the rosary for Rafaela's well-being and a quick end to her own great anguish. Chon was livid and threatened to harm Cayetano. The next day, the Village gossip was indeed that the two of them were together.

Rafaela's leap for young love and romance changed into a horrifying and painful nightmare. When Cayetano began to sexually assault her, she became frightened and asked him to take her home. He refused. Over the next two days, he repeatedly forced himself on her despite her pleas to stop and take her home. Finally, he relented and warned Rafaela that she must not tell anyone of his actions. He left her at the home of his cousins, and from there she found her way home.

When Rafaela walked into the house, Candelaria rushed to embrace her. She was relieved that her daughter was home, but at the same time she saw in Rafaela's face that she was hurt and weak. Rafaela's voice broke when she tried to speak and tears fell from her face. Candelaria pulled back and asked with great concern, "What happened to you, where have you been?"

"I was with Cayetano. He said we were going to get married. And I believed him. He grabbed me and forced himself on me. I asked him to bring me home, but he would not."

Candelaria did not say anything. Instead, she had Rafaela lie down so she could tend to her and change her into fresh clothing. Then she said, "You stay here and rest. I am going to see what I can do for you. If your father comes home before I talk to him, do not tell him. Leave that to me." Rafaela nodded.

Candelaria decided that she should speak to Father Hernandez. But before she left for the chapel, she briefly searched the house for Chon's revolver. He kept it hidden and she had not found it despite the small size of the house. She thought that perhaps a friend held the *pistola* for him.

Candelaria explained to Father Hernandez what had happened. She asked if he could meet with the Rodriguez family to ensure that Cayetano would be held responsible for his actions. Father Hernandez told her that he knew the family and that he would speak to them right away. The next day, the priest went to Candelaria's home and told her that a meeting between Marcela and Candelaria was set for the following day at the chapel. Neither Cayetano nor Rafaela would be present. Chon was also kept from the meeting because of his temperament.

When the mothers and the priest met, there was a cold awkwardness. Candelaria was certain in her cause, Marcela was aloof, with little apprehension. Father Hernandez began with a prayer asking God to guide them in their endeavor and to give all of them the courage to do what was best for their children. When he concluded the prayer, they all replied, "Amen."

Father Hernandez opened the talk by saying to Marcela, "Señora Padilla tells me that a few days ago your son, Cayetano, forced her daughter, Rafaela—who is only thirteen years old—to engage in sexual relations against her will. Señora Padilla also says that after two days Cayetano allowed her to return home. She also says that Cayetano promised Rafaela that he would marry her. How do you explain what she alleges?"

Marcela quickly defended her son. "My son tells me that Rafaela has been after him. She wants to marry him. He has a good job and is a musician, and she wants him to take care of her, so she threw herself at him. So, I'm not surprised that she was willing to go with him. When they were together, he wanted to get away from her, but she didn't want to leave. If they had carnal relations, she was willing. She could have left him any time. He did not force her to do anything."

Father Hernandez said to the women, "You both know that a family is publicly dishonored when a man takes a daughter from the home, has sexual relations with her, and then returns her to the home the next day. And if these two young people willfully had carnal knowledge of one another outside of marriage, then they have sinned against God. If Rafaela was forced to commit these acts, then she has not sinned. Cayetano surely has. I believe the only resolution that can keep these two young people in God's grace is for them to confess their sins and then marry in the Church."

Marcela responded, "Padre Hernandez, my son does not want to marry any woman, especially that girl. What does she know about being a wife or mother?"

Candelaria was conflicted. She wanted a good and secure life for Rafaela. But she did not want her daughter to endure, as she did, marriage with a man for whom she had little affection. She also wanted all her family to live in God's grace.

When Father Hernandez saw Marcela's opposition to marriage, he began the arm twisting. "Señora Rodriguez, you must remember that in this country men go to jail if they force a woman to have sexual relations, especially if the victim is so young. I know that many times the police do not care what happens in the Village, but when a young child is the victim, they go after the guilty man. Do you want that for Cayetano?" The priest's comments had a sobering effect on Marcela, who began to consider the possibility of a marriage.

Candelaria, though conflicted, remained opposed. "Padre Hernandez, I fear that Rafaela will never have any affection or respect for Cayetano. I have asked Rafaela about a marriage to Cayetano, she told me she was unsure of marriage. She doesn't know what to do."

"We must have a resolution within the eyes of the Church," Father Hernandez told her. "With the grace of God, Rafaela might find forgiveness for Cayetano's actions. And having forgiven him, they could live a Christian marriage."

Candelaria's own experience of married life with Bernardo gave lie to the priest's belief that forgiveness alone was the answer. Her faith in the Church's teachings wavered for a moment.

Everyone, except for Father Hernandez, opposed to varying degrees marriage as the resolution—including Rafaela and Cayetano themselves. All, including Father Hernandez, doubted that the result would be a lasting and loving marriage. But in the end, they compromised their hopes, dreams, and affections. The wedding date was set for Saturday, January 3, 1920, at Our Lady of Guadalupe Chapel in the Village. Until the wedding day, Rafaela would stay in the home of Andres Navarro and Maria Gutierrez, Marcela's sister. Father Hernandez concluded the meeting with a surprising demand. "Señora Gutierrez, Cayetano must pay for a wedding dress for the ceremony." Though Marcela opposed this, she did not defy the priest. Instead, she nodded in agreement.

Chon was furious with the resolution. He yelled at Candelaria, "That man is a criminal and should be shot!"

Candelaria beseeched him, "Please, Chon. Please."

"My daughter should not be entrusted to a man like him. Let me at him! I'll let my *pistola* do the talking for me. He deserves it!"

"Please calm down, Chon! Please! Can't you see that if you harm him matters will be worse for Rafaela?" Chon angrily grabbed his coat. Fearing that he intended to hurt Cayetano, she asked, "Where are you going?"

"This is not right, Candelaria, and you know that," he said, in a low, resigned voice. "I do not want to be a part of this disgrace. I want to go outside." He stepped into the cold December night and firmly closed the door behind him.

The wedding took place as scheduled. Rafaela wore a white shin-length wedding dress with long sleeves, high neckline, and sweep train. Her ensemble included a white cap and veil, white gloves, and white ankle-high boots. After the ceremony, Candelaria and Chon retreated to their home. The bride and groom, the witnesses, a flower girl, and a ring bearer posed for a professional photographer. The photo did not capture any happiness. Rafaela and Cayetano soon moved into their own small home in the Village. In a matter of weeks, Rafaela's dreams of a better life crumbled down around her.

8

Candelaria's Grandchildren, the Cold of November 1927

In the weeks that followed her wedding, Rafaela realized that Cayetano's promises of bliss were a deception. He showed little affection and was attentive only to his own wants and needs. At times, he was mean-spirited—locking her in the house while he went out to play in his band, and prohibiting her from visiting Candelaria, where she found comfort and welcome arms. Rafaela timed her visits so that Cayetano was at work, and she would be unseen by Marcela and Francisca, who spied on her for Cayetano. Candelaria knew her daughter was in a difficult situation and needed guidance. She did not take an "I told you so" attitude with Rafaela. She wanted to help Rafaela to the greatest extent possible.

Just days before Alvina delivered her child, Rafaela announced that she might be carrying a child as well. The announcement, while joyful for Candelaria, created an instant weight of worry and stress for her. The facts were inescapable; Rafaela was too young to carry a pregnancy to full term, and there were countless risks for a thirteen-year-old girl in delivering a child. When Candelaria told Chon that Rafaela was expecting, he was more concerned about Rafaela and the injustice of the marriage. He gave no thought to his new status as a grandfather.

In May, Alvina gave birth to a daughter, Hipolita, called "Pola" by her family. Alvina later spoke with Rafaela about her experiences carrying Pola and the delivery. Rafaela also spoke with Juana about childbirth, but it was unclear whether Rafaela understood the descriptions of her sister-in-law and sister. Fortunately, Rafaela carried the baby through the summer months without incident while the family anxiously waited for the mid-October arrival.

In 1920, the public school district built and operated a two-room school in the Village, and Our Lady of Guadalupe Chapel continued to provide religious services to the Mexican community. The first families to arrive in the Village had become established. They knew nearly all the residents and the people to contact on both sides of the tracks. The young people who grew up in the Village were marrying each other and baptizing their children according to Catholic and Mexican traditions and practices. From 1920 until 1939, with a few interruptions, the Village held a two-day fiesta in the Village celebrating Mexico's independence from Spain. The fiestas included patriotic speeches, national anthems, Mexican food, traditional dances, and music. Although Mexico's Revolution had ended for Villagers, there was less of a sense of going home to Mexico someday and more of a "here to stay" attitude.

In their community, separated from Dodge proper, the Villagers kept their Spanish language, food, music, and celebrated Mexican and religious holidays, sometimes solely with votive candles. Every day, one of a small group of women sacristans, including Candelaria, voluntarily cleaned and readied the chapel for services. In the winter months in the early mornings, the sacristans walked in the freezing cold to start the coal heater for services. They lit lanterns and candles and neatly set out the altar linens and priest's vestments for the Mass. They were the first to arrive in the chapel and ensured that it was warm when Padre Hernandez arrived later.

As Rafaela's October delivery date approached, she thought about the experiences Alvina and Juana had described to her months before. But on the day of her delivery, the more Rafaela's labor pains increased, the more she forgot their advice. And she could never have anticipated that Irene would be taken from her after delivery and that she would be left to care for herself.

After Irene was born, Marcela and Francisca kept Rafaela's visits with Irene to a minimum. The Rodriguez women insisted that Rafaela was unable to properly care for her baby. For years, Rafaela believed that Cayetano's failure to confront his mother and sister was in retaliation for Rafaela's disclosure of Cayetano's assaults on her.

In November 1920, Candelaria sent word to Manuel in El Paso that Rafaela and Irene had survived and were healthy. Manuel replied that he and his family would travel to Dodge at Christmas time to visit her and the new granddaughters. Candelaria realized that a gathering of her children and grandchildren was a rare event. The families arranged for a photographer to go into the Village and take a family portrait. On a mild December day, Candelaria, Chon, and the grandchildren gathered in front of their Village home. Candelaria, with her long, braided hair—now salt and pepper in color—draped around her shoulders, sat on a chair with the two babies, Pola and Irene, in her lap. Standing on either side of her were Juana's children, Nicolas, Jose, and Prudencio, Manuel's children, Rafaela and Florencio, and Abran's son, Ladislao. Only Abran's twelve-year-old son, Antonio, was not pictured. A tall Chon, wearing a black suit coat that was much too short over a white shirt and bib overalls, stood behind Candelaria.

The photograph captured one of the most joyful times in Candelaria's life. She was in the presence of the generations that would follow her, and her heart was filled with affection for them. Her life's sacrifices had positioned them for the future, and she hoped that God would grant them comfort and success and the strength and courage to overcome the many unknown challenges that lay before them. The family reunion lasted only a few days before Manuel and his family returned to El Paso and left behind the ebb and flow of life in the Village.

But the precious peaceful days of December were soon disrupted. Juana and Geronimo were struggling in their marriage. Geronimo was a devout Catholic and strict disciplinarian, but Juana found his methods excessive for the boys. He also demanded that she honor and obey him—unquestioningly, as her wedding vows required. In her early twenties with three boys, and under Geronimo's thumb, Juana became frustrated with the life she was living. She also held some resentment that she had not gotten to enjoy her teenage years of adolescence. Instead, she had spent those years as a wife and mother in Iowa and Kansas, where she always lived in poor, noisy housing near railroad tracks and the winters were long and brutally cold. Outside of the camps and railroad neighborhoods, she was made to feel unwelcome by the many stares she received and the tone she experienced in the white establishments. She was also reluctant to interact with the white population because of her limited English and Spanish accent. She believed that at least in El Paso people would welcome her. Despite living in one of the city's poorest barrios until she was twelve, she remembered El Paso as a place of friendship, music, and good food.

Geronimo wanted nothing to do with El Paso. He was able to provide for his wife and family with his work for the Santa Fe. He was proud of being the breadwinner and doing the job a man was supposed to do—take care of his family. After many arguments and her threats to leave him and take the boys, Geronimo decided to show Juana that he did not fear living without her. He decided to return to Mexico, alone. He left in May 1921 and returned to his family in the state of Jalisco. Juana thought that after a short time away Geronimo's anger would subside and that he would return. But by summer's end, he remained in Jalisco. Candelaria counseled that to save the marriage, Juana should join him and convince him to return to the family in Dodge. In the fall, Juana joined Geronimo and his family in Valle de Guadalupe, Jalisco. Rafaela and Candelaria agreed to take in the boys in Juana's absence. The time Rafaela spent caring for Juana's boys only slightly eased the pain of her separation from Irene. While Juana was away, the Rodriguez women allowed Rafaela to spend a few hours a week with Irene in their home.

By the spring of 1922, Juana and Geronimo had reconciled in Mexico. Geronimo returned to Dodge to resume work with the Santa Fe, but Juana was pregnant and due in August, so she remained in Jalisco with his family until after the birth, when mother and child could travel safely.

Lives in the Village continued their course. La Pelona, Mexico's grim reaper, visited the Village from time to time as the community of families began to suffer the loss of their loved ones, young and old alike. Most had left their homeland in the hope of a better life in the United States with the Santa Fe. La Pelona struck in El Paso as well. Felipa, Manuel's wife, died at the age of thirty on June 16, 1922, after an eight-month battle with tuberculosis. In September, Catarina Rodriguez, who had left Juarez to join her daughters, Marcela and Maria, died in Dodge at the age of eighty-seven. In a two-sentence obituary, the *Dodge City Journal* callously reported that Catarina was one hundred years old and the oldest person in Dodge and that she died in the Village of old age. The *Journal* did not identify surviving family, the date of death, or the location of burial. The Rodriguez family was unable to pay for a lot or stone, so Catarina was buried in an unmarked pauper's grave in the Mexican section of Maple Grove cemetery on Dodge's west side.

In October, Juana and her new son, Cesario, rode the Santa Fe to Dodge. Despite the reconciliation, the marriage remained unsteady. The couple had periods of affection and closeness, but other times they were frustrated and angry with one another. Rafaela was especially happy to see Juana back in the Village, as Juana's return from Mexico, even with a new baby in hand, would lighten the workload for all. And Rafaela was anxious to share the news with her sister that she was carrying a second child, due in December. Though their marriage remained without affection, Rafaela continued her marital duty to her husband.

On nights when Cayetano locked Rafaela in the house to keep her from the company of family or friends, she felt especially alone. She tolerated his controlling insecurity to avoid his anger or displeasure. She wanted Irene returned to her and believed she would need Cayetano's support. At the same time, and despite her age, she began to show her resilience by quietly resisting Cayetano's efforts to keep her away from others. She was socially trapped inside the shanty and she wanted contact with the outside. When she was pregnant with Irene, she had introduced herself to the couple that had just moved into the shanty across the lane, Valente and Josefa Rodriguez. Josefa was in her early twenties and had just given birth to a son, Jesus. Despite the difference in age between the two women, pregnancy and giving birth were the common experience that in time led to a nearby and reliable source of support. Her friendship with Josefa became stronger during Rafaela's pregnancy in the summer and fall of 1922—Josefa was carrying her second child as well.

With her second pregnancy, Rafaela's greatest fear was that the Rodriguez women might again take the new baby. She believed she had demonstrated through her care for Juana's boys that she was a capable mother, thereby depriving the Rodriguez women of the excuse they had used for taking Irene.

On December 4, 1922, Rafaela—at age sixteen, with Candelaria and Juana supporting her in delivery—safely gave birth to a son. This time, Rafaela did not follow the Catholic calendar in naming her child. Instead, she chose the name Salvador, meaning savior. The Rodriguez women made no attempt to interfere with the birth or take custody of him. At last, she knew that most precious of moments when the newborn Salvador lay on her chest.

By the time Irene was three years old, she knew that Rafaela was her mother. Neither the Rodriguez women, nor Cayetano, tried to deceive her; from the beginning, when speaking to Irene they referred to Rafaela as "tu mamá." As Irene grew older, she asked Cayetano more and more often to take her to see her mamá and Salvador. She was too young to understand the rift between her mother and the Rodriguez women, but she did know comfort and support from her mother, both of her grandmothers, and her Aunt Francisca. Irene, her cousins, Juana's three oldest boys, and Abran's two sons all grew up knowing that Candelaria's house was a fun place where they played together and were spoiled by abuelita—the only limitation was to stay out of abuelo Chon's garden. Candelaria always greeted her grandchildren with a warm hug and a snack. When it was time to leave, she sent them off with a piece of hard candy for their promise to obey their parents. In July 1924, another girl joined the family when Juana gave birth to a daughter, Teresa.

In April 1926, Juana's second daughter, Celestina, was born. The couple was now raising six children, but Juana and Geronimo's marriage remained very troubled. Adding to the turmoil, Geronimo was certain that he was not Celestina's father. In her disillusion and frustration, Juana stepped outside the marriage and on occasion was absent for days. Candelaria was unhappy with Juana's behavior, particularly leaving the care of her children to Candelaria and Rafaela. But Candelaria knew very well the hardships of a woman in a difficult marriage. Geronimo was outraged but tempered his anger and allowed Juana to return to the home because of his Christian faith in forgiveness. Candelaria could do little to bring some stability to the household but keep a votive candle lit in the chapel and pray the rosary for the family.

Irene's first language was Spanish, but she had some English vocabulary. More importantly, she knew the alphabet before she began going to school. Her Aunt Francisca had sufficient schooling in Mexico to learn to read and write. Francisca recounted that one of the great insults she suffered in her life occurred when she entered the United States and a border crossing agent demanded she prove her ability to read. She snatched the booklet from his hand and read two paragraphs, distinctly, and without error in pronunciation. The agent, realizing he had challenged the wrong person, interrupted her, and said, "That will be sufficient, Señora." She snapped back at him, "Señorita! If you please. I am not married!" She returned the booklet with a look of contempt. Francisca was a strict disciplinarian and taught Irene the alphabet and how to write her name and a few short words in Spanish. Children's books in Spanish were rare in Kansas at the time, but Francisca would read aloud simple stories and accounts from her Spanish-language Bible. Her insistence on proper and correct reading and writing laid a foundation for Irene's curiosity and the desire to read and write. On her first day of school in 1926, Irene was ready to learn.

Historians refer to the 1920s and its growth in industry and commerce, particularly in the larger urban cities on the east and west coasts, as the "Roaring Twenties." American culture was entering new social arenas in and outside of the home. Travel, rail transportation, and automobiles continued their growth, and air travel was in its infancy. Radio, lighting, and other electrical products were common in many homes. Newspapers and radio sensationalized events and exaggerated individuals into celebrities, heroes, and villains. Small amounts of this wealth, glamor, and glory reached Dodge in this era, but very little seeped into the Village. With English taught in the Village school and spoken in the workplace, English words began to drift into the Village's daily language. Lives there remained sharply focused on shelter, food, the welfare of children, their Catholic faith, and keeping Mexican culture and traditions. Comforts were few, and luxuries were rare. The bare-knuckle living and dying in the Village were manifestly apparent.

During the third week of January 1927, temperatures fell to nearly zero degrees and did not rise above thirty-two. Outside work nearly came to a complete stop. Homes in the Village were consuming large amounts of coal for heat. As their stocks of coal fell at a rapid rate, the families were vulnerable to the freezing temperatures. Desperate to keep their families warm and healthy, Chon and a coworker decided the immediate remedy for the shortage was to take coal from Santa Fe train cars. The Santa Fe often looked the other way as Villagers gathered scraps of wood, bits of coal, and grains that fell from the train or were left behind in the rail cars. But on this Sunday night, when Chon and an accomplice named Miguel ventured into a coal car to gather the coal to keep their families warm, they were arrested and charged with theft.

When Chon appeared in court the next morning, the judge asked, "Are you Asención Padilla?"

"Sí, Señor."

"Mr. Padilla, do you understand English? Do you understand what I am saying?"

"Sí, Señor."

"Good. Now Mr. Padilla, this police officer says you were taking coal from a Santa Fe coal car, and you did not pay for that coal. Is that true?"

Chon nodded and said, "Yes."

"Mr. Padilla, since you admit that you were taking coal without paying for it, I am going to find you guilty of the crime of theft. Do you understand me?"

"Sí, Señor."

"Now, before I impose a sentence, is there anything you want to tell me? Why were you stealing the Santa Fe's coal?"

Chon looked at Miguel and indicated that he did not understand what the judge was asking him.

Miguel translated for him, "Porque robaste el carbón?" In broken English, Chon told the judge, "My family has no coal. My family needs heat." The judge said, "Mr. Padilla, I understand your family needs heat, but the law says you cannot take coal from a person or business without paying for it." The judge looked at the arresting officers and asked, "Gentlemen, do either of you have anything to say?"

One of the policemen answered, "I only want to add, your Honor, that we have recorded numerous thefts of coal recently."

"Thank you, officer. Mr. Padilla, I am imposing a fine of fifteen dollars. You pay that amount to the clerk as soon as you can. Do you understand?"

"Sí, Señor." The fine amounted to approximately six days wages.

The judge struck his gavel on the dais and called out, "Next on the docket!"

Despite the conviction, Chon kept his job with the Santa Fe. He was a reliable and productive worker. He was nearly sixty, and had he lost his job, his prospects for other work would have been limited—day labor or piecework that might arise on either side of the tracks.

On February 1, 1927, Rafaela gave birth to her third child, Cecilio. He, too, was born in the Village without a doctor present. Rafaela was attended by the Village midwives and women healers, the curanderas, including Marcela and Candelaria. Despite the women in Candelaria's family giving birth without a loss of life, she remained cautious and did not assume survival was certain.

Candelaria was committed to preparing the Village Chapel for the 7:00 a.m. daily Mass. Each morning at six, she walked the 150-yard distance down the lane to the chapel. On mornings when twilight was yet to break, she carried a lantern to light her way. On cold winter days, she wore a heavy coat, scarf, and shawl for warmth. On entry, she lit the coal-burning heater, then one by one, she lit the many candles that illuminated the chapel and altar. She ensured that all was prepared for Padre Hernandez's Mass before she returned home.

There was bitter cold on the Kansas prairie on November 15, 1927, with temperatures falling to sixteen degrees. But the harsh conditions did not deter sixty-two-year-old Candelaria; she did not waver in her devotion despite the cold. By the end of the next day, she began to feel ill and asked Chon to tell one of the other chapel sacristans that she would not be able to prepare the chapel the following morning. She was very tired and began coughing. In the morning, her condition was unchanged. She got out of bed with the intention of doing the household chores, but she was too weak, and her cough persisted. On Friday, the temperature reached only twenty-five degrees. Candelaria's fatigue and raspy cough became more pronounced, she had developed a slight fever, and she was becoming short of breath. Chon, an otherwise confident man, began to worry. He sent Juana into the bitter cold to find medical help in Dodge. Dr. R. G. Klein agreed to examine Candelaria, who was now bedridden. Chon waited at the Village entrance with Juana and guided the doctor to the house. After his examination, Dr. Klein told the family that Candelaria had an illness in her lungs. He concluded that she might be suffering from a flu virus or a very bad cold. He left a few pills with no assurance they would be effective. Recommending bed rest, hot tea, soup or broth, and a cold compress to break the fever, he told the family to keep her comfortable and in bed, adding that she could develop pneumonia if she did not improve soon. He told them he would examine her on the following Monday, but the family should contact him if her conditioned worsened during the weekend.

Over the weekend, Candelaria's condition did not improve. The curanderas provided teas and broth made from traditional Mexican herbs. Their remedies provided Candelaria some relief from her symptoms and discomfort, and kept her from dehydration, but could not overcome her illness. Candelaria's fever did not break, her chest and back ached from the coughing, and she was speaking less and less. During this time, Candelaria kept her rosary in her hands. She started a new rosary with a whisper, but she tired quickly. Juana and Rafaela kept the votive candles lit on Candelaria's altar and kept the children hushed.

As promised, Dr. Klein returned to the Village on Monday to examine Candelaria. When he explained his diagnosis to the family, he spoke in a serious tone. Candelaria had developed pneumonia. If she did not improve soon, she would become gravely ill and possibly pass away. Dr. Klein had noticed the small altar with candles and images of Jesus Christ and Our Lady of Guadalupe. He told the family, "There is nothing more we can do. Her body must fight to recover. Now is the time to pray for God's mercy."

Juana asked Dr. Klein, "If she does not get better, how long will she live?"

"One or two days at most. I am so sorry for your family. I can see from all of you here that she is a good woman and a good mother."

"Thank you, doctor, for coming to see my mother, and thank you for all you are doing."

"You're very welcome."

Later that night, Juana and Rafaela sat on her bedside as Candelaria fought for breath. With a raspy voice she asked Juana, "I am dying, aren't I?"

Neither daughter could hold back the tears at her question. Juana gathered herself and said, "Mamá, the doctor said you can still fight back and recover. You have always told me, 'con Dios, todo es posible.'"

"Sí, mija, but now He is calling me to heaven. I will finally see all my children and parents." She looked at her daughters and said, "Take care of your marriages. But always take care of your children first. They are the innocent."

As the women spoke, Abran and Chon came over to her bedside. Abran's eyes were filled with tears. Chon's were filled with frustration and anger. He said to Candelaria, "If you did not work for the Church, you would not be sick. There was no reason for you to make yourself sick for them."

Candelaria slightly rolled her head from side to side and whispered, "Stop, Chon. Stop."

But Chon could not keep his emotions under control. In a voice filled with frustration he said to her, "You did not have to sacrifice yourself for them."

"Por favor, Chon, let me die in peace." Those were the last words Candelaria spoke to him.

The next day, Candelaria was unable to speak and labored heavily to breathe. Juana kept a rosary in her hands. For a time, Chon sat at her side and held her hand. His anger had subsided and he spoke to her in the hope that she might hear him. Rafaela stood at his side as he said to Candelaria, "Thank you for the life you shared with me. Que Dios te bendiga." Rafaela comforted him and put her arm around her father's shoulder. Padre Hernandez arrived and quietly administered the last rites. Abran began making a wooden casket for his mother.

As the day progressed, Candelaria's breathing was shallower but remained steady. Juana and Abran brought their children to see her while she still lived. Abran told them, "Tell your abuelita to get better and that you love her. She can hear you." After each child had taken a turn, Abran led them out of the house.

Chon, Abran, Juana, and Rafaela kept vigil through the night. On Wednesday morning, November 23, the time between each breath was steadily increasing. Juana asked Geronimo to go out into the bitterly cold weather and bring Dr. Klein. By the time the doctor arrived in the afternoon, Candelaria had stopped breathing. Her children wept and grieved as they realized they would never touch her, nor speak with her, ever again. Irene was with Rafaela and saw her mother's sorrow. At age seven, she understood sadness but not the magnitude of loss. Dr. Klein examined her and declared her death at 3:30 p.m. Before he left, Dr. Klein gave Juana and Geronimo the name of an undertaker, Joe Halpieu, and reminded them to record Candelaria's death at the county offices.

Word of Candelaria's death spread through the Village. Some of the women came to pay their respects and to console the family. When Padre Hernandez arrived, he sat with Chon and said, "I am so sorry, Asención, for you and your family. I will speak with the parish pastor to arrange her burial."

Chon responded in a monotone, "Padre, I do not have the money to pay for a burial."

Father Hernandez told him, "The Church will make arrangements with the cemetery."

Chon only nodded his head. After a moment of silence, Chon looked directly at the Padre and said, "You know what, Padre?" Apprehensive of what Chon might say, Padre Hernandez remained silent. "You encourage the people to endure their misery, but you and the Church do little to stop the misery." There was a moment of silence as Chon stared at him with contempt and waited for him to answer. Finally, the padre stood up, and said, "Chon, we will take care of her burial," and stepped away.

A generation ended with Candelaria's death. She had led her family from the yoke of centuries under the hacienda system in Mexico to the portal of opportunity to live a life of one's choosing. Two days later, the undertaker drove a wagon with Candelaria's casket to the cemetery. She was laid to rest in a pauper's grave in the Catholic section. There was no stone or marker to identify where she might lie. Neither the Church nor the cemetery created a written record of her exact final resting place. Only the city records indicate her burial in Maple Grove Cemetery. Nearly a century after Candelaria's passing, her living grandchildren and great-grandchildren, in love and respect, installed a headstone with her and Asención's names. The headstone is engraved with a depiction of Our Lady of Guadalupe.

Candelaria and Asención Padilla with eight of her nine grandchildren in the Mexican Village. Circa 1920. *Left to right*: Ladislao "Lalo" Rodriguez, Prudencio Gomez, Nicolas Gomez, Candelaria Padilla (seated), Jose Gomez, Rafaela Rodriguez, Florencio Rodriguez. Seated on Calendaria's lap, Hipolita "Pola" Rodriguez, Irene Rodriguez. Standing behind Candelaria, Asención Padilla. (Author's collection)

Two girls from the Mexican Village riding a tricycle adjacent to a train of cattle cars. Children in the Village had no access to a park, playground, or play equipment. Circa 1930. (Courtesy Micaela Rodriguez Judd)

Members of the Santa Fe Mexican Band. Circa 1925. Music and dance are important pieces of Mexican culture, and many immigrants brought their musical talent and passion to the Mexican Village. (Author's collection)

Interior of Sacred Heart Catholic Church in Dodge City, Kansas. Originally constructed in 1915. (Author's collection)

Rafaela Padilla (*center*) poses with two unidentified teenage girls from the Mexican Village. Circa 1919. (Author's collection)

Rafaela Padilla (*left*) poses with two unidentified teenage girls from the Mexican Village. Circa 1919. (Author's collection)

Wedding photo of Rafaela Padilla and Cayetano Rodriguez (1920). (Author's collection)

Rafaela Rodriguez with sons David (*left*) and Gonzalo (*right*) Rodriguez, circa 1940. (Courtesy of Rita Rodriguez)

The Rafaela Rodriguez family celebrates a toddler's birthday with a cake and candles. The women, *left to right*, are Rafaela, daughter-in-law Rosella Rodriguez, niece Celestina Gomez Pinon, and daughter Maria Paz Rodriguez. The toddlers, *left to right*, are daughter Rita Rodriguez, grandson Manuel Rodriguez, Christina Pinon, and son Mauricio Rodriguez. Circa 1949. (Courtesy of Micaela Rodriguez Judd)

Rafaela Rodriguez. Circa 1983. (Author's collection)

Family portrait of the children of Rafaela Rodriguez in Dodge City. *Seated left to right*, Mauricio, Cecilio, Maria Paz, Enedina, Ezeqiel, and Rita. Standing behind the couch, *left to right*, David and Gonzalo. Absent are Salvador and Irene. Circa 1954. (Author's collection)

Irene Rodriguez. 1938. (Author's collection)

Hipolita ("Pola") Rodriguez (*left*), Antonio Rodriguez, and Irene Rodriguez (*right*) stylishly pose. Circa 1942. (Courtesy of Micaela Rodriguez Judd)

Irene Rodriguez and Dionisio Garcia wedding portrait. 1943. (Author's collection)

Irene Garcia and Dionisio Garcia at wedding dance. 1949. (Courtesy of Micaela Rodriguez Judd)

Irene Rodriguez Garcia and Micaela Rodriguez. Circa 1955. (Courtesy of Micaela Rodriguez Judd)

Irene and Dionisio Garcia family seasons greetings portrait. 1963. Front row, *left to right*, Philip (5), Raphael (12); middle row, *left to right*, Sylvia (8), Dionisio seated holding Lisa (1), Irene seated holding Charles (3), Maria (10); back row, *left to right*, Christina (16), Geraldine (13), Marcela (19), Virginia (17). (Author's collection)

Irene and Dionisio Garcia dancing at the Mexican Fiesta in Garden City, Kansas. 1983. (Courtesy Louis Mendoza)

Irene Garcia in her kitchen on Santa Fe Street in Garden City. 1991. (Author's collection)

Enedina Rodriguez (approximately 16), on the right, and two unidentified girlfriends sit on the front end of a car. Circa 1945. (Courtesy of Micaela Rodriguez Judd)

Gonzalo Rodriguez high school graduation. 1955. (Author's collection)

Dionisio Garcia in US postal uniform. Circa 1965. (Author's collection)

Ladislao Rodriguez, son of Abran Rodriguez. Circa 1945. (Author's collection)

Rosella Rodriguez and Salvador Rodriguez, with godson, Alfred Martinez. Circa 1955. (Courtesy of Micaela Rodriguez Judd)

Mexican Village children and Francisca Rodriguez pose after First Holy Communion. Circa 1948. (Courtesy Micaela Rodriguez Judd)

Asención Padilla. Circa 1895. (Courtesy of David Rodriguez)

Wedding ceremony in Our Lady of Guadalupe Church in Dodge City, Kansas. Circa 1960. (Courtesy of Micaela Rodriguez Judd)

Our Lady of Guadalupe congregation in Dodge City, Kansas, at Sunday Mass. Circa 1960. (Courtesy of Micaela Rodriguez Judd)

Rhythm Aces Band, Dodge City, Kansas. Circa 1940. (Courtesy of Micaela Rodriguez Judd)

American G.I. Forum Independence Day parade float. Circa 1965. The G.I. Forum is a Mexican-American veterans organization formed after World War II. (Courtesy of Micaela Rodriguez Judd)

Mexican Fiesta, Garden City, Kansas. Circa 1950. (Courtesy Spencer Research Library)

Candelaria and Asención Padilla headstone, Maple Grove Cemetery, Dodge City, Kansas. (Author's collection)

Candelaria Padilla. Circa 1925. (Courtesy of Micaela Rodriguez Judd)

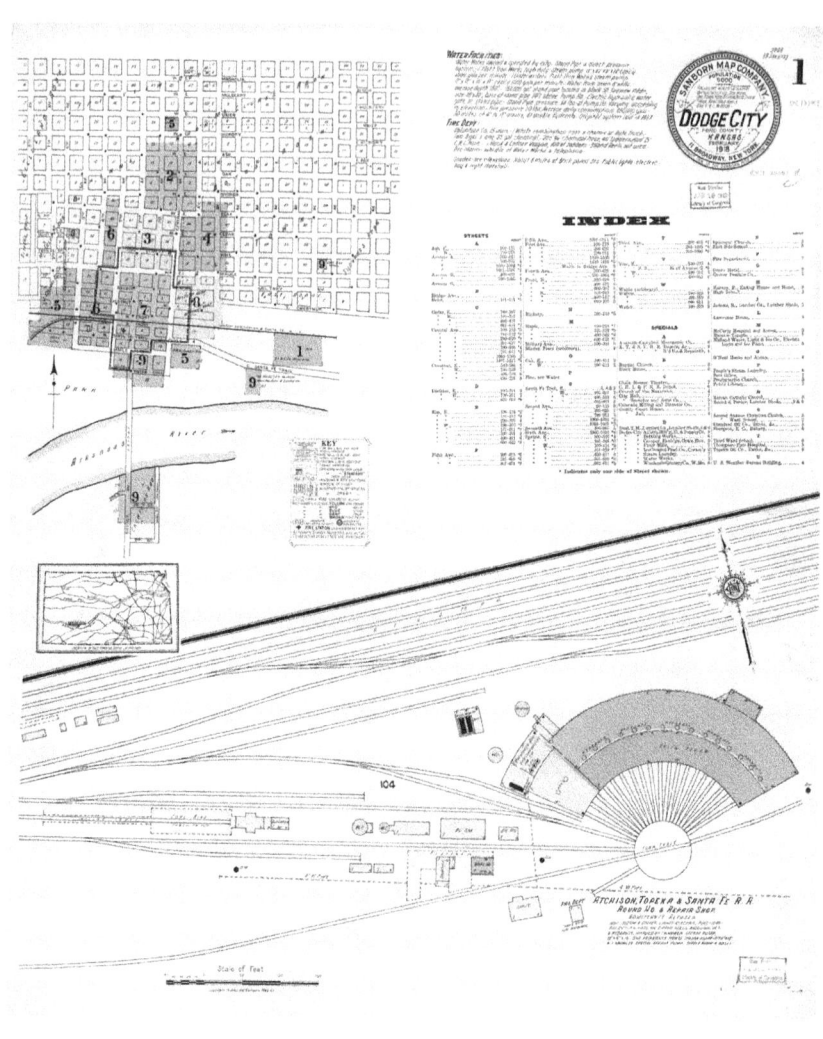

Sanborn Insurance map, Dodge City, Kansas. 1918. (Courtesy Library of Congress)

(*above*) Rafaela Rodriguez and Irene Garcia with the Munoz family. Garden City, Kansas. Front row, *left to right*, Marcela Garcia (age 10), Rafaela (age 49), Irene (age 36), Mary Ann Munoz. Back row, Michael Munoz, Ronaldo Munoz, Guadalupe Munoz. Circa 1955. (Author's collection)

(*left*) Antonio "Tony Montana" Rodriguez. 1935. (Courtesy of Micaela Rodriguez)

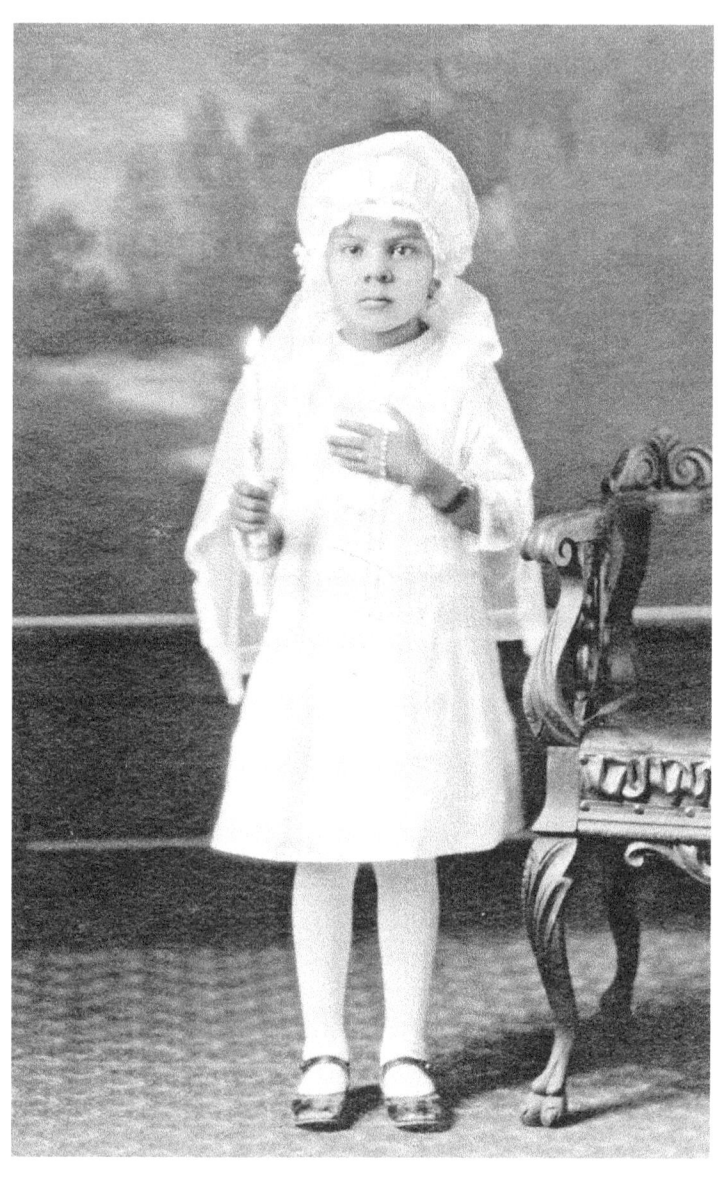

Irene Rodriguez, First Holy Communion. Circa 1927. (Courtesy of Virginia Garcia Jaramillo)

Part II
Rafaela

9

Steadfast Through the Dust Bowl and Depression, Irene's Diploma

After Candelaria's death, Chon remained in their home for a short time, but eventually he moved in with Rafaela and Cayetano. The arrangement was quite precarious given Chon's temperament and contempt for Cayetano. But Rafaela was Chon's only blood relative in the Village. He had his stepchildren, Abran and Juana; nonetheless, Rafaela insisted that he live with her and Cayetano. She also believed that Chon's presence would discourage any abusive behavior Cayetano might display toward her.

Shortly after the holiday season, Juana said directly to her husband, "Geronimo, I am not happy living here. And now, with my mother gone, I see no reason to stay." Geronimo dismissed her comments. "Look, Juana, you are unhappy all the time. You feel this way because you just lost your mother. You are sad, and that's why you want to leave. You'll feel better with a little more time."

"The way I feel has nothing to do with my mother. You were harsh with me and the children before she died, and I see no reason to go on living this way of life."

"The reason, Juana, is that we are married. We were married before God and the Church, and we will stay married."

Juana was adamant. "Geronimo, we may stay married, but we are not staying together. I told you; I am leaving you and taking the children."

At her defiance, Geronimo raised his voice and said, "No, you're not! I've had enough of this craziness. And if you want to go, go! But you are not taking the children! They are not going to see their mother live a life of sin. Try leaving and you will see! Do you think the law is going to allow you to take my children? You have no way to care for them. You have no money."

"My brother Manuel will help me in El Paso, and I can find work. And you? How are you going to take care of the children? Are you going to nurse Celestina? Wash them, bathe them, cook for them, wash their clothes? The children do not like the way you treat them! I'm done, Geronimo. Can't you see that I have no affection for you?"

"What I can see is that you are not in your right mind, whether because of your mother's death or your fairy tale that life will be better in El Paso."

Within days, Juana told Rafaela and Abran that she was leaving Geronimo and going to El Paso. She told them that she would take Celestina with her. But she could not convince Geronimo to allow her to take Teresa as well. She asked Rafaela and Alvina to help Geronimo with the children and promised to send money. Reluctantly, they agreed.

After kissing the boys and Teresa goodbye with a promise to see them soon, Juana boarded the train with Celestina in tow. Geronimo made no attempt to stop her. He continued to doubt that he was Celestina's biological father, and he believed that Juana would eventually become destitute and miss her children so much that she would come back, just as she had followed him to Mexico years earlier. Juana, however, felt relieved and pleased that she had acted to change the course of her life. She did not follow the marital path that Candelaria had lived. Putting aside her mother's wishes and the Church's command for married life, she left behind the cold winters of Kansas and Iowa. But she was also pained and saddened that she was leaving her children. As the train began to roll, she held Celestina close to keep her warm.

Juana never returned to Kansas. In the 1930 census, both Juana, in El Paso, and Geronimo, in Kansas, reported that they were widowed.

Without Juana, Geronimo managed with his teenage sons, who needed less care than Teresa. Ultimately, in 1930, tired of single parenting and harsh winters, he gathered his children and took them to his family in Mexico.

In May 1929, Rafaela gave birth to her fourth child, a daughter named Enedina ("Nina"). Rafaela had lost her mother's support with her passing, and Juana's support when she left for El Paso. Their absence left an emptiness in Rafaela's heart, but her friendship with Josefa and other women who lived nearby, and who were also raising children, filled some of that empty space. Josefa gave birth to a daughter in 1924 and a son in 1929. Rafaela stood as godmother for Josefa's son and two years later for yet another daughter. The women in Rafaela's corner of the Village were resourceful and supported each other, providing care for one another's children when needed. The children went freely in and out of each other's homes and yards, shared toys and dolls, and stayed for meals when they were too busy to go home to eat. In the company of the other young mothers, and without worry of triggering the heavy hand of her domineering father and husband, Rafaela was free to display her warmth and sense of humor.

Though Rafaela continued to fulfill her marital duties with Cayetano, they each kept the other at arm's length. There was little, if any, affection between the two. Nor did Cayetano show any interest in parenting. He left most of the discipline to Rafaela. His interests were work and practicing his fiddle.

Rafaela had noticed that at social gatherings or events where Cayetano's band performed, he had a roving eye and comfortably flirted with female admirers in attendance. On one occasion during this time, Chon learned of rumors that Cayetano had acted in a manner showing great disrespect to Rafaela. He was outraged. In previous bouts of rage, Candelaria had tempered his impulses, but after her death, Chon was on the loose. Many men in the Village over time had heard Chon's threats of using his *pistola*, but never seeing an actual firearm, they considered his comments nothing more than macho bluster. But on this afternoon, Chon got his *pistola* from its hiding place and began walking toward Rafaela's house, revolver in hand. A neighbor spotted his approach and rushed ahead to warn Rafaela and Cayetano. Although Rafaela held Cayetano in contempt, she did not want her father to shoot him. She yelled, "Get out! Now! Hurry!" He ran out the door and escaped through the backyards of his neighbors. Chon entered, pointing the *pistola*, and yelled, "Donde está ese cabrón?!" As Chon moved through the house, Irene fainted, believing that her grandfather was about to shoot her father.

The episode ended without shots fired. Rafaela convinced him to leave and take the *pistola* with him. Chon spent the next few weeks with Abran but did eventually return to an uneasy peace at Rafaela and Cayetano's house. The whereabouts of the revolver remained a mystery.

❦

The Roaring Twenties began its slide into a thundering stock market crash on Black Tuesday, October 29, 1929. The crash signaled the beginning of the economic disaster that history named the Great Depression. By 1930, the full-scale calamity of the Great Depression was underway across the country. Industrial manufacturers reduced or ended production, and approximately four million people lost their jobs as a result. Agricultural production also fell, particularly on the prairies of Kansas and the Southwest. Farming and ranching were devastated by drought and poor farming practices that led to the Dust Bowl sandstorms. Within two years of the stock market crash, the Great Depression had devastated the livelihoods of workers across the country.

In the rural communities, especially in the Dust Bowl states of Kansas, Oklahoma, Colorado, New Mexico, Texas, Arkansas, and Missouri, farmers and ranchers and homeowners suffered the full impact of the natural and economic disasters. With little or no income, they were unable to pay their mortgaged farms and homes. Banks and lending institutions foreclosed, took back the properties, and evicted the families. Many of the people who were newly homeless left their home states looking for work in California, where their arrival was often unwelcome. Some communities used law enforcement roadblocks to turn away those with no money who were escaping the disasters. Many local governments considered the new arrivals as an undeserving drain of the relief funds reserved for local residents. A few local community service groups and churches provided some aid to the arriving families, but most were left to fend for themselves and were shoveled off to camps on the outskirts of towns called "Hoovervilles."

During the years of the Great Depression (1930–1938), tens of thousands of people were abducted off the public streets and taken from their homes by US government officials without regard to their legal status. The abductions were largely from communities with large Mexican populations in metropolitan areas, especially California and Texas, but also in Midwestern states and on the East Coast. The rationale offered to support the abductions was exceedingly simplistic and without foresight: if Mexican laborers were removed, then white workers would replace them and take the jobs that were rightfully theirs. This reasoning was, and remains, a reoccurring theme politicians use to remedy periods of unemployment, a scapegoat for workers who have lost jobs or have low wages, and a further justification for racists to remove people of color from the country.

The promise of one-to-one replacement with white people popularized by the Hoover-era slogan "American jobs for real Americans" was an insidious deception of people suffering severely during the Great Depression. The heart of the abduct-and-replace equation was to allow local and federal governments to instill so much fear in Mexicans, citizens, and noncitizen populations alike that they would voluntarily leave for Mexico rather than suffer the cruelty of forced separation from their infants, children, and family members. Some of the abducted US citizens had no current ties with Mexican relatives and were unable to return to the United States for lack of necessary documents. Some hospital patients, including some unable to care for themselves, were taken to the Mexican border and left there to fend for themselves.

Estimates are that 1.5 million people were ultimately sent to Mexico via railroad, bus, or car. Most of the abducted people had no opportunity to contact their families to advise them of the circumstances of their separation and disappearance. The number and identity of people actually abducted and removed cannot be determined with certainty because government officials kept no records, unlike the records kept by German officials during the Holocaust in the decade to follow. They were granted no hearings, appearances before judges, or any notice prior to their detention. The abductions were completely without due process and fundamental fairness and violated the Constitution of the United States. Congress passed no law, nor did President Herbert Hoover issue an order authorizing or approving the abduction and removal program. But officials from the Department of Labor assisted local governments in passing laws to carry out the unwritten policy. The harsh reality is that people of color have suffered the cruelty of family separation at the hands of governments attempting to subdue and control them. That experience has a long history in the United States, including nearly three centuries of African slavery, the removal of Indigenous children from their lands and families, the internment of Japanese families during World War II, and the horrific treatment of Central American children and families lawfully seeking refuge at the southern border in the twenty-first century.

The Great Depression experience in the Village differed from those of the large Mexican populations on the West Coast and Texas. All railways suffered a downturn in business and income during the Great Depression, especially on the East Coast. But the impact was not as severe on railways in the western part of the country. Populations were relatively small, and the region was so expansive that railways remained the best transportation for goods and people. And from El Paso to Iowa, the Santa Fe operated with the labor of men of Mexican descent. Since the turn of the twentieth century, the Santa Fe had deliberately employed a manual labor workforce of Mexicans and US citizens of Mexican descent. The administrators, supervisors, and foremen of the railway were, almost without exception, all white men, while the labor force was virtually all Mexican. The Santa Fe needed its Mexican labor force to operate and stay in business, and it was not about to round up its workforce and send it back to Mexico. At the same time, men in the Village took some pride in the fact that they were employed and able to support their families without public relief.

But while the men in the Village kept their jobs, they did not suddenly become prosperous. The Santa Fe did not pay higher wages that enabled them to buy more material things. But with fewer and fewer customers, and falling prices, Dodge merchants were desperate to sell to anyone. Because working Villagers were able to buy more with the same wages, they filled the customer void. Conditions in the Village started to improve but remained poor. There was still no running water, electricity, sanitation services, or paved roads. The lone exception was the Ceballo's grocery store.

Village families whose men were unable to work for the Santa Fe because of injury or age scrambled for any work available. Men and families, including children, found seasonal work in the sugar beet fields and performed other harsh and demanding manual farm labor. A sugar beet factory operated some fifty-five miles west of Dodge just outside of Garden City. Farmers in the surrounding counties planted large crops of sugar beets, which required intensive seasonal manual labor. By auto or rail,

Villagers packing a week's food supplies and clothing found their way to the fields and factory for work.

Many men traveled across the country on railways in search of work during the Great Depression. They had no money to pay for their transportation, so they resorted to riding the rails. Without purchasing a train fare, they would climb aboard train cars or into boxcars to get to the next potential work site. The stowaways were unable to pay for meals, so at stops along the way they asked locals for handouts of food and water. Local police were often called upon to move them back to the rail yards and away from the townspeople. Dodge City remained a rail hub, and many rail riders detrained there to go to the Village in search of a meal. They entered without interference, as there were no Village police to keep them away.

Rafaela's and Abran's homes were in the first line of homes along the tracks and frequently the first approached by the stowaways. Rafaela had seen Candelaria give food to men who rode the trains without passenger fare. They were hungry and unbathed. But Candelaria, following the teachings of her faith, showed mercy to the exhausted men. Rafaela chose to act as her mother did. She did not allow the men into her home but told them to sit and wait outside in the lane while she prepared a bag of beans, eggs, potatoes, tortillas, and a jar of coffee or water. She sent Salvador and the older boys to deliver the lunch and send the hungry travelers on their way. Most Villagers responded to the rail riders with similar cautious humanity during the country's time of hardship and suffering.

Chon remained dangerously troublesome. About 1932, five years after Candelaria's passing, he began living with Alegria, a woman from the Village a few years younger than Chon, who was by then sixty-five. Before too long, Chon heard a rumor that Alegria had been exchanging affectionate glances with another man at a Village event. When he ended his work day in the afternoon, he was on the brink of rage. He stood in the doorway and said angrily, "Alegria, I must talk with you right now!"

She did not expect to hear so much anger in his voice. "Chon, what is happening? What is the matter?"

"You have been flirting and making eyes at another man!"

Alegria was surprised by the allegation and fearful of his response. "Chon, what are you saying? What are you talking about?"

"You think I don't know? You think I don't hear about it at work? Everyone knows you have been making eyes with another man."

"That is not true! I don't know what you're talking about."

"Don't deny it!" Chon demanded.

Alegria got up from the chair where she sat and said, "I did not do any such thing. You don't know what you're talking about!"

Chon shouted, "I am not going to support a woman so that she can play around with another man!"

Alegria had started to walk away from him when she saw him raise his hand on his right side. When she realized he held a revolver, she screamed, "Chon! No!" With a flash and a loud bang, Alegria fell to the floor. Chon's neighbors hurried to the house. They recognized the sound of gunfire from years of men shooting into the air in celebrations of various sorts. When they entered the house, they found Chon on his knees trying to help Alegria. He explained, "I shot her. But that was not my intention. I only wanted to scare her; I did not mean to shoot her."

At this time, there were two or three Village residents who owned a car. Chon's neighbor rushed to ask one of them to take Alegria to the hospital, where she was treated for the wound. The bullet had entered and exited her abdomen on her left side without striking any vital organs. It was not life-threatening.

Chon remained behind and made his way to Rafaela and Cayetano's home. He explained the shooting to Rafaela, to her great frustration and dismay. Later in the evening, two Ford County deputies went into the Village, detained Chon, and took him to the county jail. They seized the revolver as evidence as well.

The authorities delayed charging Chon until the severity of Alegria's wounds was determined with certainty. After a few months in jail, he was released without any formal charges brought against him.

Two factors were considered in the decision to release Chon. In the first place, law enforcement agencies avoided getting involved in Village disputes. Second, in a routine medical check of county inmates, Chon tested positive for tuberculosis, a notoriously contagious and lethal disease. The jail wanted him out immediately. Chon assured the authorities that he would go to El Paso to lessen the possibility of reprisal by Alegria's family and promised not to return until the following spring. The Santa Fe terminated his employment upon his incarceration, so the extended absence was possible.

Rafaela went to the jail when Chon was released. As she waited for him, the sheriff's office gave her his personal belongings—including his revolver, which the deputy suggested she ought to destroy. She took it from the bag and put it in her purse. Later, when Chon asked about it, she told him she did not know anything about it and that perhaps the sheriff had kept it or destroyed it. The reality was that Rafaela put the unloaded weapon in her own hiding place.

Rafaela gave birth to her fifth child and third son, Ezequiel, in the spring of 1931. On January 24, 1933, Rafaela's sixth child and third daughter, Maria Paz, was born two months premature and survived. Still in a marriage without affection, Rafaela bore her children from a sense of duty as a wife. She shared her mother's view that children were blessings from God, and should the children survive into adulthood, they would provide care for their parents in their old age. Though their care was exhausting, her children knew the security of their mother's warmth and affection. She kept away the bitterness and resentments of her marriage that might interfere with the love for her children. And there was great reason to carry bitterness and resentment. While Rafaela was carrying Maria Paz, she heard Village talk that Cayetano had a sexual liaison with the wife of an acquaintance. The rumors were later confirmed, and the liaison resulted in the birth of a daughter in October. Rafaela was crushed. She wondered how a man could be so cruel—taking her as a child and forcing her into marriage, and then humiliating her with an illegitimate child. She cried a great deal during these times. Reconciliation of their marriage became impossible, yet divorce was out of the question given her Catholic faith. Still, she had the resilience to gather herself over time and carry on for her children's sake.

By 1933, the Great Depression and Dust Bowl were punishing the big cities and the heartland. During this time, Irene had not only completed elementary school at the Village school but also had become an excellent student. Her performance in the classroom did not go unnoticed by the school's teacher, Arthur E. Scroggins. He was born in 1899 in Missouri and completed his high school education in 1916. After a year as a high school principal, he attended the teacher's college at Fort Hays, Kansas, and in 1923, obtained a graduate degree in education. Scroggins began teaching at Coronado School in the Village in the 1924–1925 school year.

Scroggins lived his beliefs in teaching, education, and enlightenment. He encouraged travel abroad so that the individual might see and understand different peoples and cultures.

Irene became one of Scroggins' favorite students; he referred to her as "my Little Indian Princess." He always encouraged her in her school work, and at times during the reading period he asked Irene to read aloud to the class. She was content to take that role and lead the class.

In April 1932, after his brief exile in El Paso, Chon returned to the Village and Rafaela's home. He also began looking for work. In an unexpected and fortunate circumstance, a young entrepreneur, C. Edward Faber, had opened two years earlier a nursery and greenhouse located a half-mile to the east of the Village on Fort Dodge Road. His greenhouse sold, among other items, flowers, plants, vegetables, and a variety of peppers and squash. Chon walked to Faber's and in broken English asked for work. He explained to Faber that he had his own garden in the Village and that he had worked in gardens all his life. Faber told him that he could offer only seasonal work, a term that Chon readily accepted. The job was nearly ideal for an aging Chon—Faber's was within walking distance, and he was able to manage the reduced workload.

The Santa Fe granted passes for its workers and their families to travel to any location on their railway. Rafaela took advantage of this benefit to get out from under Cayetano's control, if only for a two-or-three-week period. She convinced Cayetano that she was able to travel with her children without a husband's protection. Nearly every summer during this time Rafaela traveled to El Paso with Irene and one or two of the youngest children to visit Juana and Manuel. On one of their first trips, Rafaela and the children stepped off the train at the Albuquerque stop to stretch and move about. As they walked along the red brick platform, they encountered an elderly woman from one of the local Pueblo Tribes sitting on a colorful blanket with turquoise and silver jewelry spread out before her. She smiled at Rafaela and asked in Spanish, "Tus niños?"

"Sí." Touching Irene's head, she said, "She is the oldest, and these are my youngest." Rafaela asked her in return, "Do you have children or grandchildren?"

"Oh yes, all my children are living, and I have grandchildren." The two women introduced themselves—the woman's name was Maria—and a long conversation followed as each described their families for the other.

As the train sounded its boarding whistle, Rafaela bought a pair of earrings and said, "We'll talk again on my return to Kansas."

"Muy bien, Rafaela. Enjoy the time with your family," said Maria.

"Gracias. Y Dios te bendiga." Rafaela kept her word and spoke to Maria on her return that summer and every summer thereafter. Though the travel dates were never set in advance, the women marked the beginning of summer with Rafaela's arrival on the Santa Fe. Rafaela always bought a ring or bracelet, and Maria always included a small extra item in the purchase. Rafaela's meetings with Maria were pleasant assurances that soon she would be with family in El Paso.

Rafaela did not travel in the summer after Maria Paz was born. That year, Juana had given birth to a son, Jesus. She was working as a seamstress in a factory and living with a man named Gabriel Hernandez. In 1934, Rafaela returned to El Paso, taking Irene with her as usual. This time when they returned to the Village, Irene would leave Marcela's and Francisca's house to live with Rafaela. At thirteen, Irene was frustrated and unhappy with the strict religious regimen of her Aunt Francisca. She had just completed school at Coronado and wanted to spend time with her friends—girls and boys. Talking to boys was strictly forbidden by Francisca. As Irene approached her teenage years, she spent more and more time with Rafaela and Cayetano, where she was more comfortable away from the strict parenting methods of Francisca. She preferred the company of her growing number of siblings. But at the end of each day, she returned to her grandmother's home, where each evening Francisca led the daily rosary and recital of the Litany of the Blessed Virgin Mary. Irene was persistent in asking her father when was he going to take her to live with him and Rafaela. Finally, Cayetano told his mother and older sister that the time for Irene to live with him had arrived. His demand was not well received by the Rodriguez women, but eventually they relented. At long last, after nearly fourteen years, Irene's and Rafaela's wish to live in the same home, all day, every day, came true.

In early January 1935, Rafaela gave birth to her seventh child and fourth son, Gonzalo. For the first time, Rafaela gave birth in the Village with a medical doctor present. The local doctors had begun to deliver babies in the Village and the families were able to pay for their services. With the additions of Gonzalo, Irene, and Chon, living space in the two-room house became even tighter.

The Village houses and shanties were especially vulnerable to the high winds and fine dust that seeped into wooden structures during dust storms, which worsened as the droughts persisted and the decade progressed. Rafaela battled the dust storms in much the same manner as farmers and small-town residents on the prairies, using wet towels to cover her face and those of her children to keep the fine dust from reaching their airways and lungs. During the stifling summer heat, Rafaela cooked the meals and made tortillas at daybreak. For lack of electricity, even the simplest relief, a fan, was unavailable to relieve the heat of the day. Her shanty did not have a porch or trees to shade the yard and escape the heat. But she was resourceful and often took the children to Abran's shanty, where trees shaded the yard. The families set chairs outside for the adults to chat and laid out blankets for the children to play. They enjoyed cool drinks when Santa Fe throwaway ice was available. After the evening suppers, she left the dishes untouched until sunset when she could wash them in less heat.

On Palm Sunday, April 14, 1935, after a calm sunny morning, a dust storm roared out of the north and west with winds reaching sixty miles per hour. It swept down across southwestern Kansas and Dodge City and the Oklahoma and Texas Panhandles. In some locations, temperatures dropped thirty degrees. The dust cloud was hundreds of miles wide and reached from the horizon into the high afternoon sky. The cloud was so thick and black with dust that it blocked out the sun completely. People reported they could not see their hands in front of their faces. The afternoon turned into such complete blackness some believed that judgment day had arrived.

The Palm Sunday dust storm was not only the largest in size but the most harmful to residents of the Dust Bowl. The fine dust people inhaled with every breath damaged their lungs and left them susceptible to dust pneumonia, particularly those with respiratory systems weakened by old age, tuberculosis, asthma, smoking, or other lung disease. Just four months after the Black Sunday dust storm, Marcela became ill and could not breathe. She was seventy-three years old and in poor health. It became apparent very quickly that she was in great distress and possibly on her deathbed.

Marcela, who stood slightly less than five foot tall, had great affection for Rafaela's children, especially Irene. While Irene was uncomfortable at times with Francisca's strict discipline, she did not have similar reservations with Marcela. Irene loved her and her welcoming arms very much. Irene had few images of Candelaria's passing in her mind. But at Marcela's death, she had a much greater understanding of the finality and pain of her loss.

Rafaela's emotions were conflicted. She again felt the pain of Candelaria's death and knew that Marcela's son, Leon, and her sister, Maria, were hurting in the same way. But Rafaela's empathy was more reserved for Marcela, Francisca, and Cayetano, who were complicit in separating her from Irene at Irene's birth.

Marcela died of pneumonia on July 25, in her home in the Village with her children and her sister, Maria, at her side. She was buried in Maple Grove Cemetery in Dodge. The Gutierrez family was able to purchase a lot and headstone, which marks her resting place in the Mexican section.

❄

On a Sunday afternoon in the first week of September, twelve-year-old Salvador ran into the house and told Rafaela and Irene that "El Sapo," toad in English, was walking down the lane that fronted their house. Some of the older boy students at Coronado School had tagged Mr. Scroggins, Irene's teacher, with the disrespectful nickname. Irene's view—and that of most students—was dramatically different. She saw him as a teacher with an interest in their education and futures.

Irene looked out the door and confirmed that, indeed, it was Mr. Scroggins walking through the Village. She was surprised when he turned and began walking directly toward their house. She said to Rafaela, "Mamá, it's the teacher, Mr. Scroggins. He is coming to our house."

Rafaela asked Irene, "What is he doing here? Are your brothers in trouble?"

"I don't know, Mamá," Irene replied as Scroggins knocked on their door.

When Irene opened the door, Scroggins said in English in a cheerful tone, "Hello, Irene. How are you?"

"I am fine, Mr. Scroggins. What are you doing here?"

He answered in a more formal tone, "I would like to speak with you and your parents."

Irene turned to Rafaela and interpreted his request. "He wants to talk to you and Papá."

Rafaela said, "Tell your father the teacher is here." Irene stepped around the curtain divider and went into the back room to tell Cayetano.

Rafaela made space in the front room for the four of them to sit. She offered coffee to Scroggins, who politely declined.

When Cayetano walked into the room, Scroggins greeted him, "Buenas tardes, Señor Rodriguez." He nodded at Rafaela and said, "Señora." She nodded back and invited him to sit down. The two men sat down without shaking hands. Cayetano, too, had no idea of the purpose for his visit, but like Rafaela he thought the boys might have misbehaved.

Scroggins looked at Irene and asked if she would interpret for him. She nodded. He looked at Cayetano and began speaking. "Señor Rodriguez, it is my understanding that Irene has not enrolled at the high school. She is very intelligent and a great student. She can complete high school, and that will help her in the future. I came here to encourage you to send her to high school." Irene interpreted his comments while trying to hold back her surprise. Rafaela and Cayetano were surprised as well. For Village children of Irene's age, especially the boys, formal education ended at eighth grade, if not sooner. Only a handful of students continued to high school, including those few Mexican students who lived with their parents in Dodge City proper.

Cayetano showed little interest in Scroggins's comments. He asked the teacher, "Why does she need more schooling? I think she needs to stay home and help her mother take care of her brothers and sisters. She doesn't need school."

Scroggins persisted. "Señor Rodriguez, I respectfully disagree. More and more women with an education are working and help their families. With more school, she will get one of those jobs."

Cayetano remained unconvinced. After a brief, expressionless silence, he asked Irene directly, "Do you want to go to school?"

Irene hesitated for a moment. She wanted to attend, but she was cautious about crossing her father's wishes. With a slight hesitation she made a choice. "Yes. I do. That would be nice."

Cayetano turned to Rafaela and asked, "Do you think she should go to school?" Rafaela, also careful to avoid crossing Cayetano in the presence of other men, deferred to her husband. "If she wants to attend, and you approve, that is fine by me." Rafaela had rarely seen a young woman benefit from a high school diploma. At the same time, she was certain that she did not want Irene to marry before she was fifteen and suffer the hardships and heartaches that she, her sister, and her mother had experienced.

Scroggins sensed an opening in the resistance and said, "Señor y Señora Rodriguez, I am certain that if you permit Irene to get her high school diploma, she and her family in the future will live a good life."

Finally, Cayetano conceded disinterestedly. "She can go to school if she wants to."

Irene, quickly and with more confidence, chimed in, "I do want to go."

Scroggins immediately closed the discussion by saying, "Great! Wonderful! Thank you, Señor Rodriguez." He looked at Irene and directed her to go to the school and enroll. "If you have any trouble getting into the school or with your classes, tell me and I will help you."

When Scroggins stood up to leave, he considered extending his arm for a handshake. But when Cayetano remained seated, he thought better of it. Rafaela and Irene saw him out and thanked him for coming to speak with them.

The next day, Rafaela and Irene walked the mile to register and enroll her in the high school. To reach the school, they walked to the northwest corner of the Village to a short concrete underpass. The tunnel, as it was known, was built in 1910 and allowed trains to cross over a ditch that carried rain runoff to the Arkansas River. But perhaps more importantly, it was a portal that allowed Villagers to go back and forth between the Village world and the white world.

When Irene walked through the high school doorway, there was no celebration with colorful balloons, blowing horns, or floating confetti. It was the simplest of acts, yet the moment was monumental in Irene's life and her family's history. She was the first to pursue an education beyond basic elementary school. Her knowledge of the world would expand exponentially, and in the future, she would always see the world and herself in a different light.

❧

For most Mexican students, their first encounter and interaction with white students and white adult authority was in the public schools. For seven hours a day, five days a week, they were immersed in classrooms with students who differed in appearance, language, attitudes, behaviors, dress, and meals. In short order, they realized there are those who have material comforts and those who do not. Decades later, some of the children who were raised in the Village said that as children, they did not know they were poor. But the adults knew, and knew that they were resented by many Dodge residents. There are photos of Village children from Irene's era that depict happy and smiling faces. Their expressions indicate their parents and caretakers ably sheltered them from the hardship of their poverty with loving and supportive families. But there are also photos that reveal expressionless faces, tired and worn faces, and hunger.

Nonetheless, the Village parents and grandparents hoped their sacrifices might instill in their children and grandchildren an inner strength, determination, and resiliency. These qualities would enable them to withstand the hostility that awaited them on the other side of the tunnel. Initially, Irene and the two Mexican boys who also enrolled at the high school were taken aback by the differences, but the awkwardness lessened over time. In pursuit of their diplomas, they were learning lessons beyond the materials in their books.

One of Irene's surprises at the high school occurred in her gym class. Her Aunt Francisca had raised her to always act with the utmost modesty. She was to be ladylike and not play games and sports, especially if boys were participating. She was unfamiliar with basketball, tennis, and other light exercise activities in the gym class. She found those activities that focused on balance, health, and beauty far more enjoyable. She was especially pleased that the class was held in the gym out of the view of other students and the public. But her biggest shock was in the girls locker room. It was a complete surprise to her that the girls disrobed in the presence of their classmates. Even more surprising was that a few of the girls walked around without any clothing at all, and seemingly without the slightest concern that others might see them. But to Irene's relief, many of the girls wore bathrobes while they changed clothes.

After school, Irene and Cayetano asked Francisca to make gym clothes and a robe for her. Francisca was an excellent seamstress, and she was already familiar with the cut of the blouse and bloomers the girls wore in the class but unsure of the cut of the robe. Irene described the robe in detail while Francisca sketched a model. Francisca told Cayetano how much money she needed from him to buy the materials. Within days, Irene was a full participant in her gym class and less uncomfortable in the locker room.

Not surprisingly, Irene's grades in physical education were average, but overall, she was an above-average student. She enjoyed reading, as

Mr. Scroggins could attest, and she was already familiar with Latin from Catholic rites and rituals and earned As in her English and Latin classes. She earned Bs in her natural sciences and math classes. She was dedicated and diligent about her school work. She walked through the tunnel every school day, regardless of the weather. She often stayed after school to complete her homework where the lighting was better and surroundings quieter. There were also comforts at the school that remained unavailable in the Village: water fountains, indoor plumbing, and heating. She was cautious on her way home and avoided walking through the tunnel alone, especially when darkness fell early in the winter months. She watched for strangers, including rail riders, who might be at either end.

Irene was naturally quiet and never described as boisterous or loud. In high school, she was not timid and shy, but she was careful in developing friendships. In her junior and senior years, she was a member of the Girls Reserve group, a club with the goals of building character and confidence. Irene and the Reserve Group raised funds at football and basketball games and at other activities by selling candy and treats. Mother-and-daughter banquets were held, but Irene and Rafaela did not participate. For the holidays, the group prepared and distributed food baskets for the less fortunate of Dodge City. Among the friendships Irene made in high school, a few became lifelong.

By the start of Irene's senior year, in 1937, President Roosevelt's New Deal programs were leading the way to recovery from the Great Depression. But the recovery was not complete, and the US economy suffered a setback in midsummer. People who were fortunate to have been part of the recovery again lost their jobs and their homes. Meanwhile, conditions in the Village had remained fairly constant. Births, baptisms, marriages, and deaths continued at their usual pace. Those who worked for the Santa Fe kept their jobs during the setback. Villagers who were not employed by the Santa Fe continued to look for work as laborers on nearby farms and on temporary WPA and other New Deal building projects in Dodge. Children who were spared the hardship of farm labor remained with family or friends while the adults left for work. Girls and boys left behind helped with care for children and household chores. Boys and early teens entertained themselves with their surroundings, climbing atop railroad cars and jumping from car to car or crawling under supposedly parked train cars. When chased out of the railyard, they might go into the neighboring stockyard and ride the unsaddled horses. They also played a less dangerous game of baseball in a nearby empty field or lot.

Chon was fortunate; he had calmed and was able to keep his part-time employment at Faber's Greenhouse. Since Candelaria's passing, he had made short visits to El Paso during the Kansas winters to visit Geronimo, his stepchildren, Juana and Manuel, and their children. If Chon was not back from El Paso by the start of the spring season, Faber went into the Village to ask Rafaela when Asención might return from El Paso and to remind Rafaela to tell Chon that his job waited for him.

In the Village in early November, Rafaela gave birth to her eighth child and fifth son, David. Once again, a doctor was present for the delivery and both mother and son survived the birth without harm. Rafaela and the women of her generation, with better water and nutrition, medicine, and prayer, had a higher rate of survival than prior generations. With three adults, including Chon, and eight children in the house, Rafaela enlisted Irene and the older siblings to help her with household operations: cooking, cleaning, washing, bathing children, gathering coal, and fetching water. In the mornings, Salvador escorted his younger brother and sister to Coronado School while Irene made her way to the high school.

In late May 1938, Irene completed her classes and earned her diploma. Her achievement in those times was exceptionally rare and should not be regarded lightly. Only a handful of girls graduated with high school degrees. Many white teens, not only in Dodge but across the country, did not complete high school. Teen boys during the Depression were already working or trying to find work, and girls were at home learning to become homemakers and considering marriage and motherhood. High school diplomas in the Depression did not provide instant jobs, but in time, they opened the gateway to a better life.

On Rafaela's summer trip to El Paso in 1939, she brought her three youngest—David, Gonzalo, and Maria Paz—and Irene with her. At the Albuquerque stop, they detrained and went to visit with Maria and buy some of her jewelry. They walked up and down the depot platform but did not find her. Rafaela stopped in front of a woman who sat with jewelry spread out on a colorful blanket and said to her, "Buenas tardes. Excuse me, do you know if Maria is here today?"

"Wait, just a minute," the woman said. She then spoke in her Indigenous language to another woman also sitting and selling jewelry. After a brief exchange, she asked Rafaela, "Do you mean the older woman who sold bracelets and earrings?"

"Yes."

The woman's expression softened. "Lo siento, Señora. Maria passed away last winter."

Rafaela was stunned. She had not for a moment expected the woman's answer. Her eyes filled with tears. The news was heartbreaking. Their friendship was so limited by time and circumstance, yet it was a reliable and uncomplicated connection based on the two women's shared experience of love for their children and family. Rafaela thanked the woman, who again said, "I'm sorry."

Irene saw her mother's sadness and hugged her. As they walked back to the train, Irene tried to comfort Rafaela and said, "Mamá, try to think about the kindness you gave to each other."

"You're right, mija. You're right. May she rest in God's peace," Rafaela said quietly. Irene helped Rafaela and her younger siblings climb aboard. More than ever, Rafaela was anxious to see Juana and Manuel. The whistle sounded, and soon the train began moving toward El Paso.

10

Leaving the Village, World War II Begins, Irene's Marriage

Three months before Irene received her high school diploma, European nations drove the world to the crossroads of war and peace. Nazi Germany took control of the country of Austria and lit the fuse to the powder keg of world war and its companion, genocide. Decades later, author David D. Romo discovered in his research in the National Archives "an article written in a German scientific journal written in 1938, which specifically praised the El Paso method of fumigating Mexican immigrants with Zyklon B." The Nazis initially used the chemical at some of its border crossings and ultimately as the killing agent of millions of Jews in gas chambers. The only uncertainty of the impending horrific human catastrophe of warfare was its date of eruption.

On September 1, 1939, the powder keg of war exploded. Germany, under control of the Nazis, declared war and invaded Poland. After four centuries of warfare in Mesoamerica and North America, the people in the Village knew well that war moves people, both within and outside of their home countries. Wars have altered the way people live their lives as new and different values emerge. At times, the resulting changes were immediate and dramatic, and at other times, they came in slow, but constant increments.

With the outbreak of war in Europe, governments, officials, politicians, and the public debated the United States' appropriate role and response. Wartime industries, including the railroads, began preparations in the event the United States entered the war. In the Village, rumors spread that the Santa Fe and a small metalworks business needed more space to accommodate the possible increase in operations. The most likely expansion was to the east of the roundhouse, which would require moving or razing the Village. Over the years, the Santa Fe never raised the fifty cents monthly rent. The low rent gave Villagers little incentive to move into Dodge. Other than the rent, perhaps the only positives about the Village were the convenient walk to work, and the avoidance of displays of contempt directed at them by Dodge residents and businesses. But with expansion on the horizon, Village families realized they might be forced to leave and find housing in Dodge. There was no outcry from Villagers demanding to stay and raise their children in the Village. They understood they were on Santa Fe property and that the railway company could do as it pleased.

Cayetano was always aware that the family needed more living space. His plans to add on to the house ended with the rumors of expansion. There was no point if the Santa Fe was going to evict everyone and raze the Village. But with this new threat, he needed to consider a move to the north side of the tracks. A handful of Village families had already done so. Cayetano also believed that Salvador needed no further education beyond Coronado School. He was certain that if Salvador worked for the Santa Fe, he had a job for life. And with Salvador providing an extra paycheck, the family would be able to pay a monthly rent or perhaps a mortgage. He told Rafaela of his plans to save money and pay for a move out of the Village. Rafaela, of course, was relieved and hopeful.

Many of Roosevelt's New Deal programs, including the Works Projects Administration and the National Youth Administration (NYA), continued to operate. Both programs had reached Dodge City by the late 1930s. Soon after graduating, Irene began training in the NYA program. She and other Village women sewed hospital garments, doctor and nurse uniforms, bandages, and bedsheets. As the country moved closer to war, the women sewed parachutes, bandages, and military garments. They later assembled medical kits in the Brown Manufacturing plant in Dodge. For the US economy, the increased production ended the setback of 1937. For the Santa Fe, more Mexican men were added to its workforce. And for Irene, it broke her family's centuries-long practice of limiting women to work in the home.

Irene was comfortable in her NYA work setting. Her experience at a nearly all-white high school lessened the anxiousness or awkward moments with white supervisors and fellow employees. She worked with former classmates and established a network of friends. Some young women from the Village, who had few or only negative exchanges with white people, were cautious and less confident in the new workplace. But they greatly appreciated three comforts in the plant that remained unavailable in the Village: indoor plumbing, running water, and electricity.

Irene's life at home did not suddenly become free of chores. When she got home from work, she still helped with the care of her younger siblings and the chores Rafaela needed her to do. Some of Rafaela's generation were opposed to their daughters working in factories with men. Some of the men in the Village, old and young alike, believed that a woman had no business in the public workplace. Men with recent and closer ties to Mexico were more likely to hold these views. But Rafaela and Cayetano were supportive, especially after Irene's success in the high school. They did expect Irene to give a portion of her wages to them to support the family, which she did willingly. After her contributions to the family, she still had the choice to spend or save her remaining pay as she pleased.

By June 1940, Germany had defeated France, leaving Great Britain to stand alone against the German war machine. Great Britain asked the United States to provide them with war supplies and materials, including military naval vessels. Opponents of US involvement in the war argued against the aid to Great Britain. Roosevelt believed that while the United States remained legally neutral, the country was still able to supply the aid. The buildup of war materials and men was under way with railways adding laborers to move them across the country. As the debate continued, events in Asia became more perilous with Japanese efforts to expand their military control over parts of China and Southeast Asia. Roosevelt assessed the war in Europe and hostilities in Asia and signed into law a peacetime involuntary draft, the first in US history, which heightened the ire of those in opposition to US involvement. All men between the ages of eighteen and sixty-five were required to register for the draft.

Once the draft was signed into law, the familiar pathway to marriage for young adults in the Village was blurred by the fog of war. The decisions of who and when to marry necessarily included consideration of the groom's military service. Mothers, wives, and sweethearts began to acknowledge the worst possibilities and fear the loss of the men in their lives. In the years before the invasion of Poland, the concerns and worries of Rafaela and the mothers in the Village were the well-being and futures of their children.

This generation of new adults in the Village was born around 1920 and had survived the Great Depression and Dust Bowl years. For teens still in the Village, especially those without jobs, the only place to go for friends and fun was the north side of the tracks. Some of the teens ventured into the northside confidently and fearlessly, while others were cautious. They developed friendships and mixed with white classmates and with the few Black classmates as well. Though most did not graduate from high school, their attendance at junior high took them north of the tracks. They learned to speak English and easily mixed the interests of their white classmates into their Village upbringing. They enjoyed the movies, radio, big band dance music, fashion styles, sports, hamburgers, hot dogs, and Coca-Cola. Irene and her girlfriends read *Photoplay* and other magazines that followed the lives of Hollywood stars.

The members of Dodge City's first railroad generation were coming of age and were already eyeing each other for potential marriage partners. Candidates were not limited to those in the Village. All along the Santa Fe's main line, Mexican communities had increasing contact with one another and opportunities to meet and find their sweethearts. Some of the young men rode the rails to nearby towns and cities to meet their dates. Any town within thirty miles was in reasonable driving distance for a public dance or private wedding. There were no phones in the Village except at Ceballo's grocery store, so sweethearts relied on written messages and letters to communicate until the next meeting. The young adults met in public settings where brothers, cousins, or other responsible older men chaperoned young women. The ladies stood or sat together as the young men approached to ask for a dance. For a date, or potential suitor, to take a young woman from her home and return her the next day was considered an act of great disrespect and would likely result in an angry rebuke, if not an actual assault. The only resolution was to cautiously approach the family in the company of a priest to ask for the young woman's hand in marriage.

When Irene began junior high school, Rafaela had constantly reminded her of the hardships suffered in marriage at an early age. Her Aunt Francisca always preached modesty and criticized the faults and weaknesses of men. When she started high school, she took note of her mother's and aunt's words and focused on her school work rather than boys and marriage. But there was one student from the Village that caught her attention: the boy across the lane, Josefa's son, Jesse. Until Irene went to school at Coronado, she did not know Jesse or his family, as she lived with Francisca and Marcela. By the fifth grade, Irene and Jesse's younger sister by two years, Amelia, had become playmates. Their friendship grew stronger as they spent more and more time together during Irene's visits with Rafaela. At the time, Jesse was little more than an intruder upon the girls' playtime.

Irene and Jesse were in the group of Village students who attended the Dodge junior high school after Coronado, although Jesse was a year behind Irene's class. Every school day morning, the group left the Village, lunches in hand, and walked through the tunnel. But because many Village students did not attend school after eighth grade, the number of high-school-aged tunnel walkers was very few. Most days only the three or four walked to the high school, Irene and Jesse among them. Their uncommon presence in the student body helped draw them together for security and comfort in their new setting. Irene began to see Jesse in a new light. He was easygoing, with a big smile and sense of humor, and handsome at five-foot-nine with a head full of thick, black, wavy hair. They were both good students and enjoyed each other's company during the high school experience.

Rafaela watched Irene and Jesse through the years and thought that he had always treated Irene respectfully. She saw their closeness when they danced during the porch yard singalongs when the two families occasionally gathered. She believed that they might marry someday, and she was not opposed to the possibility. Rafaela found Jesse's parents to be good neighbors and parents and thought Jesse would have those virtues as well. Once Irene and Jesse reached high school, Irene talked to Rafaela about him frequently. By her senior year, Irene thought that marriage was a possibility and so did Jesse.

After high school, Irene and Jesse did not date one another exclusively. Irene was not the only young woman who found Jesse attractive, and he flirted with other young women. Still, Irene and Jesse kept up their friendship and remained attracted to one another. After high school, Jesse took a different path than most young men in the Village. Instead of working for the Santa Fe, he took a job in Dodge working in the Pepsi-Cola bottling facility.

In late 1940, Amelia invited Irene to walk with her to Ceballo's grocery. As they walked, Amelia said to Irene, "I need to tell you some surprising news about Jesse."

Her tone and expression did not suggest anything troubling. Irene, unable to guess what she might be about to hear, looked at Amelia and waited. Finally, she broke the silence. "What, Amelia? What about him?"

"He's getting married."

In disbelief, Irene said quietly, "Getting married? To who?" She knew Jesse dated, but she could not imagine which one of those girls he might marry.

"He is going to marry Blanca."

Irene was again jolted. Blanca was her friend. Beginning to accept the truth of Amelia's announcement, she asked, "When?"

Amelia knew that Irene and Jesse had teased each other about getting married someday, and she knew that Irene was hurting from the news she'd just delivered. But Amelia had more hurtful news, and she told her friend the truth. "They're getting married as soon as possible. She's pregnant."

Irene stopped in her tracks and said in shock, "Pregnant? Amelia, this cannot be true! Is that the reason he's marrying her?" Her heart was aching and her eyes filled with tears.

As they resumed walking to the store, Amelia tried to comfort Irene by putting her arm around her and saying, "I'm sorry, Irene. I'm sorry."

Days later, when Irene went to see Amelia, she encountered Jesse for the first time since Amelia had revealed his news. Irene was gracious and kept control of her emotions, concealing her broken heart. "So, Amelia says you're getting married. Is that so?"

Jesse managed to muster a quick smile and said, "Yes, that's right. I am sorry, I wanted to tell you myself, but I didn't have a chance."

"I understand Blanca is the lucky girl."

He nodded and said seriously, "Yes, I guess so."

Irene ended the awkward moment. With sincerity, she told him, "Jesse, I wish you and your bride good fortune and health. I hope you find happiness." He only listened. "I want you to know that I will always cherish our friendship, no matter what happens in the future. We will always be friends."

"I feel the same way."

"Okay, then." Then she added, "Oh, I almost forgot—congratulations on being a father."

Jesse did not know that Irene knew, but he gathered himself and said, "Thank you."

When Irene explained to her mother that Jesse's life had taken a dramatic turn, Rafaela saw her hurt and disappointment. She comforted Irene and told her not to despair. She explained that life was filled with unexpected changes, many painful, but with prayer and God's grace, people find the strength to overcome and live worthy lives. She said to Irene, "Con Dios, todo es posible."

In March 1941, Jesse married Blanca, and in the following July he responded to President Roosevelt's call and registered for the military draft.

❧

When newly hired Mexican laborers arrived at the Village and learned that the Santa Fe was threatening to dismantle it, many looked to Dodge City's east side for housing. The eastside houses were north of the tracks, a short distance from the Village. Most of the small, wood-frame houses stood on concrete slabs. They were built to suit the needs of the family that lived there, rather than as replicas of a development model. Many were without access to electricity or indoor plumbing and relied on coal-burning stoves for heating and cooking.

In 1941, Cayetano learned of a property on Avenue J on the east side, which had been purchased by a family in Dodge who then defaulted on their mortgage in 1933. The circumstances of the default were typical: the husband was the primary breadwinner, but at age seventy-two, he was retired from the railroad with no other income and the wife was a homemaker. The couple could not afford the monthly mortgage on the husband's small pension. The loan company foreclosed on the house and took title to the property but allowed the couple to remain as renters until the property sold. But potential buyers were few, as many families still suffered the financial hardships of the Depression. Most families barely endured the lean years and were unable to save for a mortgage down payment. Additionally, non-Mexican buyers who were able to pay a mortgage were reluctant to do so in a neighborhood that was quickly becoming predominately non-white.

In early spring, Cayetano approached the loan company with an offer to buy. Previously, banks and loan companies did not extend credit to potential buyers from the Village. They had no credit history for monthly mortgage or rent payments. Additionally, many of the newly hired men had no history of long continuous service with the Santa Fe. But the loan company had tired of the role of landlord and wanted the property on Avenue J off their hands. They were desperate to get Great Depression foreclosures off their books. Surprisingly, the loan company chose to ignore its past practices and agreed to sell the house on the strength of Cayetano's application. He had twenty years of continuous employment with the Santa Fe, and he had saved for a small initial payment. He had a large family and was unlikely to return to Mexico, and he was willing to agree that title to the property would not transfer until the final payment. In the event Cayetano defaulted on his payments, the loan company would keep title to the property and the payments. When the purchase agreement with Cayetano was finalized, the white elderly couple who lived there vacated the property and began renting a home located three blocks away in the growing Mexican neighborhood on Avenue K.

The move-in date for Rafaela, Cayetano, and their family was set for June 1941. After nearly thirty years, she and her family, and Chon, left the Village. The house was at the intersection of Military Avenue and Avenue J, approximately a quarter-mile north of Santa Fe's main line. The wood-frame, 850-square-foot, three-bedroom structure was built in 1910. In 1930, the house was remodeled to include running water, indoor plumbing, electricity, and linoleum flooring. The property included a small storm cellar, enough land for a midsize garden in the backyard, and a separate small guest house with no running water or plumbing.

For Rafaela, the house and property were luxurious and spacious and a welcome relief from the living conditions in the Village. The family left behind the lantern-lit space of the shanty and moved into the electric light of the house. Rafaela's children shared beds in more spacious rooms, rather than side-by-side on the dirt floors of the shanty. Cooking and heating did not require burning coal or wood. They were replaced by a small gas stove and furnace. A short time later, a swamp cooler was installed to add to their comfort. The cold and freezing trips to the outside privy were no more, and the sanitation conditions were less of a concern. Hot baths in the spacious clawfoot tub were a welcome convenience. Except for the whistles of the trains passing through Dodge on the main line, the noise, smoke, and pollution of locomotives and train cars moving about the railyard were absent. Avenue J and Military Avenue were quiet streets, especially at night.

Just as important as the physical house improvements, the home on Avenue J became Rafaela's portal to escape the restraints placed on her interests and curiosity about people and events outside the Village. Cayetano bought a radio to listen to Mexican broadcasts that reached Dodge City after dark and in the early morning hours. Cayetano's interest was the music. Rafaela, too, enjoyed the music, and after he left for work, she listened to English comedy and variety shows and the news broadcasts. Rafaela spoke little English when she left the Village, but with her children speaking English at home and the radio shows, she quickly understood more and more.

Chon never pushed Rafaela to stay in school. He thought the family was better served if she learned to help with womanly chores. But somewhere in his total disregard of Rafaela's potential, and his view that a woman's place was in the home, he found the time to teach Rafaela a basic level of reading and writing. Irene and Nina enjoyed reading the popular magazines featuring Hollywood's movie stars and the daily paper for the news. Rafaela picked up the magazines and papers they left behind and read them to the best of her ability. When she could not decipher particular words, she asked her children for the meanings. With time, she asked fewer and fewer questions.

Apart from the physical comforts, another great benefit of living in an actual house on Avenue J instead of a Village shanty was access to the public elementary school. Rafaela's youngest sons, Gonzalo and David, were the first to attend. Gonzalo's first school year was at Coronado, while David's first year was at Roosevelt—a three-level red brick building built in 1910. Roosevelt was originally called the First Ward School, and the student body was primarily from poor families, white, Black, and Mexican, both first-generation US citizens and Mexican nationals. The school was within walking distance for Rafaela's sons, as it stood only three blocks from their house on Avenue J. She sent the boys to school in new school clothes and new shoes.

Although Rafaela's family escaped the poor conditions of the Village, they were not free from the racial segregation and the slights by white residents of Dodge. Most of the Mexican families living on Dodge's east side regularly returned to the Village Chapel for religious services. Every Catholic in town understood that the new Sacred Heart Church was for the white congregation, and the Chapel was for Mexican Catholics, as Father Handly had clarified years before. Certainly, Villagers were free to attend Sacred Heart to fulfill their Sunday obligation, but the reverse was highly unlikely. The Chapel and school, which had no drinking fountain or restroom until 1940, had served Village residents to a degree. But it also facilitated the interests of the influential who wanted to keep the Mexicans in their place—close to work and separated from Dodge's white community and churches. But before the end of Gonzalo and David's first semester at Roosevelt, world events began the slow and eventual Village diaspora. The slow demise of the segregated Village and Chapel began to give way to a mix of races and nationalities on Dodge's east side.

❈

On a Sunday in the fall of 1941, Antonio Rodriguez, Irene's cousin who was three years older than her, invited Irene to come along with him on a drive to Garden City. Antonio had married Abran's daughter, Pola, in 1939. He was an exceptional character in the Village. His life's experiences were joyful and tragic, sweet and bitter, and yet, he remained a young man of good humor and shared the joy of life with those around him. He was the son of Pedro Rodriguez and Micaela Gutierrez Sanchez. Pedro was the man who guided Cayetano and Leon when they entered the United States in 1916. Antonio was four years old when his mother died of tuberculosis in November 1921, at the age of twenty-seven. Pedro, a widower at age forty-four, left his young daughter, Juana, with family in the Village and became a migrant farm worker. He took Antonio with him to California and other states in search of work. Their travels reached the state of Montana. When Antonio was about ten years of age, he and his father returned to the Village. When children in the Village asked Antonio where he was from, he answered, "Montana." When asked if he went to school, he again answered, "Yeah, in Montana." The moniker was born and stuck. Soon he was popularly known as "Tony Montana," or simply "Montana."

Though Tony stood tall in the Village for his zest for life, in actual height he stood only five-foot-two, a stature that kept the Santa Fe from hiring him. If a Mexican man did not work for the Santa Fe, the only other employment for him and his family was seasonal farm labor. In the spring and early summer, the sugar beet fields had to be thinned of plants and cleaned of weeds. The tools of this labor included short- and long-handled hoes and the fingers and hands of children. In the fall, the beets were harvested and processed in the sugar beet factory that was built in Garden City in 1906. Winters were stressful with little available work. Some families traveled to California to work in the fruit orchards and vegetable fields. As a young adult, Tony worked as his father did, in the farm fields. After his extended trips to the western states, a fifty-five-mile trip to the sugar beet fields surrounding Garden City was not a bother.

With his sociable manner, Tony soon attached himself to some of Garden City's first-generation Mexican families who labored in the fields, the Garcia and Mesa families among them. They lived in small houses on the same block on Fourth Street next to a railroad spur in Garden City's eastside Mexican barrio. Each family had six sons, and Tony became friends with the older boys of each family. The Garcias invited Tony to stay in their home and work with them in the fields and sugar beet factory.

When Tony invited Irene to come with him to Garden City that fall day in 1941, he and two other friends were going to visit Tony Mesa and the Garcia boys. During the visit at the Mesa home, one of the Garcia boys, Dionisio ("Nicho") joined the group. Tony introduced Irene to him and eventually the other brothers as well. The two closest in age to Irene were Guillermo ("Willie"), four months older, and Nicho, a year younger. Irene thought both Willie and Nicho were respectful, handsome, and good dancers to both Mexican music and big band swing music. At the Christmas Eve dance later that year, while Irene and Willie danced to the music of "Moonlight Serenade," she asked him, "Is Nicho here tonight? I haven't seen him."

Willie answered matter-of-factly, "No, he didn't come; he's at home. He's taking my mother to Midnight Mass tonight."

Irene thought, *Good man.*

During the fall, Japan was still at war with China and needed oil and other resources to maintain its effort. It was trying to expand into and then defend the newly conquered territories and countries. When the United States and other nations refused to supply the war materials, the Japanese military convinced Emperor Hirohito that to secure Japan and increase Japanese influence in Asia, war with the United States and its allies was necessary. In early December, Emperor Hirohito approved the surprise attack on Pearl Harbor. In the early morning of Sunday, December 7, more than twenty-four hundred Americans died in the aerial assault, and a number of military vessels in the US Pacific Fleet were sunk or heavily damaged. The war itself had already touched the Village—one of its sons, Rodolfo Sanchez, a corpsman who had entered the army months earlier, was under the falling bombs at Pearl Harbor.

On December 8, President Roosevelt asked Congress for a declaration of war. Congress granted his request and approved the declaration. His call to arms reached every color, race, nationality, and gender. Two months later, the army directed Jesse Rodriguez to report for duty at Fort Leavenworth, Kansas. He did so on February 10, 1942.

Men in the Village and across the country were registering for military service. Abran's two oldest sons, Antonio and Ladislao, had registered in El Paso in 1940. Cayetano, his brother Leon, and Rafaela's brother, Abran, all registered in 1942. Salvador was among the men in the Village who registered for military service on the last day of June 1942, as was Rodolfo Esquibel, a friend to Salvador and Irene. All knew in their souls that out there, somewhere on unknown battlefields, La Pelona might lie in wait for them.

Not only did the United States gather its citizens for military service, but it also rounded up its citizens of Japanese ancestry, including women and children. They were detained in relocation camps across the West and Midwest. On February 19, President Roosevelt issued Executive Order 9066, which led to the detention of at least one hundred thousand Japanese Americans. Thousands of people lost their homes and property without any court proceedings. The US government gave them little time to gather or sell their belongings, and many family members were separated and not informed of the whereabouts of their loved ones. Construction of one of the detention camps, known as Amache, began in July and opened in August 1942, in Granada, Colorado, eighty miles west of Garden City, Kansas.

The whirlwind of events after Pearl Harbor that changed lives in Dodge and the Village continued into 1942. On Mother's Day, May 10, a large spring storm, carrying a fierce tornado within, approached the city from the southwest. At about 7:00 p.m., it crossed the Arkansas River and struck Dodge's northwest side. Saint Marys of the Plains Academy stood directly in its path. The cyclone destroyed the administration and dormitory and classroom buildings beyond repair. The fierce winds ripped away portions of the roofs, crumbled a number of walls, and left the ornamental chapel in a pile of rubble and dust. Bishop Hennessey's jewel of southwestern Kansas was lost in a matter of minutes. Dodge City proper and the Village were virtually untouched.

In the summer of 1942, Dodge City and the Army Air Force agreed to build a training airfield outside of Dodge. The flat terrain in Kansas was ideal for training pilots and a strategic location for air base defense. The project brought businesses and jobs to Dodge residents, including Villagers. During this time, the Santa Fe confirmed that a significant portion of the Village would be razed to make room for a large oil storage tank. The railway was switching to diesel engines over coal and wanted a ready supply of oil. The company gave the affected Villagers notice of the impending loss of their homes. The notice might have been reasonable as to time, but it lacked a resolution for the families that were displaced after decades of the poor conditions in the Village. They were left to find their own way.

Rafaela continued to meet with her friends in the Village though she no longer lived there. They met at Rafaela's home on Avenue J and in the Village on Sundays when Rafaela returned for Sunday Mass. The warmth and joy of their friendship remained despite Rafaela's move into Dodge. Often the talk was about their sons and the war and about leaving the Village to join Rafaela in Dodge's eastside barrio.

Rafaela's warm and welcoming nature enabled her to quickly become friends with her neighbors on Avenue J. One family was German, another family was Black, and another was Mexican. Despite the women speaking three different languages, they arranged to meet at each other's home for tea and sweets. Rafaela did not bake breads and cookies, so often she brought freshly made tortillas, which the women willingly exchanged. Their teas were a kind distraction from the stress of the war.

❖

Irene and Tony continued to meet with the Garcia boys at events in Garden City and in Dodge. While Irene was meeting new friends, Salvador had found a match. He fell in love with Rosella Sanchez, and they planned their wedding for late December. The wedding announcement surprised some, but given the circumstances of the times, they chose not to wait.

As the year came to an end, the reality of the war began to weigh on the Village. More and more of the young men received orders to report for service. The men in Garden City received their notices as well. On November 20, 1942, Nicho received his order to report to the newly constructed Fort Carson in Pueblo, Colorado. Before reporting for basic training, he asked Irene if she would consider getting married. It was not a formal, ring-in-hand, on-bended-knee proposal. She did not give him a definite no, but she delayed her answer by imposing conditions before marriage: they must wait three years until he completed his military service, and he must have a separate home, as she was unwilling to live in his mother's house. Nicho agreed.

Irene and Nicho exchanged letters when he was in Pueblo. In January 1943, Nicho wrote that his asthma had worsened for lack of medicine and he was in the base infirmary. He had worked in the sugar beet fields since the age of eight and had been in many dust storms. He was caught out in the open for a short time during the Palm Sunday dust storm of 1935 and thereafter developed asthma. His condition worsened when he was in his late teens and, eager to take on a badge of manhood and emulate the leading men of Hollywood, he became a smoker. The army medical officers quarantined Nicho for six weeks in the belief that, somehow, he had induced his poor condition. They eventually determined he was medically unfit for combat and he was honorably discharged in March. While Irene was happy that Nicho would not see combat, she felt some apprehension—his service was complete, and thereby he had met one of her conditions for marriage.

With the Santa Fe's plan to raze the Village, the shrinking number of Village residents, and the school closing, the Catholic Diocese had little choice but to close Our Lady of Guadalupe Chapel. The obvious challenge for the diocese was the course of action necessary to serve the Mexican community in Dodge. One possibility was to invite the Mexicans into Sacred Heart Parish and church and forego any expansion of the current structures. Another possibility to accommodate the new parishioners was to build an addition to Sacred Heart Church. Yet another suggestion was to build, at the expense of the one hundred Mexican families, a modest church in Dodge's eastside barrio. Some in the diocese believed that Dodge's Mexicans felt more comfortable practicing their faith in their own language, culture, and neighborhood parish. Despite the universal Latin mass, language remained an issue for some parishioners. Some intolerant Catholics might have preferred to have few, if any, Mexicans in Sacred Heart Church. The certain result of an eastside parish was that the races would remain largely segregated, as they were at the Village Chapel.

In February 1943, Padre Hernandez, speaking for the Wichita Catholic Diocese, surprised the Village and Dodge with the announcement of a new church building to be built at a "better site" to replace the small chapel in the Village.

Curiously, the *Advance* article did not identify the future location of the new church, nor that the Diocese had purchased the property for the new location. Instead, the article indicated that the site had "already been procured by one of the parish members." The *Advance* also reported that a Village spokesman pledged contributions and sacrifices for the new church building despite their living conditions. The *Advance* did not clarify what the Diocese and Padre Hernandez made clear to the Villagers and Mexicans who had left the Village: they must raise the funds to pay for building their new church.

Within two months, women from the Village organized a committee to raise funds for the new church and selected Irene as the entertainment chairperson. Her position was crucial for the fundraising effort, as relatively few individual cash donations might come from the Villagers. Aunt Francisca, ever working for the Church, was selected as treasurer. Irene kept her job in the war effort, and during her off-hours organized a dance and dinner open to the public. Women from the Village and eastside barrio prepared the food for the event and collected donations of jewelry boxes, intricate embroideries, and similar items for door prizes. Irene arranged for the use of Hoover Pavilion in the public park and brought in a band to provide the music. Several dance and fiesta fundraisers were held in the years that followed.

The fundraising effort became a constant concern for the Mexicans in the Village and Dodge. Most of the women believed their work and sacrifices were entirely justified as acts of faith. Many of the men who contributed labor were driven more by construction of a fixed, long-standing, brick-and-mortar building, rather than a deeply held faith. Even young men from the Village serving in the army sent donations from overseas. The *Advance* noted that one soldier sent a one-hundred-dollar contribution.

The story of the soldier's generosity was awkwardly followed by a report that the diocese bishop and vicar general were taking a two-week vacation in Colorado.

In early 1943, the savagery and destruction of the raging war in Europe were knocking on Village doors. US troops were increasingly engaging German forces and their allies on a large scale, particularly in Northern Africa. At the same time, US, British, and French leaders met in Morocco to plan for the invasion of Europe. Their overall strategy was to defeat Germany first, then turn their efforts to Japan. The army needed soldiers, and its call for young men to train for battle included those in the Village. Salvador, three Esquibel brothers, Rodolfo, Roberto, and Miguel, and others were ordered to report to their respective military installations for basic training. Salvador assured Rafaela and Rosella that the army granted a furlough after basic training and that he would return within a few months.

Rafaela tried to suppress her fear that Salvador would suffer great harm. Candelaria had told Rafaela that her reason for leaving Mexico was to keep her children safe. There was no higher priority, but Rafaela was powerless to keep Salvador out of the war. Going to Mexico was no alternative; neither she nor Salvador were born there, and they had no home there. Some men saw military service as an opportunity to show loyalty to their new country. For Rafaela and others, warfare was a needless risk to their sons. In Dodge, she and Cayetano, despite his faults, were able to keep him safe. Rafaela felt at the time that the only protection she could provide Salvador was to cover him with an umbrella of hope and prayer.

On the morning Salvador left, she made her son his favorite breakfast of eggs, bacon, and beans wrapped in flour tortillas and a cup of hot coffee. At the door of the house, he kissed Rosella and gave Rafaela a hearty embrace and a reminder that he would return soon. He then walked down the pavement to the street, turned toward the main line, and walked to the depot.

Salvador and Rosella had been living in the guest house behind the house on Avenue J, but when Salvador left for basic training, she returned to her family's home to wait for his return. Rafaela added to her small altar in the house, alongside her image of Our Lady of Guadalupe, the image of the Sacred Heart of Jesus. She also included a tall votive glass candle blessed by Padre Hernandez.

Shortly after Salvador left for basic training, Amelia visited Irene at the house on Avenue J. They had seen each other less frequently since Jesse had gotten married and left for the army. Almost immediately Irene asked, "How is Jesse? Have you heard from him?"

"Yes, we have. And that is one of the reasons I wanted to talk to you."

At first Irene thought that perhaps Amelia was going to tell her that Jesse had been hurt, or worse. She kept herself from assuming the worst and asked, "Is he alright?"

"Yes, he is still in the States. You know the baby is almost a year old now. Well, a month ago Blanca's family told us that the baby looked like another man, and not Jesse." Irene straightened up and listened intently as Amelia continued. "Blanca's family confronted her, and she admitted that she had been intimate with the other man while she was dating Jesse."

"Are you sure about all this, Amelia?"

"Of course I'm sure. We told Jesse, and he has already filed for divorce."

Irene wondered why Jesse hadn't written to her and told her what was happening. *Why doesn't he write to me?* She said to Amelia, "My goodness. That's unbelievable. I have not heard from him."

Amelia tried to assure her, "He'll probably write to you soon."

Irene found it difficult to admit that she held some hope that Jesse might decide to consider a romance and marriage with her. Still, she thought it better to wait for him to write. She had little time, as Nicho was working to meet the conditions she had set for their marriage.

When Irene told Rafaela about the events in Jesse's life, Rafaela asked Irene, "Is Jesse going to come back and ask you to marry him?"

"I don't know, Mamá."

"Do you want him to ask you?"

"I don't know that either. I'm not sure."

"And what about Nicho?"

"I told him I would consider it, if he had his own house."

Rafaela had watched Jesse from childhood to adulthood through her friendship with Josefa. They had lightheartedly talked about Jesse and Irene getting married someday. Now, it was a possibility. But Rafaela wanted Irene to marry the man she loved and a man who could provide for her. She wanted Irene to be certain in her choice. She offered her counsel. "Mija, don't give either man a definite answer until you are certain. Have patience."

"I will, Mamá." After a pause she lamented, "This is so difficult."

"Así es la vida, mija. Only with the grace of God do we find our way."

Through the summer months, Irene did not receive any message or letter from Jesse. She could not understand why he did not write. At the same time, she and Nicho spent more time together. There was a growing closeness and affection between them and an excitement when they talked about the possibility of marriage. They went to the weekend dances that had a new tension and air about them with the boys in uniform and possible deployment to the battlefront.

When Nicho told her that his mother had lent him money to buy a small house, Irene knew the time had arrived for her final answer. By July, she still had not heard from Jesse and she assumed he had no interest in contacting her. In early August, she put any thoughts of him aside and answered Nicho with a yes. They began planning their wedding for late September.

Irene told Amelia about her wedding plans, but she did not ask Amelia to pass them on to Jesse.

Irene met with Padre Hernandez to advise him of her plans. "Padre, I have a couple of matters to discuss with you."

"Of course, child, what can I do for you?"

"Padre, I will no longer act as the entertainment committee chairman. I am sorry that I cannot continue."

"I'm surprised and disappointed," Hernandez said. Irene was an integral part of the fundraising. "Is something wrong?"

"No. No, padre. It's just that I am getting married."

Hernandez recovered quickly and gave the proper response. "Well! That is great and happy news! Congratulations!"

"My fiancé is from Garden City and we will live there."

Hernandez nodded in understanding. Irene continued, "Padre would you accompany me, and my fiancé, Nicho, and his mother, Rosa, to meet with my parents to ask for my hand in marriage?"

"Of course, my child, of course."

The meeting was an opportunity for the families to meet for the first time and learn more about the other. At the Rodriguez home, with Padre Hernandez, Irene, Rafaela, and Cayetano present, Nicho asked for Irene's hand. Cayetano said that if Irene wanted to marry Nicho, he gave his consent. When Irene said yes, Nicho promptly gave her the engagement ring. Again, his proposal was not on bended knee opening a black velvet ring box; it was far more straightforward and without glitter. The families and Padre Hernandez agreed on a wedding date of September 22.

At the end of August, Nicho sent a letter to Irene from Garden City telling her that the newly purchased house was small and needed work and that they would make the improvements as time went on. Although Garden City had no segregated Village for the Mexican residents, two barrios had formed on either side of Santa Fe's main line. The housing south of the tracks was two blocks deep, with Santa Fe Street and Maple Streets running east and west parallel to the main line. The housing north of the tracks was one block deep, bounded by Fulton Street. On both sides of the tracks, property lines of the homes abutted railroad spurs. The two barrios combined were a mile long east to west, with a business-lined Main Street dividing the barrios at midpoint. Most of the main street businesses were north of the tracks, as the southside was only two streets deep. Irene's new home stood two blocks east of Main Street and faced an unpaved Santa Fe Street. Beyond the back property line was an alley and a tall, imposing, rectangular, pitched roof, grain elevator that abutted a Santa Fe rail spur.

Tony agreed to drive Irene to Garden City to see the house prior to the wedding. On arrival, she saw an exterior painted in a plain beige color. The house was built in 1925 and set back in the middle of the lot about thirty feet. Its dimensions were nearly square, twenty-five feet by twenty-five feet, and it was wood-framed, as were most houses in the barrio except for a few small adobe houses that had been built by Mexicans who arrived earlier in the century. The interior was essentially divided into four squares, with the living room and a bedroom to the front, and the kitchen and another bedroom to the back. She was disappointed when Nicho told her the house had no running water or indoor plumbing. While the house had electricity and a gas heater, it lacked the comfort of the house on Avenue J. Each room had tile floors and two windows without curtains. She agreed with Nicho's assessment that improvements were sorely needed, and she wanted them in place as soon as possible.

Irene and Nicho were married midmorning in Our Lady of Guadalupe Chapel in the Village, with Padre Hernandez officiating. The wedding party of twelve adults was slightly larger than most Village weddings. Included were Tony and Pola, the best man and maid of honor, a flower girl, and ring bearer. In the morning, the families served hot chocolate and Mexican bread to the guests. After the ceremony, the wedding party went to a professional photo studio in Dodge. Irene wore a white satin gown that did not overpower her petite frame but gave her an effortless elegance. The dress's modest V-neck displayed her unadorned neck. Her wrist-length sleeves were fastened with white cloth-covered buttons at the cuffs. The skirt fell straight to the floor with a small flare, ending in an elegant but small train. Her head was adorned in a lace veil, gathered at the crown of her head behind her dark curls and falling to her hips. She carried a bouquet of white flowers. Nicho wore a black tux with tails and black patent leather shoes.

In midafternoon, the guests were served a meal and provided music by local musicians, including Cayetano. As the wedding came to a close, Rafaela told Irene that Cayetano wanted to impose an old Spanish-Catholic practice, "plazo de tiempo," keeping the bride with her family for an additional three days. Rafaela tried to discourage him, but Cayetano would not yield. The two women asked Padre Hernandez to intervene. He met with Cayetano, Rafaela, and Irene and explained that the plazo was an old way and that the young people of modern times did not follow it. After some reluctance, Cayetano conceded.

Before nightfall, Irene embraced Rafaela, quickly hugged Cayetano, and climbed into the Garcia boys' car with Nicho, his brother Felipe, and Felipe's wife, Luisa. Felipe drove the newlyweds to Garden City, where Irene would begin her married life in their new home.

Part III
Irene

11

Victory, the Baby Boom Arrives, Death by TB

The differences between Rafaela and Irene when they began their married lives were striking. Rafaela was thirteen years old, Irene was twenty-three; Irene had a spacious home with a front and backyard, electricity, gas, and tile floors, and more improvements soon to be installed. Irene's experience sewing parachutes and medical bandages in the Dodge factory before the United States entered the war was a positive one. She felt her efforts supported the boys in the army, and her paycheck supported her family. When she saw that her new home needed improvements, she wasted no time and applied for work at the Garden City air base to help pay for the repairs. She thought her high school diploma and her work history in Dodge might give her a slight edge in the decision to fill any open position.

Nicho's formal education did not extend beyond the eighth grade. His early school years were extremely difficult: he spoke very little English and there was no Spanish instruction. Additionally, his parents took him out of school for weeks at a time to work in the sugar beet fields. As a result, he was held back two school years. Nonetheless, he had become fluent in English by the time he reached adulthood. The primary lesson learned from his schooling was that without an education, the greater part of life was hard work. Nicho's father, Jose, had died in 1938 at the age of fifty-eight from sepsis after an appendicitis infection. Jose had worked for the Santa Fe in Garden City before an injury in 1928 sent him and the family of six boys into the sugar beet fields. Jose ruled the household with an iron fist, and after his death, when Nicho was fifteen, Rosa took the same hardened approach to maintain order.

When Nicho and Irene began their married life, Nicho did not have regular work. As a teenager, he took any work he found: seasonal work in the beet fields, yard work, shining shoes, painting, and many others. But with more and more men leaving for military service, he left the fields for work in Garden City. The jobs were often labor intensive and temporary, including construction of Garden City's Army Air Force base, which began in July 1942. Five months later, when the base was operational, he worked in the Army Air Force as a chauffeur in the motor pool parts and service department.

After her first week in Garden City, Irene returned to Dodge to see Rafaela. When they had a moment to themselves, Rafaela handed her an envelope and said, "I received this letter for you a few days ago." Rafaela allowed Irene a moment to look. It was addressed to Irene and had an Army base return address. When Irene realized the sender read "Sgt. Jesse Rodriguez," her chest tightened and she felt uneasy. She had been waiting for his letter for many months, only to receive it days after she married. She began to feel unbalanced and braced herself in case she fainted. Rafaela noticed Irene's reaction and asked, "Are you feeling well?"

Irene steadied herself and said, "It's from Jesse."

"I thought so. Are you going to open it?"

"I'm not sure. I will take it with me and decide later."

Irene was deeply curious to know the letter's contents. She assumed that Amelia had told Jesse about her impending marriage and given him her mailing address. But she resisted her curiosity until she returned to Garden City and could find a time and circumstance to be alone with her emotions and thoughts.

On Irene's return to Garden City, a letter from the Army Air Force had arrived with an offer for a position as a mechanic's helper. She was directed to report to the air base for further information and a training schedule.

She waited a week before she opened Jesse's letter. Jesse wrote that he would be coming home soon and to wait for him. She read it a second time without anger or sadness. This was the letter she had waited for, and for a brief moment she tried to imagine how they might have married. But she quickly accepted that events had closed the door to that possibility. Like Candelaria and Rafaela, she believed that there are no divorces for marriages consecrated in the Catholic Church. She loved Nicho, and in her heart and soul she wanted a successful marriage. She was newly hired by the army, and she was not so easily going to discard the commitments she had just made.

Irene wanted to keep her friendship with Jesse, but it was impossible to know the path his life might take. Only time would tell if her hope might come to pass. To end any more thought of Jesse's letter, she set it and the envelope afire in the flame of a candle, dropped the burning paper into a pail, doused them with water after they had blackened, and tossed the ashes into the refuse container in the alley.

In October, Irene began working at the air base on aircraft wing assembly. Her petite frame and light weight enabled her to maneuver on the wings with minimal effort. At times, she lay prone on the wings to reach the rivets and screws used in the assembly. She was adept at the work, and six months later she completed an instructor training course to supervise other women's work.

October 1943 was a special month for families in the Village. Many of the boys who were sent to basic training, including Salvador and the Esquibel brothers, were coming home on furlough. Rafaela was thrilled at her son's return, but his news that he would likely be shipped overseas tempered her joy. He could not reveal the destination or country, but everyone knew from letters home, the movie news reels, and newspaper headlines that the United States and its Allies had driven Germany from Northern Africa and Sicily and landed in Italy. It was clear the fighting was moving into Europe.

Irene and Nicho went to Dodge to see Salvador and Rafaela and to attend the weekend dance held for the boys in uniform. As Salvador's leave ended, he and Rosella went to his family's home for a shared meal. When it was time to leave, Rafaela asked him to take a knee before her small altar to receive her blessing. She held her hand over his head and said, "May God protect you, y te bendiga, en el nombre del Padre, del Hijo, y Espiritu Santo, Amen."

"Amen," Salvador echoed. He stood to leave, hugged her firmly and kissed her on the cheek. "Mamá, te amo. Don't worry so much. I'll write to you when I have the chance and let you know how I am doing."

Rafaela stayed at the house while Rosella and the others went with him to the train depot. Rafaela's fear and apprehension overwhelmed her. The last time he left, she had some confidence he would return soon. This time she felt no certainty at all. She cried softly for a long time. Her children tried to console her, and she held them close. Even Chon was moved by the apprehension he saw in his daughter's eyes. Now seventy-five years old, Chon usually kept himself out of family matters. But having seen a revolution and a world war, he understood that his grandson was in peril. He took Rafaela's hand in his and, in a display of confidence, firmly stated his belief that her son would return unharmed. She brought her tears to a stop with Chon's words and a prayer, "Dios, he is in your hands. Please bring him back to me."

❖

In his message to Germany on the last day of 1943, Hitler told his people that the Allies intended to land somewhere in western Europe in the coming year. Armies and civilians across the planet knew the invasion was inevitable. The unknowns were where and when. In the Village, family routines remained largely intact. Work on the Santa Fe railway continued. Locomotives, railcars, and troop transports were constantly moving in and out of the railyard and roundhouse. But there were two additions to the routine: first, the rationing of some foods, fuel sources, and war materials and, second, the constant spoken and unspoken prayer for the safe return of the men at war.

In Garden City, Irene and Nicho, paycheck by paycheck, made small improvements to the house on Santa Fe Street. Irene began to see more of the character of the man she married. As they were putting up new curtains on the windows, Irene offered a suggestion to overcome a stubborn curtain mount. She thought her idea might be helpful, but Nicho snapped, "I'll do it! Don't you think I know how to do this?" His reaction to her reasonable suggestion surprised her. She did not respond further as he fixed the mount. But she took note that he did not respond well to a comment that seemed to question his competence.

Days later, Irene encountered another unpleasant event when she went to the linen store to buy bedsheets. After making her selections, she stood in the cashier's line behind two other women. When she reached the counter, the white clerk told Irene that she must go to the end of the line that had formed behind her. The clerk added that when she finished tending to the other customers, she would then serve Irene. It was a reminder for Irene that hostility toward Mexicans existed in Garden City as well. She had dealt with these confrontations in Dodge City in the past and would continue to do so in Garden City, even as her brother risked his life for his country.

In early 1944, Salvador sent word that he and his unit were overseas and safe. He asked for their continued prayers and said that he would write more later. When Rafaela shared Salvador's letter with Irene, she asked her daughter, "Has Jesse sent any more letters?"

Irene was quick to answer. "No. No, of course not."

Rafaela pressed on. "Did you read the letter I gave you?"

"Sí, Mamá. But I threw it away. He wanted me to wait for him so we could get married. It was too late. Have you heard anything about him? Has he come home on leave?"

"No, mija, I haven't heard a word from Amelia or Josefa. We have to pray for all of the boys."

Irene nodded. "Yes, we do."

At first light on D-Day, Tuesday, June 6, 1944, the Allies began their assault on the beaches at Normandy, France. On the first day approximately twenty-four thousand allied troops rushed the heavily defended beaches. The strategy was brutally simple: the Germans would be overwhelmed and would not be able to kill enough of the onrushing soldiers to prevent the establishment of a landing base. Estimated Allied casualties on the first day were approximately ten thousand, with forty-four hundred killed. The Normandy Invasion became the largest amphibious invasion in military history. By its end, more than 156,000 men and supporting materials were brought ashore. News of the invasion immediately dominated radio and newspapers and brought more anxiety to Village mothers and wives, including Rafaela and Rosella. It was reasonable to assume that the invading forces included the boys from the Village. There was nothing the women could do except wait for any news and pray.

Three weeks after D-Day, Irene visited Rafaela. They greeted each other with a hug on the front porch of the house. Irene asked, "Mamá, has Rosella received any news from Salvador?"

"Mija, he hasn't written to her or to me. I don't know anything," she said with resignation.

"There is so much happening right now. I am sure he will write when he can."

When they sat at the kitchen table, Irene said, "I have a surprise for you." She paused to see Rafaela's expression. "I think I am going to have a baby. You're going to be a grandmother." After the initial shock, Rafaela stood up to hug her. "What good news! Gracias a Dios! When will the baby arrive?" she asked excitedly.

"I'm not sure. Maybe in November."

"What wonderful news. And Nicho? What does he say?"

"He's very happy with the news. He wants a boy, of course."

Rafaela counseled her, "Lo más importante is that the baby is healthy." Irene's joyful news drew away some of Rafaela's worry for Salvador during their weekend visit. But her apprehension was well-founded.

After the Allies took the beaches in Normandy, US forces, led by General George Patton, drove west to east across France. In the initial push, US troops encountered fierce German resistance. On July 4, Rodolfo Esquibel, Irene and Salvador's friend from the Village, was wounded in the fighting when shrapnel from a German artillery shell hit his arm. The injury hospitalized him for a month. On July 16, Rodolfo's brother, Roberto, also on the battlefield in France, wrote a letter home saying he was well. But tragically, Roberto was killed in the fighting five days later. The Esquibel family received an army letter regarding Rodolfo's wounds, and just four days later, Roberto's wife, Carmen, received the notice of Roberto's death. Carmen and the Esquibel family were in shock and agony. The community respectfully gave their sympathies to the Esquibel family. At the same time, the Village felt the fear and harsh reality of war and clearly understood that their young men were vulnerable.

The tightness in Rafaela's chest and pain in her stomach increased after learning of the loss of Roberto and of Rodolfo's wounds. She continued to pray with full intensity for Salvador and the Esquibel family, but it did not lessen her fear and anxiety. Irene felt the same anguish when she heard the dreadful news of the Esquibel brothers. When she lived with her Aunt

Francisca and grandmother Marcela, the Esquibel family home was two houses away. Her fear for Salvador rose, as well as for Jesse, her Gomez cousins, Nicolas, Jose, and Prudencio, and the boys from Dodge High School. They all were serving in the army and likely in Europe as well.

After his time in the hospital, Rodolfo Esquibel was sent to rejoin his unit in Patton's charge across France to Germany. A few months later, incredibly, by chance, he and his older brother, Miguel, encountered each other in Belgium at an army facility. It was Miguel who gave Rodolfo the heartbreaking news of Roberto's death. But Miguel also told him joyful news. Rodolfo's wife, Frances, had given birth to a baby boy three months earlier, in October 1944.

In Garden City, Irene worked through most of her pregnancy, and despite showing the baby's growing development, she continued to climb on the wings of airplanes and complete the work. She enjoyed the work and the role of a supervisor. She also believed she had a patriotic duty to support the war effort and her brother Salvador.

Irene and Nicho bought a bassinette and newborn supplies and prepared for the delivery at the house on Santa Fe Street. Nicho's mother, Rosa, and his sister-in-law, Rosalinda, who had already given birth, would attend to Irene until the doctor was called. Irene wanted Rafaela to be with her when the baby was born, but Rafaela's household of six children kept her from going to Garden City. On the morning of November 23, Irene endured a long and painful labor. The doctor arrived in time for the delivery and Irene gave birth to a baby girl. Irene named her daughter Marcela, after her beloved grandmother.

As a teenager, Irene helped care for her youngest brothers when they were toddlers, but she was less familiar with care for a newborn. When she was unsure, she preferred guidance from Rafaela, but her mother was unable to travel to Garden City. Consequently, she turned to her mother-in-law for advice. Rosa's manner was at times stern and left little doubt that she was in charge of the situation, but she was nurturing as well. Irene was eager for the day when she could travel to Dodge and present Marcela to Rafaela. But she thought it best that they wait until Marcela was at least a month old before she traveled.

In December 1944, the Allied forces in France and Belgium were at Germany's western border, while the Soviet Army in Poland approached Germany's eastern border. Some in the Allied armies believed that

Germany was finished and that Hitler would fall in a matter of weeks. The commanders were so confident that they rested soldiers who fought in recent battles and assigned newly arrived inexperienced soldiers to Belgium's southern border. Their numbers were few and they were lightly armed. Behind the lines in Paris, troops anticipated a quiet holiday given the extreme cold and foul weather.

While the Allies planned for rest and entertainment, Hitler devised a desperate last attempt for a major victory to force peace negotiations with the Allies. The plan provided for an assault to break through the lightly defended line of US troops in the Ardennes Forest in southern Belgium. The German force was massive, with more than two hundred thousand troops and more than one thousand tanks. Once the US lines were broken, the Germans would then drive northward to the vital Belgian port city of Antwerp. The maneuver would split and weaken the Allied Forces.

Hitler's assault began at 5:30 a.m. on December 16 and took the unprepared US forces by surprise. After the initial setback, US Army units regrouped and with reinforcements stopped the German advance and began pushing Hitler's forces back to Germany. Rodolfo Esquibel's unit was engaged in this epic battle that history named the Battle of the Bulge. On December 31, Rodolfo stepped on a German mine and was killed. The heartache and sorrow the Esquibel family suffered when they received the news cannot be put into words.

The Battle of the Bulge ended in mid-January. United States forces suffered nearly ninety thousand casualties, with nineteen thousand killed. It was the largest single battle by US forces in the war. Hitler's gamble failed. His last viable fighting force was destroyed and could not be replaced. The end of the war was firmly in sight. Back in the states, newsreels and newspapers described the Battle of the Bulge and the rescue of the City of Bastogne in Belgium. Again, families in the Village had to suppress their fears that one of their own might be in the battle. The anguish suffered by the Esquibel family continued as they received no news from Miguel. Although their prayers for Roberto and Rodolfo were not answered, they continued to pray for Miguel's safe return. In late January 1945, the letter from the army arrived. Mercifully, it stated that Miguel had been wounded but was receiving proper medical care. In a later letter from Miguel, he told the family that he was recovering.

The suffering of the Esquibel women and the lack of information about

Salvador's well-being tormented Rafaela. In the days and weeks to come, she might receive the notice with unbearable news. The moments in a day when Rafaela did not feel the stress for Salvador's safety were rare. Irene provided some relief when she and baby Marcela finally made their first visit to Dodge in late January. Rafaela and Irene's younger sisters, fifteen-year-old Nina and eleven-year-old Maria Paz, spent the day doting on the new baby. Irene noticed that Rafaela was especially attentive and affectionate. Nina and Maria Paz enthusiastically helped Irene with Marcela's care, the house chores, and the family meals.

Rafaela and Irene were finally alone when the rest of the family left them with the kitchen cleanup. When they finished, they sat together over a cup of coffee. Irene casually commented aloud, "I hope Salvador is well. Still no word from him?"

"Nada, mija. Nada. He is in God's hands."

"Y Rosella, how is she?"

"She is like me, she worries constantly. She is like many young women in the Village; they rushed to get married before the start of the war, only to have the husbands leave and face great harm." After a short pause, Rafaela added, "And now the babies are coming. You know how things are on the east side and the Village—someone announces they are expecting and soon other women are pregnant."

They chuckled at her observation, and then Irene asked, "Mamá, who do you know who is pregnant?"

Rafaela, holding her mug at her lips with both hands, said calmly, "Me."

Irene quickly put down her mug and said loudly, "What?"

Rafaela finally smiled, seeing that she had caught her daughter completely by surprise.

With an expression of happy excitement, Irene asked, "Truthfully, Mamá? Really? Are you sure?"

"Si Díos me da licencia. My time of the month is late and I have moments when I don't feel well."

"Díos mío," said Irene. "Does Papá know?" Rafaela's smile slipped away. "No, I won't tell him until I'm certain."

"Don't worry, Mamá. I'm not telling anyone! When is the baby due?"

"In the summer, July or August."

"I can't wait!" Irene happily replied.

Rafaela still believed that a child was a blessing from God, but she also felt reservations about the new blessing at age thirty-nine. She had given birth to her last child, David, eight years earlier. In the interim she continued to fulfill her marital duty without affection. She suffered a miscarriage after David was born that led her to believe she was unable to conceive or carry another child to full term. She thought her labors of newborn care had ended. And she did not believe a new arrival would in any way improve her marriage.

Irene was able to travel to Dodge on the doodlebug train, a small, diesel-powered train that carried passengers and small freight for short distances. For rural residents in Kansas with family in nearby towns and villages and farmers selling their commodities to local markets, the doodlebug was ideal and inexpensive. Irene and Nicho needed to walk only one block to the Garden City depot, board the doodlebug for the one-hour ride, and return at the end of the day. Irene's trips to Dodge on the doodlebug train were frequent, and she always took time to go to the Village to visit Francisca. Rafaela preferred to have Irene spend all her time together, but Rafaela did not interfere with Irene's decision to spend some time with her aunt. Francisca still lived with her younger brother, Leon, who, not surprisingly, still worked for the Santa Fe. She had found work in the laundry department of Saint Anthony's Hospital and continued to teach Sunday School for the Village children. Ever the teacher, Francisca was always quick to volunteer advice on the care of infants without request from Irene.

To Rafaela's great relief, Rosella got a letter from Salvador in February. Salvador was a quiet young man and expressed little emotion in his letters and was reluctant to share his private thoughts. He recounted even less about his military experiences and circumstances other than to say that he was well and in Europe. Rosella and Rafaela believed his letter signaled that he survived the Battle of the Bulge, if he was there at all. For both women, Salvador's latest letter calmed their fears but only to a degree. Salvador was still at war and at great risk.

In early spring, Allied forces in the west and the Soviets in the east resumed their march to Berlin, town by town, city by city. Benito Mussolini, Hitler's Italian ally, was captured trying to flee to Spain and was executed on April 28. His body and that of his mistress were hung upside down in the town square in Milan. Two days later, Hitler committed suicide in his bunker in Berlin. News of their deaths resounded across the planet and brought the war in Europe to its official end on May 8, 1945. In the Village and Dodge's east side, news of the German defeat spread quickly. Neighbors, young and old, stepped out of their homes to share the news with each other. Rafaela's celebration was restrained—she had received no word about Salvador since his February letter. Her fear of receiving a dreaded official Army notice remained, but now that the war was over, her hope began to rise. Still, she would not lower her guard completely.

In Europe, the US Army began returning troops to the States according to regulations developed the year before. Priority for the trip home was established with a point system that rewarded those with the longest active service, those who had been wounded in battle, and those who were parents. Lower-priority troops stayed in Germany to maintain the peace while new governments were established and millions of displaced Europeans moved across the continent to find family and new homes. The regulations also provided for the transfer of troops with low priority to the South Pacific to fight the Japanese Empire. Salvador was in the latter category and faced transfer to the other side of the planet.

In July, Irene and seven-month-old Marcela rode the doodlebug to visit Rafaela. Soldiers were returning from Europe, and the train depots in Garden and Dodge Cities had heavy traffic of men in uniform. At Rafaela's, Irene immediately asked if there was any more news from Salvador. "Not a word," Rafaela said. "The army has not sent any letters either, Gracias a Dios. I think some day, when I'm not looking, he'll just walk in the door."

"That sounds like Salvador," Irene said in support. After they had been talking for a bit, Irene asked, "Mamá, do you remember you told me that when a woman gets pregnant, soon the women around her are pregnant as well?" Rafaela, nodded and smiled.

When Irene did not say more, Rafaela asked, "Who is pregnant?" Then she answered her own question. "Don't tell me, you are."

Irene happily confirmed her guess. "Yes! I'm due in January!"

Rafaela hugged Irene and told her, "The Lord has blessed you again. What good news!" When the surprise subsided, she said in a tone of embarrassment, "I can't believe it. My daughter and I are pregnant at the same time."

Irene downplayed the circumstances. "Mamá, I think it's great! And an incredible blessing! You'll see. When I tell Nina and Maria Paz, they will be happy for both of us!"

"You're right. What people might say is not important." Rafaela then repeated a maxim that guided the course of her life. She said, "The most important is that these babies be healthy."

※

On the morning of Monday, August 6, 1945, the US military dropped the atomic bomb on Hiroshima, Japan. Estimates were that eighty thousand men, women, and children, both military and civilians, were killed instantly. Thousands later died from their injuries and exposure to radiation. So powerful and intense was the atomic blast that when light from the center of the blast hit a concrete surface, it bleached away paint and dirt, leaving the surface a lighter color. But if a person or object blocked the light and protected the concrete, their silhouette was imposed on the protected area for decades.

When Japan did not immediately surrender, a second atomic bomb was dropped on Nagasaki three days later, instantly killing forty thousand people. Emperor Hirohito's cabinet and military were divided between surrender and fighting on without regard to more atomic bombings. Finally, on August 15, the emperor declared Japan's surrender. The world war that would change the course of human history in so many ways finally ended. The Japanese surrender altered the US military's plans to transport ground troops to the South Pacific theater. The likelihood that Salvador and other soldiers serving in Europe would be sent to Asia was virtually nonexistent. Now that the war was entirely over, Rafaela believed Salvador might soon walk through her doorway.

Just six days after the war ended, Rafaela gave birth to one of the first baby boomers, a daughter, Jane Frances Rita Rodriguez ("Rita") at Saint Anthony's Hospital without complications. Irene, herself three months pregnant, went to Dodge as quickly as possible to help her mother with her newborn sister's care. For Rafaela, after six years in the somber shadows of the threat of war, and the war itself, Rita's birth brought light and hope.

Signs of the war's end began to appear in the weeks after the atomic bombs fell on Japan. Salvador sent a letter telling Rosella that with Japan's surrender he would likely remain in Europe for some time. Soldiers were coming home to Dodge, including Miguel Esquibel, the only one of the three brothers to return from the war. He returned in September and was discharged in October. On October 15, the US government closed the Japanese relocation center near Granada, Colorado, and released any remaining camp detainees. The camp's closure seemed to be of no consequence to Irene, but its impact would be felt in the months ahead.

At the end of the remarkable year, Rosella and Rafaela kept the vigil for Salvador's return without word from him or the army. There was some relief for Irene when Rafaela told her the Village gossip that Jesse was back in the States. Irene reacted to her mother's news with restrained relief, quietly saying, "Gracias a Dios." She avoided any exuberance in Salvador's absence.

Irene started the new year with a new baby, Virginia, born at the end of January 1946, in Garden City. Irene delivered her with the same support group and doctor as with Marcela fourteen months earlier. The only change was that the delivery occurred at her mother-in-law's house.

When the war ended, so did Nicho's work at the air base. But the war sparked an increase in local business ventures and increased the demand for employees. Nicho's work included a shift in the sugar beet factory during the fall processing season, auto repair and maintenance in a local garage, and serving as a shipping clerk with the retailer Montgomery Ward. His work at the factory and in Garden City ended his work in the sugar beet fields. He worked two jobs to offset the reduction in family income when Irene stopped working to care for the babies. The loss in pay slowed their savings for the needed house improvements.

In February, one of Nicho's friends showed him a newspaper ad for the salvage and auction of materials from Amache, the Japanese detention camp in Granada. Buyers at the auction were responsible for dismantling structures and fixtures and removal of the items from the camp. Irene did not agree with the detention of Japanese citizens and was uncomfortable thinking that she and her family might benefit from the wrongful treatment of the detainees in Granada. She also thought the trashing of building materials in good condition was wasteful. She concluded that the better course was to salvage the materials and install the improvements for the house at a lower cost. In the end, she urged Nicho to make the trip to Granada.

Nicho and another man borrowed a truck, loaded their toolboxes with all manner of pipe wrenches, saws, hammers, screwdrivers, wire cutters, and crowbars, and drove the eighty miles to Granada. Using their savings and funds from his mother, Nicho returned with materials they had sorely needed. His cache included two porcelain kitchen sinks, faucets, a bathtub and shower head, a toilet, a bathroom sink and faucets, and blue tinted linoleum sheets for the kitchen and bathroom walls. The men also gathered all the piping and plumbing that would be needed to install the fixtures.

In the following weeks Nicho carved out of the back corner of the kitchen enough space to make room for the indoor bathroom. He and his brothers installed all the fixtures, piece by piece, and dug a sewer trench with pick and shovel from the house to the city sewer line. Alfonso Mesa, an excellent carpenter who grew up on the same block with Nicho, built new shelving and cabinets for the kitchen and the porcelain sinks. The newly installed items, though remnants of the detention camp, brought welcome comfort to Irene and the babies.

At Amache, the unsold camp materials and fixtures were bulldozed where they stood and were buried in the high plains. A year earlier in late 1944, the US Supreme Court ruled in the case of *Korematsu v. United States* that the camps were lawfully established under the president's military powers. But the decision did not address whether due process or the equal protection rights under the Fourteenth Amendment were violated with the use of military powers. The United States did not build detention camps for German nationals or German Americans, nor for Italian nationals or Italian Americans. Seven decades later, the Supreme Court would overrule the *Korematsu* decision, declaring that it was "gravely wrong."

About the time Nicho went to salvage the Ameche detention camp, Rafaela sent ten-year-old Gonzalo on an errand for a package of sugar at Noll's Grocery, a small neighborhood store three blocks from the house. Gonzalo noticed that the clerk seemed unusually cheerful and friendly. From behind the refrigerated meat and poultry glass display, the clerk asked the Gonzalo, "Hey, guess what?" It didn't seem to matter that his ten-year-old listener would have no idea about the topic of his question. Gonzalo, of course, did not answer, but the clerk did not seem to care. "My son is coming home from the war! I'm so happy! I had to share the news with someone!"

Gonzalo did not know what to say to the clerk, who, before that day, had said very little to him. He said politely, "That's very nice."

"Yep. He's coming home on a ship! And guess what?"

Again, Gonzalo could not guess. "What?"

"There is another guy on the ship with him from Dodge City. He said his name was Salvador Rodriguez. Do you know anybody by that name?"

Gonzalo was taken aback. And so was the clerk when Gonzalo said, "Yes, I do. He's my brother."

"Well, I'll be! They'll be home soon! Isn't that great?"

Gonzalo grabbed the sugar, ran out of the store, and hurried home excitedly. When he arrived, he rushed into the kitchen, laid the sugar package on the table, and breathlessly said, "Mamá, I have good news!"

Rafaela did not immediately join in his excitement. She asked, "Did you bring the sugar?" When Gonzalo nodded, she asked, "What good news do you have, mijo?"

"The man at the store told me that his son was coming home from the war on a ship. He said that his son told him another guy from Dodge was with his son. And he said his name was Salvador Rodriguez!"

Rafaela could not believe it. "Are you sure, mijo?"

"Sí, Mamá. He's on his way home."

When Rafaela finally let herself believe, her tears flowed. Gonzalo tried to comfort her with a hand on her shoulder. She walked over to her candlelit, image-covered altar and knelt in front it. She said repeatedly, "Gracias a Dios. Gracias a Dios. Gracias a Dios." Soon Nina and Maria Paz were at her side comforting her as well. The tears continued to fall. Her emotions were not only the relief and elation of Salvador's return but also empathy for the other mothers and families who suffered through the war, including her sister Juana's sons, Nicolas and Jose, and especially the Esquibel family. Rafaela knew that very easily her firstborn son could have been lost. Salvador had walked through the valley of the shadow of death and survived. Three weeks later, he walked through Rafaela's doorway.

In later years, Salvador's siblings and friends asked him to describe his wartime service. But he remained under the stress of the war, and always said, "It was just another war." In actuality, he served with the 727th Railway Battalion. Their mission was to operate and maintain the trains that supplied the Army battlefronts with war materials and troops. General Patton would not have raced across Europe or come to the rescue of encircled troops at the Battle of the Bulge, without an uninterrupted supply of war materials and men. Salvador and his battalion arrived at the Ardennes a month before the start of the battle. Not only did his battalion work tirelessly to keep the trains moving to the front with materials, but they also quickly repaired the railroad lines that the Germans ripped apart as they retreated to Germany. The 727th's mission did not end in the Ardennes; they went into Germany and continued to supply the materials as the army fought its way toward Berlin. The trains also carried survivors of the death camps back to their homelands.

When the Village men who served in the war returned, they viewed their lives and homes in a different light. They had literally traveled the world and seen people in the misery of war, but they also saw people of many nations—rich and poor, city dwellers and farmers—living in better conditions than those in the Village. When the veterans reached the Village, it remained a place of poverty and unsanitary conditions and without the modern conveniences of the twentieth century. The new veterans were determined to leave the Village—the United States owed them and their families the opportunity to thrive. Some families had already left, and it was no secret that the Santa Fe and other businesses continued to eye the Village space for other uses.

❈

In early June 1945, shortly after Germany's surrender, Cayetano's fifty-one-year-old brother, Leon, and a divorcée of seven months were leaving a basement tavern located on Front Street in Dodge. The divorcée's ex-husband, Luis, accosted the couple on the stairway. He attempted to slash Leon's neck with his pocket knife, but struck instead the back of his neck as Leon turned to avoid the slash. Luis' ex-wife then pushed Luis, and Leon took out his knife to defend himself. The blades of both knives were no more than two and a half inches long. Bystanders tried to subdue Luis and pin him down while Leon continued stabbing at Luis. Luis's wounds were fatal and Leon was detained by police for homicide. Leon argued self-defense and authorities later released him. Nonetheless, Luis's relatives regarded Leon's release as unjust and swore vengeance. Soon thereafter, Leon left for California. A year later, he married the woman who ran the boarding house where he lived.

Leon's episode shocked Rafaela and Irene. In the years when Irene lived with Marcela and Francisca, Leon was the breadwinner and filled the role of man of the house when needed. He was Francisca's sole supporter before she worked at the hospital. Francisca was furious that Leon might be involved with a divorced woman and about the tragedy that followed, and she resented that he would go to California and leave her alone. Also, despite teaching Sunday School classes, Francisca had a streak of intolerance and was outraged that her younger brother would marry a woman of Creole descent. In Leon's absence, Cayetano moved Francisca out of the Village and into a small rental near his house on Avenue J. She lived alone and walked to work at Saint Anthony's Hospital, except when coworkers kindly drove her in bad weather.

In the summer of 1946, Irene's cousin, Tony ("Montana"), and Pola still lived in the Village. Pola was fighting tuberculosis, but in October, at twenty-five years old, the disease finally overwhelmed her, just as it did when Tony's mother, Micaela, died at nearly the same age. Tony and Pola had three children at the time of her death: Micaela, named after Tony's mother, Robert, and Manuel, ages four, eighteen months, and six months, respectively. Tony was a joyful man, but he had never expected that his children at a tender age might suffer the same loss that he did as a child. He continued to work in the sugar beet fields and as a day laborer to help support the children.

Pola's parents, Abran and Alvina, suffered that worst of human anguish with the death of their child. They and other family members took Pola's and Tony's children into their homes and gave them loving care. Salvador and Rosella eventually adopted Manuel. Irene was devastated by Pola's death. Irene was a cousin to both. They grew up together, and as young married couples, Tony and Pola and Irene and Nicho shared family celebrations, dancing, and social events. Both couples dreamed of better lives for themselves and their children. Rafaela couldn't believe the loss of her niece. She experienced moments of survivor's guilt. Her son, Salvador, had gone to war at great risk of death. Yet, he survived and returned to Dodge, while Pola, living in the Village, contracted tuberculosis and passed away, leaving behind her children and husband. Sadly, the disease wasn't finished with their family. Abran and Alvina continued to suffer in the months following Pola's passing when Alvina also contracted tuberculosis. Three months later, she passed away in January at age sixty-four.

After the war's end, Chon stopped working at the nursery, but he still planted a garden at the house on Avenue J. He developed cataracts and lost vision in his right eye; otherwise, at age eighty he remained fairly healthy and independent, and he continued his winter trips to El Paso. He was yet to embrace his new position as a great-grandfather to Irene's children and still lacked patience and affection for children not his own.

Irene and Nicho and their daughters, still without a car, rode the train to Dodge as often as possible. During her visits, Irene frequently visited Francisca, who still lived alone. Rafaela still considered Irene's visits with Francisca to be time taken from her, but it was in her character to hold her emotions within and not inflame the fierce resentment between the two of them. Twenty-seven years after Irene's birth, at any opportunity to catch Rafaela alone, Francisca criticized her parenting. Rafaela simply responded that her daughter was doing fine. More than once Francisca adamantly pounded her fist on the table and declared, "She is my daughter!" Rafaela answered calmly, in a matter-of-fact tone, "No, she isn't. I gave birth to her." Rafaela knew any further comment was useless, and that sooner or later, Francisca would confront her again. Irene was aware there was a rivalry between the two women, but she did not realize the ferocity of the friction.

In 1947, Irene was again expecting with a due date in October. The baby arrived early, and Irene gave birth to a third daughter, Christina, at St. Catherine's Hospital in late September. With the new baby, Irene's three daughters were under the age of five. She spent much of each day washing clothes and diapers using a wash board and tin tub but always after Nicho left for work. Every morning, she ironed and readied Nicho's work clothes and prepared his breakfasts and lunches. She followed another of Candelaria's and Rafaela's maxims: men are the breadwinners, they eat first to fuel them for the workday and to keep them healthy and in good working order.

The following spring, Rafaela again surprised everyone with an announcement that she was expecting a child in the summer. Irene was extra watchful for Rafaela, who was about to deliver a child at age forty-two. Rafaela decided that after this child, no others would follow. From that point forward, she slept separately from Cayetano. He did not appreciate her decision, but by that time Rafaela did not care to fulfill her marital duty. Their marriage had never been built on affection. In July, Rafaela gave birth to a son, Mauricio, who had three nieces older than himself.

During a fall visit, Irene eagerly told Rafaela about Nicho's new job, which had emerged out of his duties at Montgomery Ward. He often took the retailer's parcels to the post office for shipment, especially during the busy holiday season. When he delivered the parcels, he engaged postal employees in friendly conversation and proved himself helpful. When they needed an interpreter to help Mexican laborers send money orders to Mexico, the postal clerks called Nicho at Montgomery Ward. Nicho had made a good impression, and the post office hired him for the holiday season. With the encouragement of the employees, Nicho applied in the fall of 1948 for a full-time position with benefits. After a few attempts, he passed the civil service exam and was hired.

As a youngster, Nicho had stood in the lobby of the post office and peered in at the workers through the glass doors of the mailboxes. His dream was to leave the sugar beet fields to work in the post office. But even at a young age, he understood that it was likely out of his reach. But his dream became real. Neither he nor Irene could foresee the great impact this modest postal position would bring to their lives. It enabled a slow climb out of poverty and entry into a lower middle-class income. The family would have shelter, food, health insurance, education, and an opportunity to serve neighbors and their community. They purchased a car, which only Nicho knew how to drive. Cayetano never allowed Irene or any of her sisters to learn to drive. Twice, Nicho tried to teach Irene, but each time his impatience with her performance made her quite nervous. She later enrolled in a state-sponsored drivers education program and secured her license.

The car was part of a nightmarish incident the young couple escaped in 1949, when Marcela was five years old. The post office was holding a social picnic at a state park a half-hour's drive from Garden City, and Nicho insisted that his attendance might further solidify his status in the workplace if Irene and Marcela accompanied him. Marcela sat alone in the back seat as they drove on the highway. Suddenly, Irene and Nicho heard a whoosh coming from the opening of the passenger-side back seat door. Nicho immediately took his foot off the gas to brake and looked in the rearview mirror. What he saw was terrifying. Marcela was tumbling in the grass and weeds that lined the highway. He pulled the car to the side of the road and ran back to her.

Irene screamed, "Oh my God!" She sat in the car and cried into her hands, certain Marcela was dead. She felt faint.

As Nicho approached Marcela, he could see that she was on her knees, crying, and bleeding from the top of her forehead. He was so relieved to see that his daughter was alive. Nicho gathered her up and took her to Irene, who took Marcela into her arms and rocked her side to side. She pressed a cloth to the cut on her hairline to stop the bleeding. They rushed back to Garden City and took her directly to Saint Catherine's emergency room, where she received stitches. All involved expressed their certainty that the lack of a more serious injury was miraculous. Three factors figured in Marcela's escape. When Nicho took his foot off the gas, the car immediately began to slow, Marcela held on to the door handle and was suspended in the air for two or three seconds before she lost her grip, and there was no paved shoulder. The roadside growth and soil on the highway's edge softened her fall.

With Marcela's head wrapped with gauze and bandages, Nicho loaded Irene and Marcela back into the car and resumed the drive to the picnic. This was the first of a gauntlet of near misses in the years to come, both at home and on the highways, when the family slipped out of death's reach.

12

Enedina's Ordeal, Arrivals and Passings, Higher Education

In the early morning of January 1, 1949, two boys found a body underneath a railroad viaduct a mile from the Village. The discovery shocked the Village when the corpse was identified as Justo Esquibel, father of the Esquibel brothers, who fought in World War II. On Monday, January 3, the *Hutchinson News* carried a story on page eight with the headline: "Dodge City Death Determined Accidental." The text read: "A coroner's jury returned a verdict that death was accidental in the case of Justo Esquibel, 68, whose body was found by two boys under a viaduct two miles east of here on Sunday. Esquibel, retired Santa Fe roundhouse employe[e], last was seen alive Saturday. Friends of the [deceased] said they feared his death had been the result of foul play with robbery as the motive."

On the same day the *Hutchinson News* carried a second story on page eleven with a headline that read:

Solve Mystery, Find Another Dodge City—. . . The broken body of Justo Esquibel, 67, retired Santa Fe roundhouse worker was found at 8 a.m. Sunday under a railroad viaduct one mile east of Dodge City. The body was found by two boys sons of E. L. Armantrout. The body when found had one leg broken with a compound fracture, with the nose cut open, with other cuts about the body. J. C. Dunsford, coroner, said it was not possible to determine immediately the time of death or the cause of death. Police said the body was warm when found. Dunsford set a coroner's inquest for 10:00 a.m. Monday. Police suggested that Esquibel could have fallen from the viaduct or could have been knocked off. The viaduct is twelve feet high at the point. However, the police could not determine any reason for Esquibel to be on the viaduct as his home is in the Mexican village, one mile from the spot where the body was found. Esquibel was last seen alive in Dodge City at 7:30 p.m. by the Chief of Police. He is survived by his widow and nine children. Two sons died in military service.

Justo Esquibel's still-warm body was found on a Sunday morning, and in the span of twenty-six hours, the coroner's office ruled his death accidental. The coroner's and law enforcement's assumptions could not have been reasonably tested given the time between death and the coroner's ruling. The Esquibel family received no reliable answers and was left to forever question whether the machinery of justice was lacking in the investigation of Esquibel's death. The Esquibel men fought and died in World War II, not only for the country's security but also for the full measure of justice for all. The family was deserving of a thorough investigation into the circumstances of the patriarch's death.

A week after Justo Esquibel's death, Rafaela's second-oldest son, Cecilio, married Antonia Montoya in Our Lady of Guadalupe Chapel in the Village. His marriage would be the last of Rafaela's children to marry in the chapel with Padre Hernandez officiating. The old chapel was near its end. After seven years of countless dances, food sales, raffles, fiestas, and individual contributions from Mexicans and a few non-Mexicans, the fundraising committee had collected enough money to build the new Our Lady of Guadalupe Church on Avenue J. The diocese decided to move forward with plans for a modest church of buff brick in the eastside barrio. In April 1949, groundbreaking and construction began on two "procured" lots on Avenue J despite the diocese's lack of legal title. The location on Avenue J was just two blocks from Rafaela and Cayetano's home. The diocese hired a contractor who used the design plans of a prior project to build the new church. Except for a carpenter who supervised the construction, the labor for the build was supplied by men and women volunteers from the Village and eastside barrio, drawing on their masonry, carpentry, plumbing, and painting skills. They installed the roof and flooring, removed cement and mortar from bricks with a hammer and chisel, and moved the bricks as directed by the contractor.

When completed and officially dedicated in the spring of 1950, the cost of construction, excluding the labor, was $32,000, paid by the Village committee. Later, a small rectory and community center were added to the parish campus. The individual owners with legal titles to the lots transferred their titles in 1953 to the newly established Diocese of Dodge City. With a large crucifix attached to the bell tower, the new church was the tallest stone structure in the eastside barrio, except possibly Roosevelt School. The new church was essentially a replica of the Spanish churches in the small villages and towns of Mexico where stone churches stood as the highest structure among the poor adobe homes.

Rafaela and her family found their proximity to the new church a great convenience. Previously, Mexican residents on Dodge's east side who did not drive and who wanted to attend Mass on Sundays and holy days in the Village faced a long walk across unpaved paths and railroad crossings. For Rafaela, the new church was a five-minute stroll away on sidewalks or pavement. Coincidentally, Cayetano made the last payment on the house on Avenue J during construction of the new Guadalupe Church. For the first time, at age fifty-three, he became a landowner. Initially, title to the property passed only to him, but years later he added Rafaela's name. Cayetano and Rafaela had achieved a large part of the "American Dream"—homeownership. Neither family had done so in the past.

In the spring of 1950, Irene was expecting her fourth child. Irene, like Candelaria and Rafaela, believed children were a blessing and she was likely to have more. She and Nicho were practicing Catholics and did not take birth control measures. The young couple realized their home was getting smaller with each child, and so to ease the crowding, they decided to build a half-basement.

The project required the removal of six to seven feet of earth under the house. Irene and Nicho did not have the funds to pay a contractor to remove the dirt. Instead, they supplied manual labor. After each day at the post office, Nicho was under the house digging until the end of daylight. Three of his brothers and his neighbors volunteered their weekend time and labor when possible. The basement became a family and neighborhood project: neighbors also helped install the framing, drywall, and painting for the three small bedrooms. When the team of volunteers was unavailable, Irene pulled out her air base work clothes, shoes, and a pair of gloves. She set the three girls on a blanket a safe distance from the dig and waited for Nicho to fill a wheelbarrow using a pick and shovel. When the barrow was full, he walked it up a ramp of wood planks. Irene, standing on the ramp's edge, pulled on the rope tied to the wheelbarrow to help lift it to the surface.

The dig proved to be a curiosity nuisance for a few neighbors. When the dig was three feet deep, an elderly woman, Pola, who lived two houses away, peered into the hole from the dig's edge. The ground underneath her gave way, and she slid into the dig on top of the collapsing dirt. Fortunately, she was not hurt, but the wood planks of the ramp were unstable and could not support her. She had a heavy build and wasn't able to crawl out without assistance. Nicho tried to help her but had no success. He asked Irene to stay with her while he went to ask for help from his brothers, who lived a block away, and a neighbor. Their initial rescue attempts failed. Finally, two of the men reached under her shoulders, while two others jumped into the dig and grasped a leg just above the knee. On the count of three they lifted her and were able to pull her onto the surface. Pola, embarrassed but uninjured, repeatedly offered her apologies and thanked her rescuers.

When the basement was completed, Irene and Nicho told their neighbors that they were welcome to take shelter in the event of a tornado. There were sixteen homes around the perimeter of the block where Nicho and Irene lived on Santa Fe Street, the vast majority of which were wood framed and without basements or storm shelters. The neighbors, Mexican and white alike, took some comfort knowing there was a shelter nearby for them and their elderly loved ones if any of the eighty or so annual Kansas tornados threatened.

The first five years of the decade became a time of departures and arrivals for Rafaela. Her older children were marrying and departing the house on Avenue J. The arrivals were the eleven grandchildren who came to visit their abuela Rafaela. Salvador and his wife had two sons, Cecilio and his wife had a daughter, and Maria Paz, who married in 1952, gave birth to a daughter and a son. Maria Paz and her children lived with Rafaela for two years while her husband, Ramon Cervantez, served in the army.

The surrender of Germany and Japan had not ended the military tensions among and within nations. In 1947, France, with support of the British military, was fighting in Vietnam to keep the country within its empire. India ended two hundred years of British rule, only to have the newly independent nation engage in an internal conflict between Muslims and Hindus. In August 1949, Soviet scientists used stolen US intelligence and research to develop and test an atomic bomb. In October, the Chinese communist revolution began under the leadership of Mao Zedong. In June 1950, communist North Korea invaded South Korea.

These world events and their architects seemed far removed from the daily concerns of the eastside barrio and those who remained in the Village. But the United States kept a standing army to respond to the global threats. Once again, the army reached into the barrio and Village for the manpower. The army called to service Rafaela's son Ezequiel, who, as a student, was constantly at odds with Mr. Scroggins at Coronado School. Ezequiel eventually withdrew before finishing school. In 1951, the army sent Ezequiel first to Germany, and then to the Korean conflict, where he saw combat. Ezequiel's military career ultimately covered ten years, including tours of duty as an MP in the Air Force and as a crew member in the US Coast Guard. When his service ended, the former Village native returned to Dodge after living in France, Germany, Japan, Hawaii, and Guam.

Rafaela again quietly carried the heavy weight in her heart of possibly losing a child. She was frustrated with the government and the military. She lived to raise her children and keep them sheltered and fed, all with little support from her husband. But the government repeatedly put them in a position that might undo in an instant all she had done for them. She again lit the candles on her altar and prayed to Our Lady of Guadalupe for strength and protection.

On Good Friday in 1953, Padre Hernandez survived a heart attack, and after thirty-nine years of serving the Church and Village residents, he resigned as pastor of Our Lady of Guadalupe. But he continued to serve as chaplain at Saint Anthony's Hospital. The following November, the diocese appointed Father Gilbert Herrman as the new pastor of Our Lady of Guadalupe. The twenty-nine-year-old was a native of Kansas and the son of a prominent Catholic family of German heritage. He had been ordained five years earlier and had served as an assistant pastor in three other Kansas parishes. Father Hermann lived in a remodeled diocese rectory adjacent to the new Guadalupe Church.

When Nina was twenty-four, she began to display very abnormal behavior. She suffered outbursts of unexplained fear and nightmare-filled sleep; she became reclusive, timid, and depressed and clung tearfully to Rafaela. After a short while, Nina told her mother that Cayetano had abused her. Rafaela embraced and comforted her daughter. She assured Nina that she would overcome her suffering and that Cayetano would pay for his actions.

Rafaela, who rarely raised her voice for any reason, struggled to contain her anger and contempt for her husband. She confronted him, but he denied that he had committed any abuse and suggested that Nina's emotional condition was the result of the breakup with a long-distance boyfriend in Colorado. Rafaela rejected his defense immediately. She demanded that Cayetano pay for care and medical expenses for Nina.

When Nina did not improve after a few months of medical and psychological treatments, her medical doctor suggested electroconvulsive therapy (ECT), commonly known as electroshock therapy, as a possible treatment. ECT was a relatively new psychiatric treatment. Although improved and still in use, it is generally used for the treatment of depression, not abuse. The treatment on average entailed two sessions per week, for a total of six to twelve sessions in which electrical current passed through the brain.

The doctor met with Rafaela, Cayetano, Nina, and the new Guadalupe pastor, Father Herrman, whom Rafaela had invited. Like her mother, Rafaela had great faith in the counsel of their local priests. Rafaela greeted a priest by kissing his ring, as Candelaria always did. For hundreds of years, Catholics showed respect and obedience to clergy in this way, but Father Herrman told Rafaela it was not necessary.

Rafaela and Cayetano were unfamiliar with the proposed treatment. Rafaela's only concern was Nina's well-being and relied on the advice of Father Herrman. Cayetano accepted the recommendation for the treatment and Father Herrman offered no objection. Cayetano agreed to take out a loan to pay the costs of treatments—approximately ten thousand dollars.

Nina was taken to Saint Francis Hospital in Wichita for an extended stay to complete the therapy. On two or three occasions, one of her older brothers drove Cayetano to Wichita to visit Nina during her stay, but

Rafaela refused to accompany him. She wanted no part of Cayetano's concealment of his actions.

On Nina's return, her mental and emotional state slightly improved, but returning to her abuser's house left her in a very fragile position. By mid-1956, Nina began to attend six-thirty mass daily at Guadalupe Church, along with Rafaela when possible. Father Herrman noticed Nina's and Rafaela's daily presence and suggested that perhaps Nina might benefit from a stable routine of half-day housework for the parish. Father Herrman relied on female volunteers for the cooking, cleaning, laundry, and housework at the parish residence. Nina and her parents agreed, and after morning mass, Nina cooked breakfast for Father Herrman and performed other household chores. She also prepared his lunch before ending her work day at about 1:00 p.m., then returned to the house on Avenue J. In the following months, Nina continued her work for the parish without any major episodes of depression, but her stability remained tenuous.

The worst of the departures for Rafaela occurred in the spring of 1954. Chon was eighty-six years old and his health had declined in the last few years. His frame, once tall and straight, was slightly bent and thinned, and his hair had grayed. But even as his life neared its end, he remained feisty and defiant. Chon was twenty-two years old when his father died. He promised his father to care for his mother, and later promised to care for Candelaria and her children. Chon kept his promises, though with a large helping of irritability and foul temperament.

In mid-May, Chon had difficulty breathing and Rafaela took him to Saint Anthony's Hospital, where he was diagnosed with pneumonia. Rafaela and other members of the family kept vigil as he fought for breath. At his age, his body could not fight the infection. As father and daughter said their last words to each other, Chon asked Rafaela, "Mija, donde está mi *pistola*?"

Rafaela exclaimed, "Ay, Papá! You're dying, and you're worried about your *pistola*?" She did not reveal to him or anyone else where she had hidden his revolver.

Chon, the gardener-*pistolero*, took his last defiant breath on May 11. He received the Catholic last rites and was buried in Maple Grove Cemetery on a breezy Kansas morning. Irene comforted her mother during Chon's funeral mass at the new Our Lady of Guadalupe Church. She sat in solemn prayer at the passing of the last of her grandparents. Village neighbors, including Irene's dear friend, Jesse, paid their respects to this difficult man. Chon's final resting place was originally marked with a small flat headstone bearing only his name. Nearly seven decades later, the headstone was replaced with a stone that included Candelaria's name and the image of Our Lady of Guadalupe.

In his lifetime, Chon saw the Mexican Revolution, the birth of flight, a worldwide pandemic, two world wars, the development of radio and television, the Great Depression, the Dust Bowl, and the atomic bomb. The entirety of his life in the United States was lived in a time of legal racial segregation. Six days after Chon's death, the US Supreme Court swung a mighty hammer at the granite wall of racial segregation in the United States. The Supreme Court unanimously ruled in the case of *Brown v. Topeka Board of Education* that in education, the doctrine of "separate but equal" had no place and inherently violated the Constitution. In short, the separate but equal decision was a mistake, and the country has paid the price with racial strife. The court's ruling in the *Brown* case was the legal gateway to further blows against the practices of racial segregation.

After World War II, in states across the American Southwest and Midwest, many Mexican American communities organized to engage the institutions that practiced racial discrimination and denied persons of Mexican descent the rights enjoyed by their fellow white citizens. Often, Mexican American veterans who battled on the front lines of World War II and Korea were on the front lines in the battle for civil rights. They had returned from the wars with the conviction that they and their fallen comrades had earned the right to passage into first-class citizenship.

Shortly after the end of World War II, Mexican and Mexican Americans in Garden City loosely organized themselves into a social and community group called the Latin American Club. It was supported by charitable organizations, congregations, and Catholic and Protestant clergy. Two of those groups, the Blue Cross Brigade and Mutual Benefit Society of Mexico, were part of an interchurch effort to support arriving Mexican immigrants. In 1919–1920, the Brigade and Benefit Society operated out of a structure called the Mexican Mission located south of the tracks. Most of their early work focused on food, shelter, clothing, housing, and medical care for the new arrivals. In the mid-1950s, the Latin American Club began to address public issues, including racial discrimination. Many young couples with children, including Irene and Nicho, participated in the club's activities. The club sponsored dances, food booths, and queen pageants to raise funds for the poor in the Mexican community. Irene used her experience in fundraising for the new church in Dodge to help raise money for their projects.

Irene's education and experience was uncommon in the Mexican American community in Garden City. Members of the community considered her reasonably reliable for assistance in English instruction and preparation for naturalization exams, tax returns, and other government agency paper work. She became a vital resource for the Latin American Club in their projects to help those navigating the social and governmental landscape, including naturalization and citizenship. In 1957 alone, Irene guided twenty-eight persons through the naturalization process, and her effort was recognized by the congressional representative from her district.

The education of their children was important for Irene and Nicho. They believed that Marcela, their oldest child, performed poorly in her early years at Saint Mary's Elementary School because her first language was Spanish and made a conscious decision to speak only English in the home. Afterward, young Mexican couples slowly began to name their children using the English versions of their names: Miguel became Michael, Esteban became Steven, Maria became Mary. Nicho was especially conscious of the naming issue, having experienced it himself. When his older brother, Felipe, had enrolled him in school, the teacher requested that he use a name other than Dionisio. Nicho chose the name Henry, after a popular local boxer. Thereafter, in the Mexican community he was known as Nicho and in the white community as Henry or Hank.

By 1955, Irene had given birth to two more daughters, Maria and Sylvia. The girls were born without any serious complications, although Irene became ill and was hospitalized for nearly a week during one of the pregnancies. With six girls and one boy, Irene's workload and stress at home increased. Aunt Francisca gladly came from Dodge to help Irene for a few weeks after each birth. Rafaela was envious and frustrated that Francisca was able to go to Irene's aid while she remained in Dodge with her own children. Each additional child kept Nicho working a second job to make ends meet. His second jobs included evening shifts at the sugar beet factory during the harvest season and as a service attendant at gasoline stations.

Irene was thirteen years into her marriage and was now raising seven children. She assigned each of the two oldest daughters a younger sister.

The older sisters bathed, dressed, and combed the hair of their younger siblings and kept them busy at play. As each daughter got older, they took their turn at washing the dishes after meals.

After kindergarten at public schools, the children attended Saint Mary's Catholic School. The family could not afford to pay for Saint Mary's hot lunches, so they took sack lunches instead. Irene suggested that the children take burritos or tacos for lunch, as they were more filling than sandwiches, but they quickly rejected this idea. They did not want to stand out from their classmates or be subjected to ridicule. While Irene helped the younger children get ready for school, the older girls began preparing lunches. Irene organized an assembly line of sandwich makers. One sister spread mayonnaise on Wonder Bread slices, the next added the bologna, or egg salad in observance of the no-meat Fridays, the next sister added one slice of bread atop the other and wrapped them in a sheet of wax paper. Finally, the next sister added fruit or cookies and bagged the lunch. Each child grabbed a bag on their way out the door.

After the schoolchildren left for school, care for the toddlers and an infant were left to Irene. She prepared each day's meals and the snacks in between, and she kept the kitchen neat and clean after each meal with dishes washed and tables and stove cleared. When Irene was in the kitchen and the little ones were quiet or at school, she finally had time alone with her thoughts. The two kitchen windows with café curtains set above the sinks let sunlight into the home and provided a view to a busy town on the other side of the tracks. To the right of the sinks, a built-in pastry board for rolling tortilla dough slid out of the cabinet top. She made two dozen flour tortillas nearly every day for family meals. When she made tortillas in the cold winter months, she used two of the burners with hot comals, and two other burners heated the kitchen. In the summers, she started the tortillas at daylight to avoid the heat. Nicho and the children often began their days to the comforting rhythmic *clack*, *clack-clack* of her rolling pin.

Amid all the daily work and tedium, Irene and Nicho took advantage of every opportunity to listen to music, a simple but pleasurable break from the drain of the workday. They enjoyed popular English music on the radio and listened to Mexican singers and balladeers on 10-inch 78 rpm phonograph records. They loved to go to weekend dances and weddings and share the joy of the music with other young couples and family members.

A favorite weekend of dance was the Mexican Fiesta in September of each year.

On occasion, when Irene and Nicho went to dances in Dodge, Irene danced with Jesse, her longtime friend. At these dances, a man known to a husband might ask for and receive permission to dance with the other's wife, but an ask by a man unknown to the husband was a rather perilous matter. Nicho knew of Irene's long-standing friendship with Jesse and gave his permission. During their dance, Irene and Jesse had a brief opportunity to update the other on their lives and share each other's company. By 1955, Jesse was remarried and the father of two daughters and a son, while Irene had six daughters and a son. Jesse teased Irene about the number of her children.

From the start of their marriage, Nicho pursued a few individual diversions. He played softball on the Latin American Club team in a competitive town league. Team members were Mexican with the exceptions of an occasional black or white player. The contests were usually intense with each team eager to display their superiority with their softball skills. Nicho enjoyed some comradery with his fellow postal workers as a member of their bowling team. In keeping with his love of music, he played the bongos and other percussion instruments in a rumba-conga band. The band's wardrobe was complete with colorful V-neck shirts and ruffled sleeves, similar to Ricky Ricardo's band on TV's *I Love Lucy*. Irene attended the softball games and the band performances in support and took along the children when she could. But each of these diversions fell by the wayside and were soon overtaken by the demands of raising six children. In a tone of practical necessity, Irene convinced Nicho that their time should be devoted to his work, the family, and their community service. Nicho knew she was right and eliminated many of the activities, although with some reluctance.

In 1955, Irene and Nicho did manage to save enough to fulfill their longtime dream of travel to Mexico. They left the care of the children to Aunt Francisca and other relatives. They drove to Mexico City accompanied by Nicho's brother, Guillermo, and his wife, Sophia. They stopped and visited with relatives from both families in El Paso, Juarez, and Mexico City. There, they visited the floating gardens of Xochimilco, the Mayan pyramids, the cloak of Our Lady of Guadalupe in the Basilica, and they attended one of Nicho's favorites, a bullfight.

During these events and celebrations, Irene noticed that Nicho, on occasion, drank more than he should, especially in the company of male friends and pals. Some viewed his behavior as humorous and loud, but not Irene. She very rarely saw her father inebriated, and Nicho's drinking behavior made her uncomfortable. She told him privately that she would prefer he drink less, but he was annoyed and said that her concerns were unfounded and that he could hold his liquor. Irene never demanded that he completely stop, only that he consume less. She also understood that a direct challenge to his belief in dominance by virtue of his place as man of the house could evoke a loud, mean response from Nicho. Sometimes after he drank too much, she insisted that he lower his voice and tone before entering the house, where the children might see him in such a state.

※

In Dodge, Rafaela's younger children—Gonzalo, David, Rita, and Mauricio—made their way from public grade school through high school. In their public school years, the children saw clearly the differences between poor students, mostly Mexican and Black, and middle-class students, mostly white, in the simple comforts of their clothes, shoes, and school supplies. They also experienced the sting of racial intolerance, relegated to balcony-only seating at the movies and barred from swimming in the public pool. During middle school, the boys team won a city basketball tournament despite the lack of a gym. The coach took them to the drugstore luncheonette to celebrate with a malt shake, but the clerk refused to serve the Mexican players. The coach apologized to the team and took them to another shop and paid for their celebratory treats.

In May 1955, both Gonzalo and David earned their high school diplomas, Gonzalo from Dodge City High and David from Saint Mary's of the Plains. David had transferred to Saint Mary's for his senior year in search of more playing time on the football team. They became the second and third of Rafaela's children to graduate from high school. After a summer of unsuccessful job searching, the young men enrolled at Dodge City Community College and became the first in both the Rodriguez and Padilla lines to attend college. The brothers thought that after a year of college studies, the racial barriers might fall and their employment prospects might improve. Rafaela was pleased that her sons decided to stay in school, more so that they chose their own paths. At the same time, she was not convinced that a college degree was a sure key to better lives. She understood that the racial limitations placed on her sons were not so easily overcome. Cayetano was largely unimpressed. He still thought their time was wasted in the classroom and would be better spent working for the Santa Fe.

By this time, the addition of a new stove, a refrigerator, and a wrangler washing machine—a white tub on four legs with a two-roller hand crank—had lightened the burden of Rafaela's housework. But Rafaela's transition into the twentieth century was not immediate, and she still favored some traditional kitchen items over the modern electric models. She continued to make coffee by boiling water in a pot and pouring it over coffee grounds. And she preferred to heat flat cast irons to press clothing.

Rafaela also continued Chon's custom of planting a small garden of corn, squash, and chilies every spring. Her grandchildren livened up the house with their play, both indoors and outdoors in abuela's big backyard. As always, she was ready to give them a warm hug and a snack.

By the summer of 1955, most of the Village families had vacated the property, as demanded by the Santa Fe. Their demands were made in writing and by loudspeakers atop a vehicle driven through the Village. Some of the Villagers dismantled their houses and salvaged the wood and hardware to use in their new homes on Dodge's east side. Other homes were left for demolition; a few were kept intact and moved to the north side of the tracks. A handful of residents resisted and held out for as long as possible, but eventually they also left. In the end, the Village was cleared except for a few slabs of concrete foundations. Over time, small industries and businesses slowly occupied the land where, for a half-century, a determined people cared for their families and did their living, praying, and dying.

Padre Hernandez, who had led the families in their faith for nearly five decades, passed along with the Village. He died in February 1956. A six-foot-tall headstone in the Calvary section of Maple Grove Cemetery marks his gravesite. Later that year, the diocese approved funding for a full-time, live-in housekeeper position for Guadalupe parish. Nina, along with other part-time housekeepers, applied for the job. The diocese deferred to Father Herrman, who asked Rafaela and Cayetano if they objected to Nina taking the position. Nina wanted it, and Rafaela believed that her daughter would be safe and her well-being might improve if she was removed from the stress of living in the same house with Cayetano. Additionally, with the parish residence just down the street, Rafaela could visit her daughter often. The diocese approved Nina's hiring in late 1956.

Cecilio also left Rafaela's home in 1956, when the army sent him to Germany as part of the occupation force. He learned to speak a surprising amount of German while serving there. Much to the delight of their neighbors on Avenue J, the Kruger family, on his return Cecilio spoke with them in German. In effect, Cecilio traveled to the other side of the planet to learn the language of his neighbor across the street.

❧

Perhaps the most significant home appliance purchase for the home on Avenue J in 1957 was a television. Like the radio, the TV became another portal for Rafaela to see events outside the house and to avoid Cayetano's attempts to control her life. Now that her adult children were out of the home or going to school and Rita and Mauricio were in grade school, she had more time to spend as she chose. She put aside any thoughts of possibly working outside the home. She knew Cayetano would never allow it. So, she took what she could from TV to improve her English, know news events, and find entertainment. She had her favorite soap operas, *The Guiding Light* and *As the World Turns*. With her sense of humor, she thoroughly enjoyed *I Love Lucy* and, in later years, *The Carol Burnett Show*. She watched *The Lawrence Welk Show* faithfully and even a western cowboy series—*Gunsmoke*, of course. But Rafaela was not glued to the TV set. She loved to crochet and knit small items of clothing for the grandchildren, and often she sat in the shade of the porch in the summers, and in her small living room in the winters, to complete her labor of love. She also followed the instructions in sewing booklets to make intricate, delicate doilies and mats for furniture and small tabletops.

Rafaela also resumed her summertime travels. She rode the Santa Fe train to Los Angeles to see Juana, who had moved from El Paso to Pico Rivera, California. She took the train to visit Maria Paz when she and her family moved to Sidney, Nebraska. She took Rita and Mauricio with her on most trips, and on occasion Cayetano accompanied them. Each September, she asked one of her sons to drive her to Garden City to visit with Irene and to attend an evening celebrating the Mexican Fiesta. She enjoyed the music and watching the younger generations perform Mexico's traditional dances. On those occasions when Cayetano came along, they sat together, but she never gave a thought to join the couples who took to the dance floor after the dance program ended. There might have been a very rare occasion when they danced together after Irene's birth, but it remains uncertain whether they ever did. She found joy elsewhere.

When David's and Gonzalo's first year at the community college ended, they were eager to start earning the paychecks that would raise their quality of living, especially with a car. But their employment opportunities outside of the railroad remained dismal, so they both applied to the Santa Fe and took tests for positions as a carpenter's apprentice. They passed the exams, but only David was hired in late 1957. Gonzalo was shorter than David, and thin, and his stature might have influenced the decision by the Santa Fe. David was so anxious to get out of Dodge that he asked to work in Wellington, a larger facility thirty-five miles south of Wichita. The Santa Fe agreed and David left home. Gonzalo decided to return to college. Father Herrman told Gonzalo there were scholarship funds available at Saint Mary of the Plains College. Gonzalo spoke with the community college advisor, who warned him that he would face academic rigor and stricter standards at Saint Mary of the Plains. He disregarded the warning, applied, and was awarded a scholarship.

After several months with the Santa Fe in Wellington, David felt dissatisfied with his position and was ready to look elsewhere. He took a leave of absence and volunteered for the army to have some say in where he might be stationed. By 1959, he began a four-year tour of duty and was assigned to a guided missile defense unit. With the heightened tension and threats by the Soviet Union, major cities in the United States were protected by guided missiles. David served three years in the unit that guarded Milwaukee, Wisconsin.

On Wednesday, March 11, 1959, Micaela, Tony Rodriguez's daughter, walked home from school taking her regular route past her grandfather Abran's home. She often stopped and visited with him on his porch. After a short chat, he would give her his blessing and send her on her way. But on this day, Abran was not on his porch. Later in the day, his son, Ladislao, on his return from work, found him dead in his chair in the living room with rolling papers and tobacco in his hands. Abran, at the age of seventy-six, apparently died from a heart attack.

Abran's journey into the United States took him to the fields and orchards of California before he and his family settled in Dodge to be near

Candelaria. He was a carpenter and took on any type of work to provide for his family. He was a resourceful man with an ability to fashion together wood, metal, and other materials for housing, furniture, porches, livestock pens, and coffins. He was laid to rest in Maple Grove Cemetery in the segregated Mexican section where his wife, Alvina, and his daughter, Pola, had been laid to rest.

Abran had been Rafaela's only living sibling in Kansas. Her sister, Juana, was in California, and her brother, Manuel, remained in El Paso. With the loss of Abran, she felt even more alone in her marriage. With his death, she held her children and grandchildren even closer in her heart and kept a welcome door open for Abran's surviving sons, Ladislao and Antonio, and his grandchildren.

In May, Gonzalo graduated with a bachelor's degree in social sciences and philosophy. He was the first in his family, ever, to earn a college degree. Rafaela took quiet pride in the educational success of her children. She became more confident that education provided more choice in the lives they might live. But at the same time, she was not critical of her children who did not finish their education. She recognized the reality that education in the Village was limited.

A few months after Gonzalo earned his degree, the US government sent its calling card—a notice of induction into military service. He was drafted into the army and was directed to report for basic training at Fort Leonard in San Antonio, Texas.

During the years 1950 to 1960, Irene gave birth to six children, including three sons. The oldest, Raphael, was born in 1951. In 1958, she had a second son, Philip, named after Nicho's brother who had passed away the previous year. The other son was born in 1960 and named Charles Victor. Irene had preferred Victor as a first name, but she compromised when Nicho insisted on Charles. He was a fan of TV's "Rifleman," Chuck Connors. The daughters were Geraldine, born in 1950, Maria, in 1953, and Sylvia, in 1955. The amount of physical and emotional strength expended to raise the children and support a husband was incredibly difficult to measure. Irene drew on an inner strength and prayer to withstand the exhausting and numbing family care, cooking, and cleaning.

The size of Irene and Nicho's house expanded along with the number of children. In 1960, Nicho and Irene extended the front of the house eight feet and added a bedroom and more living room space. A cement company laid the concrete foundation and a carpenter installed the wood frame and roof. Nicho and his brother added the insulation, drywall, and paint. Though the added space was welcome relief, the family still shared just one bathroom.

They bought a new washing machine, but the clothes were still hung out to dry on a clothesline made of four long wires attached to salvaged pipe. They also bought a sit-down press so that Irene could more easily iron Nicho's postal shirts and pants and all the other family clothing. By 1960, they had purchased a small black-and-white portable TV. With the purchase, the children no longer went to a neighbor's home to join other children without TVs and watch the after-school Mickey Mouse program. They also installed a telephone, ending their reliance on the pay phone at the Santa Fe Depot. Rafaela was now just a phone call away. Calls for support in times of family issues or crisis or planning family events and gatherings became much less of a challenge.

Irene wanted Marcela and Virginia to develop friendships and participate in activities beyond their small barrio. She put them in girl scout brownies and tap dance classes, but unfortunately, they did not have the money to allow the girls to advance in either activity. With Nicho's support, she insisted that her daughters attend high school and earn their diplomas. Irene saw high school as an opportunity for her daughters to interact and become comfortable with classmates from different backgrounds. She wanted the girls to develop friendships and have the experiences of high school that she knew. She didn't want them to see themselves as lesser outsiders among their white classmates. The girls took with them their friendships from Saint Mary's School to junior high and high school, and that eased the awkwardness of entering a new school with entirely new faces.

Irene took the girls to buy dresses for their homecoming and prom dances. She offered suggestions for their selections without insistence and accompanied them for fitting and alterations. When the boys came to the house to escort their dates to the dance, Irene welcomed them. She asked them to sit while she pinned the appropriate colored corsage on the dress, then helped the girls attach the matching boutonniere to the lapel of the boy's suit coat. Nicho was usually at work when the boys came to the house to take the girls to the dances. So, all were spared the intimidation when Nicho expressed his expectations.

Daughters dating without a family chaperone remained highly objectionable in Mexican families, and Nicho was unusually cautious when his high school daughters attended events and parties with their classmates. Marcela and Irene convinced him to allow Marcela to hold a party at the house for her eighteenth birthday. He reluctantly agreed on condition that Irene observe the student partiers from the kitchen when they gathered and danced in the newly enlarged living room. For two hours on that cold November night, Nicho stood behind a tree in the front yard, wearing a hat and a long, dark, wool trench coat with an upturned collar, smoking, and keeping a watchful eye. He was trying to stop uninvited guests and prevent invited guests from "necking" in their cars. Irene was confident that with Nicho as sentry, and out of the party's way, there was little cause for concern. Several classmates and guests of different races and nationalities attended the party without incident. When the party ended, Marcela's classmates and friends politely thanked Irene for hosting.

Irene used her limited spare time to support and encourage members of the community to pursue education. While Marcela and Virginia watched over their siblings, Irene held English classes for new arrivals from Mexico and candidates for citizenship. She held the classes in church basements and in the small Latin American clubhouse located a block from her home. Her commitment to the classes at times limited her participation in other community service organizations, including the Altar Society of Saint Mary's Parish and the American G.I. Forum.

The American G.I. Forum had been founded by a group of Mexican veterans in Corpus Christi, Texas, in 1948. Led by Dr. Hector P. Garcia, an army medical doctor, the G.I. Forum established state and local chapters across the southwest, including in Texas, New Mexico, Arizona, Oklahoma, Kansas, and Nebraska. Shortly after its founding, an outrage sparked the war veterans in Corpus Christi into action. Felix Longoria Jr., an army soldier, was killed in the Philippines in 1945. Longoria was born and raised in the small town of Three Rivers located between San Antonio and Corpus Christi. His remains were not returned to his family until 1949. The director of the funeral home refused to allow the Longoria family to hold a wake in the funeral home because white people in Three Rivers would object. Longoria was later buried on his family's property, which abutted the segregated cemetery. The G.I. Forum and others asked for an investigation into the treatment of the Longoria family. Eventually, with the intervention of Senator Lyndon B. Johnson, Longoria was reinterred at Arlington National Cemetery with full military honors along with eighteen other soldiers whose remains were returned to the United States.

The G.I. Forum eventually established chapters in both Dodge and Garden City in the mid-1960s. The primary national mission was to ensure that Mexican American children and adults have full access to education. The forum and their objectives would play a large role in the lives of Irene and Nicho and their work for education and equality in Garden City. As the 1950s ended, the G.I. Forum became the dominant organization for the civic and political interests of the Mexican community in Garden City. Irene and Nicho gave much of their free time to the forum, with both serving terms as officers—Nicho as chairman, and Irene as chairwoman of the Women's Auxiliary. They both attended and participated in the 1960 G.I. Forum National Convention, which was held in Wichita. By that time, the Women's Auxiliary began shifting from local food, dance, and fiesta fundraisers to active support for community civil rights events, including voter registrations, education scholarships, and leadership development. Irene's work for the Mexican community instilled in her the sense that her life was more than raising children. She was following a basic tenet of her faith: use your talents and work for the benefit of your neighbor.

The Mexican community in Garden City honored the heritage their immigrant parents brought to Kansas. The community celebrated Mexico's Declaration of Independence from Spain on September 16, 1810. In the early morning hours of that day, led by a Catholic priest, the revolt to end three hundred years of Spanish rule began. As early as 1909, the new arrivals in Garden City celebrated the declaration with a city-approved fiesta held south of the tracks. An orchestra of Mexican musicians provided the music for the singing of the national anthems of the United States and Mexico and religious hymns.

By 1929, the two-day fiesta began more elaborate programming and entertainment. The fiesta days and events began with a mass and prayers, a parade, the crowning of a fiesta queen, traditional Mexican dancers, and a free concert and dance, provided by local or out-of-town bands. In the 1930s, the fiestas drew crowds of seven hundred to eight hundred, many from other towns and states, including Colorado and Texas.

Over time, the venues moved from open ground to the city park tennis courts and then to concrete slabs built specifically for the fiestas with volunteer labor. The stages and booths were colorfully painted red, white, and green and adorned with paper globes and star decorations. Many local families staffed food booths and offered many dishes to meet the public's taste for Mexican foods, including tamales, tacos, tostadas, enchiladas, burritos, menudo, and handmade tortillas de maíz or flour. Drinks included flavored aguas frescas of strawberry, lemon, cucumber, and horchata.

In the 1960s, the fiesta committees began to award scholarships and donations to Garden City's community chest. Politicians, mayors, governors, members of the US House of Representatives, and future senators appeared and spoke favorably of the Mexican community. And importantly, more and more members from the white community, not only from Garden City but also other nearby towns, supported and attended the fiestas. Irene and Nicho were not only participants; they were active in organizing and producing the events.

13

Work and Stress, Radio DJs, Floodwaters

Rafaela began the next decade with a new daughter-in-law when David, still in Milwaukee, married Miriam Wolbrink in May 1960. Rafaela was disappointed when David surprised her with his announcement that they had eloped and were married outside the Church. She also doubted the wisdom of his choice of bride on learning that Miriam was of mostly German descent. Despite interacting with her neighbors for twenty years—a Black family and a white German family on either side of her—a mixed marriage of any sort was foreign to Rafaela. The realization that David and Miriam were highly unlikely to live in Dodge also added to her displeasure.

Gonzalo's tour of duty with the army was originally scheduled to end in early 1961, but the army held him over due to the growing tensions with Cuba's dictator, Fidel Castro. After a successful military coup, Castro aligned himself with the Soviet Union. The US government, through the Central Intelligence Agency, financed and trained a battalion of Cuban exiles for an invasion of Cuba to oust Castro. In April 1961, Gonzalo found himself preparing to board a ship with troops whose mission was to provide backup support for the invading exiles. President Kennedy chose not to use US air power in support of the invaders, who were then quickly defeated. Gonzalo's mission was canceled, and within a few months he was back in Dodge. On his return, he obtained his teaching credentials and later taught in a Catholic school in Wichita.

Rafaela's marriage remained cold and without affection. She stayed on a course that kept any interaction with Cayetano to a minimum. She was quick to put a stop to any conversation or comments that might lead to a verbal dispute. She kept her tone firm, but she did not yell. Her energy and affections were all for Rita, Mauricio, and the many grandchildren who regularly visited her. Gonzalo's departure for the military left Rafaela without a driver for visits to Irene, as neither she nor Cayetano knew how to drive. Sometimes Ezequiel was available to take her to her Garden City visits, but Irene and Nicho responded with many Sunday drives to Dodge in a baby-blue 1954 Ford station wagon filled with Rafaela's grandkids.

Irene and Nicho were under considerable stress from the daily burdens of child raising and paying the bills. Irene relied on her calm determination and faith to deal with hardships. Nicho still enjoyed his job at the post office, but his second and third part-time work left him constantly exhausted. He saw no end to his current pace and place in life, and he began to vent his anger when ignited by alcohol. Irene was especially protective if he directed it at any of the children. For the most part, she was able to calm him and keep him from losing control of himself.

Irene was the lead parent in raising the children, helping them with their homework and attending parent-teacher conferences. Nicho attended the conferences only on rare occasion, as he was always at work at one of his many part-time jobs. The children were relieved when he did not attend, as he seemed to always encourage the nuns at Saint Mary's to inflict discipline on them if needed. Then he administered another dose when he got home if there was a bad report.

Irene, like Rafaela, seldom raised her voice. Her use of corporal discipline was very rare and limited to a soft sandal swat on the seat of the pants resulting in a loud, but relatively painless slap. Nicho, however, did not hesitate to swing a leather belt. One or two swats were the usual dosage, but when exceptionally angered, especially with his oldest son, he might swing his belt three to five times. This, from a barrel-chested, thick-built man who stood five foot eight inches tall. When Nicho was a boy, he worked on his hands and knees in the sugar beet fields pulling weeds with his fingers. His father swatted him on the back with a long-handled hoe if he fell asleep. Nicho considered the belt a relatively lesser means of discipline. But all the children feared its use and understood that it was very difficult for Irene to stop him.

One of the children Irene watched closely was Christina, her third daughter. She would start her freshman year of high school in the fall of 1961. Although she was quiet and shy in school, on occasion at home she would tell Nicho to stop being mean to her mother or one of her siblings, which drew Nicho's ire. But Christina escaped future conflicts with him by a stroke of good fortune. Christina's school principal at Saint Mary's, Sister Mary Carmelita, took note of her excellent grades and, unbeknownst to Christina, recommended to the pastor, and Irene and Nicho, that Christina be awarded a scholarship to attend Saint Mary of the Plains High School in Dodge City. Irene agreed without reservation—Christina would get her diploma, live with Rafaela, and avoid further conflict with Nicho. He, of course, gave his consent. He did not mind paying a small amount of room and board to Rafaela and Cayetano to lessen the cost and stress of raising another teenager.

Christina had no knowledge of the arrangement between the parish, Saint Mary of the Plains, and her parents. At the awards ceremony on the last day of eighth grade, Sister Carmelita announced the names of scholarship winners. Christina thought she heard her name called in error. But when Sister Carmelita called her up to the stage a second time, she understood. Christina was happy and filled with pride, and had no hesitations about going away to school—she was happy to do so. Irene was pleased but not so happy about Christina being away. She genuinely believed that going to Saint Mary's in Dodge was the best thing for Christina but not for herself.

Irene's oldest, Marcela, was seriously ill and hospitalized for nearly three months with rheumatic fever during the last months of her senior year in 1961. On graduation night, she was able to leave the hospital in a wheelchair and receive her diploma with her classmates. While Irene was happy and proud of Marcela's graduation, she was more concerned that Marcela fully recover from her illness. Marcela seemed to skirt more potential harm than most her age. As a toddler she not only fell out of a moving car but was also hospitalized after drinking a small amount of kerosene. Marcela's recovery and return to full strength from rheumatic fever required a full year. Irene and Nicho gave her their blessing when she left for nursing school in Great Bend, Kansas, in September 1962.

In Dodge, Rafaela's children continued to leave home as well. Gonzalo left to teach in Wichita in 1962. Rafaela's son, David, finished his military service in Wisconsin in 1962 and returned to Wellington with his wife and their infant daughter, Teresa. The Santa Fe credited David for his military service time and kept his place on the seniority list. Shortly after his return, he saw a posting for major training at the Santa Fe's "Big Shop" in Albuquerque. The Big Shop's primary task at that time was to service tracks and railcars. It was a complex of buildings built early in the century. But the buildings declined in number as locomotive engines transitioned from diesel to electric power in the 1950s. Sturdy men working in the equipment shop and the machine shop, where parts were made and repaired, completed the heavy work. David didn't want to be locked in place as a laborer in Kansas and saw the training in Albuquerque as the first step to improve his position. He asked for a permanent transfer and was selected. He immediately moved to Albuquerque and was initially housed in the Santa Fe firehouse. His family followed shortly thereafter and initially made their home in a rented house.

David had another reason to move his family to Albuquerque. During all his relocations, he kept the thought of returning to college. In Albuquerque, if the opportunity arose, he might be able to pursue his college education on a part-time basis at the University of New Mexico while working for the Santa Fe.

In November, after a difficult pregnancy, Irene delivered her tenth child, a daughter. Irene chose the name Lisa Irene. Once again, there were eight children in the home. Nicho raised the possibility of moving to a larger house and Irene working a paying job to afford a more comfortable home, but Irene opposed both ideas. Given her own upbringing in the Village, she believed the children had the conveniences they needed, and she was willing to suffer the inconveniences of a large family in a small house. The family was secure as it was. A new house would only mean more debt, and Nicho could not take on any more work to cover the added expense. She did not know if his health could withstand the extra strain.

Irene was certain that Nicho was overextended with his post office job and his evening hours at the truck stop. His work with the eighteen-wheelers was often heavy and energy-draining, and sometimes he worked until eleven or midnight. And on Saturday nights starting at 11:00 p.m., he loaded bundles of the *Denver Post* into the station wagon and delivered them to Liberal, Kansas, some seventy miles away. Usually, eleven-year-old Raphael, went along to help load and unload the newspaper bundles. But his most important task was to keep Nicho awake. Nicho kept the radio volume on high and lowered the windows for cold air in the winter, and Raphael massaged Nicho's neck and shoulders to keep him alert. On a few occasions, Irene went along on the Saturday night run to Liberal. During these middle-of-the-night trips, they listened to Mexican radio stations that played traditional ballads and love songs. It was a rare opportunity for the couple to enjoy Mexican music together.

Nicho's workload raised in Irene's mind thoughts of a disastrous possibility that appeared more ominous with each newborn: *How would I support these children if something were to happen to Nicho?* She saw troubling signs in Nicho's health. His asthma had worsened over time. It first appeared at age sixteen when he worked in the lemon orchards of California. His symptoms intensified living next to a dust-filled, pitched-roof grain elevator. Additionally, less than a city block away from the house stood an enormous concrete grain elevator with blowing dryers and a capacity to store more than a million bushels of grain. He began smoking cigarettes as a teenager and was unable to stop. Irene repeatedly asked him not to smoke in the house, but he occasionally ignored her requests. By 1962, Nicho's lung disease had progressed to emphysema, for which he took albuterol to ease his breathing. It was a medication he ingested daily with a handheld bulb inhaler.

Shortly after Lisa's birth, Nicho spoke to Irene about a rather unusual idea to earn more money. He proposed broadcasting a Spanish-language program on KNCO, one of the local radio stations. There were no daytime Spanish-language broadcasts within 250 miles of Garden City. Nicho regularly carried a transistor radio in his shirt pocket as he walked his mail route. He listened using an earpiece in his good ear. He had lost hearing in the other from an infection suffered during a bitter winter storm a few years prior. On his many night trips to Liberal, he became familiar with the delivery styles of the Mexican disc jockeys. From this minimal experience as a listener, he believed he could be a Spanish DJ.

Irene thought Nicho's idea was preposterous. She did believe that Mexican music on the local radio station would be enjoyable and a huge positive for the growing Mexican community, but she was not convinced that Nicho could be the voice of such a program. During a late meal after the evening shift at the truck stop, Irene gently addressed the possibility. She asked, "How much will you get paid?"

"Well, that depends." Irene did not find his answer helpful. She let him finish. "They will pay me by the hour minimum wage—$1.25. I will have to sell advertising for the program and I will get a commission for the ads I sell."

"Are you going to take time off from the post office to do this program?"

"I've talked to the station manager, and he said Sunday afternoons and weekday evenings would be a good time for the show.

Irene was surprised that he had already taken the initial steps to put this plan in motion. She responded, "Nicho, you've never done this before. Are they planning on teaching you how to do this?"

He was ready with an answer. "Yes, I'll sit in with a DJ and he'll show me how to run the mic and the turntables and spin the records."

She was certain he had not fully given thought to all the obvious challenges. "Is the station going to provide the music?"

"They have some old albums that a distributor sent them, but the music is not very popular. I'll have to buy new records and use what we have here at home." He knew what Irene's next question would be, so he quickly added, "They'll give me a little money to help pay for them."

Irene remained skeptical. "It would be nice if they paid for some of the expenses."

Nicho finally admitted the true problem. "The manager doesn't want to put too much money into it because he's not sure the program can pay for itself." He realized that Irene was not enthusiastically jumping on board and thought it was as good a moment as any to reveal the big ask of Irene. After a second, he said, "I will need your help."

"What are you talking about?" she said. "How am I supposed to do that?"

"I'm going to have to do the commercials. They have some commercials typed up in English, but they need to be translated. And if I get new sponsors, we'll have to write them up in Spanish and English. Then there's the list of the records I'm going to play." He looked at Irene and said, "You can do that better than me."

Irene thought Nicho was underestimating the time, effort, and expense that would be needed to put together the program, given their daily workloads and community activities. But in the end, she agreed to help on a trial basis. Nicho's arguments were not the deciding factors in her decision, however. She wanted to help in the belief that the music and program might entertain and lighten the burdens of the Spanish-speaking communities in Garden City, Dodge City, and nearby areas.

By mid-January of 1963, the *D.C. Garcia Show* was on the air. Nicho often used his first and middle initials to identify himself: *D* for Dionisio and *C* for Campos, his mother's maiden name. Initially, the one-hour show aired on weeknights at 7:00 p.m. on KNCO's FM station with eleven thousand watts of power. Within a few weeks, Nicho learned to cue the records and handle the mic without an assistant. Irene, the quiet backbone of the show, remained in the background, at home. She prepared the playlist, lined up the records in order, and wrote and translated the ads. After a full day at the post office, Nicho drove home, grabbed the stack of records and paperwork, and drove to the station. The show quickly became popular in the Spanish-speaking community, and the purchasing power of its listeners became apparent.

On a Saturday night in early March, Irene and Nicho attended a fundraiser dance. They left early so that he could make the Liberal newspaper delivery. At the dance she had kept an eye on his drinking and noticed that he was speaking loudly. On the way home, Irene saw that his driving was erratic and unsteady. She sensed danger. When they entered the house, she told him firmly, "You're not taking Raphael. You go without him."

Nicho was surprised by the tone in her demand and was unsure why she spoke to him that way. "Why not? He always comes with me." He looked over at Raphael, standing by the bedroom door ready to go. "Let's go," he said sternly.

"Nicho, he is not going with you tonight."

He raised his voice slightly. "Yes, he is."

"You can't drive. You've had too much to drink." Raphael stood still, not knowing what to do.

Nicho, standing at the front door, angrily raised his voice even more. "I have not had too much to drink! You just think I can't hold my liquor!" Nicho put on his jacket but fumbled the snaps trying to button it.

By this time, the older girls were fearful and stood close behind Irene. She tried to offer an alternative. "Why don't you ask your brother to take the papers tonight, or sleep for a little bit before you go?"

"I'm not asking my brother. I don't need him." He again looked at

Raphael and commanded, "Let's go, mijo." Raphael did not say anything, but he was willing to go just to stop the argument.

Irene said, but without raising her voice, "Nicho, he's not going."

There was a moment of silence with Irene and Nicho looking at each other. They had reached the decisive moment. Nicho finally conceded and said as if the matter was of no consequence, "Fine. I'll do it myself." He turned and went out the front door.

The girls asked Irene if she was all right. She assured them, "I'm fine, girls. I'm fine. Go to bed, everybody." Raphael was relieved the fight was over and that he did not have to endure an uncomfortable trip to Liberal with his father. Irene stayed where she was for a few minutes before the tension started to break. She had compromised with Nicho on other disputes in the past. He was quite stubborn sometimes, so she was careful to pick her battles with him. But she would not risk the safety of her child.

That night, Nicho followed his usual routine: drive the seventy miles, unload the bundles, stop for coffee and a hamburger at the 24-hour Blue Goose Café, and return to Garden City. But shortly after leaving Liberal on his return to Garden City, he found himself sitting and looking down at the light between his legs. He was confused and could not comprehend the light beneath him. After a few moments, he recognized it; it was the dome light of the station wagon. He then realized he was sitting upright, but the station wagon was not. It was lying on its roof, wheels up. He had fallen asleep at the wheel and rolled the station wagon into a deep ditch off US Highway 83. He had slipped through La Pelona's hands.

As Nicho began to crawl though the driver's side window, he felt severe pains in his neck and shoulders. His ribcage was sore as well. He felt the sting of small scratches on his forehead and cheek, but there was no bleeding that he could see. Once he was out of the wagon and able to stand, he decided that he had not suffered any injury that would prevent him from walking.

Nicho stood by the roadside for a few minutes and attempted to flag down passing vehicles. But it was 2:00 a.m. on a cold night and there was virtually no traffic on the highway at that hour. He saw a light post and the silhouette of a farmhouse a quarter-mile away and decided to go ask for help. On reaching the darkened house, he knocked on the front door repeatedly. But after the infamous Clutter family murders, dramatized in Truman Capote's *In Cold Blood*, which took place at night in the family's farmhouse outside of Garden City, nobody in southwest Kansas was going to answer the door in the middle of the night. Nicho walked back to the station wagon, and after an hour, a passing trucker pulled over and drove him to the police station in Liberal.

Irene could not sleep that night and began to worry when Nicho had not returned by 4:00 a.m., the usual time. At daylight, the phone rang. Nicho said in an exhausted voice, "I'm sorry. I didn't have a chance to call you sooner."

Irene's first thoughts were that he was alive but hurt. She asked, "Are you okay? You sound like you're hurt."

Nicho hesitated for a second before saying with great resign, "I had an accident. I fell asleep driving home and wrecked the car. But I'm okay."

"Ay, Nicho," Irene said, still in disbelief. "Are you sure you're okay? Are you at the hospital?"

"Yes. I'm sure, and no, I didn't need to go to the hospital. I'm at the police station and a highway patrolman is going to drive me home. I should be home by noon."

For a moment, Irene thought about their argument the night before and was thankful that she had withstood his demand to take Raphael on the drive to Liberal. She asked, "Is there anything I can do?"

"No. I'll take care of everything when I get home," he replied.

The next day, Nicho, bruised and aching, Irene, and Virginia drove to the wrecker's yard in Liberal to retrieve paperwork from the glove compartment and some hand tools. Irene was shocked when she saw the mangled metal of the station wagon. She couldn't believe that any person could survive the crumpled wreckage. She looked at Nicho and said, "No more *Denver Post*. You could have died."

Nicho, slightly contrite, nodded in agreement. After a few moments of thought about his age, health, and workload, he turned to Irene and said, "I may not make it another year."

Irene was unsure if he really believed what he said or if he was being overly dramatic to deflect attention from his actions. But she told him, "You will, if you quit drinking and start taking care of yourself."

Days later, Nicho replaced the blue station wagon with a tan 1959 Ford station wagon, but he never again drove newspapers to Liberal.

Nicho stayed away from alcohol in the weeks after he rolled the station wagon. His determination to remain on the straight and narrow was strengthened as his mother, Rosa, fought diabetes. He began to attend 6:30 a.m. Mass. He prayed for his mother and her health and for strength in his battle against fatigue and alcohol. In mid-April, Rosa passed away at age seventy-eight. With her passing and his renewed religious commitment, Nicho toned down his reckless behavior, at least for the moment.

❧

At the end of 1964, Marcela was one semester away from completion of her three-year RN program at Catholic Dominican School of Nursing. Virginia had graduated from high school the previous May and worked at Saint Catherine hospital as a housekeeper. Christina was in her senior year at Saint Mary of the Plains and would return home after graduation. Irene's house was again becoming overcrowded, but this time Virginia was working and able to help pay the bills. Marcela also hoped to work at Saint Catherine's and contribute to the family income. Irene and Nicho welcomed the financial relief the girls provided despite the crowded living conditions.

On December 30, 1964, Irene sent two of her children, Sylvia, age nine, and Philip, age six, to Walls IGA with a short grocery list. They crossed the railroad tracks, then Fulton Street, a four-lane business street, to reach the grocery store. After crossing Fulton on their return, they ran home on the sidewalk in front of the farmers' co-op building. Parking was behind the building, with the exit on the building's northside. The exit lane was not visible to oncoming pedestrians, and similarly oncoming pedestrians were not visible to drivers because of an adjacent building. Additionally, the exit lane was lined by a five-foot-high wall. The corner was blind to all until the nose of a vehicle began to cross the sidewalk.

When Sylvia and Philip reached the exit, a car driven by a co-op administrator suddenly emerged onto the sidewalk. Sylvia was unable to break her stride and she collided with the car, resulting in a compound fracture of her ankle. The driver called for an ambulance and tended to Sylvia. Philip sprinted home across the tracks to tell Irene. Virginia saw Philip running toward the house without Sylvia and immediately told Irene, who quickly went out to meet Philip. He was panicked and said that Sylvia had been hit by a car. Irene was terrified and, fearing the worst, started for the co-op. Virginia suggested instead that she drive Irene to the co-op and tried to calm her mother by telling her that the accident might not be that serious, as Philip was unhurt.

On their arrival, Irene saw that the ambulance had arrived and paramedics were tending to a conscious Sylvia. Irene did not faint, but she was under extreme stress and could not recall Sylvia's birthdate for the paramedic. Irene rode in the ambulance to the hospital with Sylvia, while Virginia went back to the house to care for her siblings. Postal employees tracked down Nicho on his mail route, and he joined Irene and Sylvia at the hospital. The doctors put Sylvia's leg in a cast, held her overnight, and provided a wheelchair for her recovery.

The appearance of the first responders resulted in a front-page photo and headline in the *Garden City Telegram*. A short time after the accident, the co-op placed a large mirror on the building near the exit, enabling pedestrians and drivers to see one another.

In mid-June 1965, heavy rains fell for two days in eastern Colorado. The dams and reservoirs that were designed to hold excessive rainfall failed and sent floodwaters eastward down the Arkansas River toward Garden City. By the evening on Thursday, June 17, city officials feared the floodwaters would reach homes and businesses, especially those bordering the Arkansas River. They decided to build a sandbag wall on the Santa Fe Railroad's main line tracks to protect as much property as possible. The main line was built on bedrock on slightly higher ground. City officials also understood that diverting the waters to the southside would raise the water levels in the Mexican barrios and increase the severity of damage to the homes. The city's objective was obvious but unsaid—protect the businesses downtown by keeping the floodwaters on the south side of the tracks.

The next day, the floodwaters approached Garden City as the officials predicted. Early in the afternoon, city officials went to speak to the postmaster to ask that Nicho be made available to go on radio to warn the Spanish-speaking community. The postmaster agreed, and within an hour Nicho, in Spanish, advised those living along the tracks that they should immediately evacuate their homes because of the floodwaters. At 4:00 p.m., police cars with flashing red lights, drove the length of the city's two southside streets, Santa Fe and Maple. They told residents over loudspeakers that they must evacuate.

Nicho called Irene and told her to gather their important documents and that he would be home soon to help them. Irene had the children gather and bag two days of clothing and their shoes. She boxed up the albums and records for the radio program. When Nicho arrived, he moved the large kitchen table into the living room and put the television, radio, and other electric appliances on the table top. Irene kept a cedar chest in the basement with her mementos, photographs, and her wedding dress. She asked Nicho to bring up the bulky chest, but he did not and said that he thought the contents would not be damaged. He added that in 1951, the floodwaters reached only Finnup Park and did not reach any homes on Maple or Santa Fe Streets.

Irene arranged for the older children to stay with cousins and friends, while Nicho, Irene, and the younger children stayed with friends who generously took them in. The floodwaters reached South Main Street shortly after dark and headed for the Santa Fe's main line. The sandbag wall held and spared the downtown businesses. Early the next morning, Nicho went to the wall to view the damage to the house. He saw the backs of the houses, which appeared to be floating in a shiny blue pond. The water line on the neighbors' houses on either side were four feet high. The water line did not appear as high on the house, but he could not see the basement windows. He realized then that the waters had likely flooded the basement. Their home was one of approximately two hundred homes south of the main line tracks that were damaged. Far fewer homes north of the tracks suffered damage.

Law enforcement kept anyone from entering the flood area. By Saturday evening, the river had receded and the blue pond had become a dark green, foul-smelling, debris-filled pit. Barrio residents were told that they could not return to their homes for at least a day and to boil their drinking water. Late on Sunday afternoon, city officials gave residents permission to return to their homes. Nicho made his way through heavy mud and muck to the concrete steps at the front door. He entered the house and was nearly sickened by the stench. He was correct in that the waters had not reached the main floor, leaving the table and furniture untouched. But when he peered down the basement steps, he saw standing water that nearly reached the low ceiling. It was a total loss, including the contents of the cedar chest.

The following Monday morning, before reporting to the post office, Nicho borrowed a pump from a neighbor who had emptied the water from his home. Nicho jammed the hose of the pump through the basement window and started the pump. It operated most of the day until the water level in the basement dropped too low to take in water.

Nicho, Marcela, and Virginia had to report for work in the days that followed and left the cleanup to the teenagers. Christina, who had returned from Dodge, led the cleanup crew. Irene stayed upstairs with the toddlers and supervised from a distance. Many photos, books, and keepsakes, including a new Beatles album, were warped and damaged. Nicho instructed the teenage crew to use the outside concrete stairway to drag out the waterlogged drywall, couches, mattresses, and other furniture. Nicho also directed the teens to soak up the remaining water with towels and rags and carry the buckets of water up the stairway to empty them on the street curb.

Nicho returned to the house during his lunch hour and reviewed the slow but steady progress. When he went back to work, Irene asked her children about the contents of the cedar chest. They told her that it was filled with the foul water and nothing was saved. The news pained Irene, even more than the damage to the basement they had labored to build. Her pain was mixed with anger. She had specifically asked Nicho to save the wedding dress. When she told him about the loss of the dress, he apologized, but the apology meant little to Irene. She put her anger aside to focus on the needs of the children and the cleanup. Though the hurt from the loss of her wedding dress lessened over time, it never left her.

The Red Cross drove through Santa Fe and Maple Streets and distributed medical and toiletry kits. They also provided hot meals at Saint Mary's School cafeteria and directed residents to the location where highly recommended typhoid shots were administered. Late in the afternoon, for no apparent reason, law enforcement and city officials allowed the mainly white public to parade down Santa Fe and Maple Streets. The occupants rudely gawked at the residents in their misery and filth as they tried to salvage their homes.

Irene and Nicho stayed with their friends until the basement could be cleaned and repaired. At least a week passed before insurance adjusters were able to assess the damage to the basement. With the money from the insurance and a small loan, Nicho and Irene remodeled the basement over the next two months. Among the improvements were the removal of the gas furnaces and swamp cooler, and the installation of a central heating and air conditioning unit and thin red carpet without padding on the hard tile floor.

Families on Santa Fe and Maple Streets tried to put their lives and homes back in order as the summer months passed. Irene and Nicho converted the three small basement bedrooms into one large bedroom for the four older girls and a small storage room. The crowding eased somewhat when Raphael left to attend a seminary operated by the order of the parish priests, the Missionaries of the Precious Blood. A recruiter for Precious Blood had convinced five eighth-graders and their parents that the boys should pursue a vocation in the priesthood. Many Mexican parents considered a calling to the priesthood a blessing from God and were highly supportive of their sons serving in a Catholic ministry. When Raphael expressed an interest, Irene and Nicho left the decision to him, and when he chose to join his classmates, they agreed to share the expense with Saint Mary's Parish. In late August, an assistant pastor drove a station wagon with the five boys to the seminary in Liberty, Missouri, just outside of Kansas City.

In the fall of 1965, the *D.C. Garcia Show* continued its rise in popularity. Ownership of the radio station changed hands in October with the new call letters KUP-K and a greater wattage and signal strength. As a result of the program's early success, the show was moved to the daytime AM band, and expanded to two hours on Sunday afternoons and ninety minutes on Wednesday afternoons. It was the only Spanish-language radio broadcast in Kansas at the time. The broadcasts provided the growing Mexican population not only with entertaining music but also with public service information. Irene began to go with Nicho to the station and joined him in the booth to better manage the increased advertising and musical selections. She added to her preparations a list of dedication requests from listeners within a 150-mile radius, including the Oklahoma and Texas Panhandles. Their routine and preparation became more efficient as the months passed, and the earnings began to exceed the cost of their time and expenses but never approached highly lucrative.

Rafaela's youngest daughter, Rita, who graduated from Dodge City High School in 1964, married Frank Larobina in December 1965. The amount of work for Rafaela in the home declined somewhat as each child left and when Cayetano retired in 1961. But with three of the older sons and her grandchildren still in Dodge, and Irene's visits with her family in tow, there remained constant traffic in the house. Rafaela always asked her visitors if they were hungry and was quick to put together a meal and snacks for everyone. Salvador became a postal worker, as well, and he frequently stopped to visit Rafaela at the house on Avenue J. She always offered him lunch and a cold drink or hot coffee during his lunch hour.

Rafaela's friends from her days in the Village still came to the house and chatted over sweets and coffee about the latest news in the Mexican community. Rafaela had worked with them to prepare tamales and other foods to raise funds for the construction of the new Guadalupe Church. Cayetano tolerated the visits from her friends but preferred that the women keep them short. She continued to cook and clean for him, but there was no thawing of the cold feelings. Rafaela kept her Catholic faith and walked the two and a half blocks to the church every Sunday and holy day.

When Raphael returned home in the summer of 1966 after a school year at the seminary, all ten of Irene's children were again living at home. With the older girls, now women in their early twenties, and four teenagers, there was a constant flow of family in and out of the house. Marcela worked nights at the hospital, and three of the teenagers had summer jobs. Boyfriends and friends visited throughout the day. Nicho bought a used late 1950s Buick Special to help manage the traffic and get everyone to their jobs on time. Half of the front yard served as a driveway.

At the end of the summer, Raphael returned to the seminary for another school year, and in October, Virginia, and Christina moved to Wichita for work and school. Marcela and her best friend, Ruthe Mesa, daughter of Alfonso Mesa, joined them a few weeks later. Before their departures, each of the girls knelt before Irene and Nicho, who extended their hands over them and prayed for God's blessing and His protection. It was the last time Irene's family of twelve lived together.

14

Election Campaign, Miracle Birth, Cayetano's Fall

In May 1966, Mauricio, Rafaela's youngest, graduated from high school. He was the fifth of Rafaela's children to graduate. After his graduation, Mauricio took aim at a college education, but events in Southeast Asia interfered. In his last two years of high school, the US military increased the number of troops in Vietnam from 16,000 to more than 190,000. He was facing the inevitable draft notice. He took matters into his own hands and joined the Air Force in 1968 and began a four-year commitment. By 1969, he was stationed at Cam Ranh Air Force Base in Vietnam, where he served as a mechanic for F4 Phantom jets.

With Mauricio's service, all of Rafaela's sons had served in the Armed Forces of the United States, with a different son serving in World War II, the Korean War, and the Vietnam War. The irony of their service was that the primary reason Candelaria came to the United States was to keep her children out of warfare. Later, two of Rafaela's grandsons joined the US Marines and saw combat in Vietnam. They survived, but like many of the those who served, on their return they dealt with the demons of combat.

United States historians view 1968 as one of the most tumultuous years since the Civil War. The country was fighting an increasingly unpopular war with heavy casualties in Vietnam. The brutality of the war reached the living rooms of millions when the major television networks broadcast daily reports of the jungle and urban fighting. Demonstrations against the war increased in size, intensity, and number as the year progressed.

Many civil rights leaders believed the money and attention spent on the war effort deprived the civil rights movement of the needed resources for progress. Like everyone, Irene and Nicho wanted the war to end and shared the concern that the war might slow the momentum of the civil rights movement nationally. They were still devoting a considerable amount of their time and energy to nonprofit projects, including fundraising for scholarships, foster homes, and domestic violence shelters. They promoted voting and naturalization awareness and participated in civic forums on community issues.

Garden City had made progress in its social and racial practices, albeit at times in small measure. Restaurants, merchants, movie theaters, and barber shops no longer excluded or segregated patrons of Mexican descent. Charitable community organizations and nonprofits were open to the Mexican community as well. Newspapers and television media included stories of individuals and events in the barrio. The *D.C. Garcia Show* was well established and was a clear sign of the Spanish-speaking community taking a place in the local media.

By the fall of 1968, the number of advertisements and dedications on the *D.C. Garcia Show* began to compete with music for air time. The local merchants buying ads began to broaden, from western wear to women's and menswear, restaurants, grocery stores, beauty salons, jewelry stores, and music shops. Even the local bowling alley advertised. The show also advertised upcoming public dances, concerts, and other fundraising events in the Mexican community. Rather than reduce the music time, Irene and Nicho preferred to speed up delivery of the ads and dedications. The dedications were mostly local, but with the diaspora of the Mexican children of Garden City, the program received mailed requests from former Garden City residents now living in faraway places such as Fresno, California, and Kenosha, Wisconsin. Nicho suggested that he and Irene should alternate reading the ads and that Irene should read the dedications while Nicho cued up the music. The selections included traditional mariachi ballads and popular music from Texas and northern Mexico, including Little Joe and the Latinaires and Los Huracanes del Norte.

Nicho's suggestion to put Irene on the air surprised her. She had agreed to help him from behind the scenes, and that workload increased with the show's popularity. Irene had spoken before small audiences, including community organizations and citizenship classes, but never before had she spoken in Spanish to a listening audience in the thousands. She wasn't sure that her voice and delivery were suitable or that her radio personality could match Nicho's banter. The task was intimidating. But she believed the show served the Spanish-speaking listeners, and she did not want to lose the gains and inroads the program had made with the public in Garden City. Reluctantly, she agreed to the arrangement.

Irene added a practice reading of dedications and ads to her list of show preparations. After a brief introduction, Irene's voice carried across southwest Kansas. She quickly overcame her nervousness and spoke calmly in both English and Spanish. Within a few weeks, the transition from mic to mic was without hesitation or stumble. Later in the year the post office required Nicho to work overtime due to the heavy load of holiday mail and packages, but the overtime hours conflicted with the show's broadcast schedule. Irene was the quick and obvious choice for Nicho's replacement. She took the mic, and with a station engineer cueing the records, she presented the show without major difficulties. She was pleased with her performance and thought she could still improve. She became KUP-K's de facto backup show host, and she would be called upon on occasion in the future. She was the first woman of Mexican descent to host a radio show in Kansas.

In Dodge, two of the show's loyal listeners were Rafaela and Cayetano. They were impressed by Irene's confidence and proud of her performance. Cayetano usually focused on the music when he listened to the show, but like many other listeners, he was unaccustomed to a woman hosting a radio program. Francisca listened to the show separately in her home, but ever insisting on correctness, focused on Nicho's and Irene's Spanish grammar and pronunciation. When they visited Francisca, she pointed out their errors and provided corrections, for which they thanked her politely. Though Irene and Nicho were approaching the age of fifty, their work was still under strict scrutiny by Francisca.

❈

About the time Irene was on the airwaves, Marcela and Christina decided to move from Wichita to Albuquerque, where their uncle David lived. In the new year, Marcela took a position with Lovelace Hospital and Christina took a position as an insurance claims adjuster with Allstate.

Irene and Nicho's fourth and fifth children, Geraldine and Raphael, were seniors in high school and set to graduate in May. With the news that Marcela and Christina were moving to Albuquerque, Raphael, who had left the seminary after two years, applied to the University of New Mexico. He was accepted and left for Albuquerque with his parents' blessing the day after graduation. Geraldine married Richard Duran in August 1969 and moved to Dodge. Virginia also moved from Wichita to Dodge to attend nursing school at Saint Mary of the Plains. She lived with Rafaela and Cayetano.

Irene felt the loss of her children leaving home. And she knew each child left for their own reasons. Reluctantly, she accepted that there was little she could do about the adult choices they made. She hoped that she and Nicho had equipped them with enough faith and strength to allow them to prosper. She decided that she would help them and give counsel when they asked, but she would not otherwise interfere. Irene also felt a little uncomfortable knowing that she welcomed the lower stress and reduced financial burden with the departure of her five oldest. And their absence allowed Irene and Nicho to devote more time and energy to community activities.

Other events, huge and small alike, signaled the changes in Irene's world. In July, two US astronauts walked on the moon. It was a profound achievement in human history. A far less spectacular event, but part of the daily routine that marked familiarity for Irene, was the legislation to consolidate rail passenger service into one line, Amtrak. For all of her lifetime, growing up in the Village and as a married woman, Irene had stood at her kitchen windows and marked the time with the passing passenger trains—the El Capitán, the Super Chief, and the Grand Canyon. Many communities across the United States felt the change as well. Before Amtrak, approximately 360 towns and cities were connected by rail. Amtrak's service eliminated half of those stops. Garden City and Dodge remained on the stop list.

In the fall of 1970, Irene reached a milestone: she became a grandmother. Geraldine gave birth in October to a daughter, Rachel. The women were *muy culeca*, fussing and doting on Rachel with every opportunity. Rachel was Candelaria's fourth generation born in the United States and her third generation born in Kansas.

About this time, Nicho began to talk seriously about an idea he had carried with him along with his mail bag in recent years. He wanted to run for the office of Garden City commissioner. When he had mentioned this possibility in years prior, often at the dinner table, Irene was quietly curious but held back her immediate doubts. Some of the older children thought the idea was cool, while others silently thought the idea highly unrealistic. Nicho explained to Irene that his mail route included several businessmen and public officials with whom he had become acquainted. In public, Nicho had the ability to quickly put people at ease and engage in friendly conversation. The radio program had made his name known to the non-Spanish-speaking residents of Garden City. And his and her work in the community had received coverage both in the *Telegram* and on a local TV station.

Nicho and Irene were acutely aware that men of Mexican descent in Garden City had run for public offices in the past, including the City Commission, school board, and community college board of trustees, but none were ever elected.

At the end of 1970, Nicho decided to run for the City Commission in the following spring. Irene accepted his decision knowing that she would likely expend time and energy on his effort in the face of likely defeat. But she also hoped that his run for office would encourage more Mexicans to participate in the political arena.

Nicho and Irene sought help for his campaign from Dolores Hope and her husband, Clifford Hope Jr., who had served in the Kansas legislature. Clifford Hope Sr. had served in the US House of Representatives. Dolores was a columnist and wrote stories for the *Telegram* and was active in the community. The Hopes were one of the many families who had come to know Nicho during the years he delivered their mail. Officers and members of the G.I. Forum quickly supported Nicho's candidacy. These individuals who actively served the community met at Irene and Nicho's home and formed the Friends of D. C. Garcia Committee to plan and execute a path to election.

On February 11, 1971, Nicho filed for a place on the ballot in the March primary election. The *Telegram* published a front-page article about his filing and included a biography that talked about his family, his employment as a postal carrier, the radio program, and his work with community service organizations. At the same time, the committee began to produce brochures and cards for distribution to Garden City residents urging them to register to vote and to vote for D. C. Hank Garcia.

Twelve candidates were on the primary ballot held on March 9. The six candidates receiving the most votes advanced to the general election scheduled for the following month. Irene, Nicho, and the committee believed that whether he survived the cutoff or not, the vote count would be close. They were right. Nicho's vote total placed him in the fourth position, with twenty more votes than the fifth-place candidate and thirty-nine more than sixth place. He had overcome the first hurdle. The committee's emotions quickly turned from doubt and relief to surprise, hope, and determination. His vote total put him within sixty-five votes of third place. In the general election, the two candidates receiving the most votes serve four-year terms and the third-place candidate serves a two-year term. The committee knew they were within reach of the prize. Irene thought Nicho's primary showing alone was a notable achievement and inspiration for the Mexican community, especially its younger members. She was happy for him and his success. It was a dream he pursued, and now he was halfway to the finish.

The committee immediately ramped up its campaign efforts. They had four weeks to devise a plan to raise his vote count to the third slot and put it into action. They identified and focused on precincts where Nicho received some votes but still might have the potential for more. The committee bought newspaper ads, both large and small, highlighting Nicho as a hard worker for his family and the people of Garden City and his understanding of the issues of all the people of the city. Irene hosted the radio program alone to avoid any issues of unfair access to media. Supporters and family members, including nine-year-old Lisa, thirteen-year-old Philip, and ten-year-old Chuck, went door-to-door asking for votes. The committee asked the G.I. Forum and Latin American Club members to ask friends and family to vote for Nicho and spread the word. The committee also asked individuals and influential community members to send letters of recommendation to the newspaper editor. The letters strategically appeared in the *Telegram* in the final days of the campaign.

On the evening of April 6, Nicho and the other candidates gathered with supporters at election headquarters. A local radio station reported the results as votes were received and counted. Irene was at the house getting ready for what they hoped would be a celebration at the house later in the evening. She and the children listened intently with each report of the count. The initial reports put Nicho in the middle of the pack. But with each new report his count rose and approached third position. Tension and excitement built in the house. The children were exuberant while Irene tempered her emotions to avoid a premature celebration. Nicho's vote count reached the third position and did not stop. Soon his count was in the second position. With each advance the house filled with more and more friends and supporters. All began to believe that an historic night for Garden City was at hand. With few votes remaining to be counted, it was certain that Nicho would be elected.

A short time later, Nicho called the house and asked for Irene. He said, "The counting is over. We have done it! I've been elected."

With watery eyes, she responded through her emotions, "Gracias a Dios. Gracias a Dios. I am so happy and proud of you." Holding the phone and looking to the guests in the house, she nodded her head. Cheers and clapping burst throughout the house. Tears were shed.

Nicho continued, "That's not all. I got the most votes!"

"Dios mío!" Irene responded softly. All she could say was, "Congratulations, Nicho. Congratulations. Come home. There is a crowd of people here waiting to celebrate with you."

With joy and satisfaction, he answered, "I'm on my way."

On the radio, the other candidates were asked for their thoughts on Nicho receiving the most votes. At a loss for words, they replied, "No comment."

The celebration was on at the house on Santa Fe Street. Many friends of different backgrounds, Mexican, white, and Black, who he knew from grade school to the present, came to congratulate him, give him their accolades, and express their pride at his election.

The following day, the *Telegram*'s front-page headlines reported that Nicho led the field of candidates in eleven of thirteen precincts and missed first place in another by one vote. The practice of newly elected city commissioners was to select the candidate with the most votes to serve as mayor for a one-year term. Nicho was elated with his victory but acknowledged his lack of experience as a commission member. He told the commission he would not submit his name for the mayor's position. Irene was in full agreement with his decision, knowing that Nicho was adept at learning on the job. Those who are first to rise to a position of leadership have no margin for error. Any mistake becomes ammunition for those who argue that newcomers are inherently incapable from the start.

Nicho was sworn in as commissioner and vice mayor at the next City Council meeting. The next day, the *Telegram* featured just above the fold of the front page a picture depicting Nicho and the other new commissioners taking the oath of office. In striking irony, the headline of the top story above the photo read: "Superintendent Answers Charges." The allegations, among other complaints, were that the school district discriminated against Mexican students with regard to dropout rates and limited participation in the school lunch programs.

After the election, Irene took a step back and thought about the result. She admired her husband's willingness to meet the challenge and to accept the support of others to accomplish what many people thought was nearly impossible. The voters put their political faith in him, and she made every effort to ensure that he always put his best foot forward for the city, the Mexican community, and himself. Overall, she thought the election campaign—which included her effort and contribution—was astounding.

Nicho continued working full-time at the post office while he served on the City Commission. Irene added Nicho's preparation for commission matters to her daily calendar, which still included the radio show. She had also begun to work part-time helping parents enroll their children into the local Head Start program, which provided educational and health services for low-income families. And they were still raising a family of five children with three teenagers.

The oldest of the teenagers, Maria, the sixth child, graduated a month after the election. She, too, received Irene and Nicho's blessing before she left home in the fall to attend Fort Hays State University in Hays, Kansas. Sylvia, who followed Maria, was a sophomore in high school. With Irene working at Head Start, Nicho's work on the Commission, and the remaining children in school or working after school, the traffic in and out of the home remained heavy during 1971 and 1972. Nicho especially was always moving. Some might describe his pace as burning the candle at both ends. Delivering mail, the back and forth between Commission meetings, driving to and from the radio station—all were taking their toll, and the smoking and alcohol weren't helping.

By mid-1972, Nicho was struggling to breathe and became easily fatigued. Irene convinced him to see the family doctor. After many medical tests, the doctor told Nicho that, apart from his asthma, his lungs were developing emphysema and that he was sick with high blood pressure and diabetes. The doctor told him directly that he needed to stop smoking and drinking and to change his diet. He also prescribed chlordiazepoxide, a medication to treat anxiety and withdrawal symptoms. Irene made healthier meals, but Nicho avoided them when possible. Nicho did slow his pace initially, but after a few months he was back to his usual nonstop activities.

Another dynamic family event in mid-1972 was Christina's wedding announcement. She was living in Albuquerque and planned to marry Leo Padilla in December in Garden City at the newly created parish, Saint Dominic. Irene and Virginia took the lead in planning the wedding. Five of Christina's sisters were bridesmaids, and two uncles and their wives served as *padrino* and *madrina*—sponsors of the bride and groom.

Sixteen-year-old Sylvia was one of the bridesmaids. During the weekend of events, a member of the wedding party asked Irene if Sylvia was pregnant. Irene was taken aback by the question. She was not aware of any such thing. The questioner said that, nonetheless, Sylvia appeared to be pregnant. Irene wondered what prompted the question. There was no apparent baby bump while Sylvia was dressed in her bridesmaid's gown. Her appearance did not differ from her sisters. Still, Irene could not put the question out of her mind. Her greatest apprehension was Nicho's response if it were true. He would become very angry.

Irene hoped to learn the answer without asking Sylvia directly. If Sylvia were pregnant, Irene would have to tell Nicho and deal with his anger. A few days after the wedding, Irene asked Marcela and Virginia to look under Sylvia's blouse. Days later, the older sisters followed Sylvia into the bathroom and tried half-heartedly. But Sylvia, fullheartedly, stopped them. Irene still had no answer.

Irene expected all her children to abide by the rules of the Church. Despite the changing attitudes of some in society in the 1970s, in the eyes of the Church, premarital sex was mortally sinful. Many in society viewed an unwed mother as a dishonor to the family name, especially in small communities.

On December 18, 1972, Irene began her morning routine: making breakfast for the children and driving them to their schools. But on that morning, Sylvia told Irene that she was cramping and did not feel well and wanted to stay home. She did not tell Irene that the cramps had started at midnight. Irene did not argue with her and left for the schools and her job at Head Start.

At about 1:30 that afternoon, Sylvia felt a strong urge to push. Virginia had just left for the hospital for her swing shift, leaving Sylvia alone in the house with the doors locked. Unsure of precisely what was taking place, Sylvia went into the bathroom. She sat, then stood, then squatted and pushed and saw two small legs protruding from her body. Seventeen-year-old Sylvia, alone in the house, delivered a breech baby without modern medical care or a midwife. On her own, Sylvia reached down and pulled the baby out of the birth canal. She wrapped the boy with his umbilical cord in a blanket and walked to the phone in the kitchen, trailing blood. She called Irene at her work and said, "Mom, you need to come home right now!"

Irene could hear the baby crying in the background and could only say, "Oh my God! Oh my God!" And again, "Oh my God!" She hung up the phone and drove to the house, arriving within ten minutes.

Sylvia stood while she waited for Irene. She walked to the front door, still trailing blood, when she saw Irene drive up to the house. She unlocked and opened the door for her mother. Irene was still in shock and exclaimed as she burst through the door, "Oh my God! Sylvia Marie! What have you got here?!" But Irene brought her emotion under control and her mother's instinct to protect an infant rose to the surface. She asked Sylvia, "Is that baby crying?"

"He's a boy, mom! And he is okay. We are fine!"

Irene led Sylvia and the baby to a bedroom and told her to lie down with the child. She called for an ambulance and began mopping up the blood trail that Sylvia had left as she moved about the house. While she continued to mop, she yelled out to Sylvia again, "Is that baby crying?"

Sylvia answered, "Yes, mom. He is fine."

Irene did not want to draw attention to a possible scandal and was disappointed when the ambulance arrived with sirens blaring. The EMTs asked Irene to leave the bedroom while they examined Sylvia and the baby. After a short while, they emerged and reported that mother and baby were fine. They told Irene they were going to transfer the pair on a stretcher and take them to the emergency room at the hospital. They offered to let Irene to ride along, but she turned the offer down so that she could pick up the children and prepare to tell Nicho.

As Irene waited in the front yard for Sylvia and her baby to be removed from the house, neighborhood women made their way to the house to see the commotion. Irene had to explain to her neighbors that her daughter had just given birth, alone. The women tried to comfort Irene and show their support. One elderly woman who spoke only Spanish assured Irene that her daughter and baby would be fine and that women who delivered alone were "strong women, real women." Before leaving for the hospital, Irene called Virginia, explained what had happened, and asked her to meet them in the emergency room.

At the emergency room, Sylvia delivered the afterbirth. Doctors cut the umbilical cord and gave her two units of blood. Since the baby was delivered in a nonsterile environment, he was not placed in the nursery with other newborns. Instead, he and Sylvia were assigned their own room. Irene visited Sylvia in the room for a short while, but they only spoke about the baby's condition and did not address the other obvious issues.

Birth is a miracle, but never so much as on that day.

Once Irene saw that Sylvia and baby were stable, she turned to the looming task at hand: telling Nicho. Irene called him at the post office and said, "Nicho, you need to come straight home after work. I have to talk with you."

"What about?"

"I'll tell you when you get here."

He accepted her response and said, "Fine, I'll see you soon."

Virginia was able to take the day off to help Irene deal with him. They thought that Nicho's response to the news might be tempered if he took one of the pills that his doctor had prescribed for anxiety. They planned to have him take the pill before recounting the events. They waited at the kitchen table for Nicho to get home.

When Nicho arrived and entered the kitchen, they asked him to sit down. Unconcerned, he asked, "What do you want to tell me?"

Irene said, "I want you to take a Librium first."

Her response confused, then annoyed him. "Why should I take one? I don't need one."

"Nicho, I still want you to take one before you hear what I have to tell you."

He took the pill, and said, "Okay. Now what do you want to tell me?"

Irene was careful to speak calmly and seriously. "Nicho, Sylvia is in the hospital." Before he could respond, she went on. "She delivered a baby here at the house this afternoon."

He paused for a brief moment, then asked, "A baby? Here at the house?"

"Yes. They're in the hospital and doing fine."

When he fully grasped the meaning of her words, he stood up and raged, "How did that happen? In my house?" He cursed loudly. "That's all I need right now! A daughter, not married, having a baby here, at the house! Everybody in town is going to be talking about it! How could she do this?" Still furious, but a little less loudly, he said, "I suppose her boyfriend, Ruben, is the father."

Irene knew this moment called for protection, and she interrupted his rant. She said firmly, "Nicho, do not do anything to Sylvia." She paused for a second and added, "Or anyone else." His angry comments began to slow and the volume of his voice continued to fall. Perhaps he was feeling the effects of the Librium.

For the rest of the evening, the house remained full of anger and tension, but the incredible day the family had lived ended without further incident and with baby and mother doing well.

The hospital kept Sylvia and the baby for observation for three days. Irene made only one brief visit. Again, they talked only about the baby. Irene was disappointed, angry, and embarrassed by the out-of-wedlock birth. She was careful to avoid giving Nicho the impression that she was fully supportive of Sylvia's situation or that she rejected his view of the events. Virginia visited Sylvia every day and was the conduit of communication between Irene and Sylvia. Nicho never went to the hospital to see Sylvia or the baby.

By the time Sylvia was dismissed from the hospital, she and her boyfriend, Ruben Nungaray, had named the boy Carlitos. When she and Carlitos arrived at the house on Santa Fe, there was a crib in the bedroom where they were to sleep. Irene had told Nicho that he should buy one, and despite his anger and frustration, he did so. He decided that Sylvia should marry Ruben immediately to right the situation and perhaps limit any public scandal. Irene, still angry and frustrated herself that Sylvia did not disclose her pregnancy, was unsure. She knew the Church required marriage for mothers and mothers-to-be. But she had seen with her own eyes that a marriage blessed by the Church did not mean a marriage with blessings or joy. In the end, she chose to follow the tenets of the Church and made no attempt to interfere with Nicho's insistence.

During the week after Christmas, Nicho said to Irene, "I want you to call the parish priest to arrange a date so Sylvia and Ruben can get married."

Rather than defy him directly, Irene tried to delay the marriage by asking, "How soon do you want it set?"

Without hesitation, Nicho answered, "As soon as possible." He continued sternly, "And I want her out of this house as soon as she's married."

This demand surprised Irene. Carlitos was only a week old. "They don't have any money, Nicho. If you want her out of the house, you're going to have to pay for a place for them to stay."

"Fine! I'll pay."

The parish priest told Irene that the first available date was Saturday, January 6.

Nicho was finally ready to speak to Sylvia directly. He, along with Irene, went into her bedroom. Coldly, he told her, "I am disowning you. You are not my child. You are a major embarrassment to me." Sylvia had been afraid of her father's reaction and braced herself for a harsh response. His words were more hurtful than she expected, but she kept her composure. Irene hoped that Nicho would keep his anger in check but was nonetheless surprised by his mean-spiritedness. But she could not challenge him at that moment lest she inflame his anger to a higher state. Sylvia said nothing. There was nothing to be gained by trying.

Nicho ended with a demand: "Tell Ruben to make himself available. I want to speak to the both of you together, as soon as possible." Sylvia only nodded.

When Ruben and Sylvia met with Nicho and Irene, he told them, "You need to do the right thing and get married. We spoke to the priest and you can get married on the sixth at noon. I've already found you an apartment and paid the first month's rent." He looked at Ruben and said, "I expect you to be there on the sixth. Is that understood?"

Both responded meekly. "Yes."

Nicho then said, "You have my blessing. But you don't deserve it."

Irene knew he was being overly harsh. She always hoped that he would be reasonable, but his anger and short temper got the better of him in this case.

On Saturday, January 6, the shotgun wedding was held at the new parish church. Virginia was there, along with a friend, to witness the ceremony. Lisa, the youngest sister, was also present. Irene, still uncertain about the marriage, did not want to be present and instead stayed at home with

Carlitos. Nicho worked at the post office that day and attended the ceremony in his uniform during his lunch hour.

The following week, Sylvia went back to high school. Each morning, Sylvia drove to the house on Santa Fe and left Carlitos with Virginia. Sylvia's classes ended at noon, so she was able to get him before Virginia left for her shift at the hospital. In the weeks that followed, there was an awkwardness between Irene and Sylvia. Most days their exchange was limited to child care tips and discussing how Carlitos managed through the night. Nicho was usually out of the house before Sylvia arrived, resulting in rare and brief interaction.

A year would pass before Irene and Sylvia lost their awkwardness. Carlitos was a sweet and happy infant. With each smile, new activity, and skill, he brought out the warmth of the women who cared for him. Even Nicho's coldheartedness began to thaw when Carlitos began to sit up, hold his bottle, and take tiny steps.

❧

The United States began 1973 by entering an agreement to end its involvement in the Vietnam War. The parties agreed to a ceasefire, North Vietnamese forces were to make no advances southward, South Vietnam was to hold elections, US forces would withdraw from Vietnam, and US prisoners of war were to be released. By the end of March, US troops were out of the country and on their way home. The war that brought division to the country and scarred so many young men for the rest of their lives came to an end.

Back on the home front, Garden City held its next election for three seats on the City Commission. The top vote-getter was Cecil Baker, who wanted to follow the tradition of selecting the highest vote getter as mayor. But Nicho also wanted the mayor's position, having declined it in 1971 and 1972 to acquire more experience. Three votes were needed for the mayor's seat. One of the newly elected commissioners supported Baker, while the other supported Nicho, who also had the support of the commissioner elected with him in 1971. With Nicho casting his vote for himself, he served as Garden City's first mayor of Mexican descent for the next year. Nicho's fear that Sylvia giving birth to Carlitos would hurt his political ambitions turned out to be of no consequence in any way in the contest for mayor.

For Irene, it was difficult at times to believe that a man with such rough edges with his family could persuade and charm others outside the family. His selection as mayor highlighted that contrast. Still, she could not say that her husband did not provide for their family. Together, by word and example, they instilled a work ethic in their children and the values of sacrifice and service to neighbors and community.

Months later, a Garden City resident challenged the *Telegram*'s naming Nicho as Garden City's first Hispanic mayor. The challenger argued that a cattleman from Texas, Henry M. De Cordova, served as mayor in 1884. But, he was born in New Orleans and his family ancestry was from Holland. Additionally, De Cordova, his father, and brother, all fought for the Confederacy, which meant that he was ineligible to hold public office until the Kansas Legislature removed the restriction in his last month as mayor.

Nicho's many illnesses, particularly the lung diseases, continued to weaken his system. He took his medications as ordered, but there was little improvement, only a tenuous management. Shortness of breath, pain, and fatigue were constant. Still, he kept on with a steady pace of work, the radio show, and community activities. In early November 1973, Nicho drove to the radio station studio, located about three miles west of town. He was late and decided to take Maple Street on the south edge of the city. He thought traffic might be light and that he could drive faster. But Maple Street turned into a dirt road on leaving the city, and there was no shoulder—only a ditch ran alongside it. La Pelona took note and began to follow Nicho. Nicho drove too close to the edge and it gave way. He tried to veer, but the dirt edge was too steep to hold the 1969 station wagon and it rolled into the ditch.

When the roll stopped, Nicho tried to open the driver's door and get out of the caramel-colored wagon. An ambulance and sheriff's deputy were quickly on the scene. The EMTs determined that he had no broken bones or bleeding but was likely bruised internally. They told him he would feel stiff and sore in the days ahead and to see his doctor. Irene and Virginia drove him home. Irene stayed with Nicho to watch for any medical problems that might appear. She called the radio station to say that Nicho was unavailable because of the accident. The non-Spanish-speaking tech at the station improvised and played Spanish-language records without commentary. During the ninety-minute program he broke in every fifteen minutes or so and announced the station's call letters.

Nicho did see the doctor for the pains from the rollover, but the doctor responded with more than prescriptions. Coldly and calmly, he said, "Henry, we have had this discussion before, you need to stop your smoking and drinking. If you don't stop, you'll be dead in a year." Something about the doctor's tone landed in Nicho's psyche. He knew he was sick, but he hadn't realized that death was already on the horizon. This time, the doctor's warning frightened him, and it frightened Irene as well. He wanted to live, and he was willing to endure the pain and stress of his life. He did as the doctor ordered and decided to end his addictions the hard way, cold turkey. He immediately stopped smoking and drinking. Irene was surprised by his choice of method but thankful for his decision. Little time passed before he began to experience withdrawal symptoms. Two months later, Nicho announced that he would not run in April for reelection on the City Commission.

Despite the many difficulties, higher education kept its place of importance in Irene and Nicho's family. The hope for their children's education was slowly, but surely, on its way to reality. Sylvia graduated from high school in May 1974 and walked with her class on graduation night, with Carlitos in attendance. The family's formal education showed a steady progression: Candelaria's children had little educational opportunity, while half of Rafaela's ten children earned their high school diplomas. With Sylvia's graduation, seven of Irene's children had earned theirs, with three more in the wings.

At the same time, Raphael, who had married Berta Zavala in late 1973, graduated from the University of New Mexico with a bachelor's degree. Maria temporarily interrupted her studies at Fort Hays State after the fall semester and joined Marcela in Albuquerque. Six months later, she married Jesus Perez and returned to Garden City. Maria would go on to complete her studies at Saint Mary of the Plains and graduated with a bachelor's degree in education in June of 1977. Later, she taught in an elementary school. Irene and Nicho were relieved and proud that she had the determination to complete her studies though she had married. In the fall of 1976, Irene and Nicho gave their blessing to yet another child leaving home for college, when Philip enrolled at the University of Kansas in pursuit of a degree in journalism.

David, Rafaela's son, had nearly completed the required credits for his bachelor's degree at the University of New Mexico when the Santa Fe ended a period of layoffs. He asked for a leave of absence to complete his degree, but the Santa Fe refused. The dispute led to a discussion with human resources in the Chicago home office. The personnel director asked David what he wanted in order to resolve the matter. He told them that he wanted an extension of time for his studies, and on his return, he wanted a say in who was hired and fired. The administrator agreed to the extension and advised David that if he completed his degree, he should apply for an HR position that was in development. David finished his bachelor's degree and was later hired as the employment supervisor for Albuquerque. Five months later, in October 1975, David was promoted to employment assistant manager in Amarillo, Texas. He stayed in Amarillo until July 1977, when he was promoted to the home office in Chicago.

❦

During the events of the early 1970s, Irene's uncle Leon, who was then seventy-seven years old, called Irene from California to ask for help moving back to Kansas. He had left for California in 1946, under threat of a vendetta, but now his wife had passed away and no other family could house him. Nicho had an acquaintance who owned property with a stable for a few horses and a small groomer's residence. The stables were just outside the city limits, a few minutes from the house on Santa Fe. Leon agreed to care for the horses and in return receive a small salary and live rent-free in the groomer's house. Francisca agreed to leave her own small home in Dodge to join her younger brother.

One spring day in 1975, Leon fell while working with the horses in the corral. A light rain had turned the corral into a muddy quagmire, and when eighty-one-year-old Leon tried to walk across it in his rubber boots, he sank into the mud and could not move. As he struggled to get out, he lost his balance and fell. He yelled to Francisca for help. But she, of course, was too feeble to venture into the mud and rescue him. She phoned Irene, who immediately sent Philip and Chuck to free him from the mud.

On a previous occasion, Leon was burning trash while wearing his work gloves. When he finished the burn, he went inside and laid his gloves on some papers. However, his gloves still held embers and set the papers on fire. Leon and Francisca smelled the smoke but they could not find the source. Francisca called Irene and told her, "The house is on fire!" Nicho flew out the front door with Chuck right behind him. Nicho yelled at

Irene to call the fire department. Nicho arrived at the casita expecting to see orange and yellow flames crawling out of the windows, but he saw only a little smoke. Leon had found the burning papers and thrown them into a trash can, then carried the trash can out of the house. The house was smoky, but it did not suffer smoke damage. The firefighters checked the house, declared it safe, and told Leon that he needed to ensure that any tools or items used in a burn were carefully examined when finished.

Leon's fall and the frightening brush with a house fire brought to the front a reality that Irene knew would eventually appear. Leon could no longer safely work—at the stables or anywhere else. When Leon initially returned to Kansas, Irene and Nicho had discussed the possibility of Leon living with them or building a casita for him in their backyard, but the availability of the residence at the stables temporarily ended that idea. It was revived after Leon's fall.

The back half of the lot of Irene's home had enough space for a small two-room structure for Leon and Francisca, so the question was one of construction costs, not land purchase. Irene and Nicho approached Leon and Francisca with the idea, and asked if they would be able and willing to share the costs. The elderly sister and brother were in full agreement to build and pay for costs. The construction plan for the low-cost casita was straight out of the Village playbook: find local people with construction experience and skill, supply the labor with friends and family, and use affordable and available materials. Irene enlisted her cousin Tony Rodriguez to build the casita. He had become a master-carpenter building luxury homes in Palm Springs, California, and agreed to come to Garden City to supervise the casita's construction. He never thought to charge the family for his own time and labor but asked that they cover wages for an assistant, the cost of materials, and city fees. Irene and Nicho offered room and board for the two men and Tony accepted. During this time, Irene still worked with Head Start and maintained a household that included Francisca and Leon. Without hesitation, she added to her list of chores the cooking and laundry for Tony and the assistant.

Tony set the project in motion by having Nicho and his sons and three sons-in-law dig the trenches for the cement foundation during their after work hours. Nicho brought in friends with experience to lay out the plumbing trenches and pour the cement. Tony arrived in August with his plans on notebook paper. He directed the workers and kept them moving, especially the young men who provided much of the heavy labor. Within a short time, the framing of the casita was up and the roof added on. The crew then moved to the casita's interior, installing the flooring, windows, and drywall. The last piece of the exterior construction was a walkway connecting the casita's back door to the main house. The builders also installed a buzzer between the two homes so that Leon and Francisca could easily call for assistance when needed.

After four weeks, Tony and his assistant returned to California, leaving the painting and installation of appliances to Nicho and the remaining crew. Leon and Francisca were in their new home by fall. Irene was pleased with the casita, and her aunt and uncle were in a safer place. For Irene, the only drawback was the loss of the view from her kitchen windows. For years she had enjoyed the quiet before the family and city started their days.

Another event that ended the morning tortilla-making view was the establishment of El Perico Charro Tortilla Factory in 1974. The factory altered the routines of many Mexican women, for whom a quick trip to El Perico replaced the morning hours of tedious tortilla making.

During the building of the casita, Rafaela understood that Irene wanted to help Francisca and Leon but she felt that they added to Irene's burdens. For her part, Irene continued to visit Rafaela in Dodge as in the past. Rafaela continued to visit Irene in Garden City on occasion and pay a polite visit to Francisca and Leon as well.

Though Nicho was willing to work on the project with Tony and the others, he did not have the same energy as in past years. He was often short of breath and tired, and he worked at a slower pace. When the fall season began to turn into the windy and cold days of winter, Nicho's health worsened. Irene began suggesting that he go to the doctor, but he refused, saying that he would "feel better soon." In early December, Irene and Virginia insisted that he go to the hospital emergency room. Finally, Nicho conceded. He was immediately admitted, suffering from asthma and bronchial pneumonia. Irene was afraid that he was gravely ill. She pushed aside her frustration with his refusal to see the doctor right away and stayed at his bedside until he was treated and stabilized. She returned to work and resumed her chores as head of the household. The doctor released Nicho from the hospital ten days later.

In all the difficult challenges that occurred, there were bright and happy days for Irene. During the course of 1975, four grandchildren were born, all girls. Her three married daughters, Christina, Geraldine, and Sylvia, all gave birth, as did her only daughter-in-law, Berta. Two of the baby girls lived in Garden City and, along with three older grandchildren, were frequent visitors to abuelita's house on Santa Fe Street. Another bright moment was Marcela's announcement in August that she was entering the convent of the School Sisters of Notre Dame. Marcela was a certified midwife and had delivered more than one hundred babies in her nursing career in Albuquerque. Her mission as a member of the Sisters of Notre Dame was to serve the congregation as a midwife in Catholic nursing facilities. Her decision surprised and pleased Irene and Nicho, who believed that their faith was rewarded with Marcela's decision to choose a religious vocation. Irene's only caution was that Marcela be certain about her decision.

While Irene was quite content that God had blessed her family with Marcela's entry into a Catholic religious community, she was troubled by the emotional display of her youngest daughter, thirteen-year-old Lisa. On one occasion, Irene heard Lisa in her bedroom crying and upset. Irene asked what was wrong. Lisa explained that her friend, Molly, who was five years older, said that she was getting married to her boyfriend.

Lisa said to Irene, "I'm hurt and disappointed that she is not getting married to me."

Irene was taken aback and unsympathetic. Irene said in a loud, stern voice that she rarely used, "Oh my gosh! This is ridiculous! It's not normal for a thirteen-year-old girl to cry over a young woman getting married." It was not just the "abnormality" of a girl's misplaced affection that caused Irene's harsh response. Irene genuinely feared that Lisa might lose her immortal soul and be condemned to hell if she were a lesbian. There were no other discussions between Lisa and Irene on the matter. Nicho once inadvertently referred to Lisa as "mijo." Irene admonished him and told him not to use that term because Lisa needed to be sure she was a girl, and that girls don't like other girls. There were gay individuals in the Mexican community, but most hid their sexual orientation, knowing that they would not be well accepted or rejected.

In 1976, after twenty-eight years, Nicho's health ended his work with the post office. He tired easily and was out of breath on his mail route. The change from outdoor physical laborer to house caretaker left him restless, feeling trapped and failing as the breadwinner. He wanted to work, so he took a position with the county as an after-hours courthouse janitor. But that effort was short-lived, as the cleaning chemicals affected his breathing. He suffered the same result when he took a job as a security guard at the gate of the local meatpacking plant. He simply no longer had the energy. That same year, he and Irene ended their hosting of the radio broadcasts. When station management asked for recommendations with the selection of their replacements from the community, they did not hesitate to suggest local individuals and couples who were well-received and active in the Mexican community in Garden City.

In Dodge, Rafaela and Cayetano had been living alone since Virginia had finished nursing school in 1971. Their children and grandchildren visited them, but less often as they grew older. Long-standing friendships with women from the Village and eastside barrio continued. The women regularly stopped to visit and update each other's family news and share barrio gossip. In the heat of summer evenings, Rafaela and her company sat and chatted on the small, shaded front porch.

Cayetano suffered from arthritis and by the early 1970s, his walking pace had slowed. In those years, he walked to the church and began attending daily morning mass. Rafaela regarded his daily worship as a poor attempt to undo his many transgressions. She dutifully continued to perform the household chores, rolling out the tortilla testales and cooking the meals, all the while listening to a small kitchen radio. When Cayetano drifted into memories of the past and spoke of the good days, she calmly, directly, and accurately pointed to his wrongdoings that made "good days" impossible. When she did so, he remained silent, made no denials, and did not argue. They continued to hold each other at a cold distance.

On September 24, 1977, in the early afternoon, Rafaela, her daughter Rita, and Rita's three young daughters left the house for a brief shopping trip. Rita told Cayetano to remain in the house until they returned. But apparently at some point he disregarded her words. A passing postman found him lying on the ground near the porch step. How Cayetano fell from the porch remains unexplained. He may have suffered some acute medical episode or simply may have lost his balance and tripped. His chronic arthritis resulted in an uneven shuffle that might have contributed to his fall. The postal worker helped Cayetano to sit on the porch and stayed with him until Rita returned. He complained about pain in his upper left arm and shoulder. Rita immediately took him to Dodge City Regional Hospital.

Salvador and Rafaela joined Rita at the hospital at Cayetano's bedside.

That evening, Cayetano lost consciousness and did not speak or open his eyes. His condition remained unchanged after days. By September 30, he had developed pneumonia and the doctor recommended that the family be called to see him. Irene and Virginia immediately left Garden City for Dodge. Irene could not believe the suddenness of the possibility of her father's passing. He was not in good health—he suffered from hardening of the arteries—but there were no signs of impending death. Yet within a week, she found herself at his hospital bedside along with her siblings. She had no opportunity to talk with him. In the hope that he could hear and understand her, she told him her name and that she loved him. Irene also stayed close to Rafaela.

As each of the siblings arrived over the next two days, they entered Cayetano's room and spoke to him. But still, he did not open his eyes or speak. Irene again spoke to him softly and encouraged him by saying that Maria Paz was on her way from California. The doctor told the family that with each passing hour, regaining consciousness was unlikely. They could only pray and keep vigil. At midday on Monday, October 3, Maria Paz arrived and went to see her father. She held his hand and told him who she was. He did not respond in any way. The feel of Cayetano's room and the hallway outside his door was heavily somber and gloomy. In the late afternoon, with Rafaela and their children present, he passed away at age eighty-one. Ultimately, the cause of death was hypostatic pneumonia, the collection of fluid in the lungs that occurs when lying down for long periods of time.

Rafaela and the family arranged a rosary service for Tuesday night and the burial for Wednesday morning at Maple Grove Cemetery. During the services, Rafaela, Irene, and the other women wore black dresses and footwear and covered their faces with black veils. The brothers were in black suits and wore dark sunglasses. Irene did not feel the reality and weight of her father's passing until she was at the cemetery. She cried softly during the rituals of the Catholic burial. She knew her father was a man of faults, and she regretted the mistakes he made, but there was little she could do, then or in the present. She thought about her mother's well-being and believed that so long as Rafaela lived with family, she would not suffer a widow's loneliness. And, as beneficiary of Cayetano's railroad pension, she had some financial security.

Despite the discord of their marriage, Rafaela and Cayetano had raised their children and lived their lives together over the course of fifty-eight years. Rafaela was stoic throughout the events at the hospital, rosary, and cemetery. She did not weep or sob openly, keeping any tears private. She was gracious to all who came to pay their respects. After the burial, Irene went with Rafaela to the home on Avenue J. A few months after Cayetano's passing, Rafaela visited Irene in Garden City. At lunch time, Francisca and Leon came over from the casita and joined them. At one point, Francisca sadly said, "I miss my brother. He was such a good man."

Rafaela put down her spoon, looked at Francisca, and said firmly, "No, he was not. He was a terrible man!"

The table became silent, with hardly a word spoken by anyone thereafter. Irene knew there was hostility between the two women, but she had never seen it so openly displayed.

15

The Disclosure, the Board of Education, the Last Relief

In the years following Nicho's retirement, he became a househusband and required less of Irene's attention. Irene committed more and more of her time to the field of service that gave her a great sense of worth and accomplishment—education. She took correspondence courses from colleges and universities to earn credits in education and bilingual education and attended trainings and workshops for English as a Second Language (ESL) curriculum. She worked as a teacher's aide in a bilingual classroom for the local school district, Unified School District 457. She devoted evenings to adult education and taught ESL to Spanish speakers at Garden City Community College. She championed children's issues beyond education as well, writing an op-ed piece in the *Telegram* in support of continued funding for a children's development center for disadvantaged and disabled children.

Irene's opportunity to work in bilingual education in the schools was largely due to a beef-packing plant three miles east of Garden City. Farmland Foods operated the plant in the 1970s with a workforce of nearly two hundred employees, the vast majority of them men of Mexican descent and immigrants with growing families. Like the children who were raised in the Village, Spanish was their first language and they spoke English at different levels of proficiency. But unlike in the Village, the schools in Garden City were not segregated. The Spanish speakers in Garden City were left to sink or swim in the English-only classroom without a systematic program of instruction. Additionally, as in prior decades, some parents pulled their children from the classroom to work in the sugar beet fields or with other crops. Predictably, these children performed poorly in school, and many withdrew without a diploma to enter the labor force.

But in 1974, the United States Supreme Court ruled in the case of *Lau v. Nichols* that school districts receiving federal funds must provide non-English-speaking students instruction in the English language in order to provide an equal education. In 1980, a group of Garden City parents, with the support of some teachers and aides in the bilingual classrooms, argued to the school board that funds for the bilingual program were improperly used to support the general fund. The district took the federal funds and labeled some classrooms as bilingual, but the teachers assigned to the classrooms often had little qualification or experience in a bilingual program. The classroom aides, who were paid less than minimum wage, often lacked classroom training and were used more as interpreters than instructors.

When the school board was slow to respond to the parents' complaints, the parental group sued the school district the following year. Irene did not favor filing a lawsuit. Irene knew the complaints of the parents were based in fact, but she preferred to avoid the direct legal conflict. Not only was she employed by the district, but her daughter, Maria, was then a teacher at one of the district's barrio schools. She was particularly torn because her son, Raphael, was one of the attorneys of record for the parent plaintiffs. She was also leery of public criticism and the potential negative media coverage of the litigation. She and Nicho believed the progress that the Mexican community had made might be undone with the lawsuit. Irene hoped that the school district and parent group might resolve the issues without litigation.

When a federal judge refused to dismiss the parents' lawsuit, the parents, their representatives, and the school district began the negotiations that eventually led to a settlement agreement. Implementation of some of the terms began immediately. Teacher recruiting efforts were undertaken, and classroom aides, including Irene, received more training hours and better pay. Facility improvements at barrio schools were made as well. Long-term goals and projects were established, and students were monitored for improvement in their academic performance.

Some in Garden City believed the lawsuit was counterproductive to the progress of the school district and city and set a bad precedent of conceding to the demands of a community group. But others recognized that better schools benefited not only the local children but also the hundreds of children about to arrive in Garden City after Iowa Beef Packers chose Holcomb, Kansas, five miles west of Garden City, for the new packing plant. The new plant would employ more than two thousand people, the large majority likely of Mexican descent and immigrants from many countries. In the decades to come, twenty different languages would be spoken in the school district. Drawing on its experience with the bilingual education settlement agreement, the district would ably respond to the needs of the students.

Through most of the 1970s, Virginia lived at home and was available to help Irene. In the mid-70s, she left Saint Catherine Hospital to work as a nurse in a migrant health program. She also moved out of the home on Santa Fe Street in 1978 and rented a house of her own. Irene always felt some uneasiness when her daughters left home. For centuries, the women in her family went from their father's home to a home with a husband. That was the path she, her mother, and her grandmother had walked. Rafaela's half-sister Juana, who went to El Paso and left her husband, Geronimo, in Dodge, was the rare exception. And once married, the women stayed married, even when the couple separated. In 1975, Irene was a panelist in an International Women's Year forum held at the community college. When asked about the qualities of the "ideal woman," she responded that the ideal woman was competent and competitive in her career and bilingual and bicultural. She admitted that she was ambivalent about women's radical liberation groups. She also recognized that some women believed that men should be head of the household. Many times in her life she had deferred to her father and husband, but she also picked her battles and her preference usually carried the day.

Not all of Irene's daughters followed the same path that she, Rafaela, and Candelaria had taken. Geraldine did marry right after high school, and Nicho pushed Sylvia into marriage while she was still in high school and a teenager. But the other four adult daughters, Marcela, Virginia, Christina, and Maria, left home for higher education and walked their own individual uncharted paths. Families of Mexican heritage, including Irene and Nicho's, were altering the traditional course of their lives. Irene recognized that she and her family were living lives that tried to balance the traditions of her Mexican upbringing and the customs and values in the United States.

Irene initially opposed Virginia's move out of the house, believing that living alone would jeopardize Virginia's safety and social standing. But Virginia was an independent woman, thirty-three years old, and chose to do otherwise. In time, Irene chose not to express her disapproval and instead expressed her appreciation that Virginia was nearby.

In the same year that Virginia moved out, Chuck graduated from high school. He received Irene's and Nicho's blessings and moved to Albuquerque to attend the University of New Mexico, as Raphael had done ten years earlier. The departures of Virginia and Chuck left sixteen-year-old Lisa as the last remaining child at home.

Although the children had largely moved out, holiday gatherings in the house on Santa Fe Street were large and included fourteen grandchildren. Four more were born in 1980: Maria gave birth to a daughter, Raphael and his wife had a son, and Geraldine had twin girls in May. Virginia attended some of the gatherings at Santa Fe Street with her new boyfriend, Manuel Jaramillo, who was living with her in her house. As Virginia explained to Irene, Manuel was married and had been separated from his family for some years. Consistent with her beliefs, Irene adamantly disapproved of their relationship and told Virginia so. Irene told Virginia that Manuel should not come to the house in the future. Virginia reluctantly complied.

In 1981, Lisa graduated from high school and, like her brothers Chuck and Raphael, left for Albuquerque and enrolled at the University of New Mexico. Irene and Nicho gave their blessing to Lisa as they had done for the other children. Her departure might have left Irene and Nicho alone in the house on Santa Fe, except that Raphael's marriage ended in divorce and he returned home until matters were settled. Irene and Nicho, who continued to embrace their Catholic beliefs, never approved of divorce and preferred reconciliation in troubled marriages. But they also knew that with each passing decade, divorce was less of a stigma in the Mexican community. They were civil and polite with family or friends who had dissolved their marriages while keeping their belief in the sanctity of marriages blessed by the Church.

The stigma that remained solidly in place in society and the Catholic Church was the intolerance of homosexuality. Irene suggested to Lisa that she talk to a priest about her feelings toward women. Irene had to face the issue directly when Lisa visited Garden City in 1982, after her first year in college.

The pair were sharing dinner in a Mexican restaurant when Lisa raised the subject. "Mom, I did some research on why I'm attracted women."

Irene was not expecting to discuss the issue over dinner. But she engaged. "Did you go see a priest?

"Yeah, I did, Mom. And a doctor too. And I did some research too."

Irene kept listening.

"The doctor said, 'There is nothing that can be done. There is no gay pill that could change a gay person into a straight person.'"

Irene was relying on the counsel of the priest to convey to Lisa, once and for all, that her emotions were wrong and sinful in the eyes of the Church. She asked expectantly, "What did the priest say?"

"He was very supportive. He told me that the Church does not regard a loving relationship between people of the same sex as sinful. He suggested that I find professional help to deal with my depression."

Irene could not believe that a Catholic priest would say such a thing and could not hide her surprise, anger, and frustration. She dropped her spoon on her plate and said in a raised voice, "What kind of Catholic priest was he?" She decided to end the entire discussion of the matter. She gathered herself and said, "I don't want to talk about it anymore."

After a minute of silence, Lisa asked, "Are you going to accept me as I am, or not?"

Irene paused, and finally said, "I don't understand it. And I don't know if I ever will."

Mother and daughter were at an impasse and ended the discussion at that point. Nothing could be gained with further discussion on that day. Lisa was frustrated—she did not get the breakthrough of acceptance that she hoped for. She could not bring herself to believe that a gay life was a violation of everything holy about love and marriage, and she was angry that she was being asked by her mother to accept that proposition.

❧

Shortly after President Ronald Reagan took office in January 1981, his administration announced proposed federal budget cuts for fiscal year 1982.

Federal agencies and grants that served the poor would lose $16 billion in funding. Many nonprofits across the country organized a conference to be held in Washington, DC, to strategize opposition to the loss of funding. When members of the board of directors of Harvest America, a nonprofit in Garden City that helped the poor and migrants, could not attend, they asked Irene to go in their place. They were confident Irene would ably represent them. She agreed and flew to Washington, DC, with Virginia and others from Garden City. It was Irene's first flight, and she was nervous and a bit fearful, but a trip to Washington fulfilled a dream she had carried since high school. The following morning, she rode on Washington's Metro, yet another first for Irene—a subway ride.

In Irene's four days at the nation's capital, she made time to visit the most popular buildings and monuments. Nicho's nephew, Ernest Garcia, who worked in the Pentagon for Defense Secretary Caspar Weinberger, paved the way for her tour. Ernie took Irene and Virginia into the Pentagon to see his office and into the House and Senate Chambers at the Capitol Building. From a Capitol balcony, they saw the Washington Monument and, in the distance, the Lincoln Memorial. Irene also went to the site first on her list, the gravesites of John and Robert Kennedy in Arlington National Cemetery. The vast majority of Mexican Catholics, including Rafaela, loved John Kennedy, believing he fought for the betterment of their lives. Irene and Nicho were among those who believed that both Kennedy brothers supported their work for civil rights. Irene took inspiration from their efforts to do right by the poor and disadvantaged in the country. They attended Sunday morning Mass after President Kennedy's assassination and prayed for the Kennedy family. At the gravesites, Irene remembered the pain and anguish of the president's funeral procession—the team of white horses pulling the flag-draped casket in a black wagon, his widow in a black dress, her face covered by a black veil, and John-John, on his birthday, saluting his father. She wiped away tears for each man and thought of what might have been. She returned to Garden City resolved to continue her work contributing to the well-being of the community.

In April 1975, North Vietnamese forces overran South Vietnam and created a wave of Vietnamese refugees who had supported the United States during the war. Part of that wave reached Garden City in 1983. They came to work in the IBP meat packing plant. The men took their place on the kill floor and labored to meet IBP's goal of slaughtering four thousand head of cattle in two shifts every day. Many in Garden City were surprised and unsure about where and how to house the new workers and weave them into the fabric of the city. But the school district knew what might be required. The district's bilingual education program was in place and could modify and adapt curriculum and hire personnel to serve Vietnamese students. Until the Vietnamese speakers were hired, Irene learned to say in Vietnamese basic teacher aide commands considered indispensable in elementary and middle school classrooms: "Sit down, please," and "Do not talk!"

In Dodge, Rita and her three daughters lived with Rafaela after Cayetano passed away. But in 1983, Rita and the girls moved to Chicago. Rita's brother David was living there. He worked in the Santa Fe's home office and was rising in the human resources department. When Rafaela's daughter and granddaughters left for Chicago, she lived alone in the house on Avenue J. Her grandchildren were now adults and busy living their own lives. With each passing month, she spent more and more time alone and had less and less contact with family and friends. Neighbors reported Rafaela walking in the neighborhood wearing a heavy coat in the heat of summer. A grandson found her dangerously drying a corset on a hot stove. She did not keep the house as neat and clean as she once had. At times, what little food she kept in the refrigerator was moldy or soured. On occasion she awoke at 4:00 a.m. and waited for mail delivery.

But real clarity regarding her failing mental health occurred in Irene's kitchen. On a day when they sat at the table in conversation, Rafaela leaned toward Irene and whispered, "Irene, who is that man sitting in the living room?"

Irene was puzzled. She looked at Rafaela and said, "Mamá, it's Nicho."

Rafaela said softly, in surprise, "Oh." Rafaela was in the early stages of Alzheimer's.

Maria Paz and David agreed that Rafaela should live with Maria Paz, who was living in Sacramento with her husband, Ray, their son, Jimmy, and daughter, Victoria. Maria Paz took the train to Dodge so that she could travel with her mother, but initially, Rafaela did not recognize her. Maria Paz explained that she was her daughter and was taking her on the train to California. When they arrived at Maria Paz's home in Sacramento, Rafaela did not recognize anyone.

Early in 1983, Virginia gave birth to a son, Jacob Jaramillo. Irene still disapproved of her living arrangement with Manuel and expressed her displeasure with the situation. But over time, the innocence and sweetness of the baby warmed her, and she showed her affection for her new grandson. Nicho also did not approve of Virginia's status, but his objection was more subdued than his reactions toward Sylvia had been a decade earlier. The cause for this tempered response is unclear, but he may have been too ill to respond in the same fashion. Perhaps life's experiences led him to weigh whether certain battles are worth fighting.

By the spring of 1983, Nicho was using an at-home breathing device called a nebulizer. It generated a mist from liquid medicine placed in the machine. It was letter-paper size in length and width, five inches tall, and weighed about four pounds. A plastic hose connected the compressor to a mouthpiece, and it emitted a steady noise when operated. Twice a day, Nicho sat at the kitchen table for ten to fifteen minutes breathing through the mouthpiece. Some days, the nebulizer brought great relief, other days, very little.

On a weekday night in late April, Nicho used the nebulizer before he and Irene went to bed for the night. At about midnight, Irene heard Nicho gasping for breath. He was already getting out of bed when he said in desperation, "I can't breathe." As he stumbled toward the bedroom door, he said, "My machine! My machine!" He went straight to the kitchen counter, put the nebulizer on the table, sat down, and tried in vain to start the machine. He said to Irene, "Start it! Start it!"

The commotion in the kitchen and excited talking woke Raphael, who jumped out of bed and hurried into the kitchen. He saw Nicho sitting down and facing Irene as she held the mouthpiece at his lips. She had turned on the machine, but Nicho had never explained to her how to operate it, and she did not know any further procedures to follow. Irene realized the device was of no use and told Raphael that she was calling the ambulance. As Irene spoke to the hospital operator, Raphael saw Nicho's eyes roll back into his head and his head fall forward. Nicho sat there, motionless, in his white briefs and undershirt.

Irene told Raphael to stay with him while she waited for the EMTs. She stood on the steps in front of the house with the porch light on. Fortunately, the hospital was only eight city blocks away. Raphael did not know what might be done to get Nicho to breathe. He did not know CPR, but he felt compelled to do something. He took deep breaths and blew into

Nicho's mouth, hoping some amount of oxygen might give him a breath. There was no immediate response from Nicho. Just as the EMTs made their way into the kitchen, Nicho gasped, but there was no other reaction.

Irene and Raphael stepped back from the two young men, who pried and pushed at Nicho in a way that made little sense to Irene. Early on, one of the medics tried to administer a shot to Nicho's leg. The medic pushed hard, but the needle would not penetrate his skin—instead, it broke, with part of it sticking out from Nicho's leg. Without removing the dangling needle, the medic grabbed another needle, ripped off the packaging, and again jammed it into his leg. This time the jab was successful. During the second shot, Nicho, with his head still hanging down, gasped a single gasp again. Both Irene and Raphael believed Nicho was dying in front of them. But the two gasps confused them—they didn't know their significance.

Irene rode in the ambulance when they took Nicho to the hospital with their siren blaring and red lights flashing. When she left, Irene told Raphael to call the girls and tell them she was at the hospital with Nicho.

When Raphael arrived at the emergency room seating area, he hugged Irene and asked if she was all right. She nodded that she was. She was fearful but calm. Nicho's doctor had arrived as well and was tending to him. After an hour, he emerged and spoke to Irene. "Irene, Henry is alive but gravely ill. He has suffered a major heart attack. He is stable for right now, but it's too soon to know if he will pull through. We will know in twenty-four hours."

"Thank you, doctor, thank you for all you have done."

He told her, "It's time to pray. We've done all we can do for him for now."

Hesitantly, Irene asked, "Should we call the family?"

"Yes, Irene. I think so. If you want to go in and see him, that is fine, but only for a minute and only you. He won't be able to respond to you." Irene nodded her head and thanked the doctor again. When Irene saw Nicho, his appearance discouraged her. His eyes were shut and his face swollen, and he was breathing with an oxygen mask. White medical tape attached a number of tubes to his hands and arms.

Raphael began calling his siblings. He called Nicho's brothers the following morning. His siblings were back in Garden City, or on their way, within twenty-four hours. Virginia took Irene home so that she could sleep. By mid-morning, she was back at the hospital. At least six family members were always present and kept vigil in the intensive care unit waiting room. One at a time, when permitted, they spent a few minutes at his bedside. The doctor reported that Nicho's condition was unchanged, and he could not say which direction his health might turn.

Irene and family counted the hours and prayed to reach the twenty-four-hour mark. They were more and more encouraged as the number climbed. After a day and half, the doctor reported to Irene that Nicho had improved and appeared to be out of immediate danger. He said, "Irene, Henry is a very sick man. His heart muscle has been damaged and he will have to be careful with all of his activities and diet." Irene again thanked him for all his care for Nicho. "We are going to keep him in the hospital for a few days, and if he continues to improve, we can send him home." The family was relieved and thankful. Their prayers were answered.

Nicho's recovery was slow and deliberate. He avoided any unnecessary activity while Irene took time off from work until he could care for himself. When she returned to work, Virginia, Sylvia, and Geraldine stopped by the house regularly to check on him. Irene did not return to the school for the fall semester in 1983. Nicho's postal pension and social security disability paid the bills. For the first time in their marriage, they were both at home and not working. They spent more time with Francisca and Leon, frequently sharing meals with the aging siblings and running errands for them.

For several years, Nicho had told Irene and their children that he might not live to see the end of the year. But after the heart attack in April, he believed it was a certainty. He began to hire contractors for remodeling projects he had ignored for years. After forty years, he paid for the installation of new kitchen cabinets, new wall tile, and a new table and chairs. He also put up a six-foot-high chain-link fence around the perimeter of the home for Irene's protection. Irene knew his motivation for making the improvements now, after he had been asked so many times before.

In Francisca and Leon's time in the casita, older sister Francisca was the head of the household. From their meals to their TV viewing, she had the final say. Leon saw no purpose in opposing her and deferred to her judgment on almost all matters. Francisca often voiced her concern with Leon's daily bottle of beer, but on that issue, he quietly ignored her. In June 1984, Leon reached ninety years of age. He walked without a cane or walker and was physically and mentally well for a man of his age. But in early August, his health began a rapid decline. His heart simply began to weaken. After enduring nearly a century of life's most difficult challenges, his body could no longer repair itself. He complained of fatigue and spent more and more time resting.

Reflecting on his life, Leon said to family members that Our Lady of Guadalupe had answered most of his prayers. In his bedroom he prominently displayed a picture of Our Lady, and on his dresser sat a lantern he used to signal Santa Fe trains. He remained proud of his life's work for the Santa Fe. He put his affairs in order and arranged for his burial in Maple Grove Cemetery near where his mother, Marcela, and his brother, Cayetano, were laid to rest.

In mid-September 1984, Leon was confined to his bed. Despite his weakness, he remained alert. The doctor advised that his remaining time depended on his heart and that all that could be done was to keep Leon comfortable. A parish priest came to the casita and administered the last rites and communion. Leon told Irene and Francisca that his brother, Cayetano, was coming for him. He told Virginia he wanted to be ready and asked her to shave his face. The next afternoon, on September 20, with Francisca, Irene, Virginia, and Geraldine at his side, he passed away. Days later, a hearse drove him to his final resting place in Dodge City with his mother and brothers.

Irene comforted Francisca, who at ninety-three was the last survivor of her immediate family. Irene fully understood that a generation of her family was nearing the end. But unknown to Irene, Leon's passing signaled the beginning of her children's exodus from Kansas and the house on Santa Fe Street over the next decade.

Though Irene no longer worked as a bilingual aide, her interest in and support for education remained high. During the bilingual education lawsuit, she saw that a seat on the Board of Education might further the education of the Spanish speakers. She believed that with her firsthand experience and work with principals and administrators, she was qualified to serve. She especially wanted to ensure that all families, including those whose first language was other than English and the poor, had a voice in the process. She thought at the time, *Maybe someday*. When it became apparent that Nicho didn't require full-time assistance anymore, she realized that the "someday" might arrive sooner than later. She was a known figure in Garden City, and now she had the time to serve. She decided to pull together a small group of friends and family to support a run for the board.

A board seat opened in December 1984 when one of the board members resigned. Irene's team got the signatures she needed to register as a candidate for the upcoming April election. She was one of only two candidates vying for the open at-large seat; the other members of the board were unopposed. Like Nicho before her, her campaign included newspaper advertising, letters of recommendation published in the *Telegram*, door-to-door canvassing, and distribution of brochures.

When Irene was campaigning in January, Christina returned to Garden City from Albuquerque along with her three children. After a couple of months living with Irene and Nicho, she moved in with her sister, Maria. Christina's marriage had ended, but she was nonetheless able to support her children and continue working as an insurance adjuster. Ultimately, she bought a home for her family and was another pair of helping hands for Irene and Nicho.

In April 1985, the month of Irene's upcoming election, Lisa was a struggling college student trying to pay the rent and complete her classes. She called home for help and Nicho drove to Albuquerque to bring her back to Garden City. Nicho saw that Lisa was unhappy and troubled. On the drive home he asked, "What is bothering you so much?" After Nicho's heart attack, Irene told Lisa never to tell her father that she was gay. Irene was worried that it would cause him to erupt into a rage that would overcome his weakened heart, causing a fatal heart attack. Lisa followed her mother's directive until the drive home. She told Nicho not only that she was gay but also that Irene asked her not to tell him.

Nicho's reaction was not what Lisa expected. Without hesitation he said to her, "You're my kid. I love you and want you to be happy. I'm going to back my wife, but you know that I love you." His response was unlike any of his prior responses to acts or events that went against the Church rules and teachings. Perhaps his values and views were altered by his near-death heart attack.

In the election for the school board seat, Irene received 40 percent of the votes and was defeated. The loss disappointed her, but it did not lessen her will to continue supporting the schools. Then, to the shock of everyone in Garden City, on August 1, 1985, a terrible tragedy occurred when school board member Larry Hendrix and his thirteen-year-old daughter,

Alicia, died in a car accident outside of Garden City. At the time, Irene and Nicho were in San Diego, California, attending the wedding of their son, Philip, to Marlene Linares. They were not immediately aware of the tragedy. The school board's practice was to fill a vacancy by a vote of the remaining board members. It placed a notice in the *Telegram* and asked for nominations, adding that interested persons could self-nominate for the position. Irene's supporters nominated her, and she received an endorsement from the editors of the *Telegram* based on her experience and her receiving 40 percent of the vote in the prior election. She and six other candidates were selected for interviews by the board. On September 4, the board unanimously selected Irene to complete the remaining twenty-one months of the Hendrix term. She was sworn in on September 16 and became the first person of Mexican descent to serve on the school board in Garden City. In a happy coincidence, the Finney County deputy clerk who administered Irene's oath of office was Elsa Garcia, Nicho's niece.

In contrast to the celebration when Nicho was elected to the city commission, Irene did not celebrate her appointment to a seat on the board with a joyous gathering at the house. She understood the tragic circumstances from which her appointment arose and the work for the community that lay ahead. Instead, she and Nicho, and her daughters, went out for dinner together. Nicho told her that he was proud of her and the appointment. He wanted to be more of a help to her efforts, but his health had deteriorated greatly. He breathed with more difficulty and continued to tire easily. Even with his nebulizer treatments, he slept sitting in a recliner with a pedestal fan a few feet in front of him blowing air into his lungs.

One of Nicho's few activities was singing in a small Mexican choir for Spanish masses and funerals. On Saturday, October 12, five weeks after Irene was sworn in to the school board, Nicho sang in the Mexican choir for a funeral mass. Later in the day, he went to Geraldine's home to put together a small cradle for his twin granddaughters' play dolls. Geraldine noticed that Nicho seemed to be working quickly and was short of breath. The next morning, he drove to the G.I. Forum building to count the bar sales from the night before—he was the forum's treasurer at the time. When he got back to the house, he complained to Irene that he had intermittent sharp pains in his chest. Irene wanted to call an ambulance, but he refused to let her. Irene called Virginia to come to the house to check on him.

Virginia brought her son, Jacob, with her to the house. On her arrival, she immediately told Nicho he had to go to the emergency room. He still refused to go in an ambulance. Irene told Virginia to take him while she stayed with Jacob. Virginia suggested that Irene call ahead to the emergency room (ER) and advise them they would arrive soon.

On the way, Nicho complained to Virginia of his chest pain and shortness of breath. She believed he was having a heart attack. When they arrived at the hospital, she told Nicho to wait while she got a wheelchair and advised the ER staff that he was having a heart attack. When she returned, Nicho was already out of the car and leaning against it.

Very quickly the hospital staff asked for Irene. Virginia called Sylvia to have her bring Irene to the hospital. Sylvia, with two of her children, took care of Jacob in the waiting room. When Irene and Virginia reached Nicho in the emergency room he was clutching his chest and struggling to breathe. Irene began to pray the Our Father with Virginia. The nurses gave Nicho a shot of morphine, which helped calm him down and stabilize him. By one o'clock in the afternoon, the "come home" calls went out to all the children.

That Nicho would suffer a second heart attack was entirely predictable. The first attack damaged the heart muscle and produced less oxygen for the organs and tissues of the body, including the heart muscle itself. Irene knew this day was coming. She tried to put away that apprehension deep in her mind, but that knowledge created a daily stress that rose in her consciousness.

The doctor told Irene that Nicho was in critical condition and echoed his assessment from two years prior: if he survived the next twenty-four hours, he might recover. Irene kept a glimmer of hope at his bedside. He looked relatively healthy compared to the prior attack. He was conscious and not disoriented. His face was swollen but otherwise without a constant grimace. Nicho had signed a "Do Not Resuscitate" order, so Irene knew that if his condition worsened, he would pass away.

By Monday morning, all ten children were home and the vigil began. Irene and Francisca prayed a rosary for him during the day. The siblings took turns visiting him for short periods in the intensive care unit. Nicho's younger brother, Miguel, arrived from Wichita and joined the vigil.

Over the course of Monday and Tuesday, Nicho's condition remained stable but did not improve. Morphine kept his pain in check. When Irene was with him in the intensive care unit (ICU), she could read the digital heart monitor and see a highly irregular heart beat and pulse. She spent two to three hours at the hospital in the mornings and afternoons. There were a few family members staying at the house, and she needed to check on Francisca, then ninety-four years old. Some of the children, along with Miguel, stayed at the hospital. By 10:00 p.m. on Tuesday, Nicho's heart rate had not stabilized. Shortly before midnight, a "Code Blue" sounded over the intercom. The response team headed down the hallway toward the ICU. Through the door windows, the family saw them turning toward Nicho's room. Sylvia called Irene and told her to come back to the hospital right away.

Shortly before 1:00 a.m. Nicho took his last labored breath. Just before the Code Blue, Virginia and Sylvia were at his bedside. He said to them, "Take care of my babies. I am not going to make it out this time."

When Irene arrived at the ICU waiting area, she saw the fear on everyone's face. In the ICU itself, the nurses had cleared the unit of all family. Irene was angry with herself for a moment, and said aloud, "I should never have left the hospital. I should have been with him!"

After fifteen minutes, a nurse from intensive care walked to the waiting area and asked for a representative of the Garcia family. The family chose the oldest daughter, Marcela, and the oldest son, Raphael, to go with Irene. Once there, the three were put in a small room to wait for the doctor. Of course, Irene and everyone knew that Nicho had died. When the doctor entered, he said, "Irene, Garden City has lost a great man. Henry did so much good for people. I'm sorry. There was nothing more we could do for him. You can go in and see him now if you would like."

Irene, in tears, nodded and said, "Yes. Yes, I would."

Marcela accompanied Irene to Nicho's bedside while Raphael went to the waiting room to verify what everyone knew. Irene prayed for her husband at his bedside and looked at the man with whom she had spent the last forty-two years. It was difficult to avoid being overwhelmed by thoughts and memories of the life of events they had lived together. But she kept her composure. She was solemn and serene and set the tone for their children.

When Irene and her children returned to the house on Santa Fe in the middle of the dark night, there was no sleep for the adults, only grieving. Irene thought, as did her children without saying so, that the only mercy was that Nicho's pain and struggle to breathe were mercifully at an end.

Irene spent most of Wednesday and Thursday greeting the many friends who came to the house to express their condolences. Many brought food for the family to ease the burden of cooking for the many guests. They brought so much food that Irene shared a large portion of it with the safe house for domestic violence victims. A rosary was set for Friday evening, and the funeral mass and burial for Saturday morning. During all the activity, Irene had brief moments of breaking down into sadness and tears. But after each episode, she gathered her composure and carried on with the arrangements.

On Saturday, Saint Mary's Church filled to standing room only. Nicho's choir, who had sung for a funeral Mass just the week before, now sang for him. Dozens and dozens of cars drove in a procession to the graveside service. Conditions were very cold and windy. People began to leave as soon as the burial prayers ended. Irene and her children, dressed in black and seated in a row on either side of her, accepted the expressions of sympathy from those who withstood the bitter weather. Irene was among the last to leave Nicho's grave. It was one of her most difficult days. She buried her husband on her sixty-fifth birthday.

❦

In the days after the funeral, Sylvia and Virginia helped Irene go through the paperwork in Nicho's desk. They found two small life insurance policies he had purchased for burial expenses. As the sisters continued to examine the contents of the desk, Sylvia found an insurance statement of benefits paid to a hospital in Wichita when Christina was briefly hospitalized. Christina, Marcela, and Virginia had moved to Wichita in 1966. Marcela and Christina later moved to Albuquerque in late 1968. The statement included charges for a pregnancy test but did not show the test results.

Sylvia confronted Irene and asked, "What is this?" When her mother did not answer, Sylvia concluded that Christina had delivered a baby and that whatever had transpired, Christina had been treated differently than she was treated. Sylvia persisted, "What happened to this baby?" Irene remained in tears and did not answer. Sylvia wanted answers, and said to Irene, "Why did you treat me so differently? That was unfair. You forced me to get married, but not Christina, and what happened to that baby?" Irene put her head down on the desk and began sobbing. Sylvia asked, "How could you have done this to me?"

Irene never answered her questions, and she did not clarify to either Sylvia or Christina whether she knew the result of Christina's pregnancy test. She was already grieving Nicho's death. And she felt helplessness and regret, if not guilt, that she could not provide more protection for Sylvia when Nicho reacted as he did. Even before Carlitos was born, Irene had been afraid of Nicho's reaction should he learn that one of his daughters was engaging in intimacy or became pregnant out of wedlock. It was not uncommon for a father to beat a daughter for her sexual indiscretions or confront the offending young man and force an unwanted marriage with his daughter. Back in 1968, Nicho might have driven to Wichita and demanded answers from Christina. Fortunately, Irene never had to deal with that difficult scenario. Christina was already eighteen years old and about to move to Albuquerque, and she was free to make decisions about a pregnancy.

Irene wanted her daughters to never know the pain that she and Rafaela experienced when Irene was separated from her mother at birth. Sylvia's questions convinced Irene that it was highly likely that Christina experienced the same pain of separation that she and Rafaela had suffered.

Sylvia left the room and they never discussed the matter again. She walked away believing that Christina had a child out of wedlock that was probably adopted. Within a few years, accounts from other family members would suggest that Sylvia's belief was correct.

The months that followed Nicho's death were filled with a sense of emptiness. Irene's daily routines became quieter and slower, and the spaces he once occupied, empty. But she did not miss Nicho's pain and struggles to breathe. There were many days that winter when Irene and Francisca shared their meals, just as they had six decades earlier in the Village. Francisca still had her mental faculties and was able to recite from memory the Litany of the Blessed Virgin Mary. She was mobile and able to cook meals. She struggled with the fact that she had outlived her three brothers. And now with Nicho's death, she began to talk about her death and her final wishes.

Sometimes Virginia drove her mother to Dodge to attend a diocese meeting or event. She also attended weddings and baptisms of friends and family. She visited her cousin Juana Rodriguez, sister to Tony Rodriguez. Her high school sweetheart, Jesse Rodriguez, lived near Juana, and two or three times she saw him on the porch or in the yard as they drove to Juana's home. Irene asked Virginia to pull over to the curb so that she could say hello. Jesse leaned against the car as they talked for a short while. Irene took comfort in their conversation, which always included a return to the Village and their lives there.

Irene's work on the school board allowed her to remain active in her service to Garden City. It gave her a sense of purpose and was welcome relief from the heartache and sadness at home. When her term ended in 1987, she again ran for election, but again, she won only 40 percent of the vote and was defeated. She decided to step away from positions of leadership in her community service organizations. She thought she could better serve on the front lines rather than as an administrator.

After Irene's time on the school board ended, children were again running in and out of the house on Santa Fe Street. Maria announced that she and Jesus were moving to Wichita for the upcoming school year. She was going to teach in a bilingual classroom, and Jesus was to work as a sheet metal worker. Christina, who was living with Maria, moved back into Irene's home with her three children. She planned to stay until she could buy a house. As she had done with her children, Irene made the care of her grandchildren a priority. She provided the after-school care and babysitting for the toddlers when needed.

With Christina in the house again, Irene was free to travel to see Rafaela and Maria Paz without worrying about Francisca's welfare. Irene had not seen Rafaela since she had left Kansas to live with Maria Paz. Tragically, Rafaela did not recognize Irene. Maria Paz explained to Rafaela that Irene was her oldest daughter. Rafaela just nodded politely. At the end of Irene's visit, she gave Maria Paz a goodbye hug. She turned to Rafaela for a final embrace. Rafaela politely returned it. The hug was full and long and ended with a kiss from Irene on Rafaela's cheek. Irene said goodbye knowing she might never see her mother again.

16

The Rivalry Ends, Life Is for the Living

In Sacramento, Rafaela's health continued its rapid decline. Irene's son, Philip, had moved his family to Sacramento, and when he visited Rafaela she did not recognize him. Their conversation was limited to a few short sentences. Her expression and gaze showed little awareness of their discussion. She no longer remembered her name. Maria Paz tried to help her keep what little memory remained, identifying herself and then asking Rafaela, "What's my name?" Rafaela could not answer.

When Rafaela first arrived in Sacramento, she was able to feed herself, but by 1990 she needed assistance. Rafaela walked in the backyard for exercise, sometimes with help. On one occasion she walked away from the yard but was found a short time later at the end of the block. She spoke less and less over time, but there was a subject that she frequently raised without any prompting, nor was it directed at anyone. She often said in Spanish, "My husband gave away my first baby. Why? Why? My husband's mother and his sister were mean to me." Soon thereafter, she quit speaking entirely.

In the spring, after three months of all-day care, Maria Paz reluctantly decided to move her mother to a nursing home. Rafaela needed restroom assistance and required adult incontinence underwear. She required more care than Maria Paz and her family could provide. Fortunately, Cayetano's pension followed Rafaela and eased the cost. Maria Paz and other members of her family went to the nursing home every day to visit her and feed her lunch or dinner. Sadly, it was obvious to everyone that Rafaela didn't know with whom she was eating.

In April 1990, Francisca celebrated her ninety-ninth birthday in Garden City. She remained mentally sharp and could still recite Catholic litanies from memory. She took a diuretic for some time to manage the fluid around her heart, but the medication could not stop the toll of time. As the spring turned to summer, Francisca felt increasingly weak and suffered pains in her chest. She was certain that death was near and that soon she would be with God and know her eternal reward. She laid down in her bed and told Irene that her time had come. After a week, Francisca asked Irene to feel her toes for coldness. When Irene said that they were still warm, Francisca got out of bed and went back to her routines, albeit with less activity. With a walker, she slowly moved about the casita in her petite frame that had shrunk to less than five feet over the decades.

In early summer, pivotal moments in the lives of Irene and her children began to snowball. While Irene's emotions and energies were focused on Rafaela and Francisca, Sylvia announced that after seventeen years of marriage she was divorcing Ruben. Irene's immediate thought was grounded in her Catholic upbringing—divorce was prohibited. Her second thought was whether Sylvia was able to support her four children without a husband's income. She asked Sylvia, "Are you sure you want to do that?"

Sylvia quickly responded, "Yes."

"Are you going to be able to support the kids?"

Sylvia answered with a touch of defiance. "Yes, Mom. You watch." The divorce was final in early September.

At this time, Irene received word from Maria Paz that Rafaela's condition was in steep decline. Maria Paz told Irene that if she was thinking of seeing Rafaela before she passed, she should come immediately. The doctor's prognosis was that Rafaela might have a month to live. To avoid her sister's disappointment, however, Maria Paz also said that if Irene traveled to see Rafaela, it was likely that Rafaela would not recognize her or be responsive. Irene wanted to go to Rafaela's side, but to do so would leave Francisca alone. If she became gravely ill, Irene thought one of her daughters might keep vigil at Francisca's side until she returned from Sacramento.

In the first week of October, Francisca from her bed confidently announced that this time she would not leave it alive. She still was coherent, able to pray the rosary and receive communion. But she had no strength to leave the bed. Irene told Francisca that Rafaela was also dying and asked her to keep Rafaela in her prayers. Irene saw clearly that her mother and her aunt, lifelong rivals for her love and affection, were dying at the same time. She sat at her kitchen table and softly cried for a few moments, dabbing at her eyes with a tissue. Finally, she said aloud to herself in tearful frustration, "Ay, these women . . . these women . . . even in death they're pulling me apart." In the end, Irene decided to stay in Garden City with Francisca. She did not want her aunt to die alone, and Maria Paz was with her mother in Sacramento.

On Friday, October 5, Rafaela's doctor called Maria Paz to tell her that Rafaela had pneumonia and did not appear well. The doctor also said that Rafaela was receiving antibiotics to treat the pneumonia, but it was possible she might not survive the weekend. On Monday, she was awake and a priest was called to administer the last rites. On Tuesday, she lost consciousness and did not improve. Her breathing was labored and the nurses gave her pain medication. On Wednesday morning, October 10, Maria Paz, who had kept vigil overnight, went home to rest while Ramon stayed with Rafaela. In the afternoon, before she could return, the doctor called and said that Rafaela had passed away.

The woman who at age fourteen had incredibly delivered a full-term baby without medical care, and who had raised ten children despite the challenges of poverty and a loveless marriage, had reached the end of her life. Rafaela was a woman of dignity, honest in her joy and laughter, and honest in her pain and anger. But she did not become embittered; she remained a warm and giving soul. She died on land that once was her family's ancestral home. Although born and raised in great poverty, she lived to see the success of her children and the bright promises of her thirty-three grandchildren and forty-nine great-grandchildren.

Maria Paz called Irene and told her that their mother had passed. Irene had feared the call and cried when she heard the inevitable news. She wanted so badly to be at the side of the woman who so bravely brought her into the world. Maria Paz arranged to transport Rafaela by train back to Dodge for burial. She accompanied the casket on the long ride to Dodge. On October 15, Irene joined Maria Paz and her siblings and laid Rafaela to rest. She was buried in Maple Grove Cemetery, where Candelaria lay.

On October 19, the day Irene reached the age of seventy, a priest came to the casita and administered the last rites to Francisca. Two days later, her life came to an end. Francisca believed that upon death her soul was immediately with God. A few days after laying her mother to rest, Irene followed Francisca's last requests with a funeral Mass and graveside service. In the span of three weeks, Irene buried the rivals for her love and affection, and the journeys of two generations were laid to rest in Maple Grove cemetery.

❈

Christina bought a home in Garden City the year Francisca passed away. Irene was left alone in the house and casita on Santa Fe Street. The house that once was filled with joy, the tears of laughter and sadness, and the emotions of triumph and loss had fallen silent. Irene did not want to live alone and preferred to live with family.

All but two of her daughters, Marcela and Lisa, the oldest and youngest, were raising children. Lisa was at the University of New Mexico, completing her bachelor's degree in sociology with a minor in Spanish. In May, Irene traveled to Albuquerque to attend her graduation commencement ceremonies. Marcela had obtained dispensation from Catholic authorities in Rome to leave the Sisters of Notre Dame. She was a midwife nurse at Parkland Memorial Hospital in Dallas, the hospital that tended to President Kennedy after he was shot.

Marcela lived alone in a two-bedroom apartment and suggested in early 1991 that Irene move to Dallas with her. Irene agreed and they took steps to begin the move. The first step was the sale of the house on Santa Fe Street. The closing date was set for late September. Irene agreed to vacate her house on September 30, with the buyers taking possession the following day. Shortly thereafter, a local Mexican family, known to Irene, would move into the house and begin their family's memories there.

Irene waded through her belongings to decide what should be kept, sold, or discarded. She left some items with her daughters for storage. On September 30, Virginia and Christina went to the house on Santa Fe to look and remember. Irene stood in the middle of the once life-filled living room and peered into the bare small bedrooms where her children had slept and played. She stepped into the kitchen and looked out the windows as she had done for decades. She went into the casita to make sure it was in order, clean and ready for another family. At that time, a freight train sounded its horn as it rumbled through town. Irene fought hard to avoid being overcome with emotion. She told her daughters, "I'm ready to go." She did not shed a tear until she stepped down the front steps for the last time after forty-eight years.

The next day, Irene and Marcela drove south on Main Street in Garden City. They crossed over the Arkansas River on the bridge on Highway 83 and headed toward Dallas. By happenstance, Irene's new home was on land that, like California, was once part of Mexico.

On the drive to Dallas, Marcela tried to put Irene at ease by assuring her that everything they needed was just a short drive from her apartment. The church, hospital, medical offices, grocery stores, and a mall were minutes away.

Irene, of course, knew hardly anyone in Dallas. When Marcela left the apartment for work, she had a great deal of time to herself. She could still drive, but she did not want to navigate the streets and freeways alone. Adding to the difficulty was Irene's inability to sit straight and tall. She had osteoporosis, which caused a rounding of her upper spine. The forward lean left her shorter and smaller behind the wheel. The rounding was at times very painful. She took medication for the pain and prescription medicines to strengthen her spine, but she was reluctant to take hormone treatments. Consequently, some days she quietly endured the pain.

Irene's daughters did not stay far from her. After Sylvia's divorce, she moved her family to Dallas and searched for work. Her family of five shared Marcela's two-bedroom apartment for a month while Marcela completed the purchase of a condo for herself and Irene. Sylvia found work very quickly as an office temp and was able to take over Marcela's apartment lease. Irene helped where she could so that Sylvia could pursue a career and raise her children.

Lisa spent a few months early in the year with Irene and Marcela after graduating before she returned to Albuquerque. At the kitchen table during a mid-morning coffee, Lisa asked Irene directly why she did not accept her sexuality. Sitting across from her mother, Lisa's physical presence was as imposing as her questions. She was taller than her shrinking mother and full figured. But on that morning, Irene answered Lisa as directly as she could. "I worry about your eternal soul. And I don't want any violence against you."

"Mom, what are you talking about? Nobody is going to hurt me."

Irene said, "I know a gay woman who shot the husband of her gay lover."

"That's not going to happen to me."

"Mija, I'm sorry I have a hard time understanding. It's hard for me. I'm sorry, mija." Irene continued her apology, "And I'm sorry that I said Nicho died from a broken heart when you told him you were gay. I'm sorry."

Lisa said, "I forgive you, Mom. And I love you."

"I love you, too."

A tearful hug followed, and Irene said, "But I still think you need to wear earrings and a bra." Lisa just laughed.

Irene and Lisa continued on a road to a reasonable peace and understanding. Despite Irene's view of Lisa's sexuality, she clung to her belief that the Catholic Church was the one true faith. But she told her other children to withhold harsh judgments of Lisa. She counseled them that they may find their children in a similar situation.

Three years later, Lisa changed her legal name to Zante Garcia. She continued to feel angst about her identity and thought that changing her name might put her more at ease. She wanted a name that would not readily identify gender. She wanted a unique name as well, preferably one that began with her favorite letter, *Z*. She chose Zante, the Italian name for a Greek island. Irene could not understand why the change of name was necessary and privately considered her name to be Zante-Lisa Garcia. But she eventually conceded to calling her Zante, for short.

After eighteen months of Dallas living, Irene became uncomfortable with her situation. She spent most of her time outside the condo with Sylvia's family. Marcela often worked extra hours and there was little the two of them could do together. Irene considered the possibility of renting her own apartment and was about to submit an application when Christina visited her in Dallas. Christina told her that she had asked her employer for a transfer from Garden City to New Mexico and that her request had been granted. Her preference was Albuquerque, but she accepted an assignment to Las Cruces, New Mexico. Christina added that she was going to look for a three-bedroom home with a yard and invited Irene to move to Las Cruces with her. She assured Irene that she would have her own room and privacy and the convenience of living in a smaller city with a milder climate than Dallas. Irene needed very little time to make her decision—she chose New Mexico.

Irene met Christina in Las Cruces during Labor Day weekend 1994. She went along as Christina looked for a house that would fit her family and Irene. Christina settled on a three-bedroom, two-bath house on the east side of Las Cruces. The house had a spacious backyard with a great view of the Organ Mountains-Desert Peaks. It was a setting quite dissimilar to and far removed from the high plains of Kansas. The space in the new home easily accommodated the personal items Irene brought with her. And there was space to organize and spread her papers and documents. One of Irene's retirement projects was to write a memoir of her life's events. She also wanted to travel and visit her sons in California and Arizona and her daughters in Kansas and Texas.

Irene was again living in a city where she knew no one. Christina encouraged her to participate in the city's senior programs. After some persistent coaxing, Irene decided to attend. Every weekday morning just before noon, a shuttle took Irene to the senior center, where she would spend two to three hours. Many of the people in the meals-for-seniors program were of Mexican decent and Spanish speaking, and this put Irene at ease. Many of the participants also went to the same Catholic Church, the Cathedral of the Immaculate Heart of Mary, where Irene took great comfort in attending Sunday Mass in Spanish.

In the summer of 1995, Maria and her husband, Jesus, who were living in Wichita, went their separate ways. She and her children moved to Las Cruces, where she taught bilingual education in the public schools. Soon after her arrival, she and Christina began to plan a seventy-fifth birthday celebration for Irene in Las Cruces. The plan included an invitation to all nine of her siblings, close friends, and some of Irene's Rodriguez cousins and relatives still living in El Paso and Juarez.

Irene's sisters, Nina and Maria Paz, and her brothers, Gonzalo, David, and Mauricio, attended the birthday party in October. Irene's ten children and most of her grandchildren were there, too. It was a grand opportunity for the older generation to be together once again and to share stories. The younger generation and grandchildren talked with cousins, aunts, and uncles they had never met before. Gonzalo, who also worked for the US Postal Service, came from Kansas City, Kansas. Mauricio, the youngest of the siblings, arrived from the San Bernadino, California, area, where he was working for the California Department of Transportation as a right of way agent. David traveled from Chicago to attend. He had risen to the position of manager of employment with the Santa Fe, which made him responsible for the hiring and training of all employees, from Chicago to California. Cayetano always told his sons they didn't need schooling, only the Santa Fe. Cayetano's counsel proved partly true for David. His education and work ethic completed the Rodriguez family's Santa Fe story: in the span of one generation, a rise from graveyard-shift passenger-car sweeper to corporate administrator. A year later, the Santa Fe completed its merger with the Burlington Northern Railroad. The Santa Fe Railway, which had brought into the United States at the turn of the century tens of thousands of Mexicans to work on the railroads and in agriculture for industry profits, ceased to exist on December 31, 1996.

A short time after Irene's birthday celebration, Christina decided to explain to Irene the pregnancy test from late 1969. She told her mother that she had been pregnant when she was living with Marcela and Virginia in Wichita. She became ill, and she went to the hospital, where a pregnancy test was routinely administered. When Christina learned the test was positive, she decided to move to Albuquerque with Marcela. The two of them explained the pregnancy situation to their uncle David and asked for his help in settling them in Albuquerque. She delivered a healthy girl and gave her up for adoption through the Catholic Church. Christina had already shared her story with her daughter and teenage sons. They were not upset, and this convinced Christina that the time had come to tell Irene.

To Christina's surprise, Irene showed no reaction. She did not say anything in response. She did not turn her back on Christina or walk away. Christina waited for a question, but Irene continued to remain silent. She just sat there without a word, creating an awkward moment. Finally, Christina concluded that the reason Irene did not respond was that she already knew about the pregnancy and the adoption. She thought Irene might have decided that the matter was resolved and the better path was to leave well enough alone. Irene never raised the issue or commented on who might have told her about Christina's pregnancy and the adoption. It's certain that in the years that passed, if Irene knew she had a grandchild, who was last known to be in Albuquerque in 1969, she would have prayed for her first grandchild. If she had only a belief that she might have a grandchild, Irene would nonetheless have prayed for that grandchild because of her Catholic faith. Irene learned from Candelaria and Rafaela that family, even those who might be separated by adoption, was the highest priority.

Irene visited as many of her children and grandchildren throughout the Southwest and California as possible. Perhaps the most surprising of her travels was the visit to Sylvia in Puerto Rico in December 1998. Sylvia was working as an office manager for General Telephone and Electric (GTE) in Dallas; GTE had purchased Telefónica de Puerto Rico and sent Sylvia, a Spanish speaker, on assignment as part of a team to facilitate the change in management. The company provided Sylvia with a condo on Ashford Avenue in San Juan. Her backyard was literally Condado Beach. From her kitchen windows, she could see the Atlantic surf roll onto the beach. Sylvia invited Irene to the island for a holiday vacation, but Irene was quite apprehensive about flying. She had flown only once before and never over the ocean. She eventually agreed to make the trip on condition that at least one of her daughters come along. Marcela and Christina agreed to go and guide her through the flight and the weeklong visit.

The flight was surprisingly smooth. Given the holiday season, San Juan traffic on the ride to Sylvia's condo moved slowly. Once they arrived at the condo, Irene saw that the sunshine, the blue ocean, the sound of the surf, and the sandy beach were more beautiful and amazing than pictured in magazines and in the movies. Irene walked on the beach, always in the company of one of her daughters. During her walk, she reflected on the course her life had taken from the Village to the Atlantic seashore. She looked out over the water and scanned the horizon. She was mesmerized by its colors, immensity, and power. But she had never learned to swim, and beyond getting her feet wet, she was terrified of getting in the water. Irene and her daughters cherished their week together on the island.

Irene and her children decided to ring in the new millennium in Albuquerque, as the most central location for her sons living in California and Arizona and her daughters living in Texas and Garden City. Those living outside of Albuquerque rented rooms in a hotel and the small ballroom for a family "talent show." Irene's children and grandchildren entertained the family with singing, musical performances, lip-syncing, dancing impressions of family members, a poetry recital, and a fifteen-minute short play.

Irene felt a sense of satisfaction and accomplishment as she took measure of the celebrations. For all of Nicho's shortcomings, he nonetheless insisted, along with Irene, that their daughters be independent and not be dependent on a spouse. With the exception of her youngest, each of her daughters owned their own homes and all were able to support themselves and their children. Each of them had careers and post–high school diplomas and degrees. By the time the boys were in elementary school, Nicho had made it clear, without question, that they were going to college. Irene saw that night that her and Nicho's efforts proved successful.

In May 2001, Irene learned that her younger brother, Salvador, was seriously ill. She traveled to visit him in Dodge, where he and his wife still lived. Salvador, now age seventy-eight, was suffering from cancer. Irene always dreaded the disease—she saw it as painful, untreatable, and fatal. She read a great deal on the subject. When Salvador described his ills and pains to her, Irene realized that she shared the same discomforts: shortness of breath, fatigue, exhaustion, and lack of appetite.

Irene did not tell her siblings, Salvador, Nina, and Ezequiel, or any other family members in Dodge, that she had similar signs of Salvador's illness. Instead, she used her time to visit with her siblings and say goodbye. Irene privately thought that her goodbyes at this time of her life might become final should any of them pass.

Prior to leaving for Kansas to see Salvador, Irene had complained that she felt tired. Additionally, a dark red splotch had appeared on her ankle. She went to the emergency room at the Las Cruces hospital, but an hour passed before a doctor could examine the splotch. It cleared up before the doctor arrived, and he sent her home. On the trip back to Las Cruces, Irene stopped in Albuquerque. During her stay, she told her daughters that the canker-sore-like black splotches she had seen in her mouth were symptoms of leukemia. Irene had previously described the splotches to her doctor over the phone, but he dismissed her concerns altogether.

Irene had a visit already scheduled with her regular doctor in the week after her return to Las Cruces, and she decided to wait for the appointment to raise her concerns in person. Irene slept in on the Monday morning after her return and did not feel like eating. That evening, after lying down to sleep, she walked out of her bedroom and told Christina she was in a great deal of pain and wanted to go to the hospital. They took blood samples, and when the test results did not reveal any definite findings, it became clear that Irene was going to remain overnight. She asked the doctor, "Do I have leukemia?"

He responded matter-of-factly, "Your blood platelet count was low. We are admitting you for more testing, and we're calling a specialist to review your results."

A short while later, Irene's primary doctor pulled Christina aside and told her, "Your mother has cancer. It's a type of blood cancer that senior citizens are prone to suffer. I'm sorry, mija. I'm so sorry. We will know more after the specialist reviews her chart and tests."

Christina asked, "Will she survive this?"

"If we can stabilize her now, she may have six more months." The doctor paused and said again, "I'm so sorry, mija."

The next day, after speaking with Irene, the specialist spoke to family members gathered in her hospital room. Irene was suffering from acute myeloid leukemia, a type of cancer where the body rapidly produces an unusually high number of white blood cells and reduces the number of oxygen-carrying red blood cells. Without enough oxygen, body tissues and organs deteriorate and do not function. He further explained that there were no standard treatments to stop the cancer. He offered only a slight glimmer of hope by saying experimental treatments with medications were available, but the success rate for extending the life of the patient was only 10 percent. For the moment, she would receive treatment for pain and discomfort.

Someone asked, "If the experimental medication fails, how much time does she have?"

Without any hesitation, the specialist replied, "Sixty to ninety days." He broke the moment of silence that followed his comments when he said, "If you have any questions, don't hesitate to contact me."

The next day, Irene agreed to try the experimental cancer pills with the understanding that if the medication was too painful or discomforting, she would stop. She returned home knowing that her remaining days were few. She was determined to continue her handwritten memoirs if her health allowed her to do so.

Just prior to Irene falling ill, Christina had taken a position with the Small Business Administration as an office organizer and loan assistant for victims of natural disasters. Unfortunately, days after Irene got home from the hospital, Christina was called to report to San Antonio to assist victims of Tropical Storm Allison, which struck Southeast Texas. In her absence, sisters Geraldine and Maria shared the responsibility of spending time with Irene and checking on her well-being.

Word spread quickly among Irene's siblings and family about her limited life expectancy. Maria Paz and Rita traveled to Las Cruces for one last visit with their sister. They reminisced about the lives they and their family had lived and shared moments of laughter. One of Irene's granddaughters was engaged to be married in the upcoming months, and she and her fiancé asked Irene if she wanted them to postpone their wedding to honor the *luto*, the traditional Catholic yearlong period of mourning. Irene told them emphatically, "Absolutely not. Life is for the living, and life goes on. You get married as you planned."

Irene took the experimental medication through the month of June, but the pills made her feel nauseated and uncomfortable. When her blood tests showed no improvement in her blood cell counts, she decided to end the medication. Irene knew her time was short, but she had a say on when she would die. Although it was never said aloud, it's entirely possible that Irene chose to stop the cancer medication so that her death and funeral might occur before the new school year. In that way, her children who were teachers and her grandchildren would not miss any days of school.

In July, Irene and her son, Raphael, sat on a bench in the plaza of the small historical town of La Mesilla, New Mexico. As they waited for family members to finish browsing through the plaza's curio shops and boutiques, Raphael asked Irene, "Mom, what do I need to know about death and dying?"

She looked at him and said with a parent's confidence, "Dying is a part of living." After a pause to allow her words to be considered, she added, "I will live on through my children." There was no fear or doubt in her tone. She was at peace with the life she had lived.

In late July, she was more and more fatigued and took medication to manage her pain. She maintained her mental faculties despite the array of symptoms she suffered. She continued to write her memoirs and tell her daughters her final wishes. Christina left her assignment in San Antonio earlier than originally scheduled to be with Irene in Las Cruces. On the last Sunday of July, Irene enjoyed a family dinner with three of her children and two grandchildren. They dined on Kansas-style flour tortillas, chicken, and rice. Her appetite was good that evening.

By the middle of the next week, Irene was extremely tired. She still responded to the hospice nurse and Christina, but it was clear that the process was underway. The call to the families to come to Las Cruces went out on Thursday. By Friday evening, all ten of her children, from California to Texas, were in Christina's home. Irene was able to speak to some of her children, others she acknowledged with a grip of the hand, or by opening her eyes. She lost consciousness by the end of the night. It's likely she was suffering a series of small strokes.

The sisters especially kept vigil and prayed over Irene. They checked her vital signs and noted her heartbeat. Over Saturday, August 4, her pulse slowed and weakened. It was simply a matter of time. Throughout the day, her children and grandchildren entered her bedroom, spoke to her, touched her, and kissed her. On Sunday, some attended Mass in the morning and others waited until the evening Mass at six o'clock, not wanting to be away if Irene passed in their absence. Those few who waited to attend the evening Mass left for the church a few minutes before the hour. But before they could leave the parking lot to enter the church, they were called back to the house. Irene's heart had stopped beating.

There was grief in Christina's house. But there was also relief that Irene did not linger in pain for months and that she had lived a healthy life. The family knew in advance that her time was short and were spared a sudden and unexpected loss.

A hearse from the local mortuary came to the house and took her body. Some family members stood at the curb in tears and watched the hearse drive away. A few days later, the mortuary drove Irene's body to Albuquerque. There, accompanied by her son, Chuck, and Christina, the train took her to Garden City. She was to be buried in a plot next to Nicho with a headstone bearing both names.

On Saturday, August 11, a funeral mass was held in Saint Mary's Catholic Church. Before the start of the Mass, several people expressed their condolences to Irene's children with a hug or handshake. The siblings were seated in the front row. An elderly man slowed to a stop in front of the sisters. He shook their hands and said, "I'm sorry for your family. Your mother was my high school girlfriend." The comment fell awkwardly on the ears of some of the sisters, but Virginia immediately recognized Jesse Rodriguez. When he hugged her, Virginia quietly said to him as Irene had requested a month before, "She loved you to the end." A tear fell from Jesse's eye as he returned to his pew.

After the Mass, the crowd made their way to Valley View Cemetery, where each of Irene's children dropped a rose on her casket in the grave. On Sunday, most of the children began their journeys home.

Candelaria, Rafaela, and Irene, if not by word then certainly by example, passed to the next generation the baton of hope and determination for secure lives without want. They did not travel down trouble-free roads that might have lessened their challenges. But like most immigrants, they stayed the course, suffering hardship after hardship, knowing they were sacrificing their health and their years for their children. The women were fortunate if the men in their families were stable and good-natured rather than another burden to carry. As best they could, they fostered joy and humor in their homes to shield their children for as long as possible from the harsh realities and indignities of their lives. Each of the women lived long enough to see most of their children enjoy the security and comforts for which they had fought and suffered.

There was irony in the circumstances of where the women were laid to rest. A train brought Candelaria from Mexico to Kansas, where she was buried. Similarly, a train brought Rafaela from California to Kansas where she, too, was buried. And a train brought Irene from New Mexico to Kansas, where she was laid to rest as well. But as Irene told her son, though the women are now at rest, they live on through their children and the generations that follow.

Some have said that the essence of humanity is the ability to comfort and support family and community. The lives of Candelaria, Rafaela, and Irene so ably demonstrate that humanity.

Epilogue

In early January 2017, Irene's son Raphael received a notice via email indicating a possibility that an individual identified as Helen Patricia Bonnie Priest was a first cousin. He was unaware of any person in the family with the last name of Priest, and he was skeptical of the accuracy of the notice. He thought perhaps one of his father's five brothers had fathered a child out of wedlock or outside their marriages. He conferred with other siblings and they, too, were unaware of any uncle, on either the Garcia or Rodriguez side of the family, having a connection to a woman with the last name of Priest. After three weeks, Raphael could not ignore the notice and felt compelled to contact a possible relative, despite any apparent ties.

Raphael's strong sense of family was no surprise. The Rodriguez and Garcia families had passed down through the generations the value of family ties and support. So, on January 22, he sent a short, cautious email to this unknown person. It read: "Based on our DNA . . . we have a high probability of being first cousins. Would you be interested in exchanging family names to see how we are related?" Raphael thought a response would be quickly forthcoming, but there was none.

Later in May, Raphael and his first cousin Teresa Rodriguez Kistner, daughter of David Rodriguez and a family history enthusiast, were exchanging emails regarding their respective DNA results. She relayed the names of persons listed as her first cousins. At the end of her email she asked, "So who is this woman Helen Priest? First cousins? Must be from my dad's side based on her DNA. Do you know her?" With that piece of information, Raphael was certain that Ms. Priest was from the Rodriguez side of the family. He wrote to Teresa: "I am very certain that is from the

Rodriguez side. . . . Now that she shows up in your DNA, I am convinced Helen is a daughter or granddaughter of one of our parents' siblings! But I am guessing, and I am not ready to ask any of my surviving uncles or Aunt Rita if she knows who this person is! I don't have the courage, do you?" Teresa answered, "I did send a message to Helen Priest to see if she'll respond. I'm guessing what you are—that one of our parents' siblings had a child no one knew about." Teresa's message to Helen Priest went unanswered as well.

❦

Nearly every day during her fifty-nine years, Helen Bonnie Priest thought about the family mystery of her biological parents. There was never an adoption reveal moment in her life. She and her three siblings, two brothers and a sister, grew up knowing each was adopted. Bonnie was told that her birth mother had too many children and was too poor to care for another child. As a child, Bonnie always included her birth mother in her nightly prayers and thought about her well-being, especially on Mother's Day. Bonnie was the last of the four children adopted by William and Patricia Bond. She was adopted at birth in April 1958. Bonnie was believed to be, at least in part, of Mexican descent.

Bonnie's birth certificate stated that she was born at Saint Anthony's Hospital in Oklahoma City. Her adoption was processed through Catholic Charities. There was some confusion in the adoption documents, but the legal name that emerged was Helen Patricia Bond. The nickname that was favored in her childhood was "Bonnie." William Bond was an obstetrician/gynecologist in Oklahoma City who practiced mainly at Saint Anthony's Hospital. His patients included many Catholic women and nuns. In the 1940s, he met and married Patricia, who was a nurse at the same hospital. They provided a comfortable home and standard of living for their adopted children. The children attended Catholic elementary and middle schools. But despite the appearance of an ideal home environment, the marriage ended in divorce in 1966, when Bonnie was eight years old.

Bonnie graduated from a Catholic high school in Oklahoma City and earned a bachelor of science degree in nursing in 1979 from the University of the Incarnate Word in San Antonio, Texas. She married John Asbury in 1980 in Oklahoma City and gave birth to a daughter, Jamie, in 1983. Shortly after Jamie's birth, she and John were divorced.

Epilogue

In 1985, Bonnie lost her adoptive mother, Patricia, after a lengthy battle with cancer. The void of her passing left Bonnie in deep reflection about her biological mother. Naturally, Bonnie wondered if she was still living and whether she might be found. Bonnie had never felt compelled to seriously look for her. But after much thought, and emotion, she decided that the time to risk a disappointing or painful search had arrived. It became apparent that she, too, had a sense for family ties and support. Shortly after beginning her search, Bonnie married David Priest in 1986 and gave birth to her second daughter, Alexandra (Ali), in 1990.

Bonnie reviewed what adoption papers remained available. She found an adoption order that indicated the name given to her at birth was Frances Rodriguez. There were no other revealing statements or comments. In 2005, Bonnie contacted Saint Anthony's Hospital and Catholic Charities, but both responded that they had no adoption records with those names. With the development of the internet, she periodically searched the name "Frances Rodriguez," but again without success. Bonnie became discouraged and thought that, in any event, her biological mother might reject her.

In 2013, Bonnie and David moved to Albuquerque, where she continued her nursing career. In the years that followed, David suggested to Bonnie that she submit a DNA test to possibly locate her birth mother, but Bonnie was not convinced. David persisted, and in 2016, they submitted their samples, hoping to find relatives on their family trees. Bonnie had no expectations that her sample would find her family tree. She thought, if anything, the result might verify her Mexican heritage but not identify any specific individuals.

In the early morning hours of January 16, 2019, Bonnie was updating patient files, and on a whim decided to check her emails relating to her DNA test. She was surprised to find that Raphael and Teresa had written to her. She was so excited, she woke her husband despite the early hour and said, "I think I have found my biological family!"

Raphael awoke to find an email from Helen Priest in his mailbox. It was a complete surprise. Neither he, nor Teresa, had received a word from her in the two years since their initial notice of a DNA match. Bonnie wrote:

Hello! I have not checked [my email] in many, many months, until today. I must say that I am quite delighted and surprised at finding several possible/probable relatives. I do not know any of you but perhaps that may change. . . . Some of my adoption papers that I have say my name at birth was Francis [sic] Rodriguez. . . . I am so very open to finding out more if you might know anything. [I] currently live with my husband in Albuquerque, NM. Please feel free to contact me if you'd like. It is a bit scary . . . but exciting! H. P. Bonnie Priest.

A flurry of emails between Bonnie, Raphael, and Teresa ensued over the course of the day. By midafternoon, Helen had told her cousins that she preferred to be called Bonnie. She and Raphael exchanged family photos and looked for similarities in appearance.

Raphael spoke with his siblings in New Mexico, and they responded that they were prepared to meet with Bonnie when she was ready to take that step. Bonnie replied that she would love to meet, especially with Virginia, who was also a nurse. She passed along contact information so they could arrange a visit.

The next day, Bonnie spoke with Teresa, and together they reviewed the Rodriguez family tree. Bonnie thought it very unlikely that her parents were still living, particularly because of her age and the absence of any listing of parents in the DNA report. Teresa briefly described the lives of her father and her uncles and aunts. She mentioned that Enedina, nicknamed "Nina," who passed away in 2007, never married and was a housekeeper for a priest she identified as "Gilbert Herrman or something." This struck a chord in Bonnie's psyche. She knew parish priests had housekeepers, and she thought she had seen the name Herrman listed as possible cousins in her DNA results. She asked Teresa, "Did you say Herrman?"

"Yeah."

Bonnie said seriously, "My DNA report listed Herrman first cousins."

There was a brief pause as both women made the connection. They laughed at reaching the same shocking conclusion. The key was turned and the mystery unlocked. The DNA tests established a high probability that Nina and Gilbert Herrman were her biological parents.

After their call, Bonnie searched online for more information on Nina and found her obituary. Nina had been the housekeeper for Gilbert Herrman beginning in 1956. The obituary briefly summarized Nina's life as housekeeper for Gilbert. There was no indication of whether Gilbert was still living. Bonnie later learned that he passed away in 2017, the year she made her first inquiry. Nina lived with Gilbert through the entirety of his ministry and through their retirement until her death at age seventy-seven.

Incredibly, in the span of forty-eight hours, Bonnie had come to know her biological parents, first cousins, aunts, and uncles, and she would meet her biological cousins in less than a week. Later that evening, Bonnie summarized her emotions with an email she sent to Teresa and Raphael. She wrote:

My dearest cousins: Thank you so much for your love and communication. I can hardly believe this day has come and this door has opened. Teresa, I Googled Enedina because you had written that she was never married but was [a] housekeeper to a priest for many years. It seemed to fit that if she got pregnant by a priest it would explain why Catholic Charities had no record of my birth or adoption. So when I read the obituary and saw the priest she worked for was named Fr. Gilbert Herrman, big bells rang and lights went off . . . because my DNA results, along with you and Raphael showing up as 1st cousins, there was a 1st cousin named Joseph Herrman and 2nd cousin named Christina Herrman-Stejskal. It all made sense.

I am thankful the Universe saw to bring the pieces together with you guys first. You have made me feel comfortable, safe, and warm. I have no idea about when and how I will approach the Herrmans. I first want to connect more with my Rodriguez side. . . . My head is spinning. I feel so blessed that you both describe Nina as a kind, gentle soul. I have held my mother in my heart and prayers all of my life, loving her and respecting that she chose adoption as the choice. The obituary says she enjoyed knitting, crocheting, sewing, reading and cooking, and my daughter Ali loves to knit and read and cook. . . . I love my job as a nurse and derive the most life satisfaction out of helping others.

My heart hurts that Nina lived with such a secret all of her life. How hard that must have been. I do so hope that Gilbert was good to her and loved her. If so, how tragically beautiful that must have been. . . . Much love, Bonnie.

Bonnie had connected with her family and the Las Madres lineage. She wasted no time in seeking her family's support. She and Raphael's siblings in New Mexico arranged a meeting on January 21 at Virginia's home in

Albuquerque that would include other cousins: Marcela, Christina, and Chuck. Bonnie was filled with anticipation and nervousness as she and her husband, David, approached the front door of Virginia's home. It was hard for Bonnie to imagine that she was literally at the doorstep of family she had thought about all her life. She was tense with anticipation and yet apprehensive that her family might not welcome her.

When the door opened, Bonnie was stunned. She saw herself in Virginia. The resemblance was immediate—they had the same curls in their hair and were the same height. Virginia's expressions were very similar to those captured in photos of Nina. She felt a profound attachment deep within herself. The enormity of the reality overwhelmed her. As each of her cousins hugged her, she felt more warmth and security than she could fully comprehend. There were tears of joy and expressions of affection. As the visit continued, she began to feel a deeper and broader sense of her identity and a tie to a vibrant blood family.

Bonnie met with Teresa in February, and in early March she met for lunch with first cousins Zante, Sylvia, Raphael, and three second cousins at a hotel in Dallas, where Ali lives. At that time, Bonnie invited all of them to attend Ali's wedding, set for June 8, in Dallas.

❋

Two weeks after Ali's wedding, another joyous meeting took place in Albuquerque when Bonnie met with Nina's siblings, Mauricio, Gonzalo, and Rita, along with a few more cousins. Bonnie's aunt and uncles welcomed her with warm and loving arms. Bonnie was as close as she could be with Nina and Nina's life. She would learn in time the strength of the women who came before her, Candelaria, Rafaela, and her mother, Enedina. In 2023, Bonnie visited Dodge City and, with her Aunt Rita and cousins, saw the ground where the Village stood, Rafaela's home and Our Lady of Guadalupe Church on Avenue J, and finally, Nina's gravesite.

Postscript
Las Madres Legacy

In 2004, Garden City built and dedicated a public soccer park in recognition of D. C. and Irene Garcia. A contingent of the Mexican generation that followed Irene and Nicho who were active in education issues pushed for naming a new school after them; however, the school district's policy was to name schools after teachers who served in the district. Garden City's third Mexican mayor took up the cause for their recognition and gathered enough support on the city commission to name the park after Irene and Nicho. At the time, the Mexican population in Garden City had exploded to the point where a majority of elementary students in the district were Mexican. Much of that population lived on the east side of Garden City, and city leaders believed a soccer park on the east side was an important resource for the families and children. Sylvia cut the ribbon for the opening ceremony on April 10.

In 2021, Asención's headstone in Maple Grove Cemetery was replaced with a stone that included Candelaria, installed by Candelaria's surviving grandchildren and great-grandchildren. However, Candelaria's exact resting place remains unknown.

❦

The Children of Irene Rodriguez and Dionisio Garcia
Marcela and Virginia became licensed registered nurses. Marcela specialized in labor and delivery and became a certified midwife. In her career, she delivered more than 1,600 babies. Many of those deliveries were by

women from low-income families. Virginia specialized in intensive care and kidney dialysis and provided medical care for migrant farmworkers.

Christina attended business school and had a career as an insurance adjuster for private insurance companies. Later, she became an SBA disaster relief and office organizer, including Hurricanes Katrina and Ike, and EF-5 Tornado, in Greensburg, Kansas. Christina made two attempts to obtain adoption information from Catholic Social Services in New Mexico, the organization that arranged her daughter's adoption in 1969. But their records were closed. Later, Catholic Social Services made its records available to the state. In 2013, Christina, using the state's access to the records, finally established contact with her daughter, Kirsten. They met, and since then the families have shared numerous family events.

Geraldine became a certified nurse aide and a certified nursing home care provider. She, along with her sisters, Maria and Zante, provided care in her home for Marcela for three years until Marcela passed away from cancer in 2023.

Raphael and Charles earned bachelor of business administration degrees and Juris Doctor degrees. Raphael became a legal aid attorney, public school teacher, and author. Charles became a partner in a private law firm whose clients include electric utilities and renewable energy companies.

Maria and Zante became teachers. Maria earned a bachelor of science degree in elementary education and a master of science in instructional education. Zante's teaching credentials include a bachelor of arts degree in sociology and a master's degree in bilingual education. Both sisters taught in low-income schools and served bilingual students.

Sylvia held a position as an office manager for a communication corporation before earning a bachelor of business studies and a master of pastoral ministry and office management. She provides social and religious services to a bilingual community, including the immigrant community in the Dallas area.

Philip earned a bachelor of journalism degree and served as a newspaper journalist and editor. He also served as communications director for California lieutenant governor Cruz Bustamante and later served as vice president of public affairs and advocacy at Sacramento State University.

References

Books

Menchaca, Martha. *Recovering History, Constructing Race: The Indian, Black, and White Roots of Mexican Americans.* Austin: University of Texas Press, 2001.

Mencken, August. *The Railroad Passenger Car.* Baltimore, MD: Johns Hopkins University Press, 1957.

Pablos, Julia Tuñón. *Women in Mexico: A Past Unveiled.* Trans. Alan Hynds. Austin: University of Texas Press, 1999.

Romo, David Dorado. *Ringside Seat to a Revolution: An Underground Cultural History of El Paso and Juarez, 1893–1923.* El Paso, TX: Cinco Puntos Press, 2005.

Newspapers

Catholic Advance
Dodge City Daily Globe
Dodge City Journal
El Paso Herald
Garden City Telegram
Hutchinson News
Stafford Courier
Syracuse Kansas Journal
Wichita Eagle

Oral History

Sanchez, Louis. August 18, 1998. Interview by Brandon Case. Kansas Humanities Council.

Miscellaneous

Sanborn Map Company, El Paso, El Paso County, Texas, 1908, Sanborn Fire Insurance.

Sanborn Map Company, Dodge City, Ford County, Kansas, 1911, Sanborn Fire Insurance.

Index

abductions, 164–165
agriculture, 32, 101, 164, 306
Aguascalientes, 4, 8, 11, 19, 29, 37
Albuquerque, 59, 170, 178, 246, 260, 261, 273, 274, 284
Alegria (Village woman), shooting of, 167–168
Altar Society (Saint Mary's Parish), 240
Ameche camp, 191; salvage from, 215, 216
American G.I. Forum, 240; Independence Day parade float, 153 (fig.)
Amtrak, 261
Ardennes Forest, 210, 217
Arkansas River, 19, 60, 71, 175; flooding of, 253
Arlington National Cemetery, 241, 286
Armentrout, E. L., 224
Asbury, Jamie, 314
Asbury, John, 314
Austria-Hungary, war declaration by, 87
Avenue J, 196, 219, 224, 226, 229, 236, 257; housing on, 186, 187, 188, 192

Baker, Cecil, 271
barrios, 38, 59, 97, 190, 227, 239, 259, 282; Dodge City, 192, 193, 194, 198, 224–225, 278; El Paso, 40–43, 45, 48–49, 104, 124; flood and, 253, 254; health conditions in, 57; housing in, 41; poverty in, 41, 42; servant class of, 54; water in, 48, 54–55
basement, digging, 225–226

Bath Riots, 97
Battle of San Jacinto, 9–10
Battle of the Bulge, 210, 212, 217
Bell, George, Jr., 102
Black Sunday, 172
Black Tuesday, 164
Blessed Virgin Mary, 73, 171, 297
Blue Cross Brigade, 230
Blue Goose Café, 250
boardinghouses, 41, 42, 43, 45, 48
Board of Education, bilingual education and, 291
Bond, Patricia, 314, 315
Bond, William, 314
Brigade and Benefit Society, 230
Brown Manufacturing, 181
Brown v. Topeka Board of Education (1954), 230
Burlington Northern Railroad, 306
Bustamante, Cruz, 320

Calera de Victor Rosales, 110, 111, 112
campesinos, 5, 6, 24, 30, 31, 32, 40, 111, 112
Camp Funston, 103
Capote, Truman, 250
Capper, Arthur, 93
Castro, Fidel, 243
Cathedral of the Immaculate Heart of Mary, 305
Catholic Advance, 86, 92, 194–195
Catholic Charities, 314, 315, 317
Catholic Church, 4, 85, 205, 304, 306; homosexuality and, 285

Catholic Diocese, 193
Catholic Dominican School of Nursing, 252
Catholic Social Services, 320
Ceballos, Arturo, 109, 166
Ceballos, Preciliana, 109
Central Intelligence Agency, 243
Central Plateau, 4, 8
Central Railway, 32
Cervantez, Jimmy, 287
Cervantez, Maria Paz Rodriguez, 140 (fig.), 141 (fig.), 178, 211, 213, 217, 226, 287, 298, 299, 305, 309; birth of, 169, 171; Cayetano's death and, 279; Irene and, 300, 301; Rafaela and, 300; visiting, 236
Cervantez, Ramon, 226, 287, 301
Cervantez, Victoria, 287
chemical baths, 97–98
Chicago, Rock Island & Pacific Railways, 66
Chihuahua, 31, 32, 37
Chihuahuan Desert, 36, 37, 59
Chihuahuita barrio, 40, 42
Children of Irene Rodriguez and Dionisio, The, 319–320
citizenship, 231, 240; classes, 260; declaring, 39
City Commission, 271; Nicho and, 262, 265, 273
civil rights movement, 259, 286
Clutter family murders, 250–251
Condado Beach, 307
Connors, Chuck, 238
Coronado, Francisco Vazquez de, 60
Coronado School, 105, 169, 171, 173, 178, 181, 184, 227

dances, 19, 122, 183, 190, 194, 197, 205, 219, 224, 231–232, 233, 236–237, 239, 241, 249, 259
D. C. Garcia Show, 249, 256, 259–260
D-Day, 207, 208
De Cordova, Henry M., 272
Denver Post, 246, 251
Department of Labor, 101, 165
detention camps, 191, 215, 216

Diaz, Porfirio, 19, 29, 85
Diocese of Dodge City, 225
disappearances, 165
diseases, 11, 49, 50, 52, 97, 104, 124, 130, 168, 172, 173, 189, 247, 308, 309
División del Norte, 110
Dodge City, xv, 30, 60, 61, 71, 73, 74, 76, 80, 81, 85, 86, 87, 88, 89, 91–97, 99; arrival in, 66, 67; charity efforts in, 177; commercial enterprises in, 65; described, 69, 70; discrimination in, 207; dust storm in, 172; electricity in, 108; Great Depression and, 166; growth of, 64–65, 84; influenza in, 105, 106, 208; population of, 66; progress for, 108–109; racism in, 109; Sandborn Insurance map of, 156 (fig.); Santa Fe Railroad and, 65, 66, 70, 113, 181; travel to, 212, 301; Village and, 70, 113; World War II and, 181, 191, 213, 214
Dodge City Community College, 234
Dodge City Daily Globe, 74, 91–92, 94–95; fumigations/chemical baths and, 97; influenza and, 105, 106; quarantine and, 107
Dodge City High School, 75, 209, 234
Dodge City Journal, 91, 92–93, 95, 109, 124–125; influenza and, 107; quarantine and, 106; segregation and, 110
Dodge City Regional Hospital, 278
Dunsford, J. C., 224
Duran, Geraldine Garcia, 145 (fig.), 290, 293, 309, 320; birth of, 238; education of, 261; Leon death and, 291; marriage of, 261, 283; pregnancy of, 261
Duran, Rachel: birth of, 261
Duran, Richard: marriage of, 261
Dust Bowl, 164, 169, 172, 183, 230
dust storms, 172, 193

East Side District, 75
education, 75, 91, 173, 174, 238, 239, 240, 273, 319; adult, 281; bilingual, 281, 282, 283, 287, 291, 305; equal, 282; higher, 283; high school, 169; importance of, 105; Mexican American children and, 241; physical, 176

El Paso, 52, 56, 58, 64, 67, 69, 70, 71, 80, 88, 97, 99, 102, 104, 108, 112, 113, 123, 124; crossing into, 38–39, 40; housing in, 68; infant mortality in, 53; leaving, 61–62, 63, 64; living/working in, 40; return to, 96, 101, 179, 219; water in, 48–49
El Paso County, infant mortality and, 54
El Paso County cemetery, 53
El Paso Electric Railway, 38, 102
El Paso Herald, 102
El Perico Charro Tortilla Factory, 277
El Saucillo, 4, 6, 12, 15, 18, 20, 26, 31, 48; campesinos on, 32; epidemics on, 52; haciendas on, 30; life in, 19
El Segundo barrio, 40
electricity, 67, 93, 108, 109, 166, 172, 182, 186, 187, 198, 203
elites, 5; campesinos and, 40
English as a Second Language (ESL), 281
equal protection rights, 216
Esquibel, Carmen, 208
Esquibel, Frances, 209
Esquibel, Justo: death of, 223–224
Esquibel, Miguel, 209, 210; military service and, 195, 205, 214
Esquibel, Roberto, 210; death of, 208, 209; letter from, 208; military service and, 195, 205
Esquibel, Rodolfo, 208, 209; death of, 210; military service and, 191, 195, 205
Executive Order 9066 (1942), 191

Faber, C. Edward, 170, 178
Faber's Greenhouse, 170, 178
Fairbanks, Douglas, Jr., 106
farm labor, 166, 190
Finney County, 293
Finnup Park, flood and, 254
First Holy Communion, 150 (fig.)
First Ward School, 188
Ford County, 70, 91, 94, 168; influenza in, 107
Ford County Board of Health, 106
Fort Bliss, 101, 102
Fort Carson, 193
Fort Hays State University, 169, 265, 273
Fort Leavenworth, 191

Fort Leonard, 238
Fort Riley, 103, 104
Fourteenth Amendment, 216
Franklin Mountains, 42, 69
Franz Ferdinand, Archduke, 87
Fred Harvey Hotel, 60
French Imperial Army, 8, 9–10
French Intervention, 10, 20
Friends of D. C. Garcia Committee, 262
fumigations, 97–98

Garcia, Berta Zavala, 273, 277
Garcia, Catarina, 8, 10
Garcia, Charles Victor ("Chuck"), 145 (fig.), 284, 311, 318; birth of, 238; campaign by, 263; education of, 320; fire and, 274
Garcia, Delfina, 10
Garcia, Dionisio Campos ("Nicho"), 143 (fig.), 144 (fig.), 145 (fig.), 146 (fig.), 149 (fig.), 205, 208, 209, 219, 238, 257, 282, 286, 304; accident of, 250–252, 272; basement digging by, 225–226; casita and, 276; character of, 206, 270–271; Christina and, 245; civil rights movement and, 259; community work and, 259, 261; death of, 295–296, 297; education and, 203, 239, 273, 319; fire and, 274–275; flood and, 253–256; hardships for, 244; health issues of, 234, 247, 252, 265–266, 272, 273, 276, 277–278, 288–294; house improvements and, 206; Irene and, 190, 193, 197, 204, 212, 257, 289–290, 294, 296, 297, 307–308; Kennedy and, 286; Leon and, 274; Lisa's sexuality and, 292; Marcela and, 221–222, 240; marriage of, 193, 196, 198–199, 205, 232; Mexican choir and, 293; military service and, 193; politics and, 262–263, 264–265, 271–272; as radio DJ, 247–249, 256, 259–260; Raphael and, 288; soccer park and, 319; social life of, 230–231, 233, 234, 242, 249; Sylvia and, 270, 283; Sylvia's pregnancy and, 266–270, 271; Virginia and, 288; work of, 215–216, 220, 221, 225–226, 232–233, 239, 265, 281

Garcia, Elsa, 293
Garcia, Ernest, 286
Garcia, Felipe, 199, 231
Garcia, Guillermo ("Willie"), 190, 233
Garcia, Hector P., 240
Garcia, Irene Rodriguez, 123, 124, 126, 133 (fig.), 141 (fig.), 142 (fig.), 143, (fig.), 144 (fig.), 145 (fig.), 146 (fig.), 147 (fig.), 157 (fig.), 158 (fig.), 158 (fig.), 170, 171, 179, 222, 247, 250, 252, 279, 286, 291, 293; Amelia and, 185, 195–196, 197; birth of, xvii, 122, 173, 237; birthday party for, 305–306; camp closure and, 215; campaign by, 263, 264, 265, 292; car accident and, 272; Cayetano's death and, 279, 280; children of, 231–232, 239, 261; Chon's death and, 229–230; Christina and, 245, 298, 305, 306, 309; civil rights movement and, 259; community work and, 259, 261; death of, 311; detention camps and, 215, 216; discrimination against, 207; education and, 239, 273, 281, 287, 319; education of, 127, 169, 170, 172, 173–175, 176, 177, 180, 184, 188, 231; fire and, 274–275; flood and, 253–256; Francisca and, 172–173, 176, 220, 231, 280, 301; hardships for, 244; health issues of, 303, 309, 310; Jesse and, 184–186, 197, 205, 230; Kennedy and, 286; Leon episode and, 218; Lisa and, 277, 285, 303, 304; Marcela and, 240, 245, 303; Maria Paz and, 300, 301; marriage of, 193, 198–199, 231–232; Nicho and, 193, 197, 204, 212, 257, 281, 289–290, 294, 297, 307–308; Nicho's death and, 295–296; Nicho's health and, 251, 265–266; politics and, 262, 272, 292; pregnancy of, 208, 209, 213, 215, 219, 225, 231, 238, 246; as radio DJ, 247–248, 259–260, 278; Rafaela and, 177, 186, 196, 203, 204, 208, 209, 211, 213, 220, 244, 257, 276, 277, 301–302; Raphael and, 288, 289; school board and, 282, 293, 298; soccer park and, 319; social life of, 230–231, 233, 234, 249, 242; Sylvia and, 252–253, 270, 271, 296, 297; Sylvia's pregnancy and, 266–270; Tony and, 189, 190, 192–193, 198; travels of, 233, 286, 307; Virginia and, 276, 283, 284, 298; World War II and, 191, 213

Garcia, Jose, 203–204
Garcia, Lisa Irene (Zante), 145 (fig.), 202, 270, 320; birth of, 246, 247; campaign and, 263; Helen and, 318; Irene and, 277, 285, 303, 304; Marcela and, 302; name change and, 304; Nicho and, 292; sexuality of, 277, 285, 292, 304
Garcia, Luisa, 199
Garcia, Macario, 4, 6, 7, 8, 10, 34, 35; Bernardo and, 11; death of, 71–72, 73; decision by, 13–14; flight of, 9; marriage proposal and, 12–16
Garcia, Marcela, xvi, 124, 145 (fig.), 157 (fig.), 211, 213, 215, 239, 260, 296, 304, 318, 319; birth of, 209; car accident and, 221–222; Christina's pregnancy and, 306; death of, 320; education of, 231, 245, 252, 283; flood and, 255; health issues of, 245; Irene and, 303; Lisa and, 302; Nicho's death and, 295; party for, 240; Sylvia's pregnancy and, 266; work of, 261, 277
Garcia, Maria Loera, 71, 90, 99; death of, 88
Garcia, Maria Pascula, 10
Garcia, Marlene Linares, 293
Garcia, Miguel, 294, 295
Garcia, Philip, 145 (fig.), 274, 299; birth of, 238; campaign by, 263; education of, 273; Sylvia's accident and, 252–253; wedding of, 293
Garcia, Raphael, 145 (fig.), 247, 249–250, 251, 282, 284; birth of, 238; divorce for, 284; education of, 256, 261, 273, 320; family and, 213; Helen and, 315, 316, 317, 318; Irene and, 288, 289; marriage of, 273; Nicho and, 288, 295
Garcia, Rosalinda (Rosa), 197, 204, 209, 252
Garcia, Sophia, 233
Garcia, Visente, 10, 73
Garcia, Zante. *See* Garcia, Lisa Irene (Zante)

Garden City, 166, 190, 191, 192, 193, 197, 198, 199, 203, 204, 206, 209, 213, 215; community chest of, 242; discrimination in, 207; education in, 241; flooding in, 253–255; Mexican-American community of, 231; soccer park in, 319; social/racial practices in, 259; train stop in, 261; traveling to, 212
Garden City Community College, 281
Garden City Telegram, 253, 262, 263, 281, 292, 293; Nicho and, 264, 265, 272
G.I. Forum, 241, 262, 263, 293
Girls Reserve, Irene and, 177
Gomez, Celestina, 162; birth of, 126
Gomez, Cesario, 125
Gomez, Geronimo, 79–80, 87, 89, 94, 103, 126, 178, 283; Candelaria's death and, 131; influenza and, 108; Juana and, 75–76, 78–79, 124; marriage of, 76–77, 80–81, 82, 83, 162; separation for, 161–163; work of, 85
Gomez, Jose Santana, 103, 123, 133 (fig.); birth of, 96; military service and, 209; return of, 217
Gomez, Juana Rodriguez, 19, 21, 22, 35, 39, 42, 45, 53, 55, 56, 61, 67, 68, 71, 72–73, 85, 86, 87, 89, 102, 105, 114, 115, 125; birth of, 18; Candelaria and, 28–29, 37, 38, 78–80, 81, 82, 104; Candelaria's death and, 130–131; children of, 123; Chon and, 78–79, 81; education of, 49; Felipa and, 81; Geronimo and, 75–76, 78–79, 124; Manuel and, 162; marriage of, 76–77, 80–81, 82, 83, 162; pregnancy of, 87, 94, 96, 103, 104, 122, 126, 171; Rafaela and, 283; separation for, 161–163
Gomez, Nicolas, 103, 123, 133 (fig.); birth of, 87; military service and, 209, 217
Gomez, Prudencio, 105, 123, 133 (fig.); birth of, 104, 105; military service and, 209
Gomez, Teresa, 162, 163; birth of, 126
Granada, camp at, 191, 215
Grant, Ulysses S., 9
Great Depression, 166, 167, 169, 177, 178, 183, 186, 187, 230; abductions during, 164–165

Great War, 96, 97, 98–99, 105, 107; entering, 87, 99, 101
Greensburg, tornado in, 320
Gutierrez, Catarina Aguilar, 113
Gutierrez, Francisco, 113
Gutierrez, Maria, 112, 119
Gutierrez, Refugio, 112, 113

hacendados, 6, 16, 34, 62; described, 5; military service and, 30
haciendas, 10, 23, 28, 30, 32, 34, 35, 36, 40; death on, 20; described, 4–5, 6, 7, 41
Halpieu, Joe, 131
Handly, John, 91, 92, 189; chapel/school and, 94–95; racial intolerance and, 93; on Village, 95
Harvest America, 286
Harvey House, 59–60, 65
Haskell County: influenza in, 103–104, 105, 113; migratory bird species in, 104; population of, 103
Head Start, 265, 267, 275
Hendrix, Alicia, 293
Hendrix, Larry, 292–293
Hennessy, John J., 86, 91, 192
Hernandez, Gabriel, 171
Hernandez, Hilario, 117, 118, 129, 194, 195, 197, 198, 224, 235; Candelaria's death and, 131–132; death of, 235; forced marriage and, 119; health issues of, 227; Marcela and, 118; mass and, 122; work of, 85–86
Hernandez, Jesus, birth of, 171
Herrman, Gilbert, 227, 228, 229, 237, 316, 317; Nina and, 235–236
Herrman-Stejskal, Christina, 317
Hirohito, Emperor, 190–191, 214
Hitler, Adolf, 206, 210, 212
Holcomb, packing plant at, 283
homelessness, 49, 164
Hoover, Herbert, 165
Hoover Pavilion, 194
Hoovervilles, 164
Hope, Clifford, Sr., 262
Hope, Dolores, 262
housing, 85, 186, 238; segregated, 110

Huerta, Victoriano, 85
Hurricane Katrina, 320
Hutchinson, 75, 80, 81, 82, 85
Hutchinson News, 223

Immigration Act, 98, 101, 113
Imperial Army, 10
In Cold Blood (Capote), 250
Indigenous people, 4, 5, 102, 166, 179
industrialization, 19, 32, 127, 181
infant mortality, 18, 53, 54
influenza, 103–104, 105, 106, 113; impact of, 107, 108
Iowa Beef Packers, 283
Irene of Tomar, Saint, xvii

Japanese Americans, detention of, 166, 191, 215
Jaramillo, Jacob, 294; birth of, 287–288
Jaramillo, Virginia Garcia, 145, 239, 261, 278, 279, 286, 289, 296, 297–298, 302, 306, 311, 319, 320; birth of, 215; car accident and, 272; Carlos and, 271; education of, 252, 283; flood and, 255; Helen and, 316, 317–318; Irene and, 276, 283, 298; Leon's death and, 291; Nicho and, 288, 293–294; Nicho's death and, 295, 296; pregnancy of, 287–288; social standing and, 284; Sylvia and, 253, 270; Sylvia's pregnancy and, 267, 268, 269; wedding planning and, 266
Johnson, Lyndon B., 241
Juarez, 31, 32, 35, 97, 102, 112, 113, 125, 233, 305; travels to, 36, 37–38

Kansas City, 256, 305; influenza in, 106
Kansas Health Department, 106
Kansas State Board of Health, 106
Kennedy, John F., 243, 286, 302
Kennedy, John F., Jr., 286
Kennedy, Robert, 286
Kirsten (Christina's daughter), 320
Klein, R. G., 129, 130, 131
KNCO (radio station), 247, 249
Korean War, 227, 230, 258
Korematsu v. United States (1944), 216

Kouns, C. W., 74
KUP-K (radio station), 256, 260

La Pelona, 124, 191, 250, 272
Larobina, Frank: marriage of, 256
Larobina, Jane Frances Rodriguez ("Rita"), 140 (fig.), 141 (fig.), 214, 234, 236, 244, 278, 287, 309, 314; Helen and, 318; marriage of, 256
Las Cruces, 210, 304, 305, 308, 309–310
last rites, 50, 51–52, 53, 86, 131, 229, 291, 301, 302
Latin American Club, 230–231, 233, 263
Lau v. Nichols (1974), 282
Lee, Robert E., 9
Little Joe and the Latinaires, 259
Little Mexico, 70, 110
Loera, Florencio, 56, 57
Loera, Francisco, 56, 63
Loera, Homobono, 56
Longoria, Felix, Jr., 240, 241
Los Huracanes del Norte, 259
Lovelace Hospital, 261

Madero, Francisco, 85
Mao Zedong, 227
Maple Grove Cemetery, 125, 132, 173, 229, 235, 238, 279, 291, 301, 302, 319
Maple Street, 198, 272; flood on, 253, 254, 255, 256
Maria (Juana's friend), 77, 78
Maria (Rafaela's friend), 170, 171
marriages, 116, 122, 178, 183, 212, 284; arranged, 90; birth of, 4; civil, 64; forced, 114, 118–119; interracial, 93; mental/physical fitness for, 13; war and, 193
Martinez, Alfred, 150 (fig.)
Mary Carmelita, Sister, 245
Maximilian von Habsburg, 8, 10
Mesa, Alfonso, 216, 257
Mesa, Ruthe, 257
Mesa, Tony, 190
mestizos, 4, 5, 102
Mexican Civil War, 3
Mexican Declaration of Independence, 241
Mexican Fiesta, 233, 236

Mexican laborers, 58, 65, 66, 73, 98, 186, 221, 283; delousing of, 98; hardships for, 75; hostility toward, 207
Mexican Mission, 230
Mexican Republic, 29
Mexican Revolution, 73, 88, 110, 112, 113, 122, 230
"Mexicans Object to Winter Baths" (*Dodge City Daily Globe*), 97
Mexico City, 8, 233
midwives, 46, 49, 50, 54, 55, 96, 104, 128, 267, 277, 302, 319
Miguel (Chon's accomplice), 126, 128
military service, 30, 31, 183, 186, 191, 193, 195
Miner, Loring, 103
Missionaries of the Precious Blood, 256
Monroe Doctrine, 9
Montgomery Ward, 215, 220, 221
Mount Cristo Rey, 42
mulatos, 4
mulattos, 5
Munoz, Guadalupe, 157 (fig.)
Munoz, Mary Ann, 157 (fig.)
Munoz, Michael, 157 (fig.)
Munoz, Ronaldo, 157 (fig.)
Mussolini, Benito, 212
Mutual Benefit Society of Mexico, 230

Napoleon III, 9
National Health Service, 105
National Youth Administration (NYA), 181, 182
Navarro, Andres, 119
Neeley, George A., 73
New Deal, 177, 181
Noll's Grocery, 216
Nungaray, Carlos, 270, 271, 273; birth of, 269, 297
Nungaray, Ruben, 300; marriage of, 270–271; Sylvia's pregnancy and, 269
Nungaray, Sylvia Marie Garcia, 145 (fig.), 265, 277, 290, 294, 295; accident for, 252; birth of, 231, 238; career of, 320; divorce of, 300, 303; education of, 273; Helen and, 318; Irene and, 271, 296, 297; marriage of, 270–271, 283; Nicho's death and, 295, 296; pregnancy of, 266–269; soccer park and, 319; wedding of, 269–270, 271
NYA. *See* National Youth Administration

Ocampo Alley, 48, 49, 57
Occidental Mountain Range, 113
Organ Mountains-Desert Peaks, 305
Our Lady of Guadalupe Chapel, 119, 122, 193, 198, 224
Our Lady of Guadalupe Church, xvi, 9, 51, 52–53, 68, 73, 130, 132, 152 (fig.), 195, 224, 225, 227, 228, 229–230, 257, 291, 318

Padilla, Asención ("Chon"), xvii, 21, 22, 23, 25, 26, 27, 29, 30–31, 32, 33, 34, 36, 37, 38, 40, 45, 47, 49, 50–51, 63, 73, 90, 102, 109, 118, 123, 127, 129, 133 (fig.), 151 (fig.), 171; Abran and, 88–89, 91; Alegria and, 167–168; birth of, 20; border crossing and, 39; Candelaria and, 115, 119, 120; Candelaria's death and, 130–132, 161; Cayetano and, 116, 117, 163–164; character of, 43, 44, 87, 114–115, 229; conviction of, 128; death of, 229–230; education and, 105; family matters and, 205; Fernando death and, 53, 54; gardening by, 219, 235; hardships for, 61; headstone of, 132, 154 (fig.), 230, 319; health issues of, 108, 168; housing and, 57, 68, 69–70; incarceration of, 168–169; Juana and, 78–79, 81; Macario's death and, 71–72; Manuel and, 44, 45, 62, 63; marriage of, 24, 28; Matilde and, 35, 52; Rafaela and, 55, 114, 121, 170, 178, 188; trial of, 128; work of, 43, 46, 55, 56, 60–61, 64, 67, 70, 84, 178
Padilla, Candelaria Garcia, xvii, 11, 22, 24, 25, 26, 29, 30, 35–36, 49, 63, 87, 89, 92, 102, 103, 109, 125, 126, 133 (fig.), 155 (fig.), 167; Abran and, 33, 70–71, 88, 90–91; Alvina and, 23; Bernardo and, 119; birth of, 3, 9; Chon and, 115, 120; death of, 130–132, 161, 173, 178; education of, 10, 105, 273; Felipa and, 71;

Padilla, Candelaria Garcia (*cont.*)
  Fernando's death and, 52–54; fleeing Mexico and, 39–40; hardships for, 19, 42, 43, 44, 61, 75, 96, 129; headstone of, 132, 154 (fig.), 230, 319; health issues of, 108, 130; housing and, 41, 48, 57, 69; Juana and, 28–29, 37, 38, 78–79, 79–80, 81, 82, 104; Macario's death and, 71–72, 73; Manuel and, 51–52, 62, 63, 64, 100, 101, 123; marriage of, 17, 25, 26, 28, 119, 162; marriage proposal and, 12, 14, 15, 16; Matilde and, 37, 50, 51, 52; maxim of, 219; pregnancy of, 18, 44–45, 46, 47, 54, 55; protecting children and, 99–100; Rafaela and, xv, 56, 82, 83, 114, 116, 117, 118, 121; Sanchez and, 25; travels of, 36, 37, 38; Village chapel and, 94; wedding night and, 16–17
Padilla, Cesario, 36
Padilla, Christina Garcia, 145 (fig.), 252, 260, 277, 302, 304, 308, 310, 311, 318, 320; birth of, 219; concerns for, 245; education of, 283; flood and, 255; hospitalization of, 296; Irene and, 298, 305, 309; Maria and, 292, 298; marriage of, 266; pregnancy of, 306; pregnancy test for, 296, 297, 306; work of, 261
Padilla, Fernando, 49; birth of, 46–47; death of, 52–54, 54–55, 104
Padilla, Leo, 266
Padilla, Matilde Rodriguez, 20, 21, 26, 35, 37, 39, 45, 46, 49; border crossing and, 39; Chon and, 34; death of, 52, 54–55; health issues of, 50–51; Manuel and, 38, 47
Padilla, Rafael, 20–21
Parkland Memorial Hospital, 302
Patton, George, 208, 209
Pepsi-Cola bottling facility, 185
Perez, Jesus, 298, 305; marriage of, 273
Perez, Maria Garcia, 4, 6, 7, 8, 10, 11, 18, 35, 145 (fig.), 282, 305, 309, 320; birth of, 231, 238; Christina and, 292, 298; education of, 265, 273, 283; flight of, 9; marriage of, 273; marriage proposal and, 12, 13, 14, 15

Pershing, John J., 101
Phoenix Industrial Club, 110
Photoplay, 183
Pinon, Celestina Gomez, 140 (fig.)
Pinon, Christina, 140 (fig.)
Plessy v. Ferguson (1896), 94
poverty, 41, 42, 95, 176, 221, 301
Pretty Prairie Commercial Club, 74, 75
Priest, Alexandria (Ali), 315, 317, 318
Priest, David, 315, 318
Priest, Helen Patricia Bonnie, 313, 316, 317; biological parents of, 314; marriage of, 314, 315; meeting, 318
Pueblo, 60, 65, 66, 88, 193
Pueblo Tribes, 170

quarantine, 64–65, 106–107, 193

racism, 109, 234, 235
railroads, 98, 127, 166, 167, 198; Mexican workers and, 306. *See also* Santa Fe Railroad
Rancho de San Jose, 89
ranchos, 5, 19, 21, 25, 32, 37
Raton Pass tunnel, 60
Reagan, Ronald, 285–286
Red Cross, flood and, 255
Republican Army, 9, 19, 29
Rhythm Aces Band, 153 (fig.)
Ricardo, Ricky, 233
Rincón de Romos, 4, 7, 8, 11, 19, 28, 32, 34, 35, 56, 62, 72, 88, 102
Rio Grande, 40, 45, 112; barrios and, 42; crossing, 38
Rock Island Railway, 85, 86, 87, 109
Rodriguez, Abraham ("Abran"), 19, 22, 24, 26, 30, 32, 34, 35, 56, 61, 86, 102, 104, 108, 109, 123, 126, 149, 162, 172, 189, 237; birth of, 18; Candelaria and, 33, 70–71, 88, 90–91; Candelaria's death and, 130, 131; Chon and, 88–89, 91; hardships for, 29; home of, 167; military service and, 191; Rafaela and, 238; telegram from, 70–71, 71–72
Rodriguez, Abraham: birth of, 18
Rodriguez, Alvina, 22, 23, 26, 32–33, 56, 71, 72, 88, 89, 91, 108, 238; death of,

Index

219; hardships for, 219; pregnancy of, 102, 121, 122
Rodriguez, Amelia, 204, 207; Irene and, 185, 195–196, 197
Rodriguez, Antonia Montoya, 224
Rodriguez, Antonio (Micaela's son), 113
Rodriguez, Antonio ("Tony Montana"), 88, 89, 91, 123, 142 (fig.), 157 (fig.), 198–199, 238; birth of, 56; children of, 219; Irene and, 189, 190, 192–193, 198; military service and, 191, 275–276, 277, 298
Rodriguez, Arcadio, 110, 111, 112–113
Rodriguez, Bernardo, 21, 90; death of, 19; marriage of, 11, 12–16, 17, 119
Rodriguez, Blanca, 185, 186, 196
Rodriguez, Catarina, 124–125
Rodriguez, Cayetano, 112, 126, 170, 171, 173, 189, 197, 199, 218, 221, 224, 225, 261, 291, 299–300, 306; abuse by, 161, 228, 229; Alegria shooting and, 168; birth of, 110; Candelaria's death and, 161; Chon and, 116, 117, 163–164; death of, 287; described, 113–114; education and, 235; extramarital affair of, 169; fall for, 278–279; Francisca and, 219; health issues of, 278, 279; housing for, 181, 186, 187; Irene's education and, 174–175, 176; marriage of, 116, 117, 119–120, 244, 279–280; military service and, 191; Nina and, 228, 229; plazo de tiempo and, 199; radio show and, 188, 260; Rafaela and, xvii, 110, 114, 115, 116–117, 118, 119, 121, 163–164, 220, 278; sexual assault by, 116–117, 118, 123; work of, 113, 235, 256
Rodriguez, Cecilio, 141 (fig.), 226, 236; birth of, 128–129; marriage of, 224
Rodriguez, David, 139 (fig.), 141 (fig.), 178, 189, 287, 305, 306, 313; birth of, 212; departure of, 246; education of, 188, 234, 260, 237, 273–274; marriage of, 243
Rodriguez, Enedina ("Nina"), 141 (fig.), 147 (fig.), 211, 213, 217, 305, 308, 316, 317, 318; abuse of, 228–229, 235–236; birth of, 163; education of, 188
Rodriguez, Ezequiel, 141 (fig.), 227, 308; birth of, 169

Rodriguez, Felipa Loera, 67, 69, 73, 79, 83, 87, 89, 96, 101, 102; Candelaria and, 71; death of, 124–125; draft and, 99; Juana and, 81; Manuel and, 57, 62; marriage of, 63, 64; pregnancy of, 91, 94, 96
Rodriguez, Felipe, 110, 113
Rodriguez, Florencio, 99, 123, 133 (fig.); birth of, 96
Rodriguez, Frances, 315
Rodriguez, Francis, 316
Rodriguez, Francisca, xvii, 111, 113, 121, 122, 126, 150 (fig.), 171, 194, 209, 290, 291, 295, 297, 300–301, 302; birthday for, 300; casita for, 275, 276; Cayetano and, 219; character of, 184, 219; discipline by, 127, 172; fire and, 274; funeral mass and, 301; Irene and, 172–173, 176, 231, 280, 301; Leon and, 218–219, 291; Nicho and, 294; radio show and, 260; Rafaela and, 219, 231, 280; visiting, 212, 233
Rodriguez, Gonzalo, 139 (fig.), 141 (fig.), 148 (fig.), 178, 189, 216, 217, 305; birth of, 172; departure of, 244, 246; education of, 188, 234, 237, 238; Helen and, 318; mission of, 243–244
Rodriguez, Hipolita ("Pola"), 123, 133 (fig.), 142 (fig.), 189, 198–199, 226, 238; birth of, 122; children of, 219; death of, 219
Rodriguez, Jesse, 298, 311; Irene and, 184–186, 197, 205, 230; letter from, 204–205, 207; marriage of, 196, 207, 233; military service and, 191, 209, 215
Rodriguez, Jose, 36
Rodriguez, Josefa, 125, 163, 184, 196, 207
Rodriguez, Juana, 189
Rodriguez, Ladislao ("Lalo"), 108, 123, 133 (fig.), 149 (fig.), 237, 238; birth of, 102; military service and, 191
Rodriguez, Leon, 110, 112, 173, 189, 280, 290; arrest of, 218, 219; casita for, 275, 276; death of, 291; fall for, 274–275; fire and, 274–275; health issues of, 291; military service and, 191; work of, 113, 212

Rodriguez, Manuel, 19, 26, 29, 30, 35, 37, 39, 42, 49, 51–52, 53, 59, 61, 69, 83, 85, 86, 87, 89, 91, 94, 96, 102, 104, 108, 140 (fig.), 170, 178, 179, 219; birth of, 18; Candelaria and, 100, 101, 123; children of, 123; Chon and, 44, 45; draft and, 99, 101; Felipa and, 57, 62, 124–125; Juana and, 162; marriage of, 63, 64; Matilde and, 38, 47; work of, 43, 46, 55, 70, 84

Rodriguez, Marcela Gutierrez, 110, 111, 117–118, 119, 121, 122, 124, 129, 171, 184, 209, 218, 219, 222, 257, 291; crossing by, 112–113; death of, 173; health issues and, 172; Hernandez and, 118; Rafaela and, xvi–xvii, 172

Rodriguez, Maria, 124, 173

Rodriguez, Maria Anastasia, 18, 36

Rodriguez, Maria Issac, 36

Rodriguez, Mauricio, 140 (fig.), 141 (fig.), 244, 305; birth of, 220; education of, 234, 236, 258; Helen and, 318

Rodriguez, Micaela (Tony's daughter), 237

Rodriguez, Micaela Gutierrez Sanchez, 112, 113, 144 (fig.), 189

Rodriguez, Miriam Wolbrink, 243

Rodriguez, Modesto: birth of, 18

Rodriguez, Pedro, 112, 113, 189

Rodriguez, Rafaela (Felipa's daughter), 94, 96, 104, 123, 133 (fig.)

Rodriguez, Rafaela Padilla, 67, 68, 71, 79, 85, 86, 89, 90, 94, 102, 105, 125, 126, 130, 136 (fig.), 137 (fig.), 138 (fig.), 139 (fig.), 140 (fig.), 141 (fig.), 157 (fig.), 62, 171, 179, 197, 215; Abran and, 238; Alegria shooting and, 168; birth of, 56; Candelaria and, 56, 82, 83, 105, 114, 116, 117, 118, 121, 124; Candelaria's death and, 130–131, 161, 173; Cayetano and, 110, 114, 115, 116–117, 118, 119, 121, 163–164, 220, 278, 279, 280; children of, 226, 234, 246; Chon and, 114, 121, 170, 178; David and, 243; death of, 301; education of, 75, 105, 188, 273; Francisca and, 219, 231, 280; health issues of, 108, 287, 299, 300, 301; hospitality by, 192, 257; housework of, 172, 235; housing for, 167, 181, 187; Irene and, 174–175, 177, 186, 196, 203, 204, 208, 209, 211, 213, 219, 244, 257, 276, 277; Juana and, 283; Kennedy and, 286; Leon episode and, 218; Marcela and, 172; Maria and, 170, 171; marriage of, 116, 119–120, 121, 169, 184, 244, 279–280; Mauricio and, 258; Nina and, 228; plazo de tiempo and, 199; pregnancy of, 121, 122–123, 125, 128–129, 163, 169, 171, 172, 178, 212, 214, 220; radio show and, 260; Salvador and, 195, 207, 211, 214, 217; Scroggins and, 173–174; sexual assault of, 116–117, 118; World War II and, 183, 207, 213

Rodriguez, Robert, 219

Rodriguez, Rosella, 140 (fig.), 150 (fig.)

Rodriguez, Rosella Sanchez, 195, 205, 206, 208, 214, 215, 219; letter to, 212; marriage of, 192; World War II and, 207

Rodriguez, Salvador, 126, 141, 150 (fig.), 167, 173, 206, 208, 226, 278; birth of, 125; cancer for, 308; education of, 181; letter from, 212, 214; marriage of, 192; military service and, 191, 195, 205, 207, 209, 213, 217; Rafaela and, 195, 205, 211, 214, 217; return of, 215, 217, 219; work of, 257

Rodriguez, Teresa, 246, 313; Helen and, 314, 315, 316, 318

Rodriguez, Tony. *See* Rodriguez, Antonio ("Tony Montana")

Rodriguez, Valente, 125

Rodriguez, Ventura, 36

Rodriguez, Vicente, 36

Romo, David D., 180

Roosevelt, Franklin D., 182, 186; Executive Order 9066 and, 191; New Deal and, 177, 181

Roosevelt School, 188, 189, 225

rosary, 130, 296; praying, 45, 102, 126, 131, 171, 294, 301

Sacred Heart Catholic Church, 53, 70, 73, 86, 90, 91, 92, 95, 135 (fig.), 189, 193; mass at, 94, 108; Mexicans at, 194

Sacred Heart of Jesus, 195
Saint Anthony's Hospital, 212, 214, 229, 314, 315
Saint Catherine's Hospital, 219, 222, 252, 283
Saint Dominic Parish, 266
Saint Francis Hospital, 228
Saint Mary of the Plains, 234, 245, 252, 261, 273
Saint Mary of the Plains Academy, 86, 87, 92, 191–192, 245; influenza at, 107
Saint Mary of the Plains College, 86, 237
Saint Mary of the Plains High School, 245
Saint Mary's Catholic Church, 232, 296, 311
Saint Mary's Elementary School, 231, 239, 255
Saint Mary's Parish, 240, 256
San Antonio, 238, 240, 309, 310, 314
San Jacinto, 8, 9, 10
San Jose, 14, 20, 21, 31, 37
San Jose de Gracia, 4, 10, 11, 17, 19, 61, 90
Sanchez, Francisco, 24, 25, 26
Sanchez, Marco, 77, 78, 80
Sanchez, Rodolfo, 191
Sangre de Cristo, 60
Santa Fe Mexican Band, 75, 135 (fig.)
Santa Fe Railroad, 42, 46, 74, 75, 79, 99, 110, 115, 125, 127, 170, 171, 172, 177, 185, 198, 236, 273–274, 287, 291; Burlington Northern and, 306; Chon and, 57–58, 59; delousing and, 98; Dodge and, 65, 66, 70; flood and, 253, 254; fumigations/chemical baths and, 97; growth of, 84; houses of, 67; Mexican laborers and, 58, 65, 66, 73, 166, 186; property of, 84–85; Rodriguez family and, 306; stealing coal from, 128; Village and, 166, 193, 218; wartime operations of, 181; working for, 42, 55, 58, 59, 60, 61, 62, 64, 70 72, 80, 81, 94, 109, 112, 113, 124, 168, 183–184, 187, 189–190, 204, 206, 212, 235, 237, 246, 306
Santa Fe Street, 198, 206, 209, 226, 264, 269, 277, 283, 291, 302; flood on, 253, 254, 255, 256; house on, 295, 298
Santa Fe Trail, 65

school board: bilingual education and, 282; election for, 292, 293, 394
School Sisters of Notre Dame, 277
Scroggins, Arthur E., 169, 170, 175, 177, 227; visit from, 173–174
segregation, 107, 108, 208; housing, 110; racial, 230
727th Railway Battalion, mission of, 217, 218
Sierra Madre, 113
Sisters of Notre Dame, 277, 302
slavery, 3, 5, 166
Small Business Administration, 309
Sophie, assassination of, 87
Spanish language, 122, 126, 127, 231; threat to, 98
Spanish Mission, 70
Spanish Peaks Mountains, 60
Stafford Courier, 73, 74
Suarez, José Pino, 85
Sunday School, teaching, 212, 219
Syracuse Kansas Journal, 73

Taft, William Howard, 85
tornados, xv, 61, 191–192, 226, 320
Torreón, 36–37
Tropical Storm Allison, 309
tuberculosis, 49, 124, 168, 172, 189

Unified School District 457, 281
University of Kansas, 273
University of New Mexico, 246, 261, 273, 284, 302
University of the Incarnate Word, 314
US Army, 104, 213
US Army Air Force, 192, 204
US Civil War, 9, 258
US Coast Guard, 227
US Constitution, 165, 230
US Customs, 97
US House of Representatives, 242, 262
US Marines, 258
US Postal Service, 305
US Public Health Service, 103, 106
US Supreme Court, 216, 230, 282

Valencia, Andres, 29, 30, 31, 36
Valenzuela, Anacleto, 64

Valenzuela, Virginia Luera, 64
Valley View Cemetery, 311
Vietnam War, 227, 258, 271
Villa, Francisco ("Pancho"), 88, 110, 111–112
Village, 71, 73, 74, 76, 78, 86, 91, 96, 102, 103, 104, 114, 115, 116, 119, 120, 123, 124, 135 (fig.); church at, 93, 94, 95; collapse of, 92–93; conditions in, 95, 109, 166, 167, 172, 182, 187, 188, 188–189, 192; demolition of, 235; Dodge City and, 70, 113; education in, 238; fumigations/chemicals baths in, 97–98; girls from, 134 (fig.); growth of, 84, 109; housing in, 187; influenza in, 105, 106, 107, 208; as labor camp, 109; living in, 93–94; quarantine in, 107; racism in, 109; relocation of, 85; restrictions in, 75; Santa Fe and, 166, 193, 218; school in, 94–95, 122, 169, 177, 194; World War II and, 181, 183, 191, 192, 193, 195, 205, 206, 213, 218
Village chapel, 94–95, 110, 129, 189, 194

Walls IGA, 252
water, 182; drinking, 54–55; polluted, 48–49

Weinberger, Caspar, 286
Western Division (Santa Fe), 65
Wichita, 91, 228, 237, 241, 244, 246, 257, 260, 261, 294, 296; moving to, 298
Wichita Catholic Diocese, 86, 91, 92, 194
Wichita Eagle, 104
Wilson, Henry Lane, 85
Wilson, Woodrow, 85, 99, 101
Women's Auxiliary, 241
Works Projects Administration (WPA), 177, 181
World War II, 223, 230, 258; end of, 213; impact of, 195; internment during, 166; outbreak of, 180–183, 190–191
WPA. *See* Works Projects Administration

Ybarra, Patricia, 11

Zacatecas, 8, 9, 19, 29, 36, 37, 85, 110, 114
Zimmerman telegram, 98–99
Zyklon B: fumigation with, 180